VIXENS, FLOOZIES AND MOLLS

Vixens, Floozies and Molls

28 Actresses of Late 1920s and 1930s Hollywood

by
Hans J. Wollstein

McFarland & Company, Inc., Publishers
Jefferson, North Carolina, and London

The present work is a reprint of the illustrated case bound edition of Vixens, Floozies and Molls: 28 Actresses of Late 1920s and 1930s Hollywood, *first published in 1999 by McFarland.*

LIBRARY OF CONGRESS CATALOGUING-IN-PUBLICATION DATA

Wollstein, Hans J.
    Vixens, floozies and molls : 28 actresses of late 1920s and 1930s Hollywood / by Hans J. Wollstein.
       p.   cm.
    Includes bibliographical references and index.

    ISBN 0-7864-2260-2 (softcover : 50# alkaline paper) ∞

    1. Motion picture actors and actresses—United States—Biography.
2. Actresses—United States—Biography.   3. Femme fatales in motion pictures. I. Title.
PN1998.2.W655   2005
791.43'028'0820973—dc21   98-45591

British Library cataloguing data are available

©1999 Hans J. Wollstein. All rights reserved

No part of this book may be reproduced or transmitted in any form or by any means, electronic or mechanical, including photocopying or recording, or by any information storage and retrieval system, without permission in writing from the publisher.

On the cover: Thelma White in *Tell Your Children* (1938), later retitled *Reefer Madness*

Manufactured in the United States of America

McFarland & Company, Inc., Publishers
   Box 611, Jefferson, North Carolina 28640
      www.mcfarlandpub.com

Acknowledgments

For their invaluable advice, encouragement and wisdom, I extend my gratitude to the following:

Mary Brian, Rudy Behlmer, Billy Doyle, Sam Gill (and the staff of the Margaret Herrick Library), Bob Gitt, Rose Hobart, Theo Mayes, and Anthony Slide.

I am also indebted to the Danish Film Museum (especially Janus Barfoed) for providing several extraordinary and rare photos.

Contents

Acknowledgments v
Introduction 1

1—Hollywood's Other Women   5
2—Olga Baclanova   9
3—Binnie Barnes   19
4—Evelyn Brent   31
5—Dorothy Burgess   49
6—Juliette Compton   57
7—Katherine DeMille   65
8—Claire Dodd   73
9—Mary Duncan   81
10—Josephine Dunn   87
11—Noel Francis   95
12—Wynne Gibson   103
13—Bernadene Hayes   113
14—Beulah Hutton   119
15—Rita La Roy   123
16—Nina Mae McKinney   131
17—Sari Maritza   139

18—Natalie Moorhead   147
19—Esther Muir   155
20—Ona Munson   161
21—Vivienne Osborne   169
22—Gail Patrick   177
23—Dorothy Revier   187
24—Gale Sondergaard   197
25—Lilyan Tashman   211
26—Verree Teasdale   225
27—Helen Vinson   233
28—Thelma White   241
29—Anna May Wong   247

Bibliography   261
Index   263

A fool there was and he made his prayer—
(Even as you and I)
To a rag and a bone and a hank of hair—
(We called her the woman who did not care)
But the fool he called her his lady fair
(Even as you and I)

—Rudyard Kipling, 1897

Introduction

This book is about Hollywood's "other women"—the floozies, the molls and the proverbial bad girls of the late 1920s and the 1930s. Of course, most Hollywood actresses played one or two such roles but certain of them made the type their specialty. Since censorship customarily demanded that goodness prevail, these roles were mainly in the supporting category and the actresses discussed in the following pages have for the most part been forgotten by all but a small (if vociferous) group of film buffs who delight in knowing everything about Hollywood's so-called Golden Era. In some cases the slight is well-founded: several of these actresses simply weren't very good. But whatever their acting prowess (or lack thereof), all the performers discussed here were colorful and, if nothing else, brassy scene stealers. Indeed, many had qualities sorely misused by a studio system that sustained itself by categorizing everyone. The result is that today's viewer may often ask himself, "Who was that snappy dame?" (Or words to that effect.) *Vixens* provides the answer to 28 of those questions:

Olga Baclanova—Today considered high camp and mainly remembered for her starring role as the evil sideshow ballerina in *Freaks* (1932), Baclanova had arrived on the Hollywood scene in the late 1920s with the expectation of becoming a rival to Greta Garbo.

Binnie Barnes—Beautiful, blond and British, Barnes was a splendid adversary to the precocious Deanna Durbin in *Three Smart Girls* (1936) and an asset to any film in which she appeared, drama or comedy.

Evelyn Brent—A veteran *femme fatale*, the smoldering Brent was the first actress to achieve stardom under the always vigilant eyes of the remarkable Josef von Sternberg.

Dorothy Burgess—The fiery vixen of *In Old Arizona* (1929), Burgess unfortunately suffered a bad case of typecasting and could never escape the stifling cloak of villainy.

Juliette Compton—With her clipped accent and haughty demeanor, this brunette menace was often thought to be British but she actually hailed from Columbus, Georgia. A contender for top stardom in the early 1930s, she missed the boat by exhibiting a demeanor too cold for comfort.

Katherine DeMille—Cecil's doe-eyed adopted daughter was usually limited to playing jealous squaws or hostile half-breeds, but was better known off-screen as Anthony Quinn's long-suffering wife.

Claire Dodd—Blond and dimpled and possessing a sweet, heart-shaped countenance, Dodd was nevertheless lethal when playing that 1930s specialty, the other woman.

Mary Duncan—A stage star, Duncan became one of the last of the old-time vamps during the heady days of early sound and took her final screen bow as the condescending actress in *Morning Glory* (1933).

Josephine Dunn—Blonde and seemingly vacant, Dunn could breathe fire when called upon to do so—which she was, quite often, in the early days of sound, having been unsettlingly nasty to Al Jolson in *The Singing Fool* (1929).

Noel Francis—Like Dunn, Francis was vacuous looking and often rather obnoxious. But Noel's characters were found further down the bread line and when the Production Code was suddenly "in," her proletarian molls were "out."

Wynne Gibson—Paramount thought Gibson had the makings of a great dramatic actress and awarded her Ruth Chatterton's leftovers. Alas, Wynne oozed toughness and was much more believable playing a madam than a *madame*.

Bernadene Hayes—If producers could not afford Wynne Gibson, they hired Bernadene, whose whores and floozies rarely had hearts of gold.

Beulah Hutton—The sole purveyor, it seems, of female serial villainy in the 1930s, Hutton was a little known stand-in whose contribution to screen history was otherwise decidedly minor.

Rita La Roy—A tough-looking brunette, La Roy was "Taxi Belle" Hooper, baiting Marlene Dietrich's decadent *chanteuse* in *The Blonde Venus* (1932). The role was brief, but according to the rumor mill Rita saw a great deal more of Dietrich off the screen.

Nina Mae McKinney—As the *femme fatale* in the all-black *Hallelujah* (1929), McKinney became the screen's first "cross-over" sex symbol; for the longest while, however, xenophobic Hollywood made sure she was also the last.

Sari Maritza—A Dietrich look-alike, Sari Maritza was really a nice Britisher named Patricia Nathan. When the world discovered that more than her name was invented, Hollywood dropped her like the proverbial hot potato.

Natalie Moorhead—Swathed in furs and dripping with diamonds, marcelled Natalie was all working class chic. A victim of *The Thin Man* (1934) killer, she became a darling of Poverty Row and made slouching seem seductive.

Esther Muir—What Natalie Moorhead was to armchair crime solvers, Esther was to slapstick comics. As the statuesque but duplicitous Flo in the Marx Brothers' *A Day at the Races* (1937), she even managed to upstage Margaret Dumont!

Ona Munson—Everything else Ona did paled in comparison to her turn as Belle Watling in *Gone with the Wind*. The role of Atlanta's premiere slut should have made her a star; it remains a mystery why it didn't.

Vivienne Osborne—A major stage star, Osborne probably came to the screen too late; by the time talkies came around, Vivienne was no longer in the bloom of youth and her *femme fatales* were often unintentionally amusing.

Gail Patrick—There were no Other Women of the 1930s who seemed as intelligent as Patrick. Her forthright ambitiousness in *Stage Door* (1937) made Katharine Hepburn's know-it-all neophyte look almost amateurish in comparison.

Dorothy Revier—Harry Cohn seems to have built his company around the seductive Revier in the late 1920s. But Columbia then was a far cry from what it would later become and Dorothy became known as "The Caviar of Poverty Row."

Gale Sondergaard—As the malevolent housekeeper in *Anthony Adverse* (1936), Sondergaard would win the first ever Best Supporting Actress Academy Award. There were other such roles to come, but in the end Gale suffered in comparison to the more aristocratic Judith Anderson.

Lilyan Tashman—Attired in the ultimate in decadent *haute couture*, Tashman was a triumph of style over content, sauntering her way through a series of mostly indifferent films. She was rarely given much to do, but she usually did it memorably.

Verree Teasdale—Lilyan Tashman's successor in many ways, Verree was the perfect counterpart to her celebrated husband, the suave and devastatingly elegant Adolphe Menjou.

Helen Vinson—Arrogant and almost always upper-class, Helen was the quintessential other woman—less beautiful perhaps than Claire Dodd, but more versatile and certainly a better actress.

Thelma White—Hilariously inept in the acting department, Thelma White will always be remembered as the weary procurer of young innocents in the equally hilariously inept *Reefer Madness* (1936).

Anna May Wong—Beautiful and intelligent, Wong spent a fair part of her career challenging Hollywood's treatment of minorities—a most commendable pursuit, but not one to insure a memorable body of work.

1—Hollywood's Other Women

> "It is true that I have no heart, but then I am more comfortable without one."
> —Theda Bara as home-wrecker Elsie Drummond in *The Vixen* (Fox, 1916).

It was January of 1915 when Theda Bara first burst upon the screen, almost single-handedly sweeping away the last remnants of the stuffy Edwardian age. With Europe in flames and America mobilizing, movie audiences felt free to throw caution to the wind and dash to the new picture palaces to watch Theda, her bosom heaving and nostrils flaring, demolishing men with the sheer force of her insatiable lust. Of course, the vehicle that created such a stir, *A Fool There Was*, had been played on the stage for years but theater-goers were educated, broadminded and almost always upper class. Now the common folk could see for themselves what the hubbub was all about. And they did in box office–breaking numbers. Bara, who would never escape her vamp imprint, soon had to contend with scores of imitators, some of the best of whom were engaged by her own studio, Fox. Hollywood, and indeed the world, seemed obsessed with this creature, this Vampire who brutally tore at all the old strings still attached to womanhood. But not for long. By the beginning of the next decade, the war long over and prosperity seemingly just around the corner, the industrial age spawned the flapper.

Hollywood, as usual, was loath to give up on a proven commodity—even if its time had already come and gone—but several real-life scandals involving botched abortions, drugs and even a sensational murder* forced the studios to be a bit more circumspect when it came to sex and violence. It was self-imposed censorship, to be

---

*The Arbuckle-Rappe "murder" case, the early deaths of Wallace Reid and Olive Thomas, and the murder of William Desmond Taylor.

sure, and the new edicts were constantly broken, especially among the independents on Poverty Row. But with Will Hays in his office, the flapper certainly seemed safer than the vamp—who more or less faded away along with the ridiculous Nita Naldi seducing Rudolph Valentino in 1922's *Blood and Sand*.

The flapper was a child of wartime's dependence on women in the workplace. Despite the Armistice, she was not ready to return to home and hearth. And instead of being reticent or vampish, she was now carefree, easy with a smile and a wink and "neither buxom nor a great beauty." In other words, the typical all-American girl. Of course, her one purpose in life was still to find a man, but at least her search was now accompanied by hot jazz, the Charleston and a naughty show of legs. "Actually all she did was drink a cocktail and smoke a cigarette in public. Underneath she was a good girl," said Colleen Moore, who in the mid-1920s came to epitomize the era.

Movie producers, however, soon got bolder and upon the scene came Clara Bow, Louise Brooks and Joan Crawford. They were still nice girls at heart on the screen, but their off-screen antics made headlines. (Bow, for example, was said to have laid everything in Hollywood save the linoleum!) The days of the flapper, however, were numbered. She had come to the fore during prohibition but so had the gangster. And with the gangster came his moll.

Even more so than the flapper, the gangster's moll was culled from the day's headlines. And it wasn't a pretty story at all. The moll was almost as deadly as the vamp, only she did it for money or trinkets or just the hell of it, not old-fashioned lust. If she got slapped around a bit in going about her business, why that was just par for the course; it sure beat working for a living like the dumb flapper. With hidden flasks and plenty of fake boas, the moll sauntered forth with Texas Guinan's greeting of "Hello, suckers!" still ringing in her ears.

Sultry Evelyn Brent came to define the early days of the moll. She did it with two famous films by Josef von Sternberg, *Underworld* (1927) and *The Drag Net* (1928). In the latter she was "Feathers" McCoy, all sullenness and ostrich feathers—a new standard for the sleazy mobster's girl. Of course, she was mostly the creation of von Sternberg and costume designer Travis Banton and her time in the sun was fleeting. *The Jazz Singer* had already revolutionized Hollywood by providing sound to the standard backstage melodrama and soon the Wall Street crash and the resulting Depression heralded the arrivals of new, less theatrical molls.

When movies finally talked, they did it louder and faster at Warner Bros., and it was there that the new gangster and his moll found the perfect home. Here, she was more often than not platinum blonde and he was usually a dapper little guy not unlike Edward G. Robinson or James Cagney. No longer just sultry, now the moll was Mae Clarke (with or without that pesky grapefruit) or Wynne Gibson or Noel Francis. And she had come up in the world, as well. The mean streets were no longer the moll's only haunts; she was also to be found in Art Deco boudoirs, private yachts, and lavish mansions.

The "dame" with the tough exterior and soft heart was also making herself heard. From behind the perfume counter at Macy's or leading a kaleidoscopic chorus-line, she had many similarities with her older sister, the flapper. They certainly shared the same kind of humor, but the new breed had the added advantage of sound. You could actually *hear* her wisecracks, not just read them on a title card. But you had to listen carefully—she spoke awfully fast in order to fool those irksome fellows from the Hays Office.

By 1934 Will Hays and his soon-to-be successor Joseph Breen had had about enough and fiercely clamped down on Hollywood's perceived immorality. Yet despite the dedication with which they went about fulfilling their monumental task, the bad girls of Hollywood persevered. The moll, of course, had to abandon center stage since her gangster boyfriend no longer could go about his business with impunity. But the vamp was back! Certainly, she had changed a bit through the years. Her bosom was no longer heaving, nor did her nostrils flare quite as much as in the good old days. But she was still man-hungry, still wielded power through sex. Occasionally, she was married to the hero and had to seek her prey outside of home and heart, but more often she was that historically important figure, the concubine or the other woman.

By the mid–1930s, the other woman was everywhere in Hollywood: In crime dramas, melodramas, and drawing room dramas, in screwball comedies and outright farces. She was cold, calculating, wisecracking, austere, intelligent, dumb, blonde, brunette or redhead—indeed she ran the gamut of Hollywood clichés of womanhood. Sometimes you couldn't help but root for her, especially if she was played by Claire Dodd or Helen Vinson or Gail Patrick. You had to, just look at the alternatives! The other woman of the 1930s not only lost her man to Carole Lombard (or Irene Dunne or Bette Davis)—that we could easily have accepted—but she was also beaten by such pathetic creatures as Loretta Young, Ruth Chatterton, Luise Rainer and, worst of all, Helen Twelvetrees. We still blame the screenwriters involved for that injustice!

By 1936, the vamp had come full circle. Again she was dark and dangerously beautiful and seething with passion, but now she at least could be seen in decent company. On March 4, 1937, as Hollywood honored the previous year's achievements, she proudly walked up to the podium in the person of Gale Sondergaard and received an Academy Award. With the Production Code looming ominously in the background, it was of course no surprise that the award was in the *supporting* category.

2 — Olga Baclanova

"It is certain that when she portrays a character there is going to be trouble," a reviewer once wrote of blond Olga Baclanova. "Heroes are supposed to give one or two sighs and then become victims of [her] beauty."

Baclanova came from the Moscow Art Theatre and was very theatrical. In some circles she was considered "the epitome of Russian seduction and temptation," and Hollywood immediately pegged her as a siren. Jesse L. Lasky, her benefactor at Paramount, saw her as "potentially the finest actress on the American screen," and promoted her as the successor to Pola Negri. Others deemed her a worthy competitor to Greta Garbo. Certainly, the actress had her detractors. Producer David Lewis, for example, remembered an especially embarrassing preview of her film *A Dangerous Woman* (Paramount, 1929):

> At the first appearance of Baclanova, the audience started to scream with laughter. Playing an alluring vampire, she was slightly on the aging side. And worse, she was a ham. I think she had been a well-known theatrical star in Europe, but as a film actress she was so overboard as to be ridiculous.

Lewis' opinion to the contrary, Baclanova was stunning as the battered wife in Josef von Sternberg's *The Docks of New York* (Paramount, 1928) and she left an indelible impression as the cruel and avaricious trapeze artist in Tod Browning's classic midnight show, *Freaks* (M-G-M, 1932). Few screen villains ever suffered a punishment as pitiless as did Baclanova's once-beautiful aerialist Cleopatra. Having married the circus midget out of pure greed, the sexy but heartless Cleo taunts and ridicules not only her new husband but the entire assembly of sideshow artists, openly flaunting her lurid affair with the strongman. The "freaks," needless to say, get their revenge—and what a revenge it proves to be!

Olga Baclanova was born on August 19, 1896 (some sources say 1898), in Moscow, Imperial Russia, the daughter of Vladimir Baclanoff, a wealthy manufacturer, and

his stage-struck wife Alexandra. Olga, along with five siblings, would grow up at her parents' estate outside Smolensk. At the age of ten, mainly through the influence of an aunt who was an actress, she began studying drama at Moscow's Cherniavsky Institute and was even permitted, she later stated, to attend rehearsals at the famous Moscow Little Theater.

At 16 Baclanova was one of four youngsters chosen from several hundred applicants to study at the Moscow Art Theater under the direction of the legendary Nemirovich-Danchenko. Described by her contemporaries as an "intense, high-strung personality with weird eyes, an expressive face and with an amazing capacity for hard work and long hours," she quickly became one of the school's star pupils. In 1931, writer Muriel Babcock of the *Los Angeles Times* recalled for her readers how "once, when Nemirovich-Danchenko was seized with the inspiration to put [Olga] in opera rather than drama, she prepared herself for her debut in two months of concentrated study." The months of hard work paid off, however, and Baclanova made a successful debut singing the lead in *Fille de Madama Angot*.

Vladimir Baclanoff, whom Olga always credited with her inherited interest in music, painting and sculpture, never had the chance to share in his daughter's triumphs. "It was the Revolution," Baclanova later told *Photoplay*'s Esther Dawson, explaining how her father had died prematurely. "He lost everything." Olga, fortunately, wasn't harmed herself. "The Bolsheviks were good to actors," she later said. "They gave me an apartment, I didn't have to pay for anything." Life, however, was far from glamorous in the emerging Soviet Union, even though the actress was befriended by political figures like Lunacharsky and Inokitsky and also cultivated a relationship with Komisarjevsky, the founder of Moscow's Little Theater. Daily life, she told Muriel Babcock, was reduced to "a pair of shoes and a gown one week, bread and potatoes the next."

Under such trying circumstances, it was little wonder that Baclanova jumped at the chance to tour the United States with the Art Theater under the patronage of producer Maurice Gest. Arriving in New York in 1925 with a production of *Carmenzita and the Soldier*, she quickly became the talk of the town: "She was the most Russian of Gypsies and probably the most magnetic actress who has appeared on Broadway in recent years," *Vanity Fair* raved. Baclanova was an equally successful *Lysistrata* and had them cheering for her *Carmen*, but after eight months the tour returned to Moscow. Gest, who was, Baclanova later confessed, "a little bit crazy about me," convinced her to stay behind, certain that she would appeal to Hollywood. She never admitted to having had second thoughts about leaving her homeland, but in 1928 it was revealed that part of her earnings in the United States were earmarked for support, not only of her mother in Moscow, but also of a hitherto unheard-of husband and a young son. She had married Vladimir Zoppi, an attorney, during the height of the Revolution, in order, she later claimed, to save her family. As she explained to *Photoplay*'s Esther Dawson: "It's enough to say that I needed someone to help me."

It was Baclanova's performance as a nun (of all things) in a Max Reinhardt production of *The Miracle* (1927) that finally brought her to the attention of Hollywood

Opposite: **Olga Baclanova, date unknown (photograph courtesy of Anthony Slide).**

producers. She made her screen debut in a small supporting role in *The Dove* (United Artists, 1927), a Norma Talmadge* vehicle, but was elevated to third-billing in Paul Leni's classic horror epic *The Man Who Laughs* (Universal, 1927), portraying a duchess both repelled by and attracted to the deformed circus clown Gwynplaine (Conrad Veidt, standing in, memorably, for an indisposed Lon Chaney). She was a titled lady in her third film as well, a Pola Negri potboiler entitled *Three Sinners* (Paramount, 1928). According to Baclanova herself, she stole the film from its tempestuous star and, naturally, Miss Negri was far from happy. "Baclanova, you go out!" the Polish vixen was said to have shouted in Russian. "[Negri] was very jealous," Olga told the writer John Kobal almost 40 years later. "Everybody was terribly jealous. Of me. Because I didn't know anything. I came from Russia and spoke no English and it was terrible." To keep Negri in line no doubt, Paramount quickly signed the object of all this jealousy to a long-term contract.

Baclanova's favorite silent film† was *Street of Sin* (Paramount, 1928), a taut crime drama starring Emil Jannings as a criminal who is redeemed by the love of a Salvation Army girl (Fay Wray). Olga was third-billed as the protagonist's former girlfriend, a prostitute who eventually betrays him. *Street of Sin* was far from an easy film to make. The excitable Jannings was jealous of his Russian co-star, whom he thought got too much attention from director Mauritz Stiller. (*"Ich spiele nicht!"* he had screamed when she first arrived on set.) The Svengali-like Stiller, in turn, seemed lost without his personal Trilby, Greta Garbo, and was quickly replaced with the film's writer, Josef von Sternberg. The combination of Teutonic thoroughness and Russian exoticism seemed to have worked well and Baclanova's performance was enthusiastically praised. The atmosphere, of course, proved stormy throughout, with von Sternberg admonishing his stars (excluding Wray, presumably) in crafty German.

Paramount reunited Baclanova and von Sternberg in *Docks of New York* (1928), the latter's silent masterpiece about a rough stoker (George Bancroft) whose life changes when he rescues a girl (Betty Compson) from committing suicide. A simple story, it is told with such style as to rival Murnau's *Sunrise* (Fox, 1927) for sheer beauty and visual impact. *Docks of New York* has often been hailed as von Sternberg's finest film— silent or sound—and the director, who was later to guide the early career of Marlene Dietrich, knew how to photograph beautiful women. The female leads here, Betty Compson and Baclanova, are no exceptions. The latter was cast as the wife of a sailor (Mitchell Lewis) whom the heroine is accused of killing during an attempted rape. Baclanova's finest moments as an actress come late in the film, when she confesses to having done the deed herself. "I shot him an' nobody else is goin' to get credit for it," the inter-title had her declare. "I'm his wife. He gave me the air once too often." Throughout the film, Baclanova skulks around a dingy tavern like a world-weary cat (in fact, it is a toss up between the two female leads as to who is the most emaciated), and her detached diffidence doesn't waver even when she is dragged off to jail. "I hope you'll have better luck than me," she says to the newly-wed Compson, "but I doubt it."

Despite having worked with the irascible von Sternberg before, Baclanova was

---

Baclanova recalled that Talmadge was insanely jealous of her and refused the newcomer any close-ups.

†*"I was happy they were silent," the still heavily accented Baclanova told John Kobal in 1964.*

unprepared for her treatment during the filming of *Docks of New York*. "I tried to learn my parts like a human being, and I tried to play them that way," she told film historian Kevin Brownlow. "He wanted me to play a scene a certain way—I felt this was not right. 'Why do you tell me to do that?'" According to Brownlow, Baclanova was harshly ordered to do exactly what she was told and forget everything she had learned at the fancy-schmancy Moscow Art Theatre. She tried her best, but von Sternberg was still not satisfied. "It's terrible, it's awful!" she remembered him bellowing. "We argued, and he yelled at me, and I was so scared I cried like a baby. And that, of course, was what he wanted. The scene in the picture was very good." According to Brownlow, Olga credited von Sternberg completely with getting that performance out of her and would always thereafter praise his work.

Now an established Hollywood personality, Baclanova was described by *Photoplay*'s Esther Dawson as being

> Russia incarnate—its soul, its centuries of repressed feelings, its mystery which have never been successfully fathomed. Like all Russians she lives on the inside, does not like to know many people, and comes out of herself only in her acting, her painting and her opera singing.

In other words, she was somewhat of a diva and not at all unlike her predecessor at the studio, the dynamic but often quite exhausting Pola Negri.

In 1929 Baclanova was elevated to leading lady status opposite George Bancroft in *The Wolf of Wall Street*, a quite well made drama depicting the rise and fall of a speculator. Directed by the capable Rowland V. Lee, *Wall Street* was Baclanova's talkie debut and the film even offered her a chance to sing. She played Bancroft's immigrant wife and, according to Mordaunt Hall of the New York *Times*, sported "quite a fascinating accent [although] some of her lines [were] quite indistinct."

By no means a classic, *The Wolf of Wall Street* was a great deal better than *A Dangerous Woman* (Paramount, 1929), the notorious stinker so unforgettable to David Lewis, who had then just arrived in Hollywood and had the unenviable duty of overseeing the preview. A sad throwback to the bosom-heaving days of Theda Bara, the wild melodrama starred Baclanova as a jungle siren who uses magic to lure unsuspecting young men into degradation and subsequent death. With a plot that hackneyed, it was little wonder that she was laughed off the screen.

Away from the studio, Baclanova was fighting in court with her agent Al Rosen. According to newspaper accounts, the actress had sued to be released from her five-year contract, which she claimed she had signed under the mistaken assumption that it was only to run one year. Her defense, unfamiliarity with the English language, was dismissed by Rosen's lawyer who pointed out that Baclanova claimed to be fluent in four languages, one of which, according to her screen roles, was indeed English. Surprisingly, during cross-examination it was brought out that she had divorced her first husband to become the wife of Hollywood actor Nicholas Soussanin.* The suit itself

---

**Soussanin, an American despite his Russian-sounding name, enjoyed a minor screen career which included* The Last Command *(1928),* Daughter of the Dragon *(1931),* The Man Who Broke the Bank of Monte Carlo *(1935),* Under Two Flags *(1936), and* Captain Fury *(1939).*

was eventually settled out of court but it seemed to have been rather entertaining while it lasted.

Baclanova's screen roles, meanwhile, were at this point somewhat less interesting than her private life. She did, however, enjoy a few good moments in her final film for Paramount, William Wellman's *The Man I Love* (1929). A minor melodrama about a boxer who gets to the top with the help of a faithful wife whom he subsequently dumps for a society vamp, *The Man I Love* was co-scripted by the clever Herman J. Mankiewicz, who relieved the plot's tediousness with some bright dialogue. Eying the beauteous Sonia Barondoff (Baclanova), the naive boxer Dum-Dum (Richard Arlen) asks his streetwise sidekick (Jack Oakie) who "the million dollar dame" is. "She's the hottest thing in society," Oakie replies. "Why, it ain't legal for a tabloid paper to be printed without at least two pictures of that dame." In another scene, the villain (Leslie Fenton) is overcome with desire for the alluring Sonia. "If I ever thought you didn't love me," he moans, "I'd kill myself." "Of course you would," Olga purrs, borrowing a page from Mae West. "That's the way I like to be loved."

Leaving Paramount proved a disaster for Baclanova. She had been lured over to Fox with a promise of musicals and with her operatic training she might have become another Jeanette MacDonald. The timing, unfortunately, was all wrong. The public had tired of lavish all-star musical extravaganzas and had never really taken to the slew of operettas lifted directly from the Broadway stage. Unquestionably, *Cheer Up and Smile* (1930) and *Are You There?* (1931; Soussanin had a bit part as a barber) would have damaged the careers of bigger stars than Baclanova. In the first mentioned, arguably the nadir of her career, Baclanova vainly attempted to vamp the lightweight Arthur Lake away from the equally lightweight Dixie Lee—with unintended humorous consequences. "You'll lose a pound laughing," promised *Photoplay*'s reviewer and he wasn't referring to the comedy aspects. *Are You There?* proved detrimental not only for Baclanova but even more so for its star, the otherwise indomitable Beatrice Lillie, whose antics were better suited for the stage. As a result, the film became one of Hollywood's more notorious clunkers. On top of it all, it was now the Depression and old-fashioned *femme fatales* like Olga seemed terribly anachronistic.

Supporting Adolphe Menjou and Irene Dunne, Baclanova was rather well cast as a temperamental opera diva in *The Great Lover* (M-G-M, 1931), a mild romance set on an ocean liner. She had signed with Metro earlier that year, but the studio felt that her accent was too heavy and persuaded her to return to the stage. In early October of 1931, she signed as the *femme fatale* opposite A. E. Anson in the Los Angeles production of the play, *The Silent Witness*. Lionel Atwill and Kay Strozzi had starred in Jack De Leon and Jack Celestin's original Broadway hit about a man who pleads guilty to a murder in order to protect his son. Olga, in what was essentially a bit part, played the murder victim, the protagonist's mistress.*

Baclanova returned to the screen in December of 1931 for what was to become her most famous role, the faithless Cleopatra in *Freaks* (M-G-M, 1932). Based on the short story "Spurs" by Tod Robbins, *Freaks* is the strange, almost indescribable tale of

---

When Fox made a screen version in 1933, Atwill retained his role, while another former Paramount vamp, Greta Nissen, was cast instead of Baclanova.

a beautiful trapeze artist (Baclanova) who with the strong man (Henry Victor) conspires to separate the circus midget (Harry Earles) from his money. When the circus sideshow "exhibits" learn of the pair's duplicity they hunt them down and mercilessly kill the strong man. Cleopatra's punishment proves even worse. She is mysteriously transformed into a disfigured and grotesque-looking side-show attraction billed as the "duck woman."

Freaks, to put it mildly, was not for the faint of heart and a rather unusual undertaking for the oh so genteel M-G-M. Obviously, the studio was inspired by the healthy box office returns pouring into Universal's coffers from their Grand Guignol melodramas *Dracula* and *Frankenstein* (both 1931). Irving Thalberg actually hired *Dracula*'s director Tod Browning for this undertaking and gave him free helms. It seems Thalberg had complete faith in Browning, who was awarded a budget of $360,000, a not inconsiderable amount in those days for what was essentially a genre picture. Browning certainly didn't waste any money casting his leads: Leila Hyams and Wallace Ford, whose love story serves as momentary relief from the film's more macabre goings-on, were second-tier contract players. Henry Victor and Rose Dione (who played the owner of the sideshow) had no box office appeal whatsoever. The picture's only concession to glamour came in the form of the villainess, Cleopatra. Jean Harlow had at first been tapped for the role, but was horrified by the idea and refused. Myrna Loy also turned down the role before it finally was offered to Baclanova. According to the actress herself, Browning gave her the script to read, after which he introduced her to the cast. "I meet [Earles]," she recalled for John Kobal almost 40 years later,

> and he adores me because we speak German and he's from Germany. Then he shows me a girl that's like an orangutan; then a man who has a head but no legs, no nothing, just a head and a body like an egg [Raridon, the Living Torso]. Then he shows me a boy [Johnny Eck] who walks on his hands because he was born without feet. He shows me little by little and I could not look, I wanted to faint. I wanted to cry when I saw them. They have such nice faces.

Although Baclanova grew rather fond of her strange co-stars, the filming took a toll on her nerves. "It was very, very difficult the first time," she later said. "You know, I was sorry for these people. Every night I felt sick. Because I couldn't look at them."

The sideshow cast was certainly a bizarre collection of human oddities. In addition to the above mentioned circus performers, *Freaks* also featured appearances by Koo Coo, the bird girl; Josephine-Joseph, the half-man, half-woman; Pete Robinson, the "human skeleton"; Olga Roderick, the bearded lady, and, finally, Daisy and Violet Hilton, the famous Siamese twins who would later star in an exploitation oddity all their own, *Chained for Life* (1950). Along with the amazing "human pinheads"—real life "coneheads"—these circus "attractions," under Browning's skillful direction, appeared as sympathetic human beings demanding respect and affection, not pity or scorn. *Freaks*, in retrospect, is not an exploitation picture so much as it is an old-fashioned morality play with good (the sideshow people) triumphing over evil (personified by two "perfect" specimens of the human race, the beautiful blonde aerialist and the circus strong man). It is an often very touching and moving film that was well ahead of its time.

[16]   Vixens, Floozies and Molls

Baclanova and Harry Earles in *Freaks* (M-G-M, 1932).

The critics were aghast when Metro after months of hesitation and with a good deal of corporate embarrassment finally released *Freaks* in July of 1932. "Not even the most morbidly inclined could possibly find this picture to their liking," *Variety* warned its readers. "Saying that it is horrible is putting it mildly: it is revolting to the extent of turning one's stomach, and only an iron constitution could withstand its effects." Needless to say, the film was banned in many places and M-G-M studio boss Louis B. Mayer was probably the harshest critic of all. *Freaks* simply didn't fit into the studio's family oriented type of productions and it was quickly withdrawn from distribution. Periodically, M-G-M would resurrect their "stepchild" and pawn it off as a romantic melodrama! "Can a full-grown woman truly love a midget?" new advertising would read. It didn't matter; *Freaks* remained an experience that M-G-M just wanted to forget.*

---

*The film had lost $164,000 in its early aborted run. In 1948 a financially strapped M-G-M sold the distribution rights to Dwain Esper, a notorious exploitation entrepreneur, who exhibited it under various titles including Nature's Mistakes. *The film met renewed interest and has become a staple at midnight showings.*

All M-G-M had to offer Baclanova following the *Freaks* disaster was a supporting role in *Downstairs* (1932), a mediocre comedy written by and starring a fading and alcoholic John Gilbert ("I thought he was wonderful," Olga later told John Kobal). She returned to her old studio, Paramount, for *The Billion Dollar Scandal* (1932), a prize-fighting drama, but her role as Robert Armstrong's girlfriend was brief. It was her last screen appearance in 11 years.

The Russian star returned briefly to the stage,* but soon retired to raise her son by Soussanin. Unhappily, the always rocky marriage collapsed and she divorced him in 1939 in order to marry New York publisher (and owner of that city's Fine Arts Theatre) Richard Davis. She returned to performing via a nightclub act in the early 1940s and appeared in a supporting role on Broadway in the play, *Claudia*. When Twentieth Century–Fox filmed the romantic drama with Dorothy McGuire in 1943, Baclanova repeated her role as an immigrant woman.

In the 1960s, divorced from Davis, Olga Baclanova left the United States (she had become a citizen in 1931) and settled in the fashionable resort community of Vesey, Switzerland. She died in a nursing home there on September 6, 1974.

"I don't think I was a star," Baclanova confided to John Kobal in 1964. "I never believed that I was a star. But I tell you, I don't see anybody better [today] than I saw in Hollywood when I was there. No. Some of them were so good, I was ashamed. I thought I was rotten."

OLGA BACLANOVA FILMOGRAPHY

- **1927:** *The Man Who Laughs.*
- **1928:** *Street of Sin; Three Sinners; Forgotten Faces; The Docks of New York.*
- **1929:** *The Wolf of Wall Street; A Dangerous Woman; The Man I Love.*
- **1930:** *Cheer Up and Smile.*
- **1931:** *Are You There? The Great Lover.*
- **1932:** *Freaks; Downstairs.*
- **1933:** *The Billion Dollar Scandal.*
- **1943:** *Claudia.*

In a Los Angeles production of The Cat and the Fiddle *(Belasco Theatre, October 1932).*

3 — Binnie Barnes

Blond, blue-eyed, and British, Binnie Barnes was always a threat to a 1930s heroine, no matter how innocent she herself would look. Of course, she did her fair share of long-suffering ingenues, but her forte would prove to be playing aristocratic-looking gold diggers and she usually endowed them with a great deal of sting. Even some of Binnie's shrinking violets weren't all that shrinking after all! As Alice Munro in *The Last of the Mohicans* (Reliance, 1936), Barnes showed gusto and courage—as opposed to her poor dumb sister Cora (Heather Angel) who was a true wallflower. Binnie's knack for portraying charming schemers wasn't all that surprising; she had come to prominence playing the doomed Katherine Howard opposite Charles Laughton in *The Private Life of Henry VIII*. Howard, of course, had the temerity to be unfaithful to her fat lord and master. Off with her head!

In Hollywood, Barnes proved to be one of filmdom's most charming other women. Binnie would use any means to catch her man—and yet remain a lady throughout! Deanna Durbin, for example, was in for some rough sailing when Barnes set out to capture her somewhat eligible father in *Three Smart Girls* (Universal, 1936). Later, Binnie proved a devastatingly funny, if corrupt, Milady de Winter in the Ritz Brothers' version of *The Three Musketeers* (20th Century–Fox, 1939). Through it all, she was always a pleasure to have around, despite her many dirty deeds.

Gertrude Maude Gitelle Enoyce ("Gittle") Barnes was born March 25, 1905, in London, England, the daughter of a London "bobby" and his Italian-born wife. According to later reports, she grew up in the country where, to help her impoverished and soon divorced mother (who was to have 17 children with three husbands), Binnie did farm work and slaved in factories. "I carried heavy pails of mash to the pigs, pitched hay, and milked, cooked and scrubbed," she later told Mayme Peak of the Boston *Globe*.

> I drove farm wagons to market. I delivered milk from door to door. Nowadays I can't see an old nag hitched to a heavy load in London without wanting to turn it loose for the rest of its days.

> I worked in factories, standing on my feet from dawn to dusk, making paper boxes. That was too tame, so I took up nursing, choosing the most exciting place to get my training—in an insane asylum! I never was afraid to try anything!

In her spare time, Barnes took dance lessons and discovered that she was "an uncommonly good ballroom dancer." To earn a living, she became a so-called taxi-dancer (partnering lone gentlemen for a fee), first at the Palais de Danse, later at the more exclusive Cosmo Club. She was soon promoted to hostess and would earn up to £50 a week.

Determined to go on the wicked stage, Barnes next teamed up with American "Tex" McLeod, a second-rate Will Rogers imitator, and the two embarked on a tour of South Africa. It was on this excursion that Billie Barnes (as she was billed) made her vocal debut with a throaty rendition of "My Blue Heaven." Heard frequently on radio in Johannesburg, Barnes, who possessed a rather masculine voice, was often mistakenly referred to as *Mr.* Billie Barnes; thus the name change to the more feminine sounding "Binnie."

Americanized through her association with McLeod, *Texas* Binnie Barnes returned to London with a twang and a drawl and found herself much in demand. She appeared in cabaret, vaudeville and on radio before attaining stardom singing the torch song "Deja" in Andre Charlot's 1928 *Revue*. The popularity of the show, the song, and Binnie herself opened the door for a legitimate stage career and she made her West End bow opposite Charles Laughton and Una O'Connor in *Silver Tassie* (1929). Busy as a bee, she even found time to moonlight in two-reelers with Stanley Lupino (father of Ida) while still with the show.

Binnie Barnes' timing couldn't have been more fortuitous: Noël Coward saw her in *Silver Tassie,* thought her superb and cast her as the torch singer Fanny Bridges in *Cavalcade*. Opening on September 6, 1931, and chronicling two families from the eve of the twentieth century to 1930, the epic drama was a huge success and Binnie, belting out the show-stopping "Twentieth Century Blues," was suddenly the "toast" of London.

During the run of *Cavalcade*, Barnes married London art dealer Samuel Joseph and made her feature film debut in a crime drama with Heather Angel, *A Night in Montmartre* (1931). According to some accounts, she appeared in 12 films while still starring in *Cavalcade* nightly, all of them programmers.

Barnes' diligence paid off, it seemed, when Hollywood production company Fox asked her to repeat the role of Fanny Bridges in an up-coming screen version of *Cavalcade*. According to Kirtley Baskette of *Photoplay*, Binnie blithely left the West End, sailed for New York and immediately found herself stranded.

> No one met her. She didn't know a soul. She sat in her hotel room for a week waiting for the telephone to ring. It didn't, so she finally called the Fox office.
> "This is Miss Barnes," she told them, expecting a rousing, cheery, welcome response.
> "Yeah!" came the reply. "Who are you?"
> "I'm one of the contract actresses," she explained.
> "Who signed you?"
> "Why, Mr. [Sydney] Kent."
> "Then," explained the voice, "you'll have to wait until he comes in from the Coast."

According to Baskette, Barnes returned to London with a contract release in her purse. "After all, she had just been married and that was no time to leave a nice husband for this mad America." Other sources, however, maintain that Barnes had not liked the way her role had been altered—presumably to give more emphasis to Diana Wynyard's Jane Marryot, the female lead—and walked off the production.* Whatever the case, she did in fact return to London and was almost immediately cast as the adulterous Katherine Howard in Alexander Korda's *The Private Life of Henry VIII* (London Film Productions, 1933), arguably the most successful British film of the decade.

Opening in New York City in October of 1933 (two weeks before its London premiere), the lusty re-telling of Henry VIII and five of his six wives was a triumph.† Mordaunt Hall of the *New York Times* lauded the entire production and praised Charles Laughton's indefatigable performance in the title role. The supporting cast, especially the wives, also received accolades, Barnes having been singled out as "able and charming." As a result of this film Laughton, Barnes, Merle Oberon (Anne Boleyn), Wendy Barrie (Jane Seymour), Elsa Lanchester (Anna of Cleves), and Robert Donat (Katherine Howard's lover, Thomas Culpepper) all received lucrative offers from Hollywood and went on to enjoy long careers in American films. (All, that is, with the exception of Donat, whose delicate health prohibited a hectic Hollywood schedule.) *The Private Life of Henry VIII* not only (briefly) rejuvenated a lethargic British film industry, it won Laughton an Academy Award and was itself nominated for Best Picture. Ironically, it lost to *Cavalcade*.

Before they could run off to Hollywood, Alexander Korda retained the services of Barnes and Merle Oberon for yet another bio-pic, *The Private Life of Don Juan* (London Film Productions, 1934). Starring an aging Douglas Fairbanks, *Don Juan* was a rather tepid swashbuckler and didn't come close to equaling the success of *Henry VIII*. That didn't matter much to Barnes, who had signed a lucrative contract with Universal and had already arrived in Hollywood. "Binnie left the *Don Juan* set in England at twelve o'clock midnight of a Thursday. Early Friday she was on the high seas," Kirtley Baskette reported in *Photoplay*. En route to Hollywood, Binnie busied herself by studying the script for *There's Always Tomorrow*, her first film under her new contract.

"Miss Barnes does well enough," Frank S. Nugent of the *New York Times* commented on her American debut, "but well enough is not sufficient to dominate the splendid performance that Mr. [Frank] Morgan contributes."

One of Hollywood's favorite character actors, Morgan was thrust front and center in *There's Always Tomorrow* (Universal, 1934), the story of a milquetoast whose family has pushed him into the background of their lives. Enter Binnie Barnes as Morgan's erstwhile secretary who, as she says, "makes a fuss over him, makes him feel important." Theirs becomes a gentle romance, nothing to do with anything so vulgar as SEX, but the Morgan kids naturally misunderstand the attachment Papa has for the beautiful blonde and melodrama ensues. In the end, of course, the reborn Morgan is

---

*She was replaced by Ursula Jeans.

†"Catherine of Aragon was the first," the film's introduction read, "but her story is of no particular interest—she was a respectable woman."

reunited with his wife (Lois Wilson), who, through adversity, suddenly discovers the man she once married and loved.

There's Always Tomorrow attempted to present Barnes as a sympathetic other woman—but in reality she was a mere plot machination conjured up to ignite an old man's hidden desires and partially forgotten self-respect. When Wilson re-discovers her husband's "sex appeal" (which she of course does the minute she learns of an attractive potential rival), Barnes disappears without a whimper, the sanctity of matrimony unsullied. A vibrant personality, Binnie deserved much better than playing the demure vixen to Frank Morgan's timeworn Lothario.

Universal rewarded Barnes' yeoman duty in *There's Always Tomorrow* by starring her as a singer turned jewel thief in *One Exciting Adventure* (1934), a remake of a German comedy written (partially) by Billy Wilder. Unfortunately, the film was a mere programmer that completely belied its title and Barnes was wasted yet again.

Although demoted to supporting status, she was much better served playing a glamorous Lillian Russell to Edward Arnold's James Buchanan Brady in *Diamond Jim* (Universal, 1935), a lusty if historically highly inaccurate bio-pic of a turn-of-the-century New York industrialist. And on loan to M-G-M, she played her first outright villainess as William Powell's mistress, a glamorous but brainy German spy, in *Rendezvous* (1935). During the filming of this highly entertaining World War I espionage thriller, rumors abounded that M-G-M disliked her performance to the point where the studio stopped production to look for a replacement. Filming was indeed stopped for a while, but the official reason was Barnes' bout with appendicitis. Viewed today, her performance is slinky and vastly amusing and she appears the perfect foil for the elegant Powell. A contemporary reviewer, Andre Sennwald of the *New York Times*, thought her performance "effective" and "charming" and pronounced *Rendezvous* "lively and amusing melodrama."

According to *Photoplay*'s Kirtley Baskette, Barnes enjoyed the California lifestyle to the fullest. "Binnie likes Hollywood," Baskette told her readers, "and she is having a grand time going roller skating and eating Mexican food, and going swimming at a beach place she has rented up beyond Santa Monica [presumably in Malibu]." The marriage to Samuel Joseph suffered under the palm trees, however, and the couple divorced in early 1936. Binnie, it seems, was "going Hollywood" with a vengeance. Tall (5 feet 6 inches), blonde and glamorous, she became a publicity man's delight and never turned down an opportunity for self promotion. No wonder photographers voted her "Hollywood's most obliging actress."

She was very glamorous and obliging indeed on loan to M-G-M as Robert Taylor's socialite fiancée in *Small Town Girl* (1936); and period costumes only added to her allure in *Sutter's Gold* (Universal, 1936) and *The Last of the Mohicans* (Reliance, 1936). All of these potboilers, however, were mere warm-ups to her bravura performance as the gold-digging Donna Lyons in *Three Smart Girls* (1937), the comedy that single-handedly rescued Universal from bankruptcy.

A studio without much identity but busily manufacturing a steady stream of routine Westerns and comedies, Universal was by the middle of the decade struggling in a market dominated by studios with strong theater chains which it was sadly without. Straddling respectability and Poverty Row, Carl Laemmle's old plant was badly in need of a top-draw talent. Tethered at the edge of despair, Laemmle's successors finally struck pay dirt with M-G-M reject Deanna Durbin, a pretty and vivacious 15-year-old coloratura who, to everyone's amazement, could act rings around much more seasoned entertainers. For insurance Barnes was given top billing in *Three Smart Girls*, but the film was all Durbin, sweetly scheming to get her father (Charles Winninger) back in the arms of his estranged wife (Nella Walker). According to the script, Durbin was aided in her quest by "sisters" Nan Grey and Barbara Read, but the audience had eyes only for the charming newcomer with the lilting voice and effervescent personality. As the vixenish target of Durbin's adolescent tricks, Barnes more than held her own and was a crucial, if somewhat overlooked, ingredient to the film's surprising success at the box office. Along with the droll Alice Brady (playing her mother), Binnie, according to a delighted Frank S. Nugent of the *New York Times*, "went down—undermined by pretty tears, shaken by the counter-attack of a treacherous nobleman [Mischa Auer], ambushed by a kidnap hoax—with colors still flying and a fresh onslaught being planned."

The offscreen Binnie Barnes was not vastly different from the characters she was given to portray. Binnie, according to Sidney Skolsky, "[liked] to dress in style when going out, and [figured] that time spent in a beauty shop was well spent." Not exactly an ardent feminist, she had "little regard for a woman's judgment" and was "delighted with the fact that most of her fan mail [came] from men." "As long as I can appeal to men," she told Skolsky, "I think I have a career."

In early 1937 Barnes returned to London to play the unfaithful Lady Mere in the second screen version of Gilbert Wakefield's *Counsel's Opinion*, now retitled *The Divorce of Lady X* (London Film, 1938). As opposed to the rather staid 1933 version (in which Barnes had played the lead), this was a major Alexander Korda production filmed in technicolor and featuring the cream of the crop of British stars: Merle Oberon, Laurence Olivier, and Ralph Richardson. According to Nugent of the *New York Times*, Korda pulled off the impossible by producing a British screwball comedy which was "nimble-witted" and filled with bright dialogue.

Perhaps Binnie Barnes should have stayed abroad; upon her return to Hollywood she was an incongruous Mongol queen opposite an equally ill at ease Gary Cooper in the wretched *The Adventures of Marco Polo* (United Artists, 1938). She was happier playing the snobbish Laura Cram in Columbia's screen version of Philip Barry's *Holiday* (1938), but the part was small and Katharine Hepburn, the film's star, took no prisoners. (Nor indeed did Doris Nolan, a fellow Britisher too seldom seen on screen, who played Hepburn's arrogant sister.)

Following *Holiday*, Barnes signed a stock contract with 20th Century-Fox, a studio with a penchant for corny Americana and ruled by dimpled *artistes* such as Shirley Temple and Sonja Henie. It was not exactly the ideal place for the sophisticated Barnes, who was usually wasted in secondary roles in forgettable programmers. The tedium was momentarily relieved by a smart performance as Adolphe Menjou's lively assistant in *Thanks for Everything* (1938), a screwball comedy about a millionaire posing as a hobo; and she did yeoman duty as Loretta Young's daffy rival with a penchant for beer and non sequiturs in the romantic comedy *Three Blind Mice* (1938). In the latter, as a matter of fact, Barnes garnered some of the best reviews of her career. *Times* critic Nugent, for example, thought she stole the film outright from its angular star, and urged producers to remember that she was a comedienne.

Fox paid attention and cast Barnes as Milady de Winter opposite the Ritz Brothers and Don Ameche in a frequently hilarious rendition of *The Three Musketeers* (1939). It was, of course, all-out burlesque, culminating in a scene where Binnie is picked up by the heels and shaken until relieved of a secret note; if not exactly Dumas, it was certainly prime Ritz. *Wife, Husband and Friend* (1939), in which she was an opera diva pursuing a tone-deaf building contractor (Warner Baxter), was hardly more subtle, and *Man About Town* (20th Century–Fox, 1939), with Binnie chased by a bumbling Jack Benny, continued the happy trend.

She then had a welcome change of pace, however, beating out Kay Francis, Ann Sothern, Frances Farmer, Claire Trevor and Dorothy Lamour to land the part of a tough dance-hall queen in *Frontier Marshal* (1939), Fox's first go at filming the story of Wyatt Earp (here played, somberly, by Randolph Scott). Again stealing a film from its nominal stars, Barnes was, in the words of the *New York Times'* B. R. Crisler, "uncompromisingly blond, hard and harsh-voiced" and "a miracle of rightness."

Barnes and Warner Baxter were to have been re-teamed for *He Married His Wife* (20th Century–Fox, 1940), but Baxter's star was in decline and at the last minute they were replaced with Nancy Kelly and Joel McCrea. Instead, Barnes was borrowed by Warner Bros. to play a sagacious countess in *'Til We Meet Again* (1940), a reworking of *One Way Passage*, a sentimental favorite of 1932 about a con artist and a terminally ill heiress who experience a star-crossed romance aboard an ocean liner. It was all rather dubious by 1940 and a far cry from Robert Lord's original anyway. She was misused again in Columbia's *This Thing Called Love* (1941), a star-driven comedy with Rosalind Russell and Melvyn Douglas.

On September 29, 1940, Barnes took time out from her busy schedule to marry M. J. "Mike" Frankovich, the adopted son of comedian Joe E. Brown, in whose Beverly Hills home the ceremony was held. Born in Bisbee, Arizona, in 1910, Frankovich had been a radio commentator and producer and was a former U.C.L.A. football star.* "I had to [marry Frankovich] to please or shock [columnist] Louella Parsons," Binnie said of her 35-year marriage in 1973. "Louella used to say to Mike, 'Why did you marry that dreadful woman? A nice Jewish boy like you marrying that dreadful English Catholic.' She said it backward and never did get it straight."† The newlyweds joined Louella Parson's vaudeville show and toured the country in a company that also included such disparate talent as Sabu, Robert Stack and Ilona Massey. Binnie would stop the show in every town singing English Music Hall favorites like "Why Am I Always a Bridesmaid and Never a Blushing Bride?" She also joined an all-star revival of Noël Coward's *Tonight at 8:30*, the proceeds from which went to the British War Relief Association of Southern California. In early 1942, Frankovich joined the Army and served throughout the war, attaining the rank of major.

With her husband overseas, Barnes busied herself with a series of forgettable comedies and musicals. She was once again a scheming countess, this time supporting

---

*Barnes and Frankovich would eventually adopt three children, including a British war orphan.

†Jewish-born Barnes later converted to Catholicism as an anniversary gift to Frankovich.

Hungarian import Ilona Massey in *New Wine* (United Artists, 1942); did her dance-hall queen routine in *In Old California* (Republic, 1942); and appeared gaudily costumed and rather lost amidst the empty opulence of *I Married an Angel* (M-G-M, 1942). At least these roles weren't embarrassing, but she was downright miscast as the girl Charles Laughton left behind in *The Man from Down Under* (M-G-M, 1943). To add insult to injury, the comedy-drama presented Laughton at his glorious worst and was prophetically produced by one Orville O. Dull. As for Barnes' own performance, Theodore Strauss of the *New York Times* found it "badly out of focus or simply schizophrenic."

Barnes rebounded via a couple of low-brow but rather popular comedies, *Up in Mabel's Room* (United Artists, 1944) and *Getting Gertie's Garter* (United Artists, 1945), and she was hilarious as Fred Allen's wife in *It's in the Bag* (United Artists, 1945). In the latter, according to Sidney Skolsky, she startled her co-workers by smoking a pipe between takes. "I started to smoke a pipe because I was smoking too many cigarettes," she told the gossip columnist. Despite her somewhat eccentric behavior, Barnes, according to Skolsky, was a popular addition to any cast.

> Directors, prop men and her fellow players love her. She is always there with the comeback, and she generally has a story or two to tell.
> She is easy to work with, takes direction with ease born of long experience, and only slightly annoys those directors who insist on having everything their own way. She has had few arguments with her bosses. "But they all end happily," she admits. "They win."

The separation due to the war took its toll on the Frankoviches. In early 1944, gossip columns reported that the couple were close to a divorce, but by May the storm had blown over. "It was a stupid misunderstanding such as people sometimes have," Barnes explained to the *Los Angeles Times*, disavowing any notion of an impending split.

With the war over and the Frankovich union saved, Barnes more or less abandoned her screen career to raise a family. But in between changing diapers, she, along with Lucille Ball, Constance Bennett, Dorothy Kilgallen, et al., discussed topical women's problems on Mutual Network's "Leave It to the Girls" radio show.

From 1949 on, the Frankoviches became bi-continental, spending much of their time in Europe where Barnes appeared in films produced by her husband, e.g. *The Pirates of Capri* (Film Classics, 1949), a low-budget melodrama set during the French revolution. Barnes co-starred (with Louis Hayward, another member of Hollywood's British colony who had been somewhat misused by the system) as a fearful aristocrat. Back in the United States, she replaced Gloria Swanson in the Broadway revival of the Hecht-MacArthur comedy *Twentieth Century*, but critics thought she lacked Swanson's impeccable timing and she quickly left again for Europe.

Filmed on location in Rome, *The Fugitive Lady* (Republic, 1952) featured Barnes as a proud Italian society woman. It was hardly worth the effort, according to Howard Thompson of the *New York Times*, who felt that Frankovich had "unwound this meandering claptrap, which is recounted in an interminable series of flashbacks by practically everybody in the cast, against the eye-popping magnificence of Rome's cafe society playground."

"Binnie Barnes, who is also Mrs. Frankovich," Thompson added, "does a stiff but at least restrained job as [Eduardo Cianelli's] protecting sister."

Binnie Barnes in 1951.

The Frankoviches' streak of bad luck continued with *Decameron Nights* (RKO, 1953), a tame (very tame) screen version of Boccaccio filmed in England with, as they say, an international cast. "Binnie Barnes whips around without any purpose," complained Bosley Crowther of the *New York Times,* who otherwise blamed Frankovich and screenwriter George Oppenheimer for the slow moving mess. *Fire Over Africa* (Columbia, 1954), another Frankovich production, at least had breathtaking location work and Binnie Barnes "offering an easy, realistic portrait of a bistro queen" (Howard Thompson).

In 1955 Mike Frankovich was appointed managing director of Columbia in United Kingdom and Ireland. He was promoted to vice president in 1958 and the family returned to Hollywood. By the early 1960s Frankovich had been named first

Opposite: **Charles Laughton and Barnes in** *The Man from Down Under* **(M-G-M, 1943).**

vice president in charge of worldwide production, a title he held until 1967, when he left to form a new production enterprise.

Mrs. Frankovich, meanwhile, busied herself away from the cameras and became known as one of Hollywood's better hostesses. Before she left Europe, however, she produced a quaint little melodrama about fishermen in Spain, *Thunderstorm* (Allied Artists, 1955). Carlos Thompson and Linda Christian starred, but the film received scant distribution in the United States.

Basically retired from performing, Barnes returned now and again to guest star on television and she joined Hollywood "survivors" Rosalind Russell, Gypsy Rose Lee, Mary Wickes and Kent Smith in *The Trouble with Angels* (Columbia, 1966) and its sequel *Where Angels Go—Trouble Follows* (Columbia, 1968). She enjoyed working with "old pals" but didn't miss the grind of everyday filmmaking. "Frankly, I've never been mad about acting—it just happened to be the only way I could make a living," she told the *Los Angeles Times*.

Binnie Barnes returned to the screen a final time when Frankovich convinced her to take the role as Liv Ullman's mother in *Forty Carats* (Columbia, 1973), the leaden comedy that, according to Ullman, "almost bankrupted Columbia." Frankovich, fresh from having produced *Bob & Carol & Ted & Alice* and *Cactus Flower* (both Columbia, 1969), had convinced a reluctant Ullman to tackle farce. Unfortunately, Ullman was no Garbo and *Forty Carats* no *Ninotschka*. A popular summer stock perennial, the comedy was much more suited to a glamorous leading lady such as Lana Turner, who had done it successfully on stage. With a miscast Ullman, however, audiences stayed away in droves and the only good reviews were awarded Barnes, who, as *Variety* noted, did a "wild discotheque dancing turn that would exhaust a teenager." She had not wanted the role, Binnie told the *Los Angeles Times*, but Frankovich had convinced her and besides, "not many actresses my age will admit they're old enough to be a grandmother."

Following *Forty Carats*, Binnie Barnes emerged exclusively on the arm of her successful husband, who, in 1983, was given the prestigious Jean Hersholt Humanitarian Award by the Academy of Motion Picture Arts and Sciences. Frank Sinatra presented the statuette at the year's Academy Award ceremony, referring to the happy recipient as a "Godfather of ... uh ... of ... Goodness."

Following the death of her husband on January 1, 1992, Barnes' name disappeared from the media. She lived quietly in the Trousdale Estates area of Beverly Hills, until her death on July 27, 1997.

BINNIE BARNES FILMOGRAPHY

1931: *Dr. Josser KC* (GB*; *Love Lies* (GB); *A Night in Montmartre* (GB); *Out of the Blue* (GB).
1932: *Down on Our Street* (GB); *The Last Coupon* (GB); *Murder at Covent Garden* (GB); *Old Spanish Customers* (GB); *Why Saps Leave Home* (GB).
1933: *The Charming Deceiver* (GB); *Counsel's Opinion* (GB); *The Private Life of Henry VIII* (GB); *Their Night Out* (GB).

*GB=Great Britain.

1934: *Gift of Gap* (GB); *The Lady Is Willing* (GB); *Nine Forty-Five* (GB); *No Escape* (GB); *The Private Life of Don Juan* (GB); *The Silver Spoon* (GB); *There's Always Tomorrow.*
1935: *Diamond Jim; Rendezvous.*
1936: *Small Town Girl; Sutter's Gold; The Last of the Mohicans; The Magnificent Brute.*
1937: *Breezing Home; Broadway Melody of 1938; Three Smart Girls.*
1938: *The First Hundred Years; The Adventures of Marco Polo; Holiday; Three Blind Mice; Tropic Holiday; Always Goodbye; The Divorce of Lady X* (GB); *Forbidden Territory* (GB); *Gateway; Thanks for Everything.*
1939: *The Three Musketeers; Wife, Husband and Friend; Man About Town; Frontier Marshal; Day-Time Wife.*
1940: *'Til We Meet Again.*
1941: *This Thing Called Love; Tight Shoes; Angels with Broken Wings; Three Girls About Town; Skylark.*
1942: *Call Out the Marines; New Wine; In Old California; I Married an Angel.*
1943: *The Man from Down Under.*
1944: *Up in Mabel's Room; The Hour Before the Dawn; Barbary Coast Gent.*
1945: *It's in the Bag; The Spanish Main; Getting Gertie's Garter.*
1946: *The Time of Their Lives.*
1947: *If Winter Comes.*
1948: *The Dude Goes West.*
1949: *My Own True Love; The Pirates of Capri.*
1951: *Fugitive Lady.*
1953: *Decameron Nights* (GB).
1954: *Fire Over Africa* (GB).
1955: *Shadow of the Eagle* (GB); *Thunderstorm* (GB; prod. only).
1966: *The Trouble with Angels.*
1968: *Where Angels Go—Trouble Follows.*
1973: *Forty Carats.*

4—Evelyn Brent

Evelyn Brent was what they used to call "smoldering." Few references to the actress, in fact, seem to avoid the term. Publicist and film historian John Springer, however, while dutifully mentioning her "smoldering" eyes, preferred the word "sullen." DeWitt Bodeen, who got to know the veteran performer on the set of *The Seventh Victim* (RKO, 1943), attributed the "Brent mystique" to the fact that in her dark brooding eyes "there was always that attractive, enigmatic, but bitter smile of resignation." Whatever her allure, Evelyn Brent, as Mr. Bodeen also noted, "remained a vitally interesting film personality for more than three decades in the New York, London, and Hollywood film worlds."

Brent certainly had her fair share of success, especially in the late 1920s when Josef von Sternberg chose her as the quintessential gangster's moll in two near masterpieces, *Underworld* (Paramount, 1927) and *The Drag Net* (Paramount, 1928). But in a career that began in the early teens and ended on live television in the late 1950s, there were more downs than ups. In countless programmers her sullen, if not downright morose, villainy seemed a bit too hardened and cold. Louise Brooks, a co-star in *Love 'Em and Leave 'Em* (Paramount, 1927), found her to be "tense." Brent had just arrived in Hollywood from New York (courtesy of her husband, studio executive Bernie Fineman) and was awarded the big build-up when teamed with the insightful Brooks. "Evelyn was indeed in a class by herself," Louise would write.

> After all these years the possibility of stardom put her in an emotional state of anxiety, the result of which being that she acted with an intensity better suited to Mata Hari before the firing squad than [the shop girl she played in *Love 'Em and Leave 'Em*].

Brent, in retrospect, had good reason to be "tense": according to contemporary reviews, Louise Brooks stole the picture from right under her nose.

Every once in a while, however, Evelyn Brent was cast in the right role in the right film and everything clicked. She was perfect playing rather decadent showgirls in crime dramas such as *Interference* (1928), Paramount's first "all-talkie." *Broadway* (1929), a loan-out to Universal which she had vehemently resisted, greatly benefited from her hard-boiled, smoldering participation.

Paramount, her home studio, unfortunately cleaned up house in 1930 and got rid of most of their holdovers from the silent era, including Brent. Without a strong organization to push her, Evelyn, admittedly one of the less driven stars of the era, saw her career nosedive. She briefly returned to the studio in 1937 and an old friend, director Robert Florey, did his best to resurrect whatever was left of her career by casting her in the kind of roles she had earlier perfected under von Sternberg. It was, however, much too late and Evelyn Brent spent the remainder of her days in Hollywood—13 long years—on that dead end street known colloquially as Poverty Row.

Evelyn Brent was born Mary Elizabeth Riggs in Tampa, Florida, on October 20, 1899. "I was born when my mother was fourteen," she told Gladys Hall of *Motion Picture Classic* in 1928. "She was married when she was thirteen. My father was seventeen." Her mother, she claimed, had been an Italian immigrant and her father was a New Yorker of Irish descent. Yet her friend Dewitt Bodeen, in the June-July 1976 issue of *Films in Review*, favors a different version, which the actress related in the later years of her life.

Elizabeth Riggs' mother, according to Bodeen, was a teenager from Syracuse, New York, and Elizabeth, or Betty as she was called, was born out of wedlock in her grandmother's house in Tampa. If Bodeen's theory is more believable, it is also less colorful than Brent's earlier depiction of how her father, an inveterate gambler, was killed on the race course and his body dumped without explanation on the family doorstep. Colorful, yes, but probably untrue.

Evelyn Brent was fond of telling how her mother had gradually gone insane and had died in a sanatorium. The scenario is remarkably like the experiences of her contemporary and onetime rival at Paramount, Clara Bow. Brent, it appears, knew early on how to make her from all accounts squalid but mundane early years more interesting and dramatic. In the above-mentioned interview with Gladys Hall, she relates how the Riggs women left Florida for Syracuse and later Brooklyn. In the latter location, she said, they lived in an overcrowded tenement where life was hard and bitter.

> I never had any childhood. I never was a child, I never was childish—and I knew it. Life had turned a frightful profile to me and I couldn't get away from it. Doubtless it was then that my face settled into the smoldering, secretive lines it is reputed I have today.

Brent would often claim that she was left penniless at the age of 14 when her mother died. But according to an earlier interview, she had been studying at Hunter College (not exactly a place known for sheltering impoverished orphans), when she discovered that working in films was more interesting than becoming a school teacher—her goal up to that time. In reality, Betty Riggs was still a high school student when she started fashion modeling. Soon after, she joined a group of girls who every day traveled to nearby Fort Lee, New Jersey, in search of motion picture work. The teenage girls would take the ferry in the morning and return in the evening—sometimes with a few dollars earned as extras, more often without. Silent screen star Blanche Sweet fondly remembered the ferries:

"I always used to get up at the bow of the boat," she told the *New York Times* in 1977. "Going back—often it would be night time; the lights twinkling over in New York—with millions of dreams."

Betty Riggs was among the lucky few whose dream came true. After only a couple of trips she obtained several days' work (at $3 a day) as a background extra in *A Gentleman from Mississippi* (World, 1914), a vehicle for stage star Thomas Wise. Evelyn Brent would in later years dismiss the entire experience, referring to the film as "A Man from Mars."

As Betty Riggs, she soon began obtaining featured parts at World and Metro. (She was a maid in Maurice Tourneur's *The Pit*, World, 1914).On the advice of Olga Petrova, a great dramatic star who had befriended the newcomer on the set of *The Heart of a Painted Woman* (World, 1915), Betty Riggs signed a stock contract with Metro for $25 a week. It was a big break for the novice actress and couldn't have come at a more opportune moment: she and her roommate, another aspiring actress, had been out of work for some time. "We were down to—nothing," she recalled later. "Nothing to eat for three days. I was very ill, too, with pleurisy. And it was then, at that time, that I tried to commit suicide by cutting my wrists." Apparently, it was more a cry for help than a true suicide attempt. And the offer from Metro naturally made any thought of leaving this world disappear.

> They were casting an allegorical story at Metro [she later remembered] and wanted a young, unformed adolescent girl to play the symbolic role of Sin. She had to be very slender and wear nothing at all but a long black wig. I said I couldn't possibly do such a thing. They offered me $25 a day to play the part. It would go on for close to two weeks, they said. I couldn't resist that. I did it.

The title of this "allegorical story" is forgotten (if indeed it was ever made), but Metro was sufficiently impressed with the young actress to change the name Betty Riggs to the more marquee-ready Evelyn Brent and launch her on a career as an ingenue. As Evelyn Brent she supported her benefactress Petrova in *The Soul Market* and *Playing with Fire* (both 1916); went to Alaska for location work on *The Spell of the Yukon* (1916) with Edmund Breese; and starred opposite Lionel Barrymore in *The Millionaire's Double* (1917), a comedy that benefited from a brisk June Mathis script." It was absolutely the happiest day of my life," she told *Photoplay*'s Ruth Biery of being cast opposite Barrymore. "And my last job in many months," she quickly added. She had been sufficiently unimpressive in *The Millionaire's Double* for Metro to lose interest in her potential for stardom. Instead, she tested for Lewis Selznick. "But [the Selznick casting directors] said I hadn't enough experience and hired Martha Mansfield. That seemed my last chance. There seemed nothing whatever left for me."

Brent's recollection is slightly faulty regarding her sudden lack of opportunity; indeed, she continued to appear for Metro and other companies throughout 1919 and even worked for Selznick—as the second female lead in *The Glorious Lady* (Select, 1919), a society drama starring the unfortunate Olive Thomas.* Nonetheless, these were troubled times for the young actress; according to her surprisingly frank 1928

The wife of Jack Pickford and a former Ziegfeld girl, Thomas died of a drug overdose in 1920.

interview with Gladys Hall, she had begun to take up with rich older men but claimed that she never really had any fun as a "kept" woman. She also nearly died in the tragic influenza epidemic that decimated the entertainment industry in 1918 and 1919.

In late 1919, still recovering from the disease, Brent traveled to Europe with "a rich, kind-hearted woman friend." The trip proved to be a watershed event in her life. "After Paris, which was gorgeous, we went to London," she recalled. "And London is my home. Not by right of birth but by right of—well, who knows. I belong there. And in London I had the happiest time I ever had in my life."

Her time in London also proved her most productive, artistically. Through an acquaintance in the theater world, she discovered that the part of a vivacious American girl was up for grabs in the London production of Frances Nordstrom's comedy *The Ruined Lady*. With a recommendation from a friend, the ballroom dancer Maurice, she approached the show's producers and ultimately won the part. *The Ruined Lady* opened at the Comedy Theatre on June 25, 1920, and was a hit. As DeWitt Bodeen later told it, "Evelyn Brent woke up the morning after the opening night to find that she, an American girl, was the most talked-about young actress in the West End."

Inevitably, her success led to movie offers, and when *The Ruined Lady* ended its extended run, she signed for two films to be made almost back to back. Her salary was £30 a week, "which was phenomenal for me and which I only got because I had American experience. You could get anything at that time, on that premise."

None of her British films were of any importance but they kept her name in the headlines and she usually earned good reviews. Of her debut film, *The Shuttle of Life* (1920), a society melodrama with C. Aubrey Smith, the *Bioscope* reviewer commented,

> Miss Evelyn Brent, a newcomer to British films, plays her part with quiet restraint which emphasizes the pitiful struggle to retain her self respect and gains complete sympathy. Miss Brent has charm and extreme beauty, and we shall look forward with great interest to her future career.

In 1921, Brent appeared in two films opposite then popular Chilean actor Adelqui Millar, *Laughter and Tears* and *Circus Jim*, both of which were filmed on location in the Netherlands. The former even boasted of exterior scenes shot in Venice. Her finest British-made film, *The Spanish Jade* (1922), a melodrama set in the Old Spain, was lensed on location in Catalonia.

By 1922, unfortunately, American films had seized a big chunk of the overseas market and the much poorer British film industry suffered from the competition. "I couldn't find a thing to do," Brent recalled later. "Finally, there came a chance on the stage in a play starring Cyril Maude. It was my last hope."

The hope was dashed when she again came down with pneumonia and pleurisy, this time combined with rheumatic fever. So instead of a triumphant return to the West End, Brent spent four weeks recuperating in the English countryside. When she finally was well enough to return, she discovered she was penniless. "She was thin, ill, haggard," Ruth Biery wrote dramatically in *Photoplay*. "The legitimate stage did not want her. The motion pictures were still closed [due to Hollywood competition, presumably]."

Brent was rescued in the nick of time by the Cunard Steamship Line, which was to film a commercial on the voyage between England and New York. Offered £50 and free passage for her participation, she quickly accepted and returned to New York at least in some style.

Meanwhile, Douglas Fairbanks had liked her performance in *The Spanish Jade* and now signed her to a personal contract. On Fairbanks' suggestion she immediately left New York for California, accompanied by her husband, B. F. (Bernie) Fineman, a Paramount executive. Evelyn and Fineman had been childhood sweethearts in Brooklyn, and had been reunited in London.

The contract with Fairbanks, as promising as it must have appeared at first glance, soon proved a detriment. The star hadn't made up his mind what his next film should be—and while he cooled his heels, everybody merely waited. United Artists, the company Fairbanks had co-founded with his wife, Mary Pickford, D. W. Griffith and Charlie Chaplin, was geared more toward quality than quantity and Evelyn Brent was paid a salary for doing basically nothing—a frustrating situation for an actress eager to re-establish herself in the American film industry.

Still, Fairbanks did what he could for his contractee: she was photographed in gorgeous costumes for an intended Arabian Nights story and was also mentioned for a projected sequel to *The Mark of Zorro* (1920). Nothing came of either, but at least the publicity kept her name in the columns. Fairbanks (or was it Bernie Fineman?) also made sure that she was elected a 1923 WAMPAS* Baby Star—only the second year such a selection took place.† Yet, idleness still did not suit the ambitious actress and Fineman asked for and was granted her release from the Fairbanks contract. "I had hung around the studio for six months and not a camera turned," she later explained. "That's death to an actress—to be off the screen that long." Hollywood "insiders," however, insisted that her release from the contract came as a demand from Mary Pickford. Doug's interest in Evelyn, it was whispered, had been not altogether professional.

Whatever the scenario, Brent was soon on her way back to New York having accepted a supporting role opposite the veteran House Peters in *Held to Answer* (Metro, 1923), a melodrama about a man of God who is wrongly accused of theft. She was well received in her role and wanted to stay in New York. Alas, Hollywood still beckoned, and before the year's end she was back, this time armed with a contract from Fox.

Brent was to make six films for Fox, all of them programmers. Usually she was the rather passive heroine leaving the action to such stalwarts as John Gilbert or Western star Buck Jones. By the end of 1924, she had had enough and left Fox to sign with FBO (Film Booking Office). It was a good move. Not that FBO's output was more prestigious than the Fox programmers—it was hardly that—but the studio offered her a chance to exercise her forte: playing seething women of low moral standards. Brent made 13 programmers at FBO and was top-billed in all of them. She had become a star at last.

Certainly, the FBO films had a sameness about them: in six, she was cast as a

---

*Western Association of Motion Picture Advertisers.

†The 1923 group also included Eleanor Boardman, Laura La Plante and Jobyna Ralston.

jewel thief, and she was a chorus girl in four. Not to mention *Three Wise Crooks* (1925) and *The Jade Cup* (1926), in both of which she played a chorus girl turned jewel thief. Still, the films were popular enough and made money.

By early 1927 Brent's husband, Bernie Fineman, had left Paramount and could now champion his wife at that studio, the largest in Hollywood, free from allegations of nepotism. Paramount, happily benefiting from FBO's buildup, signed her to a long-term contract. Career-wise, the three years with the company proved Evelyn Brent's most satisfactory.

Paramount initiated Brent's contract by sending her back to New York to film the romantic comedy, *Love 'Em and Leave 'Em* (1927). Adapted from a hit stage play, the film offered Brent as Mame, a hard-working salesgirl who has to put up with an amoral sister, played vigorously by newcomer Louise Brooks. As mentioned above, Brooks was far from impressed with her co-star. The two actresses first met at a costume fitting: "—In came Evelyn Brent who had just arrived in New York from Hollywood," Louise Brooks later wrote.

> For a shocking half hour I sat amazed watching [the studio wardrobe mistress] and her assemble a complete wardrobe for the film in which she played the lead, and my sister. From a pipe stand of worn size 12's they selected her clothes; and from the shoe shelves they selected my castoff slippers (we wore the same size 4). All this time her manner was warm and friendly, but I found later she was like a Baked Alaska—very cold inside.

Ironically, in her second Paramount outing, *Love's Greatest Mistake* (1927), Brent was directed by Brooks' husband Eddie Sutherland. Again she played a downtrodden heroine, this time blackmailed by a villainous William Powell. In *Blind Alleys* (1927), she was the other woman and lost hero Thomas Meighan to Greta Nissen. Yet, she achieved star billing opposite Meighan and above the otherwise highly touted Norwegian vamp, a clear indication of Paramount's confidence in her drawing power. The chemistry between the veteran Meighan and Brent was strong enough for the studio to reunite them the following year in yet another popular triangle drama, *The Mating Call*.

None of Brent's films of this period, however, was as satisfying, or indeed memorable, as the three she did for Josef von Sternberg. The actress had worked with von Sternberg (then known as plain Joe Stern) back in England where he had been a set designer on one of her films. Brent herself, however, credits the work she had done for Tod Browning at FBO [*The Dangerous Flirt* and *Silk Stocking Sal*; both 1924] as being the main reason why von Sternberg chose her as "Feathers" McCoy, the quintessential gangster's moll in *Underworld* (Paramount, 1927).

> I think that it was Tod Browning that started the "Queen of the Underworld" thing. I probably got the von Sternberg *Underworld* on the strength of Tod's pictures. I know von Sternberg had seen them.

Paramount, meanwhile, pushed Estelle Taylor, another of their resident vamps, for the role, but von Sternberg was adamant and Brent went down in history as the first "modern" *femme fatale*.

Opposite: **Evelyn Brent, circa 1925 (photograph courtesy of the Danish Film Museum).**

Kept by one gangster and cheating on him with another, "Feathers" McCoy was a character straight off the front pages—a creature distinct from the theatrically smoldering vamps of earlier days. Contemporary, tough and pragmatic, she was a girl from the tenements who had clawed her way up, not in society, but outside of it. Brent, as we have already seen, had a long list of wicked girls to her credit but they had all been stock characters—chorus girls who suddenly went bad for the love of a man, or were naively persuaded into a life of crime. Here, supported by the authentic writing of Ben Hecht (who would do even better in "talkies") and von Sternberg's famous *mise-en-scène*, Evelyn was able to bring her character to life with a realism that, in the words of critic Lawrence Reid, was "wrought from imagination and feeling." With George Bancroft as the gangster "Bull" Tweed and Clive Brook as his best friend and "mouthpiece," *Underworld* set a standard for hard-boiled gangster fiction that would endure until the mid–1930s, when the Production Code deemed such "glorification of public enemies" a cinematic taboo. *Underworld* had everything, from fast automobiles and sleazy dames with hidden flasks to a balletic climax in a hail of bullets—clichés of the genre even then, to be sure, but used here for the first time with a sense of estheticism and imagery.

Von Sternberg, known as a hard taskmaster and even harder to please, supervised the production down to minute details, such as "Feathers" McCoy's mode of dress. According to Brent, costume designer Travis Banton already had a thing for feathers and furs (his later collaboration with Marlene Dietrich certainly supported that theory), and von Sternberg's vivid description of the gangster's moll only added to his creative fervor. Said Evelyn:

> The hats were made of coq feathers and velvet leaves edged in rhinestones, and no hair showed. That saved a lot of time. Travis said it would be sensible, knowing how hard you work. It started a vogue.

The costumes, the murky, wet streets, the sleazy joints—everything helped carry the story along and Evelyn Brent was forever in awe of von Sternberg's genius, despite the fact that the dictatorial director often treated his cast as just so much furniture to be moved around. "He had a great feeling for a picture," she later explained. "The actors were not as important as the sweep of the story, [they] moved against it." A truth, the actress felt, that von Sternberg seemingly forgot when he later "created" Marlene Dietrich.

Recently separated from Bernie Fineman, Brent attended the premiere of *Underworld* on the arm of Gary Cooper, her leading man in *Beau Sabreur* (Paramount, 1928), an action adventure filmed before the von Sternberg drama. In fact, Brent had done retakes on *Beau Sabreur* at night while filming *Underworld* by day. "You were under contract, you got the same salary," she later explained. "You didn't get paid for two pictures, you got your regular salary."

In *Beau Sabreur* Brent played an American author who falls for a dashing legionnaire (Cooper). While the film, advertised as a sequel to the popular *Beau Geste* (Paramount, 1926), was generally well received, Brent was considered rather cold and, according to *Variety*, "left the imprint of having been miscast."

Offscreen, however, she was far from cold towards her co-star and they quickly became a public item. "I liked Gary Cooper very much, he was a doll, he really was," she later said. A "doll," maybe, but apparently not marriage material. When her divorce from Fineman became final, Brent suddenly left for New York, leaving Coop to find solace with the more kinetic Lupe Velez.

Brent returned to Hollywood for her second film with von Sternberg, *The Last Command* (Paramount, 1928). This time she played Natascha Dobrowa, a Bolshevik actress who first seduces her Imperial interrogator (Emil Jannings) into letting her go, but later, having fallen in love with her erstwhile tormentor, sacrifices herself so he may live. Doomed to perish in a runaway train, Brent awaits her death with a stoicism worthy of Garbo (to whom she was now often compared), and under a lesser director than von Sternberg her lack of expression would have been ludicrous. Here it only heightens the drama and the scene has been favorably compared to Garbo's inscrutable climatic close-up in *Queen Christina* (M-G-M, 1933).

In *The Last Command*, Evelyn Brent and von Sternberg created a multifaceted woman—part revolutionary, part erotic lure who makes the mistake of falling for her prey. When Natascha finally laughs (in the film's only comedy scene, which finds the entire Imperial General Staff caught taking turns snooping through a keyhole), the effect is again reminiscent of Garbo, this time as *Ninotschka* (M-G-M, 1939). It was a bravura performance, yet suitably deferential to Jannings' inaugural Academy Award–winning performance as an Imperial warlord turned Hollywood extra.

Some critics consider Brent's performance as "The Magpie" in von Sternberg's second classic gangster film, *The Drag Net* (Paramount, 1928), to be her finest. *The Drag Net* tells yet another hot-off-the-presses story, this time of a dedicated cop who is framed in the killing of his partner. In due time, however, the real culprit is exposed—by his sleazy girlfriend, "The Magpie."* Brent was reunited with von Sternberg regular George Bancroft (as the cop) and the duo (with excellent support from a young William Powell as the killer) again deliver keen portrayals of Prohibition-era victimization.

Evelyn Brent enjoyed working with Bancroft, her leading man in both *Underworld* and *The Drag Net*. At the top of his appeal in the late twenties, the journeyman actor had amazed even his own studio by becoming Paramount's number one box office attraction. Big, brawny, and, according to Brent, boneheaded, he proved one of von Sternberg's more enduring "creations," his appeal lasting until the mid-thirties. Remembered Brent:

> He was like a kid. I don't think he realized what the picture was going to be, and if it hadn't been for [von Sternberg], he wouldn't have been good at it. The strength that Joe put into it, he made George put into it. George couldn't have done it himself because he wasn't that kind of person. He had the reactions of a little boy.

Like Bancroft, Evelyn herself was never better than when under the "spell" of the Svengali-like von Sternberg, as her other 1928 releases, *A Night of Mystery* and *His Tiger Lady* (both with Adolphe Menjou) aptly illustrate: in both she was utterly conventional and, as DeWitt Bodeen would later point out, merely sullen. The latter was

---

*Paramount advertised "The Magpie" as "Queen of the hijackers and said to be the brains of the mob; hard and shrewd but [with a] set of ethics that includes fair play; lives with gang leader but has told him she would leave him whenever she met a better man."

a remake of Menjou's earlier *The Grand Duchess and the Waiter* (1926) and demonstrated once and for all that comedy wasn't her calling.

In late 1928, Brent surprised everybody by suddenly marrying Harry Edwards, a producer of programmers and sometime director (*Tramp, Tramp, Tramp,* First National, 1926). As the actress felt it necessary to explain:

> Harry Edwards is the one ideal man for me. He has a great wealth of sympathy. We like doing the same things. Sometimes I wake up in the middle of the night and want to walk, particularly if it's raining. He doesn't think me mad. He walks with me. Marriage is grand when you've somebody who understands you. Even when I was married to Bernard Fineman I was alone. But with Harry it's different. We have so much fun together.

In her professional life, reality proved less idyllic: Like everyone else in Hollywood, Brent was forced to deal with the talkies. Paramount picked her to star in their first "all-talking" drama—a courageous choice considering her somewhat limited stage experience. The vehicle chosen was *Interference* (Paramount, 1928), a drama about a blackmailing adventuress. First produced as a silent, the drama was refilmed with special effects ace Roy Pomeroy handling the dialogue. It was a difficult process, to say the least. "If we had a street scene, a lot of people, we had to shoot it silent and then dub it later," Brent recalled in the early seventies.

> They had microphones all over the place—everybody had one. And if you got up to walk toward other people, you had to remember to stop talking before you left this mike and pick it up when you reached another one. Otherwise, your voice would go in and out.

Brent handled the challenge like an old pro, and although the drama, like most early sound films, was overly static, her voice registered well: in fact, it was exactly the right pitch for the roles she had been playing—deep, husky, and sensual. Clearly, Brent was not to become a victim of technology like so many of her contemporaries.

Cleared for sound, as it were, Universal borrowed her for one of that studio's first talkies, *Broadway* (1929). Unfortunately, having no stake in her future as a star, Universal gave her second billing to the forgettable Glenn Tryon and she vehemently protested the loan-out. As a consequence, a rift developed between Brent and Paramount that would never be repaired.

Finding herself suddenly labeled temperamental, Brent's career at Paramount went into an immediate decline. She did her usual tough-girl routines, but her remaining 1929 films were mainly indifferent programmers: *Fast Company*, a comedy with Jack Oakie; *Woman Trap*, third-billed to the mediocre Hal Skelly and newcomer Chester Morris in a gangster melodrama directed by William Wellman; *Why Bring That Up?*, miscast opposite low-brow comedians Moran and Mack; and *Darkened Rooms*, top-billed in a poor drama about a phony spiritualist.

Josef von Sternberg, meanwhile, wanted her for the part of Taxi Belle Hooper, Dietrich's vaudeville rival in *The Blonde Venus* (1932), a casting coup that would certainly have put her back on the map. However, by the time cameras were finally ready to roll, the mercurial director had trimmed the part down to the bare bone (there was only room for one diva in a Dietrich film) and Brent was still considered too important a star to waste on what was now essentially a bit part.*

The year 1930 began promisingly enough when Ernst Lubitsch selected her to do a comic Apache number with Maurice Chevalier in a segment of the all-star *Paramount on Parade*. Chevalier even got to slap the quintessential gun-moll around a bit: "That cute little slapping sequence," she would reminisce for John Kobal 42 years later,

> I don't know how it all came about 'cause all of a sudden I was doing it, and I liked Chevalier so much. I had admired him so, for so many years, I thought he was so wonderful. We had fun doing it, and I had never worked music before—it was timed to the music of "My Man" like an Apache number. Between Lubitsch and Chevalier, they made it very easy for me to do. I was scared to death when I started it, because I had never done that type of thing before, but they made it so easy.

Despite her enthusiasm, *Paramount on Parade* proved Brent's final film for the studio as a star. The actress herself attributed her abrupt departure to bad outside advice. The industry as a whole was suffering from a drop in attendance brought about by the Depression and every studio had to deal with cutbacks. "We were called in and asked would we stay on for the next year at the same salary, and I was advised to say no. Which went against what I felt—but I listened when I shouldn't have," she recalled in 1972. "I think that's been true of a lot of people."

Adding to her troubles were longtime rumors that she and Paramount executive Jesse L. Lasky never saw eye to eye. Like other Paramount bigwigs, Lasky found her extremely temperamental, a quality she always denied. "I, temperamental?" she is quoted as having said, "I only happen to have a mind of my own, and I say what I think."

Whatever the reason, Brent ultimately left industry giant Paramount for RKO, a struggling studio created to take advantage of RCA's sound technology. In 1930, however, RKO was still several years away from its heyday of Astaire and Rogers musicals and Katharine Hepburn dramas, not to mention Orson Welles and Val Lewton. All Brent was offered was more of the same—only on smaller budgets. She played a night-club hostess seeking revenge on the man who killed her father in *Framed*; was Cherry Malotte in a new not very popular version of *The Silver Horde*; played a streetwalker redeemed by a sugar daddy in *Madonna of the Streets* (an ignoble loan-out to Columbia); and was rather interesting as a prostitute serving gauche salesmen in *Traveling Husbands*† (1931).

Brent left RKO in late 1931 to be a freelance, a rather vulnerable situation in a Hollywood still in transition. *The Mad Parade* (Liberty, 1931), a women-at-war melodrama fraudulently advertised as a distaff *The Big Parade*, did nothing to reverse the downward trend. Worse yet was something called *The Pagan Lady* (Columbia, 1931), a piece of drivel about a sleazy barmaid who falls for an evangelist. And this time she had no excuse: it was produced by her husband, Harry Edwards. Owing a great deal

---

*She was replaced with Rita La Roy.

†She replaced an ailing Mae Clarke.

to W. Somerset Maugham and his Sadie Thompson, the melodrama had been a stage hit for Lenore Ulric; unfortunately, that was back in the teens and the material seemed awfully dated by 1931.

From this ill-fated production venture, Brent's career continued its drastic decline. She had little to do in her only "A" film of 1932, *High Pressure*, a comedy from Warner Bros. starring her old friend William Powell. She was Powell's girlfriend, but it was the sort of part that could have been played by any ingenue on the lot. She was more at home as Edmund Lowe's unfaithful mistress in *Attorney for the Defense* (Columbia, 1932), but that film was a programmer at best.

From Columbia, Brent drifted further along Poverty Row to Majestic for two potboilers, *The Crusader* (1932) and *The World Gone Mad* (1933). Both dealt with crooked district attorneys, crusading reporters, and gangsters, and while Brent received top billing, she was given very little to do other than repeat her now overly familiar gun moll impersonation.*

Evelyn Brent had gone from top stardom at Paramount in 1929 to what amounted to supporting roles at Poverty Row in less than two years, an incredibly fast descent. Virtually overnight, a star had ceased to exist. Her career, mused the film historian John Kobal, gave the impression of someone who fell into good luck without ever having the sense to capitalize on her accomplishments and consolidate her position.

Dejected, Brent left Hollywood for a two year national vaudeville tour—happily discovering that her name still meant something on a marquee. Playing mostly outlying areas, Evelyn, according to DeWitt Bodeen, met

> fans, exhibitors, and distributors, to whom she talked about Hollywood and the movies. The result was that letters deluged Hollywood studios, asking, "Why don't you make more movies with Evelyn Brent?"

Despite the outpouring of requests for her return, there were few takers. Perhaps out of a sense of obligation, her old studio, Paramount, offered her the standard heroine role in *Home on the Range* (1934), a sentimental Western loosely based on Zane Grey's *Code of the West*. No longer considered a draw by the studio for whom she was once a major star, she received billing below former child actor Jackie Coogan and Randolph Scott.

Brent blamed only herself for her less than triumphant return to Hollywood. "The most dangerous thing an actress can do is to absent herself from the screen for any great length of time," she wrote in 1938.

> I speak from experience. When I returned [from the vaudeville tour], I wasn't a star anymore. I had stayed away too long. Hollywood had new studios and they were filled with new faces. New production methods had replaced the old. Nobody was making crook pictures [sic]. So I found myself starting again at the bottom of the ladder. I was glad to get extra roles and small parts. It was quite a comedown.

It also wasn't quite as bad as all that—at least not right away. Like so many other

---

*The ingenue was played by Mary Brian and, unlike Louise Brooks, Brian retains only fond memories of working with Brent, whom she considered a "true professional."

former luminaries, Brent found more or less steady employment on Poverty Row, with a few supporting roles at major studios thrown in for good measure: she played the callous daughter of an aging violinist in *Symphony of Living* (Invincible/Chesterfield, 1935), a tearjerker based, as they say, "on a true story!"; was an equally callous heiress in *Without Children* (Liberty, 1935); took fifth billing (below a young Betty Grable) in a Wheeler and Woolsey farce, *The Nit Wits* (RKO, 1935); and did her gangster's moll routine in something called *Speed Limits* (Regent, 1935).

The year 1936 brought only more of the same: she was second-billed (to Kermit Maynard) as a saloon belle in Ambassador's *Song of the Trail*, but in reality her role was minimal; was a temperamental actress in *It Couldn't Have Happened (But It Did)*, a backstage murder yarn from Invincible/Chesterfield; played an unfaithful wife in *The President's Mystery*, a Republic release about bigamy advertised as having "been suggested by Franklin D. Roosevelt"; and was Lilli Marsh, a female crime boss felled by one of her own henchmen in *Hopalong Cassidy Returns,* the first film under a new contract with her alma mater, Paramount.

Ironically, both Brent and Louise Brooks (who was also on the comeback trail having thumbed her nose at the Hollywood establishments once too often) ended up on the cutting-room floor in Paramount's star-studded *Hollywood Boulevard*. Brooks was also eliminated from *King of Gamblers* (Paramount, 1937), whereas Evelyn's 16th-billed gang-moll bit made it through the final cut. But Paramount didn't exactly keep her around long, letting her go after bit parts in potboilers such as *The Last Train from Madrid* (1937), a Spanish Civil War melodrama with Dorothy Lamour; *Night Club Scandal* (1937), a backstage whodunit (she was the murder victim) with John Barrymore; and *Daughter of Shanghai* (1938), a crime drama with (who else?) Anna May Wong.

In but one of these Paramount programmers was there a glimmer of the Evelyn Brent of yore: *Tip-Off Girls* (1938), a gangster melodrama about truck hijackers. She was Rena Terry, a moll who uses sex to lure unsuspecting truck drivers to pull over and be robbed. Despite its intriguing premise, it was still rather a sad send-off from the studio for which she and von Sternberg had created the unforgettable "Feathers" McCoy. Certainly, Paramount had offered her better opportunities than anybody else, but the studio had been paid back handsomely at the box office. To many (including her friend DeWitt Bodeen), Paramount's shabby treatment of the former star was reprehensible. Yet, Brent herself always spoke well of the studio.

From Paramount she went, briefly, to Universal for the serial *Jungle Jim* (1937), as the villainess "Shanghai Lil," and for *Sudden Bill Dorn* (1938), a Buck Jones Western. There was a renewed flicker of interest in mid–1938 when Brent tested for the role of the prostitute Belle Watling in *Gone with the Wind* (M-G-M, 1939), but, of course, the part eventually went to Ona Munson.

Instead of immortality in Atlanta, Brent achieved something less in Mexico City as the Empress Eugenie opposite Guy Bates Post's Napoleon in *The Mad Empress*. Directed by one Miguel C. Torres, the drama detailed the star-crossed love story of Empress Carlotta (Medea Novara) and Emperor Maximilian (Conrad Nagel), with Brent's Eugenie only a minor character. About to be released, the film was suddenly bought up by Warner Bros., who was producing their own story of the royal tragedy,

Juarez (1939)*. Quietly slipped into release in the wake of *Juarez* in December 1939, *The Mad Empress* received scant attention.

Evelyn Brent gamely continued her screen career all through the forties but the roles grew increasingly smaller. She had the title role (a female gang boss known as "The Illustrious One") in a little item entitled *Daughter of the Tong* (Metropolitan, 1939), but it was something of a last hurrah. More typical were *Emergency Landing* (PRC, 1941), a wretched programmer in which she took third billing to Forrest Tucker and Carol Hughes, and *Wide Open Town* (United Artists, 1941), a Hopalong Cassidy series entry which was more or less a remake of the earlier (and superior) *Hopalong Cassidy Returns*.

The independent production team of William Pine and William Thomas, working out of Paramount of all places, hired her for a couple of action flicks, *Forced Landing* (1941) and *Wrecking Crew* (1942), and she was Jack Holt's leading lady in the serial *Holt of the Secret Service* (Columbia, 1942), an action melodrama "designed to please adult audiences as well as younger theatergoers." While at Columbia, she stayed on for an unbilled appearance as a nurse in *Ellery Queen and the Murder Ring* (1941), with Ralph Bellamy.

Writer DeWitt Bodeen met Evelyn Brent on the set of *The Seventh Victim* (RKO, 1943), an atmospheric if overly complicated drama about cultists in Greenwich Village for which he had written the screenplay. According to Bodeen, producer Val Lewton and director Mark Robson were "delighted to have her in the unit. She was most charming, and looked very svelte as the one-armed devil worshipper, Natalie Cortez." Later, Lewton showed Bodeen a letter from a fan who had been shocked when he found out that the actress "had lost an arm." "So that's why she wasn't making pictures the last few years," the letter read. Evelyn, it seems, hadn't lost her touch and had made the most of her minuscule role as a disfigured concert pianist. Sadly, *The Seventh Victim* was her last film of any importance.

"I had made a small fortune at one time," Brent once wrote.

> How I lost it doesn't matter, but now that I'm back in pictures I'm living modestly and saving my money. One never appreciates the value of a bank balance until it ceases to exist.

Living modestly was not hubby Harry Edwards' idea of marriage, however, and the couple had separated in the mid–1930s. Hoping for a reconciliation, Evelyn had long refused a divorce, but in 1947 she finally consented. She didn't stay single for long, as it turned out, but quickly wed comedian Harry Fox,† the former husband of Jenny Dolly of the Dolly Sisters. The couple remained together until the comedian's death at the age of 70 in 1959.

---

*Juarez, starring Paul Muni in the title role and Bette Davis as Carlotta, featured Gale Sondergaard as the French Empress Eugenie.

†Fox had enjoyed a minor screen career which included 365 Nights in Hollywood *(1934),* $10 Raise *(1935),* Fugitive in the Sky *(1936),* Smart Blonde *(1937), and* Hollywood Hotel *(1938).*

Opposite: Evelyn Brent in *The Law West of Tombstone* (RKO, 1938).

Brent spent the final years of her screen career at the Poverty Row studio Monogram. In less than stellar surroundings, she appeared with the Bowery Boys in *Bowery Champs* (1944); was Johnny Mack Brown's leading lady in *Raiders of the South*, and Gilbert Roland's in *Robin Hood of Monterey* (both 1947). Her final Hollywood film was *The Golden Eye* (1948), the third to last entry in the interminable *Charlie Chan* series (she was a gun-toting nurse!). In 1950, as a favor to an old friend, director William Beaudine, she briefly appeared in *Again, Pioneers*, an independently produced religious film.

Brent didn't retire completely from the entertainment industry, however. In the 1950s she joined the Thelma White Agency for a short time as an artist's representative.* She was briefly in the news again in 1960, when Ben Hecht, writing for *Playboy* magazine, suddenly revealed that she had died! Reminiscing about *Underworld*, Hecht declared that, sadly, he was the only one connected with the film still alive. "I'm a bit surprised at Ben," Evelyn told Hal Humphrey of the *Los Angeles Mirror*.

> He was always known as a good newspaperman. Wouldn't you think he could have done some checking? Clive Brook [her *Underworld* co-star] is rather upset too. He wrote me from England.

From being an agent, Brent braved the new world of television, appearing, among other things, on the long-running series *Wagon Train*. The veteran actress, however, found the experience unnerving: "The whole thing is too fast and frantic now," she complained.

> The electricians and grips remembered me and said hello, but everyone else just sat around and glared. This can make an actor shaky all morning and affect his performance.

She quickly turned her back on further television work.

Permanently retired from acting, Evelyn Brent began showing up at various classic film gatherings, reminiscing about her starring days. "I wonder why I kept making pictures," she would say. "Perhaps I thought some day I'll make a good one."

DeWitt Bodeen met her again at a screening of *The Last Command* and marveled at how well the film, and Brent's performance, held up. "Her role still glittered with that special, exciting diamond-like fervor which was always hers," he would write in *Films in Review*.

In the late sixties, Evelyn and a companion, actress Dorothy Konrad, moved into a small apartment in Westwood Village. Film historian Anthony Slide met Brent there and found her to be a gracious woman who still retained much of her former beauty.

Another, somewhat less temperate writer, John Kobal, must have met Brent on a bad day:

> This woman [he wrote], neat and prim in her red-checkered dress, would have looked more natural standing in a farmhouse in a Depression photo. There was little left of the *femme fatale* who had excited audiences as the luscious, but deadly "Feathers" McCoy in *Underworld*, Hollywood's first true Gangster's Moll.

Brent and White had appeared together in Spy Train *(Monogram, 1943).*

In increasingly ill health, Brent moved in and out of the Motion Picture Country Home and Hospital. She would die in her own house, however, suffering a heart attack on June 4, 1975.

In the late twenties, Evelyn Brent was one of Hollywood's most promising leading ladies, pioneering the kind of role that would soon make Joan Crawford and Barbara Stanwyck (with whom Brent is often compared) top box office draws. Why, then, was her own time at the top so brief? Why, as John Kobal points out, was she on all the magazine covers in 1930 but virtually forgotten by 1931? Louise Brooks gave Josef von Sternberg sole credit for Brent's short-lived fame: "He was the greatest director of women there ever was," she said.

> Most directors can direct certain women marvelously, and some can't direct them at all. But he could direct every woman he touched, he could make her lovely. He could take the most gauche, awkward, sexless dame and turn her into a dynamo of sex.

This Svengali-like quality was exactly what Brooks saw in von Sternberg's direction of Evelyn Brent:

> I made a picture with her [*Love 'Em and Leave 'Em*], and Evelyn's idea of acting was to march into a scene, spread her legs and stand flat-footed and read her lines with masculine defiance. Oh, I thought she was dreadful, and then I saw her in *Underworld*, and Sternberg softened her with all these feathers, and he never let her strike attitudes at all. He made her move.

EVELYN BRENT FILMOGRAPHY

As Betty Riggs

1914: *The Pit.*
1915: *The Shooting of Dan McGrew.*

As Evelyn Brent

1916: *The Lure of Heart's Desire; The Soul Market; Playing with Fire; The Spell of the Yukon; The Weakness of Strength; The Iron Woman.*
1917: *The Millionaire's Double; Who's Your Neighbor? To the Death; Raffles: The Amateur Cracksman.*
1918: *Daybreak.*
1919: *Fool's Gold; Help! Help! Police! The Other Man's Wife; The Glorious Lady; Into the River* (short); *The Border River* (short).
1920: *The Shuttle of Life* (GB*); *The Law Divine* (GB).
1921: *The Door That Has No Key* (GB); *Demos* (GB); *Sybil* (GB); *Laughter and Tears* (GB); *Sonia* (GB); *Circus Jim* (GB).
1922: *Trapped by the Mormons* (GB); *Married to a Mormon* (GB); *The Spanish Jade* (GB); *The Experiment* (GB); *Pages of Life* (GB).
1923: *Held to Answer.*
1924: *Loving Lies; The Shadows of the East; The Arizona Express; The Plunderer;*

*Great Britain.

The Lone Chance; The Cyclone Rider; The Desert Outlaw; Alias Mary Flynn; The Dangerous Flirt; My Husband's Wives; Silk Stocking Sal.

1925: *Midnight Molly; Forbidden Cargo; Smooth as Satin; Lady Robinhood; Three Wise Crooks; Broadway Lady.*
1926: *Queen of Diamonds; Secret Orders; The Imposter; The Jade Cup; Flame of the Argentine; Love 'Em and Leave 'Em.*
1927: *Love's Greatest Mistake; Blind Alley; Underworld; Women's Wares.*
1928: *Beau Sabreur; The Last Command; The Showdown; A Night of Mystery; The Drag Net; His Tiger Lady; The Mating Call.*
1929: *Interference; Broadway; Fast Company; Woman Trap; Why Bring That Up? Deserted Rooms.*
1930: *Slightly Scarlet; Paramount on Parade; Framed; The Silver Horde; Madonna of the Streets.*
1931: *Traveling Husbands; The Mad Parade; Pagan Lady.*
1932: *High Pressure; Attorney for the Defense; The Crusader.*
1933: *The World Gone Mad.*
1934: *Home on the Range.*
1935: *The Nit Wits; Without Children; Symphony of Living; Speed Limited.*
1936: *Penthouse Party; Song of the Trail; It Couldn't Have Happened (But It Did); The President's Mystery; Hopalong Cassidy Returns.*
1937: *Jungle Jim* (serial); *King of Gamblers; Last Train from Madrid; Night Club Scandal; Daughter of Shanghai.*
1938: *Sudden Bill Dorn; Tip-Off Girls; Mr. Wong, Detective; The Law West of Tombstone.*
1939: *The Mad Empress* (Mexico); *Panama Lady; Daughter of the Tong.*
1941: *Emergency Landing; Forced Landing; Wide Open Town; Dangerous Lady; Ellery Queen and the Murder Ring.*
1942: *Holt of the Secret Service* (serial); *Westward Ho! Wrecking Crew; The Pay-Off.*
1943: *Silent Witness; Spy Train; The Seventh Victim.*
1944: *Bowery Champs.*
1947: *Raiders of the South; Robin Hood of Monterey.*
1948: *Stagestruck; The Mystery of the Golden Eye.*
1950: *Again Pioneers.*

5 — Dorothy Burgess

Slender, dark-haired Dorothy Burgess—"an attractive package of dynamite," her publicity proclaimed—was everywhere in the early days of sound pictures. In 1933 alone, she appeared in 14 films for 12 different companies, almost exclusively portraying her special brand of rather tawdry sirens. She had first caught the attention of picture-goers as the fiery and faithless *femme fatale* Donna Maria of *In Old Arizona* (Fox, 1929), a role that proved all but impossible to live down. Forever typecast as an exotic vixen, Burgess found leading roles in major productions extremely hard to come by. Her kind of "ladies of the night" were inevitably relegated to supporting roles—the Production Code, if no one else, saw to that! Consequently, the musical comedy star who had once headlined with Ruby Keeler in *Bye, Bye Bonnie* on Broadway, wound up her career in the hovels of Poverty Row.

Dorothy Burgess was born in Los Angeles on March 4, 1905, the daughter of actress Grace Burgess and a niece of the stage star (and later M-G-M mainstay) Fay Bainter. She grew up in New York City and followed family tradition by enrolling in Mrs. Dow's School of Acting. At the age of 15 she made her professional debut as a specialty dancer in the popular *Music Box Revue*, eventually graduating to speaking parts in comedies. Her breakthrough came as Helen Hayes' understudy in *Dancing Mothers* (1924). When Hayes decided to leave the production in mid-run, Burgess took over the part, Ruby Keeler–like, for its seven remaining months, receiving excellent notices. She was reunited with Hayes later that year in another popular play, *Quarantine*. The following season she had a successful run in the comedy *The Adorable Liar* and in 1927 starred in *Bye, Bye Bonnie*, a musical that also featured Ruby Keeler (doing the "Tampico Tap") and William Frawley.

Burgess came to Hollywood's attention in 1928 while appearing in a Los Angeles production of *The Squall*. Sound films were becoming ever more important and the industry had begun to look toward the speaking stage for new talent. When it was discovered that a Broadway celebrity was appearing right in their midst, Hollywood producers scrambled to secure her services. The winner in this instance was the Fox Film Corporation, which had just unveiled the Movietone sound system ("a distinct forward step in the art of the talking picture"), and was getting ready to film a Western with, as the publicity pledged, "not only realistic settings but also the *natural sounds* of the great outdoors!"

The subject for this monumental event was to be a screen version of O. Henry's *The Caballero's Way*, renamed *In Old Arizona* (Fox, 1929). Burgess was tapped for the important role of Tonia Maria, the drama's sultry and ultimately treacherous *femme fatale*. "Every part is a *speaking part*," the ads for the film boasted.

> Featured in the leading roles are two brilliant screen stars and a fascinating stage favorite—*Edmund Lowe* as Sgt. Dunn, the heartbreaking cavalryman; *Warner Baxter* as the Cisco Kid, outlawed Don Juan of the desert; and, in her first screen role, *Dorothy Burgess* as Tonia, the fiery, fickle, light o' love who pays the price of infidelity in one of the most startling denouements ever filmed!

In Old Arizona lived up to its hype and even garnered a Best Actor Academy Award for Warner Baxter.* The reviews of Burgess' screen debut, on the other hand, were slightly ambiguous. "Miss Burgess gives a legitimate display of the coin and man-crazy lass, but may be unconvincing to some as to star appeal power because of the sole ragged costume," *Variety*, for example, commented.

The success of *In Old Arizona* firmly established Dorothy Burgess as a screen vamp and Fox immediately cast her as a cheating wife in *Pleasure Crazed* and as a society siren in *Song of Kentucky* (both 1929). Not surprisingly, the former musical comedy actress rebelled at such typecasting and left the studio to be a freelance.

Being at large proved rather detrimental for the 5 foot 3-1/2 inch tall brunette, who continued to portray designing vamps but now without the benefit of a well-crafted studio buildup. In September of 1930, Pathé announced that she was to co-star with William Boyd in the Western *The Painted Desert* (Pathé, 1931). As a rancher's daughter who stands tall in the middle of a range war, Burgess would have had the opportunity to show that she could play something besides scheming vixens. Regrettably, the Pathé brass got cold feet and replaced her with the dreary but safe Helen Twelvetrees. So instead of standing by her man in *The Painted Desert*, Burgess reverted to type in *Swing High* (Pathé, 1930), in which she attempted to lure handsome Fred Scott away from a still very tedious Twelvetrees.

Realizing the value of a contract, Burgess signed with Warner Bros., but that studio treated her with as much respect as had Pathé. Her scheming vixen in the programmer *Recaptured Love* (1930), however, was promising enough for Warners to cast her as the *femme fatale* in *Blonde Crazy* (1931), a first rate crime comedy with James Cagney. For some reason, the studio unfortunately suddenly changed the script, cut the part to the bone and replaced her with Noel Francis. As it turned out, Warner Bros. was not exactly in dire need of vixens in 1932. In fact, the roster was full of girls who could play tough—including Glenda Farrell, Noel Francis, Renee Whitney, and

---

The film itself was nominated for Best Picture, but lost to M-G-M's The Broadway Melody. *Baxter's win has been labeled somewhat of a freak occurrence and the actor never capitalized on his good fortune, winding up a middling career playing Columbia's Crime Doctor in a series of low-budget whodunits.*

Mae Madison. Dorothy Burgess was almost interchangeable with these starlets (only Farrell would eventually separate from the pack) and was relegated to supporting parts in *Play Girl* and *Taxi!* (both 1932), typical rapid-fire Warner programmers. Billing-wise, she fared much better on Poverty Row, picking up leading roles in such potboilers as *The Stoker* (Allied Pictures, 1932) and *Out of Singapore* (Goldsmith Prod., 1932).

In *The Stoker*, Burgess co-starred as Margarita Valdez, a Nicaraguan plantation owner who hires an American (Monte Blue) to protect her plantation from bandits. Of course they fall in love, but only after a great deal of muscular action, during which she manages to save his life. Andre Sennwald of the *New York Times* accepted the melodrama for what it was: *The Stoker*, Sennwald wrote, "is an action picture strictly, which is another way of calling it uncerebral. It is not burdened with any particular theme, message or dogma."

That statement was, in fact, appropriate for all of Burgess' programmers. *Variety*, unfortunately, was not quite as charitable. "Miss Burgess slinks through [*The Stoker*] talking, at frequent intervals, pidgin English," the reviewer noted, "but for the most part forgetting [the] dialect."

With *Out of Singapore*, Burgess seems to have reached the bottom-of-the-barrel. A poor melodrama of a ship's first mate (Noah Beery) who murders his captain (Montagu Love) in order to "accidentally" sink the vessel and collect the insurance money, *Out of Singapore* starred her as the captain's placid daughter who does little but stand about while the crime is about to be committed. (The meatier role of Concha, the villain's rejected lover who comes to the aid of the law, was played by one Miriam Seegar.) Apparently, Burgess was so busy trying to redeem her image, that she made good opportunities pass her by. Happily, not many people actually saw the film; released by William Steiner on a states' rights basis, it seems to have gotten very few bookings.

Dorothy Burgess was especially busy during 1933, yet the downward trend in her career continued; all she could get were supporting roles at major studios and a few leads in slipshod Poverty Row productions.

Burgess was in her element in her first release of the year, a little item from Mayfair entitled *Malay Nights*. As Eve Blake she is an unwed mother and the kept mistress of a gangster (Ralph Ince) when picked up by a wealthy pearl fisher (Johnny Mack Brown). Unfortunately, her new protector rejects her when it appears that she hasn't quite given up her wanton ways. So while Eve is prostituting herself in a Singapore dive, the two men, now rivals for her love, duke it out in accepted "B"-movie fashion before the hero realizes that his heart's desire has reformed after all and is now worthy of his love. *Malay Nights* was typical of the fare offered to small town America—simple, old-fashioned and brimming with implied sex and violence.

What Price Decency (Equitable, 1933) was even more lurid. As Norma, Burgess is an American harlot working the streets of London when suddenly "shanghaied" aboard a freighter bound for Africa. En route, she is blackmailed into marrying a sadistic Dutch trader (Alan Hale), who later keeps her as a virtual prisoner in his mosquito infested trading post. Fortunately, the poor girl is rescued in the nick of time by a handsome Irishman (Walter Byron), and when her marriage suddenly proves to be fake, she confesses her sins and eagerly returns to civilization with her newfound love.

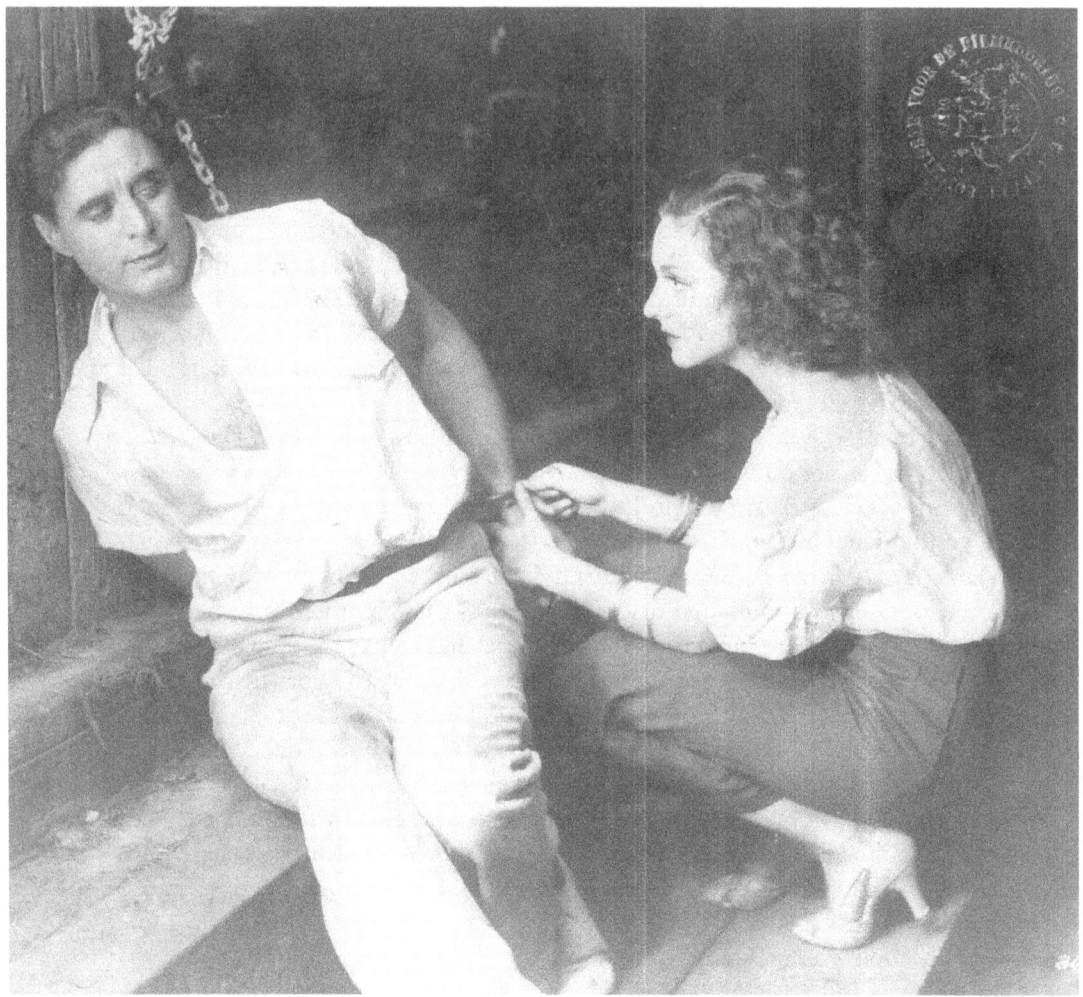

George Walsh and Dorothy Burgess in *Out of Singapore* (Goldsmith, 1932).

What Price Decency turned out to be especially loathed by the highbrow critics. "An amateurish and tedious production," Mordaunt Hall of the *New York Times* fumed, while *Film Daily* found it an "indifferent production carelessly thrown together." *Variety*'s "Waly" went even further, claiming that "few Indies are as bad as this one." Needless to say, *What Price Decency* did little to improve Burgess' status in Hollywood.

Meanwhile, in *It's Great to Be Alive* (Fox, 1933), she had a major role in one of the strangest films ever released by a major Hollywood studio. The unusual plot centers on Carlos Martin (Raul Roulien), an irrepressible rogue who suddenly, by a strange twist of fate, becomes the last man alive. Soon women all over the world are hunting the poor chap, but his main nemesis proves to be a lady gangster known as Al Moran (Burgess), who manages to catch him and proceeds to auction him off to the highest bidder. *It's Great to Be Alive* was, of all things, a musical, and the handsome exotic Roulien was touted as a new Maurice Chevalier. Unfortunately, both the film and

5—Dorothy Burgess [53]

Loretta Young, Dorothy Burgess and (extreme right) James Cagney in *Taxi!* (Warner Bros., 1932).

Roulien himself did badly at the box office and this valiant attempt at something different disappeared within weeks of its release.

(A Spanish-language version of the film, renamed *El último Varón sobre la tiara*, had Mimi Aguglia taking over from Burgess as the lady gangster. Neither version, unfortunately, has survived, which is a shame since an extant letter from the Hays Office to Fox suggests that *It's Great to Be Alive* might at the very least have been an interesting oddity. The film's main problem, the censorship board warned, was the "overemphasis on sex brought out through a situation wherein a world of sex starved females suddenly find one lone male whose presence brings about a series of humorous but nevertheless, rather baldly suggestive events.")

In mid–July, 1933, Dorothy Burgess suffered a sprained back during a fight scene with Sally O'Neil and Mary Carlisle on the set of Universal's *Ladies Must Love*, a comedy about four gold diggers in Manhattan. According to the *Los Angeles Times*, the actress, although experiencing "considerable pain," did not realize the severity of her injury and reported to work the following day. The result was a physical and mental breakdown. Luckily (for Universal at least) Burgess had already completed her scenes and the comedy was released on schedule (to indifferent reviews) in September of 1933.

Dorothy Burgess was one of several actresses tested by M-G-M for the female lead opposite Wallace Beery in *Viva Villa* (M-G-M, 1934). Filming had already begun when director Howard Hawks was replaced with Jack Conway and as Hawks went, so did most of his principal actors, including Mona Maris, the original Theresa. The studio tested Myrna Loy, Lila Lee and silent screen vamp Carmel Myers, in addition to Burgess, but in the end chose Fay Wray. A prestigious project such a *Viva Villa* (a 1934 Best Picture nominee) would certainly have helped restore Burgess to Hollywood's good graces; she needed an escape hatch from the interminable programmers that were slowly but surely ruining her career.

Instead of going on location to Mexico with Wallace Beery, Burgess journeyed, courtesy of the Fox back lot, on the *Orient Express* (1934), an imitation *Grand Hotel* on wheels in which she played a pushy sob sister — a performance which Andre Sennwald of the *New York Times* considered "a libel on the sisters of the craft." Author Graham Greene, whose novel *Stamboul Train* had constituted the foundation for the screenplay, hated the entire production. "It was a bad film," he later wrote, "one of the worst I had ever seen; the direction was incompetent, the photoplay undistinguished, the story sentimental."

In December of 1933, Dorothy Burgess joined the cast of *A Modern Hero* (Warner Bros., 1934), the only American film directed by the Austrian G. W. Pabst. The genius who once had guided Hollywood's Louise Brooks through two of the late silent era's most acclaimed works, *Pandora's Box* and *The Diary of a Lost Girl* (both released in 1929), here struggled mightily with the ponderous story of a circus bareback rider (Richard Barthelmess) who uses women as his stepladder to success. Burgess appears sixth-billed as Hazel Flint, a socialite whose loveless marriage to the Horatio Alger–ish protagonist abruptly ends when she uncovers his humble beginnings. Andre Sennwald of the *New York Times* wasn't exactly overwhelmed, but found the melodrama to be "earnest, sketchy and spiritless."

Burgess sneered and seethed darkly as the mysterious and colorful Juanita Lane, a psychiatrist's wife with a yen for voodoo who becomes the high priestess of a strange cult in *Black Moon* (Columbia, 1934). The thriller was described by Andre Sennwald as "admirably equipped to throw a double-barreled scare into the innocent entertainment hunter." *Motion Picture Herald*, on the other hand, worried about the picture's effect on a susceptible public. Warned the trade paper:

> In that the colored natives involved in the film are rather harshly pictured as bloodthirsty worshippers of black gods who indulge in sacrificial orgies, the film may meet with objection in those situations where colored people make up a portion of the patronage.

Such fears, however, proved to be not only patronizing but also in vain: *Black Moon* made very little noise at the box office and quickly disappeared from circulation.

Burgess had a change of pace with *Circus Clown* (First National, 1934), a silly Joe E. Brown farce in which she played Babe, the lion tamer. The role, however, was little more than a bit and she did not need much inducement to abandon films in favor of a return to the legitimate theater.

In June of 1934, Dorothy Burgess made her stage comeback in a Los Angeles production of *Lulu Belle* and then starred in a revival of *The Squall*, the play that had brought her to Los Angeles five years earlier. In August she left for New York City and a role opposite George M. Cohan in *Gambling* (released by Fox in November of 1934), a screen version of his stage play. Burgess played Dorothy Kane, a singer suspected of having murdered a young girl. By the fade-out, however, she is vindicated and prepares for a new life with the girl's father (Cohan). *Gambling* was produced by theater owner Harold B. Franklin, a longtime friend of Cohan, and was meant to be the first of four starring projects for the veteran hoofer. That, unfortunately, was not to be: *Gambling* was an unmitigated disaster, and the outmoded script was not the only culprit. Andre Sennwald of the *New York Times*, for example, complained that

> [the film] is deficient in many of the technical fundamentals in which the usual Hollywood product manages to be so unobtrusively suave. Narrated in an inexpert succession of medium and close-up "shots," it qualifies as a photographed stage play rather than a brilliant example of camera technique.

Gambling's only saving graces, it seems, were Dorothy Burgess' performance ("[she] catches several authentic emotional notes," Sennwald wrote) and the costumes designed by Hattie Carnegie. The part of Dorothy Kane, as it turned out, proved to be Burgess' last screen assignment of any importance.

Except for a supporting role as a rumored adulteress in *Village Tale* (RKO, 1935), a rural melodrama starring Randolph Scott, Burgess now turned her full attention toward rejuvenating her stage career, returning to Broadway for the first time in seven years to replace Edith Barrett in *Piper Paid* (1935). By 1940, however, the no longer young *femme fatale* found good roles hard to come by and she returned to the West Coast.

The reappearance of Dorothy Burgess did not exactly create a stir in Hollywood where fame is notoriously fleeting. Happily, a few veterans remembered her from the old days and cast her in bit parts in such potboilers as *I Want a Divorce* (Paramount, 1940), a domestic drama starring the husband-and-wife team of Dick Powell and Joan Blondell. Blondell, of course, was a friend from their days together at Warner Bros. and often went out on a limb for a fellow "Warnerite." However, following a small supporting role in *Girls in Chains* (PRC, 1943), Burgess had had enough and left the screen for good.

With her acting career behind her, Dorothy Burgess started on a new life—as a novelist. In January of 1945 she published a novel entitled *Say Uncle*—a thriller dealing with, appropriately enough, vampires. "I worked six hours a day for eight months," she told the *Hollywood Citizen News*. "You work on what you write until you think it is perfect, and then you write some more."

With her husband, a physician, the former actress lived for many years in retirement in Palm Springs, California. In March of 1961 she was brought to Riverside County Hospital with tuberculosis, succumbing to the disease on August 20, 1961. The erstwhile screen vixen was 56.

Dorothy Burgess arrived in Hollywood at the dawn of sound and, having been awarded the plum role of Tonia in *In Old Arizona*, should have had a clear shot at stardom. With a strong stage background, there was no reason for her to fail—except for Hollywood typecasting. In retrospect, Fox was squarely to blame. With its penchant for dewy-eyed heroines like Janet Gaynor and Marian Nixon, that particular studio was not the right place for an exotic looking actress such as Burgess. Not that they ever did consider her an actress; she was eternally thought of as the fiery border belle whose treachery almost ruins the gallant Cisco Kid. Consequently, Dorothy Burgess proved one of the most misused performers of the 1930s.

DOROTHY BURGESS FILMOGRAPHY

1929: *In Old Arizona; Pleasure Crazed; Protection; Song of Kentucky.*
1930: *Swing High; Recaptured Love.*
1931: *Lasca of the Rio Grande.*
1932: *Play Girl; Taxi; The Stoker; Out of Singapore.*
1933: *Malay Nights; Ladies They Talk About ; What Price Decency? Strictly Personal; I Love That Man; Rusty Rides Alone; It's Great to Be Alive; Easy Millions; Hold Your Man; The Important Witness; Headline Shooter; Ladies Must Love; Night Flight; On Your Guard; From Headquarters.*
1934: *Orient Express; Miss Fane's Baby Is Stolen; Fashions of 1934; A Modern Hero; Affairs of a Gentleman; Black Moon; Circus Clown; Friends of Mr. Sweeney; Hat, Coat and Glove; Gambling.*
1935: *Village Tale; Manhattan Butterfly.*
1940: *The Lady in Question; I Want a Divorce.*
1941: *Lady for a Night.*
1942: *Lone Star Ranger.*
1943: *Man of Courage; Girls in Chains.*

6—*Juliette Compton*

"Juliette Compton is laboring in the so-called Hollywood vineyard of art under two handicaps which she is taking in stride," columnist John Scott told his *Los Angeles Times* readers in 1931.

> One is her resemblance to Greta Garbo, which has caused her annoyance at the hands of souvenir collectors, who strip her car of ornaments ever so often, and the other is the fact that she made her stage debut in England [sic].

Most filmgoers, in fact, believed that the 5 foot 7 inch tall brunette with the clipped upper-class accent and arrogant demeanor was indeed British. The roles she was given to play did nothing to dispel the myth. In most of her films, Compton portrayed a well-bred *femme fatale*, her disposition every inch the cultured other woman. Whereas men found her fascinating, women hated her at first sight.

Unfortunately, Juliette Compton's reign proved short-lived. Maybe her oft bespoken resemblance to Garbo hastened her decline; after all, while Garbo was mysterious, glamorous *and* vibrant, Compton was mostly just glamorous. When Paramount let her go in early 1932 her career nose-dived, and had it not been for a notorious divorce suit that hinted at adultery, statutory rape, and transvestitism, she would have disappeared from the public consciousness all together.

Juliette Compton was born in Columbus, Georgia, on April 3, 1899. A child of privilege, she was educated by private tutors and at an exclusive girls' school. According to later publicity she was stage-struck from a very young age and early on made up her mind to become a Broadway star. "Juliette Compton is an actress because she had courage, and obeyed an impulse," a May 1931 Paramount press release stated.

> The impulse was to slip out of a crowded New York railway station and leave her world behind. When the train that was to have borne her to the family summer home in Maine puffed out of the station yards, she was not on it. Registered at a hotel under an assumed

name, she was looking over a list of theatrical agencies, wondering where she should apply first.

The dark, Southern beauty had little difficulty obtaining work and made her stage debut supporting Fay Bainter in the 1917 musical *The Kiss Burglar*. A season with the *Ziegfeld Follies* followed, after which producer John Murray Anderson brought her and several other young women to England to appear in the somewhat similar C. B. Cochrane shows. She toured with Cochrane for three years and appeared in several West End productions with Sir Gerald Du Maurier. "Tallulah Bankhead was in one of these plays," Compton told the *Los Angeles Times* in 1931.

> Tallulah is from Alabama and this, besides other reasons, caused quite a bit of rivalry between us. In the show we were both supposed to be "sexy," if you please. My costume was suitable to whirling about, and Tallulah's was not, so I more or less won out. Since those days we both have gone in for more dramatic portrayals.

Appearing nightly with Sir Gerald, Compton made her screen debut by day as the other woman in *Human Desires* (Gaumont British, 1924), a triangle drama with Marjorie Daw and Clive Brook. She went on to appear in 10 additional British silents but became a star playing the wicked Lady Castlemaine in Herbert Wilcox's production of *Nell Gwyn* (British National, 1926). The experience typecast her and determined her future career, but also resulted in a lifelong friendship with the British producer and his wife, Anna Neagle.

It was 1929 and Hollywood's newly built sound stages beckoned. Once there, Compton freelanced for a while—she was the other woman coming between Betty Compson and George Barraud in *Woman to Woman* (Tiffany, 1929)—before signing with Paramount.

Despite her reputation as a stage star, Paramount immediately categorized Juliette Compton as a supporting player. The studio had quickly discovered that she could play arrogant society women and conniving bitches better than any other actress on the lot. At the same time, however, her highly publicized resemblance to Garbo, while flattering, proved almost fatal at a studio that already possessed Marlene Dietrich, the Swedish star's acknowledged chief competitor. Dietrich and Compton, incidentally, met briefly in Josef von Sternberg's *Morocco* (Paramount, 1930), but Juliette's performance as a jealous native girl was not very memorable.

Plans to feature Compton opposite Clara Bow and newcomer Terrance Ray in *After School*, a gangster melodrama with an original story by Dashiell Hammett, came to naught when Bow was forced to withdraw after a bitter and much publicized court battle with Daisy DeVoe, her former secretary. Compton did appear opposite the former "It" girl, but her role as Piccadilly Bessie in *Kick In* (Paramount, 1931) was minor.

Throughout 1931, Compton made onscreen life miserable for Paramount leading ladies such as Eleanor Boardman (*Women Love Once*), Frances Dee (*Rich Man's Folly*), and Vivienne Osborne (*Husband's Holiday*). But while the titles varied, the plots remained basically the same: rich woman loses spineless husband to sophisticated

Opposite: **Juliette Compton in 1930.**

vamp (Compton, of course), then discovers true love. *Unfaithful* (Paramount, 1931) was typical and neither better nor worse than most. Ruth Chatterton was the wife, Paul Cavanagh the husband, Compton the mistress, a Bohemian arts patron, and Paul Lukas the decent guy who rescues the heroine from a life of disillusionment. Miss Chatterton was Paramount's most distinguished exponent of "women's" pictures, but her choice of roles was beginning to stifle her otherwise quite acceptable talents. Both victims of Paramount's typecasting and general neglect, Chatterton and Compton developed a lasting friendship.

Compton got "down and dirty" as Muriel Preston, Fredric March's tough ex-girlfriend in *Strangers in Love* (Paramount, 1932), a comedy-drama about mistaken identities. Muriel, as it turned out, was not averse to a little blackmail to get what she wanted—which in this case was to get rid of her rival, comely secretary Kay Francis. Playing a girl of a decidedly lower social position, however, did not sit well with the aristocratic Compton and the results were indifferent at best; Mordaunt Hall of the *New York Times* judged her "miscast."

Paramount was quick to respond. An intraoffice memo, dated February 13, 1932, bluntly stated that "the company will not exercise its option on Juliette Compton." Like most decisions in Hollywood regarding contract players, her dismissal was done behind closed doors. "Please keep [the decision] *confidential* for the time being," the memo continued, "as the studio does not want this info to leak. This info should not be given to Miss Compton."

Ironically, Compton's final film for Paramount, *Devil and the Deep* (1932), starred her erstwhile rival Tallulah Bankhead. Unhappily, the melodrama, a lurid triangle affair set in North Africa, was a dud and Bankhead, whom Paramount had considered a sure bet for cinema stardom, soon joined Compton on the cinematic unemployment list.

As a freelance, Compton was offered the same kind of roles that Paramount had saddled her with, but at a much lower salary. In something called *The Man Called Back* (K.B.S. Film Corp., 1932), she played Vivien Lawrence, a socialite who lures a drug-addicted doctor (John Halliday) astray. Produced on the cheap side, *The Man Called Back*, according to the reviewer for the *New York Times*, failed to "add a great deal to the welfare of the screen industry."

Compton's best remembered post–Paramount role was that of Ethel Chichester in *Peg o' My Heart* (M-G-M, 1933), a lavish reworking of J. Hartley Manner's 1912 novel of a poor Irish colleen (Marion Davies) who suddenly becomes heir to a fortune. Essentially *Cinderella* in Victorian garb, *Peg o' My Heart* recounts how, in order to receive her inheritance, Peg must live a certain time in England with the snobbish Chichester clan, constantly being humiliated by Ethel Chichester, a man-hungry tart; how the good-hearted Peg still attempts to help the perfidious Ethel with her complicated love affairs even though the woman obviously despises her; and, finally, how she gets the goods on her tormentors, accepts a marriage proposal, and collects the £2,000,000. Despite being one of Marion Davies' better vehicles, *Peg o' My Heart* left a Depression weakened audience totally indifferent, but Mordaunt Hall of the *New York Times* was in a generous mood, conceding that the film had "charm and entertainment" and that Compton was "excellent."

For all intent and purposes, Juliette Compton's screen career ended with *Peg o' My Heart*. Although she still received prominent billing as the Duchess of Devonshire in *Berkeley Square* (Fox, 1933) and as Clothilde in *The Count of Monte Cristo* (United Artists, 1934), the roles themselves were small and insignificant. She played one final upper-class snob in *Behold My Wife* (Paramount, 1935), a comedy-drama starring Sylvia Sidney.

As the haughty Diana Curzon, Compton doesn't care much for her new sister-in-law (Sidney), a native American princess. Later in the film, the two women fight over the same no-good home wrecker (Monroe Owsley), with Juliette ending up a murderess and her rival taking the blame. The film was rather lurid and implausible and most reviewers rejected it as bad melodrama. *Behold My Wife* proved to be Compton's last film for five years. Instead the actress concentrated on family life with her Australian-born husband, James Bartram.

Juliette Compton in 1934.

In 1940, she was enticed out of retirement by her friend Herbert Wilcox who, with his wife Anna Neagle, had escaped war-torn England to film under more peaceful circumstances in Hollywood. Wilcox, who had earlier guided her through the definitive Compton portrayal of Lady Castlemaine in *Nell Gwyn*, now cast her in the small supporting role of Emily Grey in the musical *Irene* (RKO, 1940). Compton enjoyed the experience enough to resurface as the gossiping Lady Spencer in *That Hamilton Woman* (United Artists, 1941), a historical drama with Vivien Leigh and Laurence Olivier (produced by another British refugee, Sir Alexander Korda). It proved to be her final film appearance.

Now completely retired from performing, Compton suddenly found herself in the headlines again in early 1942—and screaming headlines they were. "Mate Liked to Photograph Himself in Girls' Clothes, Says Ex-Actress," the *Los Angeles Times* announced on March 5.

Countless eccentricities, including a penchant for photographing himself in women's clothing, were attributed yesterday to her husband James Bartram, 48, by Mrs. Juliette Hall Bartram, 41 [sic], former actress, when she continued her testimony in the trial of the couple's contested suit for divorce.

"I told him that it was not healthy and natural for a man like him, who went to Oxford and had thousands of pounds spent on his education to spend his time in that manner," the *Times* quoted the distraught former actress as having testified on the stand. Bartram, she would further claim, also conducted himself rudely in the company of her nearest friends, especially the dignified Ruth Chatterton. In December of 1936, according to the plaintiff, the Bartrams, along with other notables, including actor Charles Boyer and his wife, Pat Paterson, were invited to a dinner party at Miss Chatterton's home. During the meal Bartram turned to Chatterton, pointing to a diamond necklace she was wearing and remarked: "Must you wear the entire chandelier around your neck?" The embarrassment following such a remark, Compton claimed, was almost too much to bear.

There was more to the case than mere rude behavior and transvestitism, however. Mr. Bartram, his wife complained, insisted on the employment of one Sheila Sutton, a girl of 17 when they met. Bartram, who was alleged to have had more than a working relationship with the teenager, used to call the young girl "a child of mystery."

The sensational case was finally settled in the summer of 1944, with Juliette Hall Compton Bartram awarded sole custody of the couple's teenage daughter, Juliette Mary.

Following the lengthy divorce proceedings, Compton disappeared from the news, concentrating instead on her lifelong interest in theosophy. She died in Los Angeles on March 19, 1989.

JULIETTE COMPTON FILMOGRAPHY

1924: *Human Desires* (GB*); *The Gayest of the Gay* (GB); *Nell Gwynn* (GB); *The Wine of Life* (GB).
1925: *Trainer and the Temptress* (GB); *Afraid of Love* (GB).
1926: *The Chinese Bungalow* (GB); *White Heat* (GB).
1927: *The Fake*.
1928: *The Woman Tempted* (GB); *The Scarlet Daredevil* (GB).
1929: *Woman to Woman*.
1930: *Ladies of Leisure*; *Anybody's Woman*; *Morocco*.
1931: *The House That Shadows Build* (documentary); *Unfaithful*; *Kick In*; *The Vice Squad*; *Women Love Once*; *Rich Man's Folly*; *Compromised*; *Husband's Holiday*.
1932: *No One Man*; *Strangers in Love*; *Westward Passage*; *The Man Called Back*; *The Devil and the Deep*; *The Match King*.

*GB=Great Britain.

1933: *Peg o' My Heart; The Masquerader; Berkeley Square.*
1934: *Grand Canary; The Count of Monte Cristo; Behold My Wife!*
1935: *No More Ladies.*
1940: *Irene.*
1941: *That Hamilton Woman.*

7—Katherine DeMille

Dark haired Katherine DeMille was always seething with either hatred or jealousy or both. Usually typecast as an exotic vixen, she rarely got her man—not even in the films directed by her adoptive father Cecil. But (according to Paramount publicity, at least) she didn't mind. "The day when an actress in Hollywood felt she must be the lead or an ingenue has passed," she is quoted as having said in the early 1930s.

> It doesn't hurt anyone to play "heavies," particularly when they are starting out in pictures. Anyone can walk in and out of a scene, and look pretty. But the best experience can be had in parts with character to them. I may want to play something else later, but I don't mind being "typed" temporarily as a villainess.

DeMille, unfortunately, would remain "typed" throughout her screen career.

She was born June 29, 1911, in Vancouver, British Columbia, the only child of Captain Edward Gabriel Lester and his French wife Cecile Culani. Katherine would have very few memories of her parents since Captain Lester perished in World War I and Mrs. Lester died shortly thereafter. At the age of nine, the beautiful, black haired child was adopted by Hollywood director Cecil B. DeMille, a friend of her father's, and his wife Constance. Katherine would join a household that already had three biological children but would always be considered a true DeMille.

According to later publicity, Cecil constantly tried to convince his daughter to appear in his films but she always demurred.* "We both have strong tempers," she explained in 1934, having again turned down yet another offer—this time for a role in *Cleopatra*.

> At home, we are the greatest of friends. We play together and discuss motion picture problems each from our own point of view—and without rancor. I can talk back to him and get away with it at home. I shouldn't want to risk the danger of arguing with him on

---

She is, however, credited with a walk-on in Madame Satan *(M-G-M, 1930).*

the set, where our relationship of daughter and father would cease and he would become the director and I the actress.

So turning down her father's *Cleopatra*, DeMille had her official screen debut in the supporting role of Rosita in David O. Selznick's *Viva Villa* (M-G-M, 1934), making it very clear that Selznick had not hired her out of friendship with her famous father. "Believe it or not, I've earned whatever place I've made in pictures through my own efforts," she was quoted as saying (having just signed with Cecil's home studio, Paramount).

> I got myself the job in *Viva Villa* opposite Wallace Beery and I connived to get myself a Paramount contract without father knowing about it. I don't know of anything more contemptible than the person who gets work merely because of family connections.

She had, she said, tried to get on *Viva Villa* as a script girl, but was persuaded by director Howard Hawks to accept the role of Rosita. Hawks, however, was replaced with Jack Conway early on, and with him went most of the cast, except Beery and, having never acted professionally before, Katherine DeMille! Not that her inexperience mattered much: the film belonged thoroughly to Beery, who gave a bravura performance as the famous Mexican outlaw-revolutionary.

Having settled into her new Paramount contract with a bit in *The Trumpet Blows* (1934), DeMille seethed with screen jealousy when her boyfriend, the proprietor of the Sensation House saloon (John Miljan), leaves her for the obvious charms of chanteuse Mae West in *Belle of the Nineties* (1934). According to some fanciful Paramount publicity, West had picked DeMille herself after having tested 50 girls for the part of the avaricious Molly Brant. It was but the first of many such roles for the doe-eyed actress who, according to Andre Sennwald of the *New York Times*, "contributed excellently to the comedy."

Next, DeMille was borrowed by Darryl Zanuck's 20th Century company to play Marie, Clark Gable's double-crossing girlfriend in the screen version of Jack London's *Call of the Wild* (1935). She had only a couple of scenes in the beginning of the film, but there were censorship problems. The Breen office, it seems, complained about Gable's Jack Thornton living with DeMille without the benefit of clergy, and even more about her character doing a bit of prostitution on the side. Consequently most of their scenes together ended up on the cutting-room floor. DeMille's only remaining scene had Gable singing "My Gal Sal" to her and was apparently deleted, after the previews because of the film's length (and, presumably, Gable's less than stellar singing talents). Katherine, meanwhile, kept her on-screen billing in all release prints—a rather unusual turn of events for a novice actress, to say the least.

DeMille again and again demurred when asked if she would ever work with her famous father. "No," she said on several occasions, "not until I change my mind, which probably means never."

"Never" came around sooner than expected. In February of 1935 Cecil B. DeMille began production on his epic story of *The Crusades* (Paramount, 1935) and cast his daughter as the disagreeable Princess Alice of France, the intended wife and queen of Richard I of England (Henry Wilcoxon). Alice was so ornery, in fact, that to avoid marrying her Richard joined the "Christian men, kings, knights and commoners [who], with motives ranging from the purest faith to the blackest treachery and greed, left their homes by the thousands and sought to wrestle the Holy Land from its Moslem possessors..." (Cecil B. DeMille).

Despite very little screen time (again), Katherine DeMille received good notices for her role in *The Crusaders*; according to her father it was "one of the best pictures I have ever made." It was also one of the director's few financial failures.

Cecil DeMille, who had threatened to retire in the aftermath of his first major flop, was coaxed back to Paramount in late 1935 to begin pre-production on *The Plainsman* (1937), the epic (if highly fanciful) story of Wild Bill Hickock (Gary Cooper), Calamity Jane (Jean Arthur) and Buffalo Bill Cody (James Ellison). Katherine DeMille suddenly left all thoughts of nepotism aside and begged her father for the role of Buffalo Bill's young bride Louisa. Cecil, however, did an unexpected turnaround and discouraged her, advising her to get some theater experience.* An obedient daughter, she took his advice and accepted an engagement with a Stockbridge, Massachusetts, company, in a production of *Topaz*.

Returning to Hollywood, a slimmer and more dedicated Katherine pronounced that she was through with playing vixens. "I grew tired of playing heavies and shady ladies," she later explained.

> I wanted to change my type and figure so that I could wear modern gowns and play modern, sympathetic roles. I feel assured now that the loss of weight is permanent and that there will still be further reduction.

Katherine DeMille's svelte new look earned her a small supporting role in the Mitchell Leisen's *Hands Across the Table* (Paramount, 1935), a sparkling "screwball" comedy starring Carole Lombard as a fortune hunting manicurist. Katherine, cast as a society girl in what amounted to a glorified walk-on, kept her chin up despite the skimpiness of the situation. "It's a small part," she admitted, "one of the smallest I have played. But I am glad to get it in order to prove the change that I have undergone."

Paramount was willing to give the "new" Katherine DeMille a chance and gave her second-billing as Larry (Buster) Crabbe's sweet sister in a Zane Grey Western, *Drift Fence* (1936). Unfortunately, the film was merely a routine programmer and escaped the attention of the influential New York critics. And although she again received co-star billing (this time to William Gargan) she had very little to do in *The Sky Parade* (Paramount, 1936), a male oriented action adventure based on the popular serial *The Air Adventures of Jimmie Allen*. According to *Variety*, she was included "simply because even kids can appreciate a good looking gal."

Leaving Paramount to sign with 20th Century–Fox, DeMille was quickly reinstated as a villainess. As the jealous servant girl Marguerita in the fourth (and most lavish) rendition of Helen Hunt Jackson's near-classic *Ramona* (1936), she tries in vain to keep the heroine (Loretta Young) away from the handsome Indian leader Alessandro (Don Ameche). A story of miscegenation among Spanish settlers and Indians in

---

*The role of Louisa instead went to Helen Burgess.

Katherine DeMille (photograph courtesy of the Danish Film Museum).

1870 California, *Ramona* was mainly praised for its groundbreaking use of color. Frank S. Nugent of the *New York Times*, however, found that DeMille "smoldered handsomely as a jealous maiden."

In *Banjo on My Knee* (20th Century–Fox, 1936), DeMille was yet again cast as a jealous maiden. This time she was the exotic Leota Long, Barbara Stanwyck's fierce rival for Joel McCrea's affections. But despite a potentially powerful role (complete with a fist fight between the two women), she all but disappeared into the crowd in an overblown love story that couldn't determine whether it was a melodrama or a musical-comedy, but whose highlights ended up being a Hall Johnson Choir rendition of "The St. Louis Blues" and Anthony (Tony) Martin singing "There's Something in the Air."

Although she received second billing to Warner Oland in *Charlie Chan at the Olympics* (20th Century–Fox, 1936), the fourteenth entry in the long-running series, DeMille again had very little to do as a mysterious woman accused of being both a spy and a murderess (she was eventually proven innocent on both counts). In *Love Under Fire* (20th Century–Fox, 1937), a vulgar story about jewel thieves romping through a Spain in the throes of civil war, she was reunited with Loretta Young and Don Ameche, but found herself billed below Borrah Minnevitch and His Gang of accordion players! She was much better served by *The Californian* (20th Century–Fox, 1937), a Western in which she played Chata, the willful wife of a bandit leader (George Regas). A thinly disguised bio-pic of California rebel Joaquín Murieta (here named Ramon Escobar), *The Californian* starred Ricardo Cortez and Marjorie Weaver and was deemed "a good secondary feature" by *Variety*.

On October 2, 1937, Katherine DeMille wed Anthony Quinn, a young newcomer she had met on the set of her father's *The Plainsman*. Born in Chihuahua, Mexico, in 1916, Quinn had made his Hollywood debut in 1936 before being selected by Cecil B.

"Gabby" Hayes, Mary Hart, Roy Rogers and Katherine DeMille in *In Old Caliente* (Republic, 1939).

DeMille to play a Cheyenne warrior in *The Plainsman*. He went on to a career that must have surprised even his father-in-law, earning two Academy Awards as best supporting actor.* Later his father-in-law cast him in important supporting roles in *The Buccaneer* (1938), *Union Pacific* (1939), and *Unconquered* (1947), and he starred in the 1958 remake of *The Buccaneer*. When Cecil, who also executive produced this, his final film, took ill before principal photography had commenced, directing reins went to Quinn, who unfortunately was not quite up to the task.

In late 1937, Katherine DeMille was suddenly replaced by Gloria Stuart in the appropriately named *Change of Heart*, and Fox terminated her contract. Freelancing, she played a peasant girl in Walter Wanger's Spanish Civil War melodrama *Blockade* (United Artists, 1938), but was pregnant for most of the year (with the first of four children by Quinn), returning to the screen in December to play enemy agent Carol Rayer opposite Jack Holt in Larry Darmour's *Trapped in the Sky* (Columbia, 1939), a minor espionage thriller about the invention of an electronically driven airplane. Her only other screen appearance in 1939 was in a Roy Rogers "B" Western from Republic, *In Old Caliente*. She was briefly considered for the role of Louvette Corbeau in her

*Viva Zapata *(1952) and* Lust for Life *(1956)*.

father's mammoth production of *North West Mounted Police* (Paramount, 1940), but the role eventually went to Paulette Goddard. Instead, she was Gilbert Roland's evil "native" wife in *Isle of Destiny* (Fine Arts/RKO, 1940), yet another low-budget aviation melodrama, and returned to independent producer Larry Darmour for a small supporting role in *Ellery Queen, Master Detective* (Columbia, 1940).

Throughout the 1940s, Katherine DeMille concentrated mostly on child rearing, leaving the acting chores to her husband. She did, however, replace Barbara O'Neill in a supporting role in Universal's *The Dark Streets of Cairo* (1941) and was, according to *Variety*, nicely cast; and she once again played a jealous native girl, in *Aloma of the South Seas* (Paramount, 1941).

Again concentrating on family life, DeMille was coaxed out of retirement to play her real-life husband's onscreen wife in *Black Gold* (Monogram, 1947), a quiet horse racing drama and Quinn's first starring vehicle. Also in 1947, she returned to Paramount to play an Indian girl in Cecil's *Unconquered*. In 1949 there was an independently produced courtroom drama entitled *The Judge* (she took second-billing to Milburn Stone).

On March 19, 1953, while Anthony Quinn was on location in Mexico, DeMille was on hand to pick up his Best Supporting Actor Oscar for *Viva Zapata!* "I can hardly believe I'm here," she gasped. The audience at the Pantages Theater tended to agree: Richard Burton of *My Cousin Rachel* had been the heavy favorite to win the coveted statuette.

The DeMille marriage, it seems, was an anomaly for its time: *very* "open"! At least it was on the part of Quinn, who usually dated his various leading ladies with full publicity. Quinn's 1953 mistress was his co-star in Universal's *City Beneath the Seas* and *East of Sumatra*, the exotic DeMille look-alike Suzan Ball who, like most of his conquests, found him "very passionate and very possessive."

Katherine DeMille made her final screen appearance in 1956 as an extra in *The Man from Del Rio* (United Artists), a Western starring her husband and Katy Jurado. She seems to have stood meekly by while Quinn romanced the troubled Inger Stevens* on the set of *The Buccaneer* (Paramount, 1958), and the "happy" marriage suffered an even bigger blow on June 15, 1963, when a headline in the New York *Daily News* blared that "QUINN ADMITS LOVE CHILD." The accompanying article revealed that the actor had fathered two sons with Yolanda Adelatori, a wardrobe girl he had met while filming *Barabbas* in Rome in 1961. Despite the fact that, as the *New York Times* reported, "the situation created something of an international outrage when it became public," the DeMille-Quinn union survived until 1965.†

Following her long-awaited divorce, Katherine DeMille, very much retired and living in Beverly Hills, has concentrated on her lifelong interest in theology. Then in May of 1995, Anthony Quinn, sued for divorce by Yolanda (and presumably fearing a suit for a hefty settlement), claimed that his divorce from Katherine DeMille was never legal! The tabloids have so far failed to interview Katherine on the matter.

All through his marriage to DeMille, Quinn seemed drawn to starstruck ingenues. The aforementioned Suzan Ball, for example, succumbed to cancer at the age of 22 (her final word, according to gossip, was "Tony"). Inger Stevens, later famous as television's "Farmer's Daughter," died a suicide after a string of high profile love affairs with co-stars such as Quinn, Bing Crosby and Harry Belafonte.

†*Quinn subsequently married Adelatori.*

7—Katherine DeMille

Despite her illustrious name, Katherine DeMille was given short shrift in Hollywood, which is a shame since in several films she proved more memorable than the celebrated stars she supported. With her exotic looks, however, DeMille was yet another victim of Hollywood typecasting and deserved a better fate.

Katherine DeMille Filmography

- **1930:** *Madame Satan.*
- **1934:** *Viva Villa; Belle of the Nineties; The Trumpet Blows.*
- **1935:** *All the King's Horses; The Black Room; The Call of the Wild; Hands Across the Table; The Crusades.*
- **1936:** *Drift Fence; The Sky Parade; Romeo and Juliet; Ramona; Banjo on My Knee.*
- **1937:** *Charlie Chan at the Olympics; The Californian; Love Under Fire; Under Suspicion.*
- **1938:** *Blockade.*
- **1939:** *Trapped in the Sky; In Old Caliente.*
- **1940:** *Ellery Queen, Master Detective; Isle of Destiny.*
- **1941:** *The Dark Streets of Cairo; Aloma of the South Seas.*
- **1947:** *Black Gold; Unconquered.*
- **1949:** *The Judge.*
- **1956:** *Man from Del Rio.*

8 — Claire Dodd

Blonde, dimpled Claire Dodd was so pretty—yet, so calculating. There was never any doubt that here was a lady with an objective—and an objective that invariably spelled trouble for a Hollywood heroine. Dodd would saunter into a situation, coolly size up her opponent, and then go in for the kill in order to get her man. Usually, it would be a man who "belonged" to somebody else. Regrettably, the mores of the 1930s forbade a successful outcome of such aggressive acts, and women like Dodd were almost always suitably punished. Consequently, Claire regularly saw herself defeated by sappy heroines like Ruth Chatterton or Kay Francis. Not that they had more class than she; they just had better agents.

Claire Dodd's heyday was at Warner Bros. in the mid–1930s, when the hard-boiled gangster's moll had given way to the calculating other woman or the bitchy wife. The quintessential Dodd performance can be found in a little throwaway programmer entitled *The Payoff* (Warner Bros., 1935). As the adulterous wife of a crooked wrestling promoter, Dodd, according to Andre Sennwald of the *New York Times*, stole the show single-handedly:

> Miss Dodd has played vindictive women all during her screen career, but this one is her masterpiece. Her crowning achievement is when she learns that her husband, whom she has deserted in favor of a notorious gambler, is in the grip of a four-day bender at a waterfront gin mill. She coolly calls up Bellevue Hospital and demands that he be removed to the dipsomaniac ward.

This was typical Dodd behavior. Despite her dimples and cunningly sweet smile, she could play the artful bitch better than almost anybody else in Hollywood.

Claire Dodd was born on December 29, 1908, in New York City. According to later publicity,

> she lived all over the United States, with her education entirely in the hands of a tutor. She went to Europe with her parents as a child—but can't remember much about that.

Claire Dodd in 1931.

From Florida to New York to California, she has lived a pleasant and comfortable life, without a single adventure or an unusual background.

And the publicist, for once, didn't even try for just a little embellishment!

Dodd made her theatrical debut in 1928, appearing as a show girl in Florenz Ziegfeld's *Whoopee* starring Eddie Cantor. Two years later she made her screen bow supporting Helen Vinson and Philip Reed in a minor crime drama from Majestic entitled *It's a Deal*. She appeared as a model for a few seconds in *Our Blushing Brides* (M-G-M, 1930), and then joined the Goldwyn Girls (a group of beauties who that year also numbered Virginia Bruce and Betty Grable) in the screen version of *Whoopee* (United Artists, 1930). None of these films brought her recognition and she was relieved when Ziegfeld requested her return to Broadway for his upcoming production of *Smiles* starring Marilyn Miller. Dodd stayed for the run of the show, but took time out on May 12, 1931, to marry New York real estate broker Jack Milton Strauss. When *Smiles* folded, she quickly accepted a contract with Paramount.

That studio brought her back to Hollywood where she did much posing for publicity pictures but very little acting. She had bits in programmers: *The Secret Call* (about telephone operators); *Girls About Town* (gold diggers); *Working Girls* (waitresses); and *Two Kinds of Women* (socialites and gold diggers). In early 1932 First National (then a division of Warner Bros.) borrowed her for small parts in *Under 18* (she played a model named Babsy) and *Alias the Doctor*, and liked her enough to request sharing her contract with Paramount.

Immediately, her roles got meatier. She posed as Melvyn Douglas' wife to save him from a jealous Mexican in the aviation drama *The Broken Wing* (Paramount); was Chou-Chou, a glamorous actress whom Lily Damita impersonates in *This Is the Night* (Paramount); stole Kenneth Thomson away from Kay Francis (who, of course, ended up with the much nicer David Manners) in *Man Wanted* (Warner Bros.); was a tantalizing socialite (her first of many), gamely trying to seduce the vapid Manners in *Crooner* (First National).

Dodd came into her own as one of Hollywood's preeminent other women in 1933. She was Leo Carrillo's "kept" mistress (and a thorn in the side of Bette Davis) in *Parachute Jumper* (Warner Bros.), an action melodrama with Douglas Fairbanks, Jr.; and was Gladys La Mann, a gangster's moll battling Joan Blondell for the attention of Chester Morris, in *Blondie Johnson* (First National), a crime drama.

Even better, however, were a couple of loan-outs to Columbia, where she was very convincing as Carole Rogers, an alcoholic nightclub singer trying to seduce naive Gene Raymond in *Ann Carver's Profession*. Ann Carver was played by Fay Wray and her profession was that of a lawyer—which, of course, she cheerfully gives up to become a good wife and mother. Dodd's Carole, on the other hand, has no such inclinations and pays a horrendous price: During a fall brought about by a drunken stupor, her pearl necklace catches on a sofa and she chokes to death!

Her other Columbia effort of 1933 was not quite as dramatic: In *My Woman*, she is again a society vamp with a yen for seemingly unattainable men. This time her victim is Wallace Ford, with the suffering wife played by the always doleful Helen Twelvetrees. As it turns out, Ford is a fun-loving guy and succumbs to Dodd's provocative charms, whereas Miss Twelvetrees finds romance with the more stable Victor Jory (a touch of offbeat casting, to be sure!).

While she lost out to archrival Helen Vinson for the role of Robert Barrat's mistress in *The Kennel Murder Case* (Warner Bros., 1933), Dodd sparkled in *Footlight Parade* (1933), Warner's highly successful follow-up to both *42nd Street* (1932) and *Gold Diggers of 1933*. In this lavish backstage musical, famous for Busby Berkeley's kaleidoscopic choreography (especially the gigantic "By a Waterfall" number) and its lilting Harry Warren–Al Dubin score, Dodd portrays a seemingly well bred actress on the make. Only Joan Blondell, her old school chum, is aware of Dodd's blue-collar roots and scheming mind. James Cagney, Blondell's boss and unrequited love, buys the vixen's act hook, line and sinker, and even proposes marriage. His protective "Girl Friday," however, quickly sizes up the situation and literally kicks her rival out of Cagney's hotel suite.

> "But where do I go?" A stunned and incredulous Claire Dodd asks.
> "Outside, countess," Joan swiftly replies. "As long as they have sidewalks, *you* have a job!"

Dodd was cool and elegant as a glamorous actress dallying with Ruth Chatterton's philandering husband (Adolphe Menjou) in the melodrama *Journal of a Crime* (First National, 1934). Chatterton, needless to say, proved too formidable a rival and Claire ended up getting shot for her indiscretion.

She could easily have suffered the same fate crossing swords with Barbara Stanwyck over Joel McCrea in *Gambling Lady* (Warner Bros., 1934), but this time she escaped such harsh punishment. Not that she didn't deserve some penalty here as well: when McCrea is innocently accused of murder, she refuses to give him an alibi—although they had been together on the crucial night—unless Stanwyck grants him a divorce (which she unselfishly does). Happily, everything gets neatly untangled before the fade-out.

Next, Dodd did two films opposite the oafish but likable Pat O'Brien: She was a socialite briefly dallying with a prizefighter in *The Personality Kid* (Warner Bros., 1934) and replaced a suspended Bette Davis as a female con-artist who matches wits with her male counterpart and eventually makes a sucker out of him in *I Sell Anything* (First National, 1934). In the latter, she gave one of her most polished performances and proved to possess a fine flair for comedy.

She was equally commendable as Tanis Judique, the scheming temptress who briefly takes advantage of Guy Kibbee in the second screen version of Sinclair Lewis' morality play *Babbitt* (Warner Bros., 1934); but a loan-out to Universal for *The Secret of the Chateau* (1934), a silly dime-store thriller that promised far more than it delivered, was beneath her talents and a waste of anybody's time. (As a consolation of sorts, she did, however, receive star billing.)

Again on loan-out, Dodd played Randolph Scott's snobbish fiancée in RKO's screen version of Jerome Kern's buoyant *Roberta* (1935). Luckily for Scott, when she drops him (because of his hayseed ways), he is picked up by Irene Dunne's Russian princess. All this, of course, is merely coincidental to the comedy and terpsichorean splendor of Fred Astaire and Ginger Rogers at their best. Curiously (in retrospect, at least), RKO was still unsure of the great dance team's box office potential in this, their third outing, and safeguarded their investment by giving the popular Dunne top billing. Viewed today, the Dunne-Scott-Dodd triangle only gets in the way of the film's real fun, but Dodd still manages to stand out doing her now patented selfish socialite bit. The RKO people liked her enough to enter into a contract-sharing agreement with Warner Bros.

Dodd made quite a departure from her usual *femmes fatales* as Perry Mason's devoted secretary Della Street in *The Case of the Curious Bride* (First National, 1935), the second of six whodunits based on Erle Stanley Gardner's popular crime novels about an invincible defense attorney. Warren William repeated as Perry, but Dodd had taken over from Helen Trenholme, whose Della had been but a minor character in the premiere effort, *The Case of the Howling Dog* (Warner Bros., 1934). First National had Dodd reprise the role opposite William the following year in *The Case of the Velvet Claws*, and she thereby became the only actress to portray the part twice on screen.* This time, however, the always lovelorn Della actually gets her man, and the film concludes with the happy couple embarking on their honeymoon!

The chemistry between Dodd and Warren William in the *Mason* films was good enough for Warners to think of her when Dolores Del Rio suddenly walked off the set of *Don't Bet on Blondes* (1935), a comedy about a bookie who insures a father against his actress daughter's marrying within the next three years. The guarantor naturally falls for the girl himself, loses a fortune but gains a wife. It is all very slight and most

---

The character of Della Street was played on screen by Genevieve Tobin in The Case of the Lucky Legs *(1935); June Travis in* The Case of the Black Cat *(1936); and Ann Dvorak in* The Case of the Stuttering Bishop *(1937). Barbara Hale, of course, played the character in the long running television series and in a series of made-for-television movies.*

reviewers found the cast superior to the material. Frank S. Nugent of the *New York Times*, for example, thought that the players deserved much better: "Miss Dodd, Mr. William and the supporting cast* act in such a quiet, charming, restrained, almost grave way that they make the triviality of the plot seem almost exasperating."

If nothing else, the *Perry Mason* films and *Don't Bet on Blondes* proved that, when called upon, Dodd could be as conventionally dull as the typical Hollywood starlet. Thankfully, she was soon back to being a vixen—an area in which she had few equals. On loan to Paramount for the first (1935) version of Dashiell Hammett's *The Glass Key*, she was the hard-boiled Janet Henry, a senator's daughter caught between her father's ambitions and her loathing for the gangster who holds their fate in his hands; she was a jewel thief who gets involved in a complicated marital hide-and-seek in *The Goose and the Gander* (Warner Bros., 1935), managing to upstage Kay Francis in the process; and, of course, there was the aforementioned *The Payoff* (Warner Bros., 1935), the film in which she vindictively had her husband (James Dunn) carted off to the dipsomaniac ward.

Dodd was conventional again, unfortunately, in *Murder by an Aristocrat* (First National, 1936), a trite whodunit released as "A Clue Club Picture"; and, on loan to Republic, she was a snobbish debutante metamorphosed into an ordinary ingenue by the love of a sailor and an adorable toddler in *Navy Born* (1936). There were a few other films, but the roles were small since Warners found it increasingly hard to hide the fact that the actress was pregnant. In late 1936 she gave birth to a baby boy, Jon Michael Strauss.

After a break to take care of her new baby, Dodd returned to the screen in July of 1937, on loan to M-G-M, portraying the kind of *Women Men Marry* but then dump in favor of sappy ingenues like Josephine Hutchinson. George Murphy was the "dumper," and he actually has reasonable justification: His wife was sleeping with his boss. Offscreen, Dodd went through the pain of a divorce herself, when her marriage to Milton Strauss was terminated in March of 1938.

Still committed to RKO (but no longer associated with Warner Bros.) Dodd continued to play her specialty—ambitious schemers—but on loan-out to other studios: she was the countess of something-or-other, momentarily steering John Boles away from poor songbird Gladys Swarthout in *Romance in the Dark* (Paramount, 1938), and she lurked mysteriously about as the mistress of a murdered book collector (George Zucco) in *Fast Company* (M-G-M, 1938). The latter was a rather derivative whodunit starring Melvyn Douglas and Florence Rice as a husband-and-wife detective team. Quicker than you can say *The Thin Man,* Mr. Douglas unmasks the guilty party, who, to no one's particular surprise, proves to be Miss Dodd. Claire, however, does not go down meekly; before the police can arrive, the cold-blooded lady tries to rid herself of her adversary by throwing a knife at his heart. Fortunately, she has a lousy aim.

She was less lethal but equally unsuccessful in love as a glamorous actress trying to steer Robert Montgomery away from small-town girl Janet Gaynor in *Three Loves*

Which included Errol Flynn in only his second Hollywood film; the actor had made his American screen debut playing the murder victim in The Case of the Curious Bride.

Has Nancy (M-G-M, 1938); and was then a murder victim herself in *Charlie Chan in Honolulu* (20th Century–Fox, 1939). In *Woman Doctor* (United Artists, 1939), her quarry was the decent Henry Wilcoxon, but she obviously stood no chance against the dignity and brains of Dr. Frieda Inescort.

All these roles were merely routine and none tested her acting abilities in the least. However, Dodd seemed no longer to care: she had met the man of her dreams, automobile distributor H. Brand Cooper, and in early 1940 they married. "She fell in love with my father and left the studio forever," her daughter Austeene Cooper later said.

Well, not quite. Leaving RKO (who must have earned a fortune lending her to other studios), she signed with Universal. It was to prove a step down for the actress who, after a somewhat promising start as Allyn Joslyn's shrewish wife in a Bing Crosby musical, *If I Had My Way* (1940), was put to work in some of the studio's less than stellar "shockers." There was to be no *The Wolf Man* (1941) for Claire, who instead did yeoman service as Basil Rathbone's wife in the ridiculous *The Black Cat* (1941). Murdered early in the pedestrian proceedings by a greedy Gladys Cooper, Dodd had very little screen time; in fact, in one nonspeaking scene her character was actually "played" by Marlene Dietrich, who was on the set visiting her current beau, actor Broderick Crawford. According to Universal chronicler Michael Fitzgerald, Dodd turned up missing one day and was briefly replaced by the accommodating German star, on a break from being *The Flame of New Orleans* one soundstage away.

From *The Black Cat*, Dodd descended yet another step on the Hollywood ladder to play the focal point of Lionel Atwill's lust in the appalling *The Mad Doctor of Market Street* (1942). Atwill ("the maddest doctor of them all," as Forrest J Ackerman so aptly described him) was the shabby film's only saving grace, delightfully hamming it up and apparently oblivious to the sad state of the material. Dodd was not so fortunate; her badly written role could have been played by any B actress on the lot.

With these pedestrian "horror" films as bookends, Dodd suffered through some of the studio's then popular but in retrospect rather humdrum wartime fillers. She was the conventional heroine opposite Abbott and Costello in *In the Navy* (1941); suffered through 12 chapters of the serial *Don Winslow of the Navy* (1941); and was on a stagebound riverboat in *The Mississippi Gambler* (1942). From Universal, she went straight to Columbia as a foil for the fading Joe E. Brown in a wartime farce, *The Daring Young Man* (1942), but then wisely gave up her career to raise a family.

A cousin of the actress, the late Virginia Mowery, once told this writer that Claire Dodd rarely discussed her screen career once she had retired but still kept her scrapbooks and various publicity photos. She died in her Beverly Hills home after a two year bout with cancer on November 23, 1973, survived by her husband, daughter Austeene and three sons.

Together with Helen Vinson, Claire Dodd was the ultimate Hollywood "other woman." In film after film, potboiler after potboiler, Dodd, to her everlasting credit, could be counted on to add some much needed spice and direct an acid barb or two toward the sugary leading lady who, more often than not, deserved no better.

Opposite: **Claire Dodd in 1941.**

Claire Dodd Filmography

1930: *It's a Deal; Our Blushing Brides; Whoopee.*
1931: *The Secret Call; Girls About Town; Working Girls.*
1932: *Under 18; Two Kinds of Women; Alias the Doctor; The Broken Wing; This Is the Night; Man Wanted; Guilty as Hell; Crooner; The Match King.*
1933: *Lawyer Man; Hard to Handle; Parachute Jumper; Blondie Johnson; Ex-Lady; Elmer the Great; Ann Carver's Profession; My Woman; Footlight Parade.*
1934: *Massacre; Journal of a Crime; Gambling Lady; Smarty; The Personality Kid; I Sell Anything; The Secret of the Chateau; Babbitt.*
1935: *The Case of the Curious Bride; Roberta; The Glass Key; Don't Bet on Blondes; The Goose and the Gander; The Payoff.*
1936: *The Singing Kid; Murder by an Aristocrat; Navy Born; Two Against the World; The Case of the Velvet Claws.*
1937: *Women Men Marry.*
1938: *Romance in the Dark; Fast Company; Three Loves Has Nancy.*
1939: *Woman Doctor; Charlie Chan in Honolulu; Slightly Honorable.*
1940: *If I Had My Way.*
1941: *The Black Cat; Don Winslow of the Navy* (serial); *In the Navy.*
1942: *The Mad Doctor of Market Street; Mississippi Gambler.*

9—Mary Duncan

Long before there was a Margo Channing of *All About Eve* (1950), there was the formidable diva Rita Vernon of Zoe Akin's *Morning Glory*. Pandro S. Berman and RKO produced a screen version of the Broadway play in 1933 as a vehicle for newcomer Katharine Hepburn. Hepburn, of course, played the naive but spirited amateur actress who leaves her comfortable New England town for New York City and the theater. Inevitably, once there she encounters actresses of an altogether different mold. Enter the imperious Rita Vernon. And, oddly enough, exit her screen creator, Mary Duncan.

Duncan had come to films near the end of the silent era and quickly had to fend for herself in a rapidly changing industry. From the outset, she had been typed as a *femme fatale*—despite her so innocent sounding name. Mary had been mean to Janet Gaynor in Murnau's *Four Devils* (Fox, 1929), and might as well have spanked Rin-Tin-Tin for all the good it did her! The audience never forgave her. The following year she vamped Otis Skinner in *Kismet* (First National, 1930), another tough spot for a young actress: Skinner was 72 years old and rather past his prime and their scenes together were ludicrous. As a consequence, Duncan's career proved short-lived. Not because she didn't try—few tried harder—but the type of roles in which she excelled seems to have vanished along with silent screen titles.

Mary Duncan was born on August 13, 1903, in Lutrellville, Virginia, the daughter of William and Ada Duncan. She was educated at a finishing school, at Wirtland Seminary in Richmond and (a fact which her publicity never seems to have missed) at Cornell University. Preparing to become a lawyer, Duncan, who had acted in a few amateur productions while at college, suddenly left for New York City (just as Katharine Hepburn later would in *Morning Glory*), where she sought out the renowned acting coach Yvette Guilbert. An internationally famous *chanteuse*, Madame Guilbert, according to *Motion Picture*'s Charleson Gray, "knew a spark when she saw it." She gave her newest protégée such special attention that, at the end of the course, Duncan had won a two year study under Lily Lehman, another celebrated musical performer.

(According to later press releases, mesdames Guilbert and Lehman were not the only luminaries to discover the newcomer: The Italian diva Eleanora Duse also showed interest in tutoring her, but, alas, Madame Duse died before anything had been decided. Opera star and former screen vamp Helen Garden, meanwhile, claimed that Duncan was "the only one of the young actresses with 'It.'")

With such unanimous praise from legendary artists, it was no wonder that Mary Duncan decided to turn down an offer from Florenz Ziegfeld and instead spend two years with Leo Dietrichstein, "obtaining schooling that was as valuable to her as was a similar study to another youngster, William Powell, who got his start with the gifted Teuton" (Charleson Gray in *Motion Picture*). Dietrichstein went on to cast Duncan in his school production of *Toto*, and she played opposite him in *The Great Lover*.

Following her stint with "the gifted Teuton," Duncan finally made her professional debut, appearing with an English touring company. She did a season of stock at the old Alcazar Theater in San Francisco, and then made a rather auspicious Broadway bow as Poppy in John Colton's controversial play of gambling and intrigue in the Orient, *The Shanghai Gesture*.

During the successful run of *Gesture* she was persuaded to make a screen test for the Fox Film Corporation. William Fox, the discoverer of Theda Bara, the first successful screen vamp, enthusiastically signed her to a contract; when the play folded in mid-1927 she happily packed her bags for a future in Hollywood.

To give their newest contract player some much needed exposure, Fox launched Duncan in a couple of programmers with Madge Bellamy, before co-starring her opposite studio heartthrob Charles Farrell in Frank Borzage's allegory, *The River* (1928).

A powerful and sometimes lyrical love story, *The River*, a silent, was unfortunately all but ignored in the burgeoning era of sound films and consequently suffered at the box office despite critical acclaim. As for Duncan herself, *Variety* found her "perfectly cast and accomplishing the various moods required."

According to *Photoplay* writer Herbert Howe, Hollywood quickly embraced Mary Duncan as a "stalker of men, not because of the maniacal nymph she had played in *The Shanghai Gesture*, but because in Hollywood drawing rooms *les hommes* gravitate helplessly to whichever corner Mary chooses."

With publicity like that, it was no wonder that the eminent German director F. W. Murnau chose her from the Fox roster to portray the *femme fatale* who comes between Janet Gaynor (Fox's ingenue *par excellence*) and Charles Morton in the circus melodrama *Four Devils* (1928).

The sentimental story of *Four Devils* centers on four youngsters training to become acrobats. Marion (Janet Gaynor) loves her trapeze partner Charles (Charles Morton) and all is bliss when in comes the Lady (Duncan) to spoil things. Mercilessly vamping the poor sap, the Lady almost gets her way but, since this is Hollywood, innocent love will triumph.

Four Devils was Murnau's second collaboration with Gaynor, but this tepid part-talkie was no *Sunrise* (Fox, 1927) and was a distinct disappointment at the box office. The blame, however, was laid squarely at the feet of Murnau and Gaynor whereas Duncan emerged as Fox's newest star vamp.

In keeping with her newly gained status, Duncan received star billing in *Thru*

Charles Farrell and Mary Duncan in *The River* (Fox, 1929) (photograph courtesy of the Danish Film Museum).

Different Eyes (Fox, 1929), but that proved actually to be a bit misleading. Directed by the capable but less than brilliant John Blystone, the melodrama involved a murder trial, shown, *Rashomon*-style, through the eyes of the various suspects. Consequently, the film was more an ensemble affair than a star turn. Duncan's character, however, was true to form: once abandoned penniless and with child, she seeks revenge and murders her former lover (Warner Baxter). In between the mayhem, however, she had an opportunity to warble a few ditties, which she did, according to Mordaunt Hall of the *New York Times*, "in a pleasingly natural fashion."*

Next, Duncan took second billing to Baxter in *Romance of the Rio Grande* (Fox, 1929), a Western about a Californian who returns home to take possession of his family's hacienda. Baxter, who was to earn an Academy Award for his portrayal of the Cisco Kid in another Western, *In Old Arizona* (Fox, 1929), was fast becoming the studio's highest ranked male lead and starring opposite the dashing Ohio-born actor was considered quite a coup. Unfortunately, *Romance of the Rio Grande* was not in a league with *In Old Arizona* and, worse yet, Duncan's role as the vamp took a decided back seat

---

*In accordance with the times, Mr. Hall went on to comment on Duncan's microphone abilities in general: "Miss Duncan is, as one might expect, uncommonly able. Her voice is pleasing without being in the least affected. She appears to be quite at home before the usually awe-inspiring microphone."

Mary Duncan in *Kismet* (First National, 1930).

to the love interest played by Mona Maris. *Variety*'s anonymous reviewer felt compelled to inform his readers that

> Mary Duncan gets another bad break. This former legit actress arrived in Hollywood before dialogue and has been handicapped by her assignments and the manner of handling her generally. She is not easy to cast. Here she does well what there is for her to do, but it's entirely non-progressive performance and unsympathetic. It is made quite clear that she unconventionally receives gentlemen callers in her boudoir.

Shocking indeed! However, the reviewer only anticipated the distinct change in attitude that would take place in Hollywood within a few years. Dialogue brought with it a heightened sense of realism and such things as naughty goings-on in bedrooms would soon become less explicit and more insinuated. As a result, the 1930s would become the decade of the tease and "the Lubitsch touch."

By now, Duncan had come to realize that she was being type-cast—basically asked to play the same role over and over again, not exactly a novel complaint in Hollywood at that time (or today for that matter). "Mary brings a distinct and thrilling personality to the screen, although she has been given too many parts dressed in black satin and chest heaves," Herbert Howe of *Motion Picture* complained in 1930. In order to escape her stifling situation, Duncan fought for and received the female lead opposite Charles Farrell in Murnau's upcoming drama, *Bread*.

Based on the play *The Mud Turtle* by Elliott Lester, *Bread* was the downbeat story of a young farmer (Farrell) who goes to the Big City in order to sell his wheat (the film's visuals seem obsessed with wheat and wheatfields) and to find a wife. Returning to his home with a new bride (Duncan), the farmer quickly learns that you can take the girl out of the city but you can't take the city out of the girl. Before long, the young wife battles over everything with her suspicious father-in-law (David Torrence) and, to put some spice into her dreary existence, beds a tough farmhand (Tom Maguire). Supposedly an attempt to show real people instead of two-dimensional Hollywood cut-outs, *Bread* was begun as a silent and had ambitions of becoming another *Sunrise*. Instead it was released as a part talkie, purged of most of its pretensions and bearing the less than stirring title, *City Girl* (Fox, 1930). It proved yet another disappointment for Duncan, but at least she finally got into some sensible clothes and actually portrayed a well rounded and not altogether unsympathetic character.

According to a friend, actor Owen Davis, Jr., Duncan was "a shrewd baby, no kidding. Nobody pulls nothing on her, if you know what I mean." She was shrewd enough, it seems, to realize that whatever her forte was on screen, Fox was in all likelihood the wrong place. Since the mid-1920s the studio had concentrated on making the kind of sugary dramas that had made first Janet Gaynor, and more recently Marian Nixon, a star. And, looking ahead, Fox's biggest box office draws through most of the coming decade would prove to be Will Rogers and Shirley Temple! In that homespun atmosphere, actresses with Mary Duncan's more exotic predilections were obviously apt to get sidelined. Granted, there was always room for a good villainess even in a Shirley Temple movie, but the roles would necessarily be smaller and being nasty to Shirley could prove rather lethal—as Astrid Allwyn (*Dimples*, *Stowaway*) and others would later discover. Consequently, Duncan left Fox in search of greener pastures as a freelance.

Veteran actor Otis Skinner had made a career playing Haji, the beggar-magician in *Kismet* who tries to pass his daughter off as a princess in order for her to catch a wealthy husband. The now 72-year-old Skinner had performed the role on Broadway (in 1911), on tour, and on screen (1920). In 1930 First National presented him in a sound-film version with Loretta Young as his daughter Marsinah and Duncan as the merciless vamp Zeleeka. The film cost a fortune and was splendidly designed in the best "Thousand and One Nights" style. Unhappily, it was all for naught: *Kismet* was played completely straight and the sight of Duncan vamping the grandfatherly Skinner was met with derisive laughter.

Following *Kismet*, Duncan went to Universal for a Betty Compson vehicle entitled *Boudoir Diplomat* (1930), the kind of chatty melodrama so popular in the earliest days of sound, but now already out of style. Little better were two for M-G-M: *Men Call It Love*, a society drama with Adolphe Menjou, and *Five and Ten* (both 1931), a Fanny Hurst tearjerker with Marion Davies. And there was *The Age for Love* (United Artists, 1931), Howard Hughes' expensive but dull ode to Billie Dove (with a screenplay by Ernest Pascal and Robert E. Sherwood, no less).

In these and other potboilers, Duncan suffered the same career decline as most silent screen vamps. From playing man-hungry leads, she was increasingly cast as the other woman and had less screen time and lower billing. The kind of roles she was offered, the heroine's sophisticated nemesis, would become a staple throughout the 1930s, providing lucrative careers to more subtle actresses—notably Gail Patrick and Binnie Barnes. This new breed of "man-eaters" fought their battles with wit, poise and a devastating sense of fashion. Completely gone were the nostril flaring, bosom heaving histrionics so prevalent in their silent screen predecessors.

In early 1932 Duncan signed with RKO for four films, all but one unworthy of her talents. *State's Attorney* (1932) was a fictionalized account of the career of scandal ridden New York D.A. William J. Fallon, a perjurer who, unfortunately for him, ran afoul of William Randolph Hearst. John Barrymore hammed it up in the lead role, with Duncan cast as one of his conquests. In *The Phantom of Crestwood* (1932), she was among the suspects in a dull but gimmick-laden murder mystery based on a popular radio show. At the close of 1932 she was one of the *Thirteen Women* (in reality there were only ten), stalked by a murderous sorority sister (Myrna Loy), whom they had once ostracized. The plot was rather preposterous and it didn't help that Loy played her half–Indian mystic with all the finesse of a burlesque queen. Duncan appears as June Raskob, a trapeze artist who is so spooked by Miss Loy's appearance that she accidentally causes her sister's demise.*

Mary Duncan was indeed very good as Rita Vernon, the temperamental stage star in *Morning Glory* (1933), and it is something of a mystery why this should have been her final appearance on screen. Mordaunt Hall of the *New York Times*, for example, found that she gave "a highly credible conception of a successful actress who essays to force demands from the producer at the eleventh hour."

Offscreen, Duncan did not "force demands" on her own behalf. On September 2, 1933, she married Stephen "Laddie" Sanford, a millionaire polo player.† The Sandfords traveled extensively and became members of the international jet-set, the former Mary Duncan having retired from show business with few, if any, regrets. The last of the true screen vamps, Duncan died in Palm Beach, Florida, on May 9, 1993.

Mary Duncan Filmography

1927: *Very Confidential.*
1928: *Soft Living; The River; Four Devils.*
1929: *Thru Different Eyes; Romance of the Rio Grande.*
1930: *City Girl; Kismet; The Boudoir Diplomat.*
1931: *Men Call It Love; Five and Ten; The Age for Love.*
1932: *State's Attorney; Thirteen Women; The Phantom of Crestwood.*
1933: *Morning Glory.*

---

*The film's sole lasting merit is the fact that it contains the only screen appearance of Peg Entwhistle, the actress who leaped to her death from the famous "Hollywoodland" sign.

†Apparently it was Duncan's second marriage; she had earlier divorced a Lewis Wood, Jr.

10—Josephine Dunn

"Not only was she beautiful, she was regular," columnist Dorothy Manners wrote of Josephine Dunn in late 1928. "She was so regular she didn't realize how beautiful she was."

Josephine was blonde and, as publicist John Springer once put it, "narrow-eyed." The position of her sky-blue eyes apparently suggested something akin to shiftiness and explained why she was always relegated to unsympathetic roles. The typecasting of Dunn started early in her screen career; already in the late twenties she had remarked: "I have played mean roles for so long that I'm beginning to lose my sweet disposition."

The early highlight of Josephine Dunn's career came in 1928 when she was Al Jolson's leading lady in Warner's *The Singing Fool*, the successor to the groundbreaking *The Jazz Singer* (1927). Cast as a sultry nightclub singer, Dunn acted rather spiteful toward Jolson, and as a consequence (as Springer also points out) her career never seemed to recover. She was the female lead in Universal's first all-singing, all-dancing musical, *Melody Lane* (1929) and was chosen a 1929 WAMPAS Baby Star. Unfortunately, *Melody Lane* was not the expected success and the Baby Star competition was more of a publicity gimmick than a real barometer of popularity. So instead of soaring to stardom, Dunn found herself playing supporting roles in "A" films and minor leads on Poverty Row. By 1932 her screen career was, for all intent and purposes, over.

She was born Mary Josephine Dunn on May 1, 1906, in New York City, the daughter of Richard and Agnes Dunn. Although most of her childhood was spent in Denver, Colorado, she returned to New York to finish high school at Holy Cross Convent. The nuns, she would later acknowledge, graciously supported the child's artistic goals and Dunn made her Broadway debut at the age of 15, appearing in the chorus of *Good Morning, Dearie* (1919), a revue starring Oscar Shaw. She quickly obtained a modicum of recognition as a chorus-girl and would subsequently appear in *Stepping*

Stones, Kid Boots, The Green Gang, The Demi Tasse Revue (Jeanette MacDonald was also in the chorus), and *Dear Girl*, in addition to several editions of the famous *Ziegfeld Follies*.

In case anyone thought otherwise, Dorothy Manners later assured her readership that Josephine had remained a good Catholic girl throughout. "When nice fat gentlemen offered her a motor car and an apartment on Park Avenue, she thought they were kidding and laughed it off," the columnist wrote in 1928. Dunn, Manners suggested, preferred instead the more uplifting company of "rather Bohemian writers and newspaper critics."

In reality, Josephine Dunn's private life was far from sedate. In 1925 she married William P. Cameron, a wealthy Philadelphian who later claimed that she deserted him after only four days of wedded hell. Soon after, the "good Catholic girl" eloped with Clyde E. Greenhouse, an Oklahoma oil magnate. That union lasted until 1931.

In late 1925, Josephine Dunn was among 16 young hopefuls chosen to attend Paramount's new acting school in Astoria, New York. There, on the studio's newly built lot, she and future stars Charles "Buddy" Rogers, Richard Arlen, and Thelma Todd were to be groomed for appearances in the company's upcoming productions. The "graduation assignment," as it were, were roles in *Fascinating Youths* (Paramount, 1926), a comedy about a wealthy hotel owner who falls for a girl from the wrong side of the tracks. Now dubbed the Paramount Junior Stars, the class of '26 was joined by established Paramount contract players Richard Dix, Adolphe Menjou, Clara Bow, and Thomas Meighan—all appearing as themselves. *Fascinating Youths*, alas, was not an overwhelming success and, as a consequence, several of the Junior Stars, including leading lady Ivy Harris, were let go and quickly forgotten.

Next, Dunn and fellow Junior Star Jack Luden were briefly seen in a beach scene in *It's the Old Army Game* (Paramount, 1926), a sketch farce starring W. C. Fields and featuring newcomer Louise Brooks (Paramount Junior Star, class of '27). Having shown adequate promise in these walk-ons, Dunn, along with Arlen, Rogers, Todd, and Brooks, was dispatched to the studio's Hollywood headquarters.

Once they were in California, Paramount didn't spare their new contractees and Dunn appeared in six films for the studio in 1927. She and fellow Junior Star alumnus Walter Goss (later known as Roland Drew) were promoted as a romantic team in the mild comedy *Fireman, Save My Child*; in *Swim, Girl, Swim*, she supported real life long-distance swimming champion Gertrude Ederle; and in *Get Your Man* she played a socialite who loses her beau ("Buddy" Rogers) to Clara Bow. None of these programmers did much for her career, and Paramount dropped her option by the end of the year.

Away from the stiff competition at Paramount, where she had had to contend with such increasingly popular blonde vixens as Greta Nissen and Thelma Todd, Dunn's career took a step in the right direction—or so it seemed at first. Under a nonexclusive contract to M-G-M she co-starred with William Haines in *Excess Baggage* (1928), a comedy-drama about a vaudevillian who marries a movie star. At the time it was considered quite a coup to be cast opposite the popular Haines. "It was so

Opposite: Josephine Dunn, circa 1929.

wonderful I went around in circles for days," she gushed to columnist Dorothy Manners, recalling the day she had received the good news. In retrospect, it is hard to understand her jubilation. *Excess Baggage* lived up to its title, being, according to *Variety*, only "a moderate program picture." Josephine, on the other hand, was lauded for her great beauty plus "an ability to get the desired pathos into the story."

Dunn's talkie debut was auspicious: Warner Bros. borrowed her to play the nightclub singer to whom Al Jolson dedicates a hit song in *The Singing Fool* (1928), the follow-up to the fabulously popular *The Jazz Singer* (1927). Like its predecessor, *The Singing Fool* was only a "part-talkie," and again its *raison d'être* was Jolson's inimitable singing. Here the Broadway star belts out "I'm Sittin' on Top of the World," "There's a Rainbow 'Round My Shoulder," "Golden Gate," and, of course, "Sonny Boy."

Although Betty Bronson was billed above her, Dunn was definitely the film's female lead. Yet, she was also its villain. Marrying Jolson out of pity, she bears him a child ("Sonny Boy") but then abandons both husband and baby for a career overseas. Leaving the struggling Jolson to cope with an adorable tot (played by child star David Lee) to pursue her own fame and fortune was definitely not the thing to do in 1928 and audiences everywhere booed and hissed. The role was to haunt the actress for the remainder of her career.

Whereas movie patrons adored Jolson, David Lee and *The Singing Fool* itself, most reviewers adopted a more sober approach to the picture. "Al meets two women in the picture and talks to them," *Variety*'s critic commented, highlighting the still astounding novelty of sound. "Josephine Dunn didn't talk so well and she looked pretty steely-hearted, even for a blonde." On the other hand, the scribe finished his report, "Joe Jackson's dialog is no smash!"

In the wake of *The Singing Fool,* Dunn was voted a 1929 WAMPAS Baby Star* by the Hollywood publicist. Not that the honor counted for much in her case: Returning to M-G-M (and silents), she appeared in two mild comedies featuring the waning team of Karl Dane and George K. Arthur, *All at Sea* and *China Bound* (both 1929) and was reunited with Haines in *A Man's Man* (1929). It was by now quite clear that sound had come to stay and none of these films did much business.

Not that sound was necessarily a guarantee for success either, the proof of which came when Universal cast her as Eddie Leonard's leading lady in that studio's first musical, *Melody Lane* (1929). Leonard, a former Minstrel performer, completely failed to click with moviegoers ("Eddie Leonard brings no vitality to a dead yarn," *Variety* complained), and the songfest, a trifle about a husband-and-wife vaudeville team, bombed at the box office.

Dunn's final silents were made at Fox. *Black Magic* (1929), a lurid melodrama set on a South Seas island, was, according to *Variety*, "a not too intelligent picture [made] for not too intelligent audiences." *The Sin Sister* (1929), was even worse: A strange mixture of slapstick and bosom-heaving melodrama, the film had a group of travelers stranded somewhere in the Arctic and stalked by a crazed Eskimo!

The group that year also included Jean Arthur, Anita Page, Helen Twelvetrees and sisters Sally Blane and Loretta Young.

Opposite: Josephine Dunn, early 1930s (German postcard).

By 1930 the now freelancing Dunn had suffered the fate of most surviving silent screen vamps. that of being reduced to supporting roles in "A" films with an occasional lead in a low-budget independent production. In *Madonna of the Streets* (Columbia, 1930), she and fellow vixen Evelyn Brent are "party girls," one of whom goes straight. Josephine, suffering a case of lower billing, played the unrepentant one. In *Air Police* (Sono-Art/World Wide, 1931), a virile melodrama starring serial ace Kenneth Harlan, she portrayed a nice girl and had higher billing but even less to do. "Josephine Dunn isn't seen much," *Variety* noted, "and then appears to be miscast. That doesn't matter, for it's a man's picture."

She was more visible but equally at sea in her first film of 1932, a terrible programmer from producer John R. Freuler called *Murder at Dawn*. Freuler was more at home in Z-Westerns and it showed: *Murder at Dawn*, which had Dunn and debonair leading man Jack Mulhall trapped in a haunted house stocked with pseudoscientific gizmos, was defeated by appalling writing (by former silent screen actor Barry Barringer), uninspired directing (Richard Thorpe), substandard acting, and ratty sets. It played like a bad serial.

Dunn returned to Paramount for two pictures released in early 1932. She had a rare comedy turn as a drunken gun-moll who accidentally comes into possession of some stolen "jools" in *Two Kinds of Women*, a melodrama about a senator's daughter (Miriam Hopkins) who is involved with the inevitable gangsters. Even the stodgy Mordaunt Hall of the *New York Times* found her performance amusing.

She returned to her old disagreeable self, however, in Ernst Lubitsch's charming *One Hour with You*. A frothy and tuneful version of Lothar Schmidt's play *Nur Ein Traum, Lustspiel im Drei Akten* (1909), *One Hour with You* probed the burning question, Can a happily married man stay happily married when his wife's friend from school puts the make on him? Andre (Maurice Chevalier) adores his wife Colette (Jeanette MacDonald), but is easily persuaded to stray by the coquettish Mitzi (Genevieve Tobin). So as not to be too tempted, Andre switches Mitzi's placecard with that of Mlle. Marcel (Dunn) during the preparations for a dinner party. Colette, of course, is a witness to the duplicity and is livid, knowing the young lady's dubious reputation. When the bleach-blonde vamp arrives, the jealous wife is ready for the attack:

> MacDonald (turning on a dose of insincere charm): "Oh my dear, how are you? I'm so glad to see you. You look stunning!"
> Dunn (flattered): "Do you really think so?"
> MacDonald: "Yes, gorgeous! I'm simply crazy about that dress. And you're looking so well too—you must have gained!"

And with that *bon mot* she leaves the mademoiselle fuming. If looks could kill, Miss MacDonald would not have been alive to meet Nelson Eddy!

Josephine Dunn's final film appearances of 1932 were as William Collier, Jr.'s girlfriend in Monarch's *The Fighting Gentleman*, a programmer about a "grease-monkey" trying to make it in the boxing arena, and as a saloon-hostess in *Between Fighting Men*, a Ken Maynard "B" Western from Sono-Art/World Wide.

In January of 1933 Dunn married Philadelphia attorney Eugene J. Lewis. This, her third marriage, was equally short-lived, lasting only until 1935. That same year she went to the altar a fourth and final time—with Carroll Case, a son of Frank Case, the owner of New York City's famous Algonquin Hotel.

In between marriage and divorce, Dunn spent most of her time playing summer stock. As a favor to her old friend Ernst Lubitsch, she returned to the screen for a few short moments playing herself in *Mr. Broadway* (Malcomar, 1933), a musical *cum* travelogue written by and starring Ed Sullivan. Dunn was briefly seen together with Lubitsch, Lupe Velez, Johnnie Walker (the film's producer), and Lita Grey Chaplin in a party scene filmed on location at the Central Park Casino. She was a bit more visible in something called *Playthings of Desire* (Pinnacle, 1934), an ultra–low budget melodrama in which she played a man-hungry socialite. Filmed independently in Tampa, Florida, in mid–1933, the programmer received scant distribution and quickly disappeared.

Josephine Dunn's final film was a rather sensational exploitation melodrama entitled *Birth of a Baby* (Special Pictures, 1938). Despite being deemed "sociologically and medically of great value" and "heartily endorsed by Eleanor Roosevelt," *Birth of a Baby* featured a rather clinical depiction of childbirth and quickly became a *cause célèbre*. Banned in many places,* the film was actually scheduled to be shown at the White House. Unfortunately, somebody got to the First Lady and four hours later the viewing was canceled with the explanation that the President "could never sit through a film as long as *Birth of a Baby*"! Other locations, it would appear, were more liberal. In several instances the film was distributed for "private showings, in accordance with Section 1082 of the Education Law"!

For Josephine Dunn the brouhaha over *Birth of a Baby* kept her name on theater marquees for decades after she had officially retired. The "scandalous" film, it appears, managed to circumvent various ordinances and quickly went into wide release. Commerce, after all, will usually triumph.

Josephine Dunn's marriage to Mr. Case was, on all accounts, a happy one—at least they were still married in the late seventies. The former actress died at the Motion Picture Country House and Hospital in Woodland Hills, California, on February 3, 1983.

JOSEPHINE DUNN FILMOGRAPHY

1926: *Fascinating Youth; It's the Old Army Game; Sorrows of Satan.*
1927: *Love's Greatest Mistake; Swim, Girl, Swim; Fireman, Save My Child; She's a Sheik; Get Your Man.*
1928: *We Americans; The Singing Fool; Excess Baggage; A Million for Love.*
1929: *All at Sea; China Bound; A Man's Man; Melody Lane; Big Time; Our Modern Maidens; A Most Immoral Lady.*
1930: *Safety in Numbers; Second Honeymoon; Red Hot Rhythm; Madonna of the Streets.*
1931: *Air Police.*

---

*The New York Board of Regents barred the film from being exhibited "in any private or public place of amusement."

1932: *Two Kinds of Women; Murder at Dawn; One Hour with You; Forbidden Company; Big City Blues; The Fighting Gentleman; Between Fighting Men.*
1933: *Mr. Broadway.*
1934: *Playthings of Desire.*
1938: *The Birth of a Baby.*

11—Noel Francis

There was something disturbingly calculating about Noel Francis. Maybe it was her eyes, always sizing up her man as if he was an opponent to conquer. Although a platinum blonde, she was not quite as beautiful or glamorous as Jean Harlow, but she usually played the same type of underworld "molls" and "dames." However, while Harlow was a certified star by 1932, Francis was primarily, as one writer put it, "relegated to the lower depths as someone encountered along the way." And that wasn't the only difference. Whereas Jean received perfect lighting and was swathed in mink at lavish M-G-M, Noel talked tough at the proletarian Warner Bros. Nevertheless, at the height of the gangster cycle in the early 1930s, she was kept extremely busy by both Warners and Paramount, going from one tough girl role to the next. Most of these parts were small, if colorful, but once in a while, as in *Smart Money* (Warner Bros., 1931), in which her character steers Edward G. Robinson away from the straight and narrow, hers was the very soul of a faithless Depression vixen.

Noel Francis Sweeney, her publicity would later reveal, "was born on an estate set in the waving cotton fields of Texas where the city of Temple now rears its commercial spires." The date was said to be November 21, 1910,* and her father to have been a wealthy cotton broker. She would grow up in Dallas and later attend Southern Methodist University there. Enrolled at Columbia University in New York City, she suddenly decided on a theatrical career. So instead of attending classes she concentrated on singing and dancing lessons, determined to make good on Broadway.

According to legend, the 5 foot 7 inch blonde was discovered by showman Florenz Ziegfeld, who "persuaded her to join his *Follies* on the condition that she could leave any time she tired of the theater." Francis, however, to her family's great consternation (her father is said to have disinherited her on the spot), had found her métier and sailed straight from the chorus of the 1926 edition of the *Ziegfeld Follies* into the hit musical *No Foolin'*. Her success was assured when she appeared with the comedy team of

---
*The actual year was probably closer to 1905.

Noel Francis in 1931.

Wheeler and Woolsey in *Rio Rita*, earning her first speaking part and splendid reviews.

It was Francis' singing voice, however, not her thespian talents that brought her to the attention of Hollywood. The year was 1929 and, with the recent arrival of sound, musicals were all the rage. She signed with Fox and was quickly ushered into the *Fox Movietone Follies of 1930*, a hodgepodge songfest about a lumberjack with show business aspirations. The Swedish-accented Philadelphian El Brendel headed the cast and Francis, playing a discount prima donna, received fourth billing. It was instant typecasting from which she would never escape, despite Mordaunt Hall's pronouncing her in the *New York Times* "quite captivating."

Unhappily, *Fox Movietone Follies of 1930* was not the expected success. By the time of its June 1930 release, audiences had finally tired of static musicals with but the slightest hint of a plot and were now demanding stronger stories and more in-depth characterizations. The novelty of sound was no longer the exclusive reason for a visit to a movie theater.

Fox had hired Francis on her merit as a musical performer and with the sudden dearth of song-and-dance films the studio didn't quite know what to do with her. She was assigned a small supporting role in *Up the River* (Fox, 1930), the prison drama that introduced Spencer Tracy to the moviegoing public, but her good-time gal bit was lost in the commotion of Tracy's screen debut. A turn as a saloon belle in a George O'Brien program Western also failed to ignite any excitement and with nothing else to offer, the studio dropped her option.

The abrupt departure from Fox turned out to be a blessing. Francis was quickly picked up by Warner Bros., an organization much better able to exploit her special brand of earthiness than Fox with its penchant for unsophisticated Americana. The home of the celluloid gangster, Warner Bros. was known for producing topical dramas brimming with fast-paced action and snappy dialogue.

In typical Hollywood fashion, Warner Bros. started out by lending their newest contract player to other studios, easily earning back their initial investment. Francis dallied a bit in Lowell Sherman's *Bachelor Apartment* and was a gold digger coming between Mary Astor and Robert Ames in *Smart Woman* (both RKO, 1931).

She was all set to appear as Mary Brian's chorus girl sidekick in *The Runaround* (RKO, 1931) when she was suddenly replaced with Marie Prevost. The reason for her abrupt departure is unclear, but in all probability she was needed at Warners, who had finally cast her in a small but pivotal role opposite Edward G. Robinson in *Smart Money* (1931).

The tale of a small-town barber who is taken in by big city gamblers, *Smart Money* had all the polish of a scratched gramophone record, but it was exactly the kind of fast and furious gangster melodrama for which the studio was deservedly famous. Francis appears as Marie, a faithless blonde who has no qualms helping Robinson lose his bankroll. Economically directed by Alfred E. Green, the drama was peopled with the usual array of Warner toughs (including James Cagney as Robinson's henchman) and was another success in the studio's gangster cycle. The reviews fully echoed public sentiment: "[*Smart Money*] has a lot of entertainment quality to recommend it," *Variety*'s "Bige" commented, crediting some of the film's success to an array of vixenish supporting players that also included Evalyn Knapp and Margaret Livingston. He then singled Francis out as being "a certain comer in talkies."

Francis went directly from rolling a barber in *Smart Money* to duping a bellhop (James Cagney) in *Blonde Crazy* (Warner Bros., 1931), a comedy that had an inordinate resemblance to its predecessor. *Blonde Crazy*, however, was adorned with songs, including "I'm Just a Fool in Love with You" (sung by Joan Blondell in her first starring role). It was yet another box office triumph for the studio.

Noel Francis' final film of 1931 was another loan-out, this time to Paramount. Along with Sylvia Sidney and Wynne Gibson she was among the *Ladies of the Big House*, an early attempt to realistically portray the inside of a women's prison. It was, to say the least, a strange film for the sophisticated Paramount to produce, but the topical Warner approach to filmmaking was so potent at the box office that other studios felt impelled to emulate it.

Francis appeared in 12 films released in 1932, but only four or five are worth mentioning for her participation. Again on loan-out, she was awarded her first lead in *Flames* (Monogram, 1932), a silly fire-fighting melodrama filmed on a shoestring. The plot (according to *The American Film Institute Catalog, Feature Films 1931–1940*) is easily summed up:

> Gertie [Marjorie Beebe] and Pat [Francis] fall in love with firemen Charlie [Johnny Mack Brown] and Fishy [George Cooper]. When Pat works late one night, her boss [Richard Tucker] propositions her. That same night a fire develops in the office building, and Charlie rescues Pat, saving her life.

According to contemporary reviews (the film, it seems, no longer exists), *Flames* could have been a great deal better had it not been so cheaply made. "Had some thought been devoted to the story, instead of resorting to the easiest way and following stereotyped lines," *Variety*'s "Wally" noted, "*Flames* could be recommended as good program material for the [first run houses]. "The same reviewer, however, had a minor gripe regarding Francis' appearance in her first starring role: "[The] director," he observed, "used poor judgment in exposing her to a semi-closeup during crying scenes because Miss Francis does not cry prettily."

Meanwhile, Francis was having quite a difficult time of it back at Warners. The battle for roles there was fierce since the studio seemed to have more tough-talking contract blondes than anyplace else in Hollywood. The competition, unfortunately, blew her out of the water. There was Joan Blondell, for example, already elevated to leading roles. Blondell, with her saucer eyes and heart-shaped face, suggested a certain vulnerability to offset the toughness, a very winning combination. Glenda Farrell, the quintessential wisecracking blonde and one of the best comediennes around, had also begun to separate from the pack. Francis was in constant competition with these ladies, but also had to contend with lesser names such as Evalyn Knapp, Claire Dodd, Renee Whitney, Mae Madison and Barbara Leonard. Increasingly, she came out the loser and her appearances in such films as *So Big* and *The Mouthpiece* (both 1932) were little more than bits.

As always, she was much better served on loan to other studios. Universal, for example, borrowed her for the female lead in, of all things, *My Pal the King* (1932), a Tom Mix "Western" set in a Ruritanian kingdom! This time the irrepressible Mix is a happy-go-lucky rodeo rider who brings his show to Alvonia, an old-fashioned operetta monarchy, where he becomes the defender of a ten-year-old king (Mickey Rooney) about to be overthrown by an evil count (veteran actor James Kirkwood). Luckily, Tom and the diminutive King Charles manage to get out of their dire predicament with the help of the beautiful Princess Elena (Francis), the king's aunt. An unusual film, to say the least, but it must have been gratifying for Francis to play a nice girl for a change.

Francis returned to the world of gangsters and murder in *Guilty as Hell* (Paramount, 1932). As Julia Reed, a gun moll, she actually brings to justice a homicidal psychiatrist who has killed her gangster husband (Ralph Ince). The drama was popular enough for Paramount to remake it in 1937 as *Night Club Scandal*, with veteran vamp Evelyn Brent as Julia.

Francis stayed at Paramount for *Under Cover Man* (1932), a taut melodrama about the son (George Raft) of a murder victim who attempts to ferret out the guilty party. Noel, as Connie, a night club hostess, gets the opportunity to be knocked about by both the hero (Raft) and his main suspect (Lew Cody). According to Mordaunt Hall of the *New York Times*, she did "valiant work" in her usual hard-boiled way.

Francis' most important film of 1932 was by far *I Am a Fugitive from a Chain Gang*, the Warners' ground-breaking exposé of conditions in a Southern penitentiary. Paul Muni was nominated for an Academy Award for his harrowing portrayal of a World War I veteran who is wrongly convicted of a fatal robbery attempt and sent "up the river." Noel is but one of several deadly females Muni encounters after he breaks out of prison and assumes a new identity. Hers is far from the most important distaff role in the film (that went to Helen Vinson), but her association with a much admired Academy Award nominee (it was also named the best film of 1932 by the *National Board of Review*) should have been a boon to her career.

By 1933, unfortunately, Warner Bros. had completely lost interest in Francis'

Noel Francis (center) in *Stone of Silver Creek* (Universal, 1935) (photograph courtesy of Janus Barfoed).

potential—to the point where she was demoted to bit parts in programmers released by First National, the studio's "B" movie outlet. Instead of appearing in films like *Chain Gang*, her name was found way down the cast list in such potboilers as *Frisco Jenny* (First National, 1932) and *Bureau of Missing Persons* (First National, 1933). Noel's final film under the old Warner Bros. contract was released late in the year and *Son of a Sailor*, a silly Joe E. Brown comedy, did nothing to persuade the studio to keep her around.

Freelancing, Francis was given the second female lead in *Her Resale Value*, a little item about small-town girls lured to the Big City with promises of modeling jobs. Produced independently by Fanchon Royer and released by an outfit calling itself Golden Arrow Productions, this no-budget film played the bottom half of double bills during the summer of 1933, after which it ignominiously slithered away.

Francis was top-billed in two programmers released by Tower Productions,

Reform Girl and *The Important Witness* (both 1933). The former, a lurid crime drama, saw her as a prison parolee who accepts a $10,000 offer from a crooked politician (Ben Hendricks, Jr.) to frame his opponent, an upstanding civic leader (Hale Hamilton). The unscrupulous vixen then gains entrance to this stalwart politician's home by impersonating his long-lost daughter who had been kidnapped in childhood. By the strange twist of fate so typical of cheap Hollywood movies, she actually *is* his daughter and a happy ending is ensured when she accepts the hand of her father's brash campaign manager (Richard "Skeets" Gallagher). Incredibly, this stale melodrama was re-released in 1952 under the even more exploitative title *Vice Raid*.

In *The Important Witness*, Francis and fellow 1930s vamp Dorothy Burgess play roommates who get in too deep with gangsters. The plot was more convoluted than her prior Tower effort, but the result was about the same: a cheap programmer made solely for the double-bill market. However, *Variety*'s "Chic" had some concerns of his own: "[The] plot has its soft spots, which need explanation," he remarked in his review, "and there is some questionable bathroom comedy." Other than that, he suggested, the film was "well knit and smoothly told."

Francis returned to mainstream filmmaking with small supporting roles in *Only Yesterday* (Universal, 1933), a remarkably realistic portrait of the life of an unwed mother (Margaret Sullavan in a much heralded screen debut); *Blood Money* (20th Century, 1933), a crime drama so lurid it was banned in many places,* and *Good Dame* (Paramount, 1934), a melodrama set in a carnival (she played a "kooch" dancer.)

Her final film for 1933 was *What's Your Racket*, another cheaply produced gangster thriller, this time from Mayfair Pictures Corp. Typecast as always, she played a tough nightclub hostess whose father was once framed by a notorious gang. To get the goods on the villains, she disguises herself as a young boy, thereby getting her hands on some information that prove her father's innocence. This little item seems to have disappeared from sight even quicker than the average low-budget "indie" production.

The year 1934 continued a sad trend for Noel Francis: bit parts at major studios and leads or second leads on Poverty Row. *Strictly Dynamite* and *Fifteen Wives* are cases in point. The former was a Jimmy Durante comedy from RKO and her bit part ended up on the cutting room floor. *Wives*, on the other hand, was a cheesy murder mystery from a fly-by-night company called Invincible and had her second billed as a radio star suspected of murdering a bigamist.

More bit parts followed: She was a surgeon's wife in *The White Parade* (Fox, 1934), had one line in the first version of *Imitation of Life* (Universal, 1934); and was a "B" girl named Chon-Chon in a bizarre thriller from Universal, *The Man Who Reclaimed His Head* (1934).

Except for a little-heralded return to Warner Bros. in a standard tough girl role in *The White Cockatoo* (1935), and the indie *Mutiny Ahead* (Majestic, 1935), Noel Francis ended her career in, of all things, Westerns. She was the daughter of a mine owner in *Stone of Silver Creek* (Universal, 1935); a rancher's daughter in *Left-Handed Gun* (Universal, 1936; released 1937), and, reverting to type, a saloon hostess in *Sudden*

---

*On the other hand, a judge in Maryland reversed a prior ban by pronouncing the film "objectionable on the grounds of extreme stupidity and dullness rather than [for moral reasons]."

Bill Dorn (Universal, 1937), her final film. All three Westerns starred her friend Buck Jones.

With *Sudden Bill Dorn*, Francis seems to have turned her back on the entertainment world. Disappearing completely into private life, the former screen moll died in her Los Angeles home at the age of 48 on October 30, 1959.

Noel Francis' once promising career stumbled when Production Code restrictions more or less put an end to the freewheeling crime cycle. By 1934 Hollywood could no longer "glorify" the gangster but instead had to show the underbelly of American society from the viewpoint of the authorities. And out with "Public Enemy Number One" went his moll.

NOEL FRANCIS FILMOGRAPHY

1930: *Fox Movietone Follies of 1930; Rough Romance; Up the River.*
1931: *Resurrection; Bachelor Apartment; Smart Money; Smart Woman; Blonde Crazy; Ladies of the Big House.*
1932: *The Expert; So Big; The Mouthpiece; Man About Town; Flames; Night Court; My Pal the King; Madison Sq. Garden; I Am a Fugitive from a Chain Gang; Manhattan Tower; Under-Cover Man; Frisco Jenny.*
1933: *Her Resale Value; Hold Me Tight; The Important Witness; Reform Girl; Bureau of Missing Persons; Only Yesterday; Blood Money; What's Your Racket; Son of a Sailor.*
1934: *Good Dame; The Line Up; The Loudspeaker; Fifteen Wives; The White Parade; Imitation of Life; The Man Who Reclaimed His Head.*
1935: *The White Cockatoo; Mutiny Ahead; Stone of Silver Creek.*
1937: *Left-Handed Gun; Sudden Bill Dorn.*

12 — Wynne Gibson

Blond Wynne Gibson played either sappy or tough. Fortunately, she was mostly the latter, and in the 1930s she had few equals in portraying hard-boiled prostitutes—as in *If I Had a Million* (Paramount, 1932), the multi-story comedy in which a millionaire decides on his deathbed to donate a million dollars to a group of people chosen at random from the telephone book. Gibson's Violet Smith, a down-and-out streetwalker, uses her "inheritance" to check into a luxury hotel where she can sleep in an opulent bed "without having to keep on her stockings!"

Often, she was the other woman, but not the kind that polite society could easily forgive. Her "ladies" had too many rough edges and their taste in attire lacked the sophistication of more upscale vixens such as, say, Claire Dodd or Helen Vinson. Usually men treated her crudely and sometimes even cruelly; as Dorothy Manners of *Motion Picture* wrote in 1931:

> In the year and a half she has been in talkies, Wynne Gibson has been cast out of more actors' lives than any other girl on the screen. She has been forcefully ejected from the scenario apartments of such players as William Boyd, Gary Cooper, Paul Lukas and William Powell. In two pictures, *The Gang Buster* and *City Streets* [both Paramount, 1931], she speaks the same line—as William Boyd and Paul Lukas, respectively, toss her into the hall and close the door in her face (courtesy of the Paramount scenario department). Looking very menacing and "other woman-ish," Wynne puts her hands on her hips, curls her soubrette mouth, draws every inch of her five feet nothing into the air and hisses, "So? You think you will get rid of me! You'll see!"

Those are the kind of roles and dialogue for which this audacious actress should be remembered—and not the sappy *"Madame X"* clones of *The Strange Case of Clara Deane* (Paramount, 1932) or *I Give My Love* (Universal, 1934). Wynne Gibson as a suffering mother was a little hard to take.

She was born Winifred Gibson on July 3, 1899, in New York City. After her education at the Wadleigh School for Girls, she became interested in the theater through some school friends who had appeared in several musical shows.

Well, at least that was the official Paramount publicity version of Wynne Gibson's entrance into the world of show business. She herself always claimed that it was photographer Julian Alfred who suggested that she find stage work "because her size [5 feet 2 inches], personality and buoyant good looks presaged success in theatrical work." It was Alfred, she said, who recommended the teenager for a job in a chorus line. Her parents were shocked when she told them of her chorus girl turn in *Tangerine*, but Gibson was determined. "If you won't interfere by telling them my age and getting me fired, I promise to fire myself after six months if I haven't risen above the chorus," she told them.

Promptly reneging on her pledge, Gibson stayed with the show until she was hired as one of the "Six Little Wives" (at $75 a week), touring vaudeville houses up and down the East Coast. One source claims that her indignant father caught up with her in Washington D.C., and swiftly brought his errant daughter home. Gibson herself, however, later told Dorothy Manners that she quit the tour to do a specialty dance in a production of *June Love*. Ray Raymond saw her in that and made her his partner on a six month vaudeville tour. Following that, she created a vaudeville act together with fellow hoofer Billie Vernon, the future Mrs. James Cagney.

On June 2, 1921 Wynne Gibson opened on Broadway in the chorus of Lew Field's *Snapshots of 1921*, which is often quoted as her official stage debut. She remained with Fields for a year, and then toured the country in *The Gingham Girl* (1922-1923). At long last graduating to star billing, she went on tour with a company of *Little Jessie James*, when, as luck would have it, she was called back to New York to replace Nan Halperin in the original Broadway production of the show.

When *Little Jessie James* folded in late 1924, Gibson went straight into a National Theater production of *When You Smile* (playing a sob sister), and starred opposite Hal Skelly in the Chicago production of *The City Chap* (1925). There were several shows that folded out of town,* after which she appeared at Los Angeles' El Capitan Theatre with Perry Askam and her old friend Ray Raymond in *Castles in the Air*.

According to most sources, she next spent a year touring in Europe (with what is never revealed), but by 1927 she had returned to New York, performing in the musical *Oh, Johnny*. That was followed by a tour of *The Clam Diggers* with the veteran Fritz Leiber.

In 1929 Gibson starred opposite Richard Bennett at Broadway's Longacre Theatre as Pauline Clare in *Jarnegan*. During the play's Philadelphia tryout she had traveled to New York City and back every day for a week, making her screen debut as "boop-boop-a-doop" singer Helen Kane's sister in *Nothing but the Truth* (Paramount, 1929). Produced at Paramount's Astoria studios, the drama starred Richard Dix (in his "talkie" debut), one of the few screen stars who preferred the bustling ambiance of New York to the eternal sunshine of Hollywood.

Gibson, however, did not mind the sun, and realizing that movies could be as

---

*"I got to become a regular friend of the sheriff's," she later said. "Every time he served a closing notice on our show, he would exclaim, 'What? You back again?'"

gratifying as the stage (and certainly much more lucrative), she relocated to Hollywood and got herself an agent. "I was glad to get away from the East," she told fan magazine writer Dorothy Manners in 1931.

> When I boarded the train to come to Hollywood, I felt like an adventurer starting a new life. And, believe me, it really was an adventure. There was no contract in my purse, or even a verbal agreement with my manager that I would find work on the Coast. But I had cut all the old ties and I was in the frame of mind to take a chance on anything.

According to Manners, Gibson didn't want to take a chance playing a villainess in Cecil B. DeMille's *Madame Satan* (M-G-M, 1930). "My sense of humor had not then come to my rescue," the actress later explained.* Instead, she signed with M-G-M, but that studio *did* have a sense of humor and promptly cast her as the *femme fatale* opposite Lawrence Gray in *Children of Pleasure* (1930). And, on loan to RKO, she was a gangster's moll in *The Fall Guy* (1930), a comedy with Jack Mulhall. After that, however, M-G-M dropped her option.

There were no other offers and Gibson returned to the stage, starring in the Los Angeles production of *Molly Magdalene* (1930). Luckily, after a three month run she was rediscovered by Paramount. "I feel I've been very lucky—walking into a contract with Paramount so soon," she later told Dorothy Manners.

> It happened by my making a test for them—a very ga-ga and innocent little girlish test. I out–Brianed Mary Brian† on that strip of film. The first director to see it was Eddie Sutherland.
> "That's the girl—that's the girl I want for the other woman in *The Gang Buster!*"
> A studio casting official was standing beside him. He protested: "But that girl's an ingenue!"
> "So are other women," said Mr. Sutherland.

The Gang Buster (Paramount, 1931), was indeed Gibson's first film for her new studio, but Eddie Sutherland had been replaced by Harry Beaumont by then. A spoof of gangster films, the comedy starred the likable Jack Oakie as a country bumpkin who inadvertently traps a gang of crooks headed by, of all people, William Boyd (years before the white-haired actor donned his black garb to become Hopalong Cassidy). Gibson played Boyd's former girlfriend who turns against him after being brutally shot in the shoulder (and, as mentioned above, having had a door slammed in her face). As a comedy *The Gang Buster* wasn't much, and neither was the studio's next Oakie showcase, *June Moon* (1931), where Gibson played the discontented wife of a composer (Ernest Wood).

She was much better in *Man of the World* (Paramount, 1931), a comedy-drama set in Paris, in which she helps William Powell run a scandal sheet and does a bit of blackmailing on the side; or in *City Streets* (Paramount, 1931), a classic crime drama

---

Lillian Roth eventually played the other woman in Madame Satan.

†*Having started her career as Wendy in* Peter Pan *(1924), Mary Brian had become Paramount's foremost ingenue. The two actresses later became friends and in 1932 Gibson appeared in a home movie "produced" by Russell Gleason as a birthday present to Miss Brian.*

Wynne Gibson, early 1930s.

about a carnival sharpshooter (Gary Cooper) who falls for the daughter (Sylvia Sidney) of a notorious racketeer.

Benefiting from an original story by Dashiell Hammett (his first written directly for the screen), the production had originally been conceived as a vehicle for Clara Bow. Regrettably, the "It" girl was in the middle of the notorious court battle with Daisy DeVoe, her larcenous former secretary, and was forced to withdraw from the project. With Bow sidelined (and suffering a near fatal career slump as a result), director Rouben Mamoulian started over with a new cast, retaining only Cooper. Gibson replaced Juliette Compton as Aggie, the tough gun moll, whose scenes with brutal gang lord Paul Lukas are among the film's highlights.

Working under difficult circumstances, Gibson managed to give an impressive, hard-boiled performance, but, unfortunately, it got lost amidst the excitement over Sylvia Sidney's sensational screen debut.

Bow had recovered enough from her very public skirmish with DeVoe to star in *Kick In* (Paramount, 1931), yet another crime drama but vastly inferior to *City Streets*. The former "It" girl was visibly intimidated by the presence of microphones, and as a result her lead role had to be downgraded in favor of the supporting cast. (In fact, the original director, Lothar Mendes, was replaced by Richard Wallace when the rushes showed that he had shifted the focus completely from Bow to leading man Regis Toomey.)

Staying well outside the fray, Gibson delivered another strong portrayal of an abused slum girl. This time the abuser was James Murray, playing her ex-con boyfriend. A key scene has a wounded Murray hiding from the police in her apartment and bleeding all over the place. When the law suddenly busts in, she quickly cuts her finger to the bone in order to explain the blood stains on the couch. The result was arguably the tough drama's emotional centerpiece.

The women Gibson was given to play this early in her screen career would do almost anything to keep their men, no matter how compassionless and cruel these mashers proved to be. What else could they do? The country was suffering under the Depression and human contact, no matter how uncaring, was human contact. That kind of realistic portrayals of Depression-era women, who had to fend for themselves in a gloomy world, was fast becoming Gibson's bread-and-butter, and she played them as well as the famed Warner Bros. heroines. "I shouldn't complain about movie realism," she told a reporter in 1932. "I've handed out some mean slaps myself in a couple of pictures."

One of the pictures she was referring to was obviously *Ladies of the Big House* (Paramount, 1931), the quintessential women-behind-bars melodrama. Again she appeared opposite Sylvia Sidney, the darling of the working class. As Sidney's vicious fellow prison inmate, she has proof of her cell-mate's innocence which she cunningly uses to her own benefit—and with dire results for Miss Sidney. In retrospect, *Ladies of the Big House* is one of the best acted films of the early 1930s—with no small measure of its success due to the gritty performances of the Misses Sidney and Gibson.

So far, Wynne Gibson had played underworld figures and less than glamorous *femmes fatales*, but in early 1932 Paramount, for reasons known only to the higher echelon, suddenly decided to make her over into another Ruth Chatterton.

The vehicle chosen for this transformation was *The Strange Case of Clara Deane*. Gibson played Clara, a clothes designer whose choice in men proved, to put it mildly, unfortunate. Mordaunt Hall, reviewing the film for the *New York Times*, appropriately summed up the contrived plot:

> *The Strange Case of Clara Deane* is scarcely an exciting picture. It boasts of a plethora of old-fashioned hokum and strenuous efforts are made by both Max Marcin, the adapter, and Louis Gasnier, the director, to draw tears, but how successful they will be is problematic. Here, another mother, like *Madelon Claudet*,* is pursued by misfortune. She marries a thief, goes to prison for a crime for which [she] is guiltless, loses sight of her daughter and finally shoots and kills her husband.

It was, of course, *Madame X*, *Stella Dallas*, and *Back Street* all over again, but Gasnier, a veteran dating back to the early silent era, directed with his usual heavy hand and the material was sub-par. Reviewer Hall did, however, allow for some good performances and lauded Gibson (whom he thought did "excellent work") and Pat O'Brien (as the brutal husband) for their efforts.

Gibson was on much surer footing as the fun loving Phyllis Adrian who nabs a playboy (Phillips Holmes) in an alcoholic daze in *Two Kinds of Women* (Paramount, 1932). Miriam Hopkins, as a naive senator's daughter loose in the big city, is, of

---

*The long-suffering heroine that had earned Helen Hayes the 1931 Academy Award.

course, more the marrying kind and Gibson again loses her man, albeit without a whimper for a change.

Since she was rapidly becoming known for her keen portrayals of the other woman, the actress took time out from her busy schedule to expound on the species for the inquiring Dorothy Manners of *Motion Picture*:

> It's hard to generalize about the other woman type. I don't feel that the women I portray on the screen are the really dangerous women in a man's life. Scenarists and dramatists make Other Women too obvious—too threatening. I do not believe that the woman who is the other woman in real life pursues such violent tactics as that famous line of mine: "So you think you'll get rid of me? I'll show you." The screen errs in making the other woman deliberate. The funny part of it is that the other woman could happen to any of us. We do not plan it. I think there are very few women indeed, who have entered the life of another couple and deliberately planned from the beginning to wreck their home.

Offscreen, Gibson didn't have to worry about the other woman entering her own life. Despite rumors in August of 1932 of an impending betrothal, she remained a lifelong bachelorette.

Warner Bros. considered borrowing Gibson for the female lead in *I Am a Fugitive from a Chain Gang* (1932), but the plum role eventually went to Helen Vinson. Instead, she played the whore who comes into a windfall in the multiepisode comedy *If I Had a Million* (Paramount, 1932). Unfortunately, few people actually saw that performance, since the Hays office prudishly made Paramount delete the segment in most release prints.

Gibson's performance as George Raft's low-class girlfriend, whom he dumps in favor of the classier Constance Cummings in *Night After Night* (Paramount, 1932), escaped the censor's scissors intact—but this was Mae West's screen debut and the voluptuous, wisecracking West took no prisoners. During the filming, however, Gibson took a much publicized stroll around the Paramount lot and ended up as an extra in the orgy scene of Cecil B. DeMille's *Sign of the Cross* (Paramount, 1933).*

In her final film of the year, *The Devil Is Driving* (Paramount, 1932), Gibson appeared second-billed as the girlfriend of a dealer in stolen cars (Alan Dinehart). This time, however, she is at long last awarded a happy ending—after first having dumped the "fence," cracked the crime ring and fallen for a lowly mechanic (Edmund Lowe). Mordaunt Hall, reviewing the programmer for the *New York Times*, did not exactly go overboard with praise when he found her "acceptable in her role."

Gibson played one of her more disagreeable women in *Crime of the Century* (Paramount, 1933), a whodunit in which she shrewishly drives her doctor husband (Jean Hersholt) into a life of crime. She was more benign as stage star Margot Brienne in *Her Bodyguard* (Paramount, 1933), pursued by men everywhere but realizing in time that marriage and homemaking are much more important than a career. It was a comedy and as such was well received by the ubiquitous Mordaunt Hall of the *New York Times*, who, in a charitable mood this time, thought Gibson "vivacious and attractive" and found the film to be "capital warm-weather entertainment."

Aggie Appleby, Maker of Men (1933), for which she had been borrowed by RKO as

---
*The provocative scene was deleted for the film's re-release. Happily, it was recently restored by UCLA.

a replacement for an ailing Helen Mack, was also a comedy, but not nearly as successful. Down on her luck, Aggie falls in with the equally destitute Adoniram Schlump (Charles Farrell) and then goes about transforming him into a salable commodity in the job market. Again she loses her man, this time to ingenue Betty Furness. A typical Depression-era fairy tale, *Aggie Appleby* was, according to Mordaunt Hall, "evidently written with an eye on the box office."

Leaving Paramount in late 1933, Gibson tried freelancing, but met with less than stellar results. RKO had signed her for two film, *Success at Any Price* and *Crime Doctor* (both 1934), but then, for unknown reasons, canceled her contract. The studio lived to regret that decision: In *Crime Doctor* Gibson's replacement was Mary Astor, but Astor had to bow out due to illness; Columbia then brought in silent screen star Corinne Griffith, but the difficult former diva did not get along with her co-star Otto Kruger and walked out on the project. Finally, the desperate studio borrowed Karen Morley from M-G-M and the film was released to only moderate success. While Morley was a capable actress, she just didn't possess the mercenary quality that the role demanded and which Wynne Gibson had to spare.

Gibson's final film of any importance was *I Give My Love* (Universal, 1934). Yet another story of motherly devotion and self sacrifice, the melodrama was adapted from an original story by Vicki Baum but turned out to be a close cousin of *Clara Deane*. Once again, Gibson comes down with a case of unwanted pregnancy, is left by her no-good husband (John Darrow), and takes up with an understanding soulmate, this time her art teacher (Paul Lukas). Suddenly the husband comes back into her life, and Gibson has to shoot him in self-defense. When she is finally released from prison, she finds herself alone and destitute. Of course her now grown son accidentally discovers her walking the streets (but does not know that she is his mother), and following several scenes of brave self-sacrifice, she is at last reunited with a forgiving family.

Andre Sennwald of the *New York Times* had, like everyone else, seen it all before—many times. "Motherhood, that uncomplaining punching bag of cinema tragedians, remained about where it stood originally after an earnest tussle with *I Give My Love*," he reported from the front.

> Tears, both crocodile and glycerin, filled the screen in sodden close-ups, and during the course of the story almost every member of the cast had a good cry. Wynne Gibson was the mother and she played it to an advanced age without cracking a smile.

By the end of 1934, movie offers had dried up and, like many other Hollywood has-beens, Wynne Gibson tried her luck in England. She played a movie queen who falls for a Navy officer (Gordon Harker) in *Admirals All* (RKO, 1935); and was a female reporter caught among spies in World War I Turkey in *The Crouching Beast* (RKO, 1936).

Neither of these programmers did anything for her, and she hurried back to Hollywood. Unfortunately, there would be no *If I Had a Million* in her future (not even an *I Give My Love!*), but she was kept busy in low-budget crime dramas such as *Racketeers in Exile* (Columbia, 1937) (in which she appeared as a gangster's moll bearing the delightful name Babe DeVoe); *Trapped by G-Men* (Columbia, 1937); and *Gangs of*

Wynne Gibson, late 1930s.

New York (Republic, 1938). There was a brief return to sentimental soap opera with Gene Stratton-Porter's *Michael O'Halloran* (Republic, 1937), but the story of a selfish woman who adopts two orphans proved too low-budget to have much of an impact.

Gibson continued to appear in routine programmers throughout the early 1940s, but her time had obviously come and gone. She struggled through, valiantly, in such poor fare as *Street of Missing Women* (Columbia, 1940), with Ann Dvorak; *Forgotten Girls* (Republic, 1940), in which she was a cruel mother who railroads her daughter into taking a murder rap; *Double Cross* (PRC, 1941); *A Man's World* (Columbia, 1942); and, her final film, *The Falcon Strikes Back* (RKO, 1943).

In 1941 she had taken time out to tour with the play *Good Night Ladies*. By the mid 1940s, with her screen career behind her, Gibson turned to radio and enjoyed a thriving career in soap-operas, appearing in *When a Girl Marries*, *Modern Romances*, and *Whispering Streets*. In the 1950s, she tackled television (*Studio One*, *Producer's Showcase*), served as a board member of A.F.T.R.A., and, together with her housemate, the former actress Beverly Roberts, she formed a theatrical producing company. The veteran actress died of a stroke at Laguna Niguel, California, on May 15, 1987.

WYNNE GIBSON FILMOGRAPHY

1929: *Nothing But the Truth.*
1930: *Children of Pleasure; The Fall Guy.*

1931: *The House That Shadows Built* (documentary); *The Gang Buster; June Moon; Man of the World; Kick In; City Streets; The Road to Reno; Touchdown! Ladies of the Big House.*
1932: *Two Kinds of Women; The Strange Case of Clara Deane; Lady and Gent; Night After Night; If I Had a Million; The Devil Is Driving.*
1933: *The Crime of the Century; The Sign of the Cross: Emergency Call; Her Bodyguard; Aggie Appleby, Maker of Men.*
1934: *Sleepers East; The Crosby Case; I Give My Love; The Captain Hates the Sea; Gambling.*
1935: *Admirals All* (GB*).
1936: *The Crouching Beast* (GB); *Come Closer, Folks.*
1937: *Racketeers in Exile; Michael O'Halloran; Trapped by G-Men.*
1938: *Gangs of New York; Flirting with Fate.*
1939: *Miracle on Main Street; Cafe Hostess; My Son Is Guilty.*
1940: *Forgotten Girls.*
1941: *Double Cross.*
1942: *Man's World.*
1943: *Mystery Broadcast; The Falcon Strikes Back.*

*GB=Great Britain.

13 — Bernadene Hayes

In *That's My Story*, a minor Universal potboiler of 1937, news-hound William Lundigan gets himself thrown in jail in order to get an exclusive interview with a notorious gang moll. Playing this tough broad was blonde Bernadene Hayes, who by that time was already an old pro in the game. Today, Hayes is mostly remembered by fans of the Hopalong Cassidy "B" Western series (she did three of them), but it was as a generally weatherworn tart that she would make her main contribution to the 1930s. Unfortunately, the films in which she was given anything of importance to do or say were for the most part minor and are all but forgotten. That is a pity, however, since Bernadene did her kind of roles better and with more gusto than most of her competitors.

Having appeared in more than 35 films between 1934 and 1942, Hayes' career slowed down considerably in the mid–forties. Happily, she came back to give it her all one more time as Longshot Lillie, the rather seedy lady fence in *Dick Tracy's Dilemma* (RKO, 1947). By 1950, however, she was playing frumpy hausfraus in films with titles like *Bunco Squad* (RKO, 1950). And if there ever was a picture that belonged to the scrap heap, it was *Bunco Squad*!

Bernadene Hayes was born on May 4, 1912, in St. Louis, Missouri, and was, according to her later publicity, a direct descendant of President Rutherford B. Hayes. The future screen actress started her career at the age of nine when she played a small part in a local production of *Ten Nights in a Barroom*. Bernadene later admitted that her parents had been very much against her entrance into show business. If so, they must have been doubly shocked when her younger sister Lorraine soon followed in her footsteps.*

When not performing Victorian melodrama on stage, Bernadene attended public school in St. Louis and later claimed to have entered Washington University where she remained for one year. She happily quit school when offered a job as a singer on radio station KMOX, St. Louis.

---

[1] *As Lorraine Randall she would enjoy a minor screen career in the late 1930s (see below).*

By all accounts, Hayes should have been *seen* as well as heard: in 1929 she was voted the "Most Beautiful Radio Artist" by advertisers in Chicago. Two years later she earned the title of "Miss Radio" and quickly abandoned broadcasting for Broadway, appearing with some success in *Midwest* and *Mother Sings*. By 1934 she was on the West Coast, singing with a band at the Hollywood Roosevelt Hotel. Appearing nightly in the midst of "Tinsel Town," the beautiful blonde band singer was quickly tapped for pictures and she paid her dues with bit parts in *The Human Side* (Universal, 1934), *Folies Bergere de Paris* (20th Century–Fox, 1935), and *Broadway Melody of 1936* (M-G-M, 1935).

A case of early typecasting, Hayes played her first moll in *She Gets Her Man* (Universal, 1935), a comedy starring the capricious ZaSu Pitts, but she was merely glimpsed for a few seconds. She was a bit more visible in *The Judgment Book* (Beaumont, 1935), an independently produced "B" Western in which a newspaperman (Conway Tearle) cleans up a lawless frontier town. Hayes plays Madge, the daughter of the local printer and Tearle's love interest. Needless to say, she had little to do other than stay out of the fray and marvel at Tearle's exploits.

Career-wise, Hayes came into her own in 1936, perfecting her tough-girl image in films such as *Absolute Quiet* and *The Accusing Finger*. In the former, a not uninteresting M-G-M "B," she is Judy, an escaped convict who with her partner Jack (Wallace Ford) takes over a Western ranch, viciously keeping the owner (Lionel Atwill) hostage. To placate his brutal captors, the wealthy and influential (but quite cowardly) ranch owner promises to ask the governor for a pardon and the convicts begin planning a return to their former life as vaudeville artists(!). It is all a ruse, of course, and the betrayed escapees perish in a rain of bullets.

Despite the rather violent goings-on in *Absolute Quiet*, director George B. Seitz imbued his film with a great deal of humor, letting both Hayes and Wallace Ford play their roles with their tongues firmly planted in their cheeks. B. R. Crisler of the *New York Times*, for one, admired their efforts,

> Bernadene Hayes, as the tough "moll" who dominates the weak gunman and is herself subtly dominated by [Atwill], shows promise of becoming a good secondary investment for some producer of underworld opera. We strongly recommend her.

Hayes was killed off fairly quickly in Paramount's *The Accusing Finger*, but prior to her untimely demise she convincingly portrayed the harridan wife of a district attorney (Paul Kelly). Refusing to grant her hapless husband a divorce so he can pursue a romance with his pert secretary, she is conveniently shot to death by a desperate jewel thief.

In late 1936, Hayes signed a three picture deal with a new production company, Grand National Films, Inc. The fledgling company had been organized by former Pathé executives and had recently secured the services of James Cagney, who had left Warner Bros. over a contract dispute. Boldly starting out with more star power than its Poverty Row conception would have suggested, Grand National brought Cagney back to the screen after a year's absence in *Great Guy* (released January 1937).

A fast-paced programmer in the time-honored tradition of Cagney's earlier

Mae Clarke, James Cagney, Bernadene Hayes and Joe Sawyer in *Great Guy* (Grand National, 1937).

G-Men (First National, 1935), *Great Guy* was a crime drama dealing with, of all things, the Bureau of Weights and Measures. The furious plot involves around a gang of racketeers who are cheating grocery shoppers by weighing down chickens with lead slugs and such. The gangsters unsuccessfully try to bribe the head of the agency, an ex-prizefighter (Cagney). Hayes appears as Hazel, the gun moll girlfriend of a corrupt politician (Robert Gleckler).

Unfortunately *Great Guy* was produced by Grand National and not Warner Bros. and the drama lacked the vim and vigor, not to mention superior writing, so typical of the latter studio. Worse yet: Although Mae Clarke (of *Public Enemy* fame) was back as Cagney's leading lady and a good portion of the action took place among fruits and vegetables, there was nary a grapefruit in sight! Happily, the bad guys, including Hayes, Gleckler, Henry Kolker, and Joe Sawyer, were very much up to par and, along with the indefatigable Cagney, assured the picture decent returns at the box office. Whatever its shortcomings, *Great Guy* remains the short-lived Grand National's best remembered production.

Bernadene Hayes in 1937 (photograph courtesy of the Danish Film Museum).

Neither of Hayes' remaining films for the studio, *Girl Loves Boy* and *Sweetheart of the Navy* (both starring the tepid team of Eric Linden and Cecilia Parker) was quite as memorable. Living up to its dreary title, *Girl Loves Boy* (1937) was a tepid rural romance about a boy (Linden) who, despite numerous warnings, marries a sexy golddigger (Hayes) instead of the nice girl-next-door (Parker) whom he really loves. The picture ends well for the young innocents, however, when it is learned that the golddigger is already married—to a notorious con artist (Jameson Thomas).

Hayes was more benign in *Sweetheart of the Navy* (1937), in which she played Miss Parker's wisecracking friend, but the film was tepid at best. Since Grand National's general output was more in the caliber of *Girl Loves Boy* than *Great Guy*, the studio was soon in financial trouble and it folded in March of 1940, less than four years after its promising arrival.

North of the Rio Grande (1937) returned Bernadene Hayes to the realm of "B" Westerns. It was the eleventh entry in the popular *Hopalong Cassidy* series of above average oaters produced independently by Harry Sherman for Paramount release. This time, Hopalong (William Boyd) trails the villains responsible for his brother's death. High on his list of possible suspects are Stoneham (Stephen Morris), a train robber operating under the alias "The Lone Wolf," and Faro Annie, a saloon belle played by Hayes with a Mae Westian swagger. One of the very best in the series, *North of the Rio Grande* featured several popular "Bar 20" regulars, including Windy (George Hayes), Cassidy's grizzled sidekick, and Lucky Jenkins (Russell Hayden), the series' romantic juvenile. This entry had the added benefit of Lee [J.] Cobb (in his screen debut) as a railroad president and Lorraine Randall (Bernadene's sister) as Hopalong's pert sister-in-law. It was Harry Sherman who renamed Miss Randall, feeling that the cast was already overrun by Hayeses!

Bernadene reappeared in the twelfth *Hopalong Cassidy* entry, *Rustler's Valley* (Paramount, 1937), but only via leftover footage from *North of the Rio Grande*. She did return to the series' Kernville location two years later for the twenty-seventh edition, playing a standard sagebrush heroine in *Santa Fe Marshall* (Paramount, 1940), a

Western enlivened considerably by the presence of veteran character actress Marjorie Rambeau as the leader of a gang of outlaws.

Hayes returned to hard-boiled drama as the accused murderer Bonnie Rand in *What's My Story* (Universal, 1937), a programmer starring newcomer William Lundigan. The picture is typical of the kind of bread-and-butter pulp fiction that sustained double-bills during the late 1930s: Cub reporter Howard Fields (Lundigan) gets himself arrested hoping to get an interview with Bonnie Rand, who is charged with murdering her playboy boyfriend. The dim-witted reporter mistakes fellow journalist Janet Marlowe (Claudia Morgan) for Bonnie and falls in love. Believing the sob story "Bonnie" concocts on the spot, he tries to prove her innocence by telephoning in his "exclusive." The real Bonnie, meanwhile, is in the midst of a prison break and appears on the scene to take the two reporters hostage. With the law in hot pursuit, Bonnie brings the couple to her secret hideout where she and an accomplice (Murray Alper) shoot it out with the police. The police win, the crooks are apprehended and the two reporters decide to share the future together. The end.

The former radio singer finally got a chance to utilize her vocal talents warbling a few Stephen Foster ditties in *My Old Kentucky Home* (Crescent Pictures, 1937), a rural melodrama in which she played Gail Burke, a golddigging nightclub hostess. Produced independently by E. B. Derr for Monogram release, *My Old Kentucky Home* told the incredible tale of a hayseed (Grant Richards) who goes blind after having accidentally been doused with acid by a suicidal but lovelorn Hayes. The boy, unfortunately, is in love with his childhood sweetheart (Evelyn Venable) and the triangle drama drags on for the film's 70-odd pointless minutes.

Next, Hayes went behind bars in *Prison Nurse* (Republic, 1938), a grim little thriller dealing with a typhoid epidemic in a state penitentiary. *Prison Nurse* was a fortunate outing for the actress: Almost ten years later, when her career had hit the doldrums, the film's producer, Herbert Schlom, would assign her the role of Longshot Lillie in *Dick Tracy's Dilemma*. Schlom had good reasons to remember Hayes, who offered the unpleasant *Prison Nurse* its few moments of comedy relief. It remains a great pity that she was given so few chances to show her flair for wry comedy.

In 1939, Bernadene Hayes would leave Poverty Row for two high profile M-G-M productions, *Idiot's Delight*, with Norma Shearer and Clark Gable, and *Lucky Night*, with Robert Taylor and Myrna Loy. In the former she appeared as a member of Gable's travelling girl troupe, joining the star in his famous (or infamous, as the case may be) rendition of "Puttin' On the Ritz"; in the latter she showed up as a "B" girl named Blondie, but, as usual, made the most of her brief opportunity to bring a bit of earthy glamour to the otherwise lofty proceedings.

In the early forties, with film offers few and far between, Hayes left Hollywood to tour with a nightclub act. She returned to the screen as Kane Richmond's leading lady in a Monogram "quickie" entitled *Don't Gamble with Strangers* (1946), a cautionary tale of a pair of crooks who take control of a gambling joint; it was all very seedy and the film quickly disappeared from view. She was much better served with her supporting role as Longshot Lillie opposite Ralph Byrd in *Dick Tracy's Dilemma* (RKO, 1947). A glamorous, if a bit shopworn, lady fence, Longshot Lillie feigns grave dismay when apprehended by the ubiquitous Tracy: "I'm no criminal, Mr. Tracy," she swears, "I'm a lady!"

No more a lady, it is soon revealed that she can have several thousand dollars stashed away in her car for the purpose of buying stolen furs by a known killer named the Claw (Jack Lambert). Bernadene's appearance here, brief as it is, is a great deal more effective than that of Kay Christopher, the film's rather vapid Tess Truehart. It was, alas, her final chance to shine.

Hayes played a few minor roles in programmers like *Women in the Night* (Film Classics, 1948), a cheaply produced war drama starring Tala Birell, and the aforementioned *Bunco Squad* (RKO, 1950). The latter was a minor crime drama designed to exploit Howard Hughes' newest discovery, Joan Dixon. Ironically, Hayes had earlier appeared as an immigrant woman in *Caught* (M-G-M, 1949), a melodrama whose protagonist (played by Robert Ryan) had an uncanny resemblance to the bizarre millionaire.

Hayes' final screen appearance came in *Wicked Woman* (United Artists, 1953), a then controversial sex drama in which Beverly Michaels played the exact kind of "B" girl so often portrayed by Hayes in the thirties.

Bernadene Hayes appeared in a few live television programs before retiring from performing in the late 1950s. The veteran actress died of heart failure in Los Angeles on August 29, 1987. She was survived by a daughter, four grandchildren and three great-grandchildren.

BERNADENE HAYES FILMOGRAPHY

1934: *The Human Side.*
1935: *Folies Bergère (de Paris); The Whole Town's Talking; Love in Bloom; Alias Mary Dow; She Gets Her Man; The Judgment Book; Broadway Melody of 1936; Rendezvous; Trigger Tom.*
1936: *Absolute Quiet; Parole! The Accusing Finger; Along Came Love.*
1937: *Great Guy; Girl Loves Boy; That's My Story; Sweetheart of the Navy; North of the Rio Grande; Rustler's Valley; The Emperor's Candlesticks; Idol of the Crowds; Trouble at Midnight.*
1938: *My Old Kentucky Home; Prison Nurse; You and Me.*
1939: *Idiot's Delight; King of Chinatown; Lucky Night; Panama Lady; Some Like It Hot; 6,000 Enemies; The Day the Bookies Wept; Heroes in Blue.*
1940: *Santa Fe Marshal; Sailor's Lady; Manhattan Heartbeat.*
1941: *The Gay Vagabond; The Deadly Game; Sing for Your Supper.*
1942: *This Gun for Hire; Nazi Agent; I Live on Danger.*
1944: *Mr. Winkle Goes to War.*
1946: *Don't Gamble with Strangers.*
1947: *The Thirteenth Hour; Dick Tracy's Dilemma; Living in a Big Way; The Crimson Key.*
1948: *Woman in the Night.*
1949: *Caught.*
1950: *Bunco Squad.*
1953: *Wicked Woman.*

14—Beulah Hutton

"It was unfortunate," author Jon Tuska wrote of the 1931 Mascot serial *Danger Island*,

> that young people should carry with them as a legacy from their time spent in darkened movie houses watching chapter plays like this, the conviction that women had either to be protected or were motivated primarily by greed. Chapter plays were scarcely the only kind of screen entertainment demarcating women in this fashion but women clearly joined the ranks of the socially oppressed, a reversal from those trends in serial plot lines which had once permitted serial queens to proudly shatter such stereotypes.

The classic silent screen serial was, in fact, built upon the notion that a strong woman could battle the evil forces of this world as well as a man. Pearl White had popularized the genre with her pioneering serial, *The Perils of Pauline* (Pathé, 1914), and her popularity brought forth such petite but vibrant and headstrong rivals as Ruth Roland, Marie Walcamp, and Allene Ray.

Ordinarily these athletic actresses found men to be both their allies and adversaries but every so often they would run into an evil and nefarious female. Neva Gerber, for example, went up against just such a creature in the crime-fighting serial *Officer 444* (Goodwill, 1926). Throughout its ten chapters Gerber is menaced by the sinister Frog, ruler over a vast criminal empire. As his chief henchman the Frog employs a beautiful, but deadly woman known as the Vulture, a worthy adversary, it would appear, to Miss Gerber when the two women duke it out while a runaway train is hurtling down the track towards an unconscious Officer 444. Despite having to battle the fierce and brutal Vulture, the heroine manages in the nick of time to reach the switch, de-claw the Vulture, and save the day for law and order.

The Vulture was played by the dark haired Ruth Royce and *Officer 444* was but one of eight serials this intriguing character actress would make during the silent era.

Beulah Hutton and Lucille Lund in Pirate Treasure (Universal, 1934) (photograph courtesy of the Danish Film Museum).

Royce, however, retired with the coming of sound and, at first, seemed to have had no heirs. That is until *Danger Island* and Beulah Hutton.

Who was Beulah Hutton? Sad to say, she remains a mystery woman. Naturally she was dark haired and of course she was athletic. Hutton had appeared in a few bit parts in feature films and worked as a stand-in for established leading ladies. But as an actress in her own right, she could only claim three serials made at Universal 1931–1934.

Actually, Beulah Hutton's participation in her first serial, *Heroes of the Flames* (Universal, 1931), was minor. A less than thrilling Western starring Tim McCoy, *Heroes* also featured veteran serial heroine Grace Cunard, whom Universal seem to have hired out of nostalgia. Hutton appears near the bottom of the cast list as a saloon belle.

She was much more in evidence in *Danger Island* (Universal, 1931), a 12-chapter serial directed by genre expert Ray Taylor. The typically fantastic screenplay details the fight for a vast radium deposit. The dying professor Adams (Tom Ricketts) informs his beautiful daughter Bonnie (Lucille Browne) that she will soon inherit a rich radium mine located on an African island. Attempting to secure the abundant deposit for themselves, playboy Ben Arnold (Walter Miller) and his exotic looking girlfriend Aileen Chandor (Hutton) feign friendship with the newly orphaned Bonnie. Soon the damsel is in distress and to her rescue comes honest Henry Drake (Kenneth Harlan), who, as a reward for his chivalry, is almost sacrificed in a strange voodoo ritual concocted by Ben and Aileen. Meanwhile, the two villains fight among themselves and Aileen decides to turn traitor and defect to the other side. With her help, Harry and Bonnie are finally able to rid the world of the villainous Ben and plan a future together.

Not since the days of Ruth Royce had serial fans had the opportunity to hiss at such a formidable villainess as Beulah Hutton. The coming of sound had unfortunately ushered in an era of demure and passive heroines, whose helplessness and dependence on men was a far cry from the days of Pearl White and Ruth Roland. Consequently, the antagonists were now mostly men; it was unseemly for a hero to battle a woman—even a "Black Widow" like Ruth Royce. The emergence of Beulah Hutton changed things for the better—but only slightly. Like most of her sisters in feature films, Hutton, as Aileen Chandon, was forced by the screenwriters to redeem herself before the fade-out, a turnabout that betrayed the character the writers had spent so much time building up. Miss Royce would never have changed allegiance, not even to save her own skin. But it was a new era and *Danger Island*'s heroine, Lucille Browne, was no Pearl White or Neva Gerber. In fact, like all 1930s serial heroines, she was little more than a glorified prop—a prize for the villain to possess and the hero to rescue. Hutton's Aileen Chandon, as despicable as she was throughout most of the serial, at least possessed a brain and could fight her own battles.

Beulah Hutton didn't betray her master in *Pirate Treasure* (Universal, 1934). Again directed by Taylor, *Pirate Treasure* was the oft-told tale of the search for a treasure hidden on a South Seas island. Dick Moreland (played by stuntman Richard Talmadge) inherits a map showing a buried fortune from one of his ancestors and sets forth on his quest. Also seeking the treasure is scheming lawyer Stanley Brasset (Walter Miller), whose attempts at bumping off fearless Dick all misfire. In desperation the lawyer dispatches his most sadistic assistants to get the job done. However, the two crooks, Tony (Al Ferguson) and Marge (Hutton), are so loathsome that the island's natives rebel and help Dick rid the world once and for all of Brasset and his minions.

Following her short career in serials, Hutton played bit parts as secretaries and telephone operators and functioned as Claire Trevor's stand-in in *Wild Gold* (Fox, 1935), and Virginia Field's in *Think Fast, Mr. Moto* (20th Century–Fox, 1937). After that she disappeared into obscurity.

The strong, athletic serial queen and her adversary, the Black Widow villainess, first came to the screen just prior to World War I. As we have seen, the genre changed from a female to a male domain in the 1930s, and with it so did villainy.*

However, by the end of the decade, when war again seemed eminent, women

---

Carlotta Monti (W.C. Field's longtime mistress) portrayed a glamorous but avaricious (and weren't they always) priestess in Buster Crabbe's Tarzan the Fearless *(Principal, 1935), but her screen time in this serial was all too brief. Most of the villainy was left for the hissable Frank Lackteen as an evil slave trader. That same year, in another backlot jungle, Margo D'Use attempted to rule the Dark Continent in* The Lost City, *a cheaply produced serial from the misleadingly titled Super Serial Productions. Unfortunately for Miss D'Use she chose George (later "Gabby") Hayes as her chief henchman and failed in a big way.*

protagonists and theatrical femme fatales returned to prominence. Frances Gifford, as the *Jungle Girl* (Republic, 1941), led the parade of more self-reliant serial queens, followed by Kay Aldridge (*Perils of Nyoka*, Republic, 1942) and Linda Stirling (*The Tiger Woman*, Republic, 1944). As for *femme fatales*, *Perils of Nyoka* offered Lorna Gray as Vultura, the queen of a band of vicious natives; *The Adventures of Smilin' Jack* (Universal, 1943) had the elegant Rose Hobart portraying the nefarious Fraulein Von Teufel (German for devil!); and in *Raiders of the Ghost City* (Universal, 1944), Virginia ("Mrs. Olson") Christine played Lionel Atwill's evil accomplice.

But the deadliest of all was Carol Forman of *The Black Widow* (Republic, 1947). The heir apparent to Ruth Royce and Beulah Hutton, Forman wreaked havoc throughout five chapter-plays in the late 1940s and early 1950s, culminating with the original *Superman* serial (Columbia, 1948), in which she was cast as "The Spider Lady," a frightening, if glamorous, female out to achieve world dominance. Unfortunately, by then the serial genre was already in decline. By the mid–1950s, television had finally achieved what no villain, male or female, had: the death of the serial queen.

Beulah Hutton Filmography

1931: *Heroes of the Flames* (serial); *Danger Island* (serial).
1932: *Back Street.*
1934: *Pirate Treasure* (serial); *Name the Woman; Wild Gold; Fugitive Lady.*
1936: *High Tension.*
1937: *Think Fast, Mr. Moto; Charlie Chan on Broadway.*

15 — Rita La Roy

Rita La Roy was Taxi Belle Hooper, Marlene Dietrich's rival in *Blonde Venus* (Paramount, 1931). She was also, it was whispered, Dietrich's lover offscreen. However, if that was the case, why wasn't the role larger? It had been in the original script (and Evelyn Brent was all set to play it), but by the time Josef von Sternberg had finished tinkering, the film was all Marlene. Still, Taxi Belle was on the receiving end of Dietrich's snappiest lines, and their few scenes together were a distinct relief in an otherwise overly sentimental melodrama about mother love.

Rita La Roy, someone once remarked, was a brunette Natalie Moorhead. Like Moorhead, she was somewhat of a clotheshorse and was usually cast as a calculating bitch. But since she wasn't a platinum blonde like Natalie, she almost always played women of a higher social position, Taxi Belle Hooper being a notable exception. La Roy appeared in more than 30 feature films between 1929 and 1934 but, like most vamps of the era, she was usually only awarded supporting roles. Nevertheless, she was the brightest thing about several potboilers of the early thirties, including an atrocious Amos 'n' Andy comedy, *Check and Double Check* (RKO, 1930). This blackface farce is unfortunately one of the few of her films still shown today.

She was born Ina Stuart in Paris, France, on October 2, 1901. According to some possibly fanciful press releases her father was Sir James Stuart, a "dispossessed British aristocrat," and her mother, also named Rita La Roy, a dancer at the Paris Opera who died in childbirth. Sir James, it appears, was an alcoholic who was forced to sell his chateau in France and move to Canada with his young daughter. He failed in whatever it was he did in Alberta and they moved again, this time to Tacoma, Washington, where he took up farming. As she would later confide to Hale Horton of *Motion Picture*, La Roy's upbringing was quite dramatic and at one point she had even tried to kill her abusive father with a shotgun. Several times she would run away from home but was always promptly returned.

Sir James died when his daughter was 13. Alone in the world, she was placed in an orphanage, from which she escaped by taking "a hundred-mile stroll through the mud to Tacoma." Once there, she waited on tables, worked in a five-and-dime, and tried vaudeville. According to later publicity, "it did not take long for Rita to become an experienced trouper," and for the next two or three years she "traveled all over the Northwest and Canada performing with various stock companies."

For some reason, La Roy suddenly left the stage and returned to Tacoma where she became a fashion designer and later even operated a small boutique. But the theater was in her blood now, and she returned to stock soon enough, this time in Portland, Oregon.

By the late 1920s, Rita La Roy had worked her way to Los Angeles. Breaking into films, it seems, was easy for the now veteran barnstormer, who, after a few bit parts, was given the female lead in *The Delightful Rogue* (RKO, 1929), a comedy-drama about a pirate (Rod La Rocque) who falls for the daughter of the man he had shanghaied. Despite the cheapness of production and performances alike, RKO liked her well enough to offer a contract.

Rita La Roy appeared in six feature films for RKO in 1930, almost always in unsympathetic supporting roles. Among them was the now infamous *Check and Double Check*, the "comedy" that brought radio's Amos 'n' Andy to the screen. Viewed today, the film's blatant racism is hard to take—and so is the fact that the stars (Freeman Gosden and Frank Correll) appear in blackface. La Roy figures prominently in a subplot as a scheming woman out to make sure that her no-good brother (Ralf Harolde) gets hitched to a wealthy debutante (Sue Carol).

According to interviews during these early years in Hollywood, Rita La Roy considered screen acting little more than means to an end. "I'm in pictures just to make money," she admitted to Hale Horton of *Motion Picture*. "If I ever discover I can make more money doing something else, I'll do it quick."

"In pictures just to make money," La Roy accepted any production that wanted her—even if that meant a stroll down Poverty Row for such exploitative little items as *Playthings of Hollywood* (1930), from indie producer Willis Kent, or *Leftover Ladies* (1931), a no-budget Tiffany release. The former was very typical of the kind of fare offered the grind houses during the early years of sound. The scenario, taken from *Film Daily* (the film itself doesn't seem to have survived), read like the cheapest of pulp fiction:

> Three sisters [Phyllis Barrington, La Roy, and Sheila Mannors] go to Hollywood where one gets a job as a secretary to an oil magnate, another is hired by a department store and the third becomes an extra in movies. Two sisters fall in love with the same man. The sister who loses the man takes a trip with her boss, an oil man, and by accident the other sister and her boyfriend travel to the same place. When the boss suffers a heart attack and dies, the sister who is his secretary is accused of his murder. Eventually, everything is straightened out and she is cleared.

That was all there was to the film, but with an exploitative title that promised far more than the Hays Office would allow it to deliver, it was surely all but guaranteed to do well in smaller venues. La Roy undoubtedly played the sister accused of murder.

In between these detours to lesser companies, La Roy continued on at RKO where she appeared as Natalie, a dangerous spy who impersonates Genevieve Tobin's maid in *The Gay Diplomat* (1931), a romantic melodrama set during the Bolshevik revolution. In *Traveling Husbands*, she was one of the prostitutes (top-billed Evelyn Brent played another) who caters to out-of-town salesmen.

Leaving RKO in July of 1931, La Roy ventured over to Fox, where she was a sagebrush vixen coming between George O'Brien and Sally Eilers in *A Holy Terror*, a quite well made contemporary Western with an interesting supporting cast that included a young Humphrey Bogart. In the more upscale *The Yellow Ticket* (Fox, 1931), she was Fania Rubinstein, a Jewish prostitute in czarist Russia, who inspires small town schoolteacher (Elissa Landi) to acquire a whore's "yellow passport," the only way a young Jewish woman was permitted to travel from the country to St. Petersburg.

Ugly rumors surfaced around this time about La Roy's private life. The actress furiously complained to the press that she was "rather fed up" with the Hollywood gossip mongers:

> They make insinuations concerning my girlfriend and myself when I've never had a girlfriend in my life; they wisecrack about my being on the make for every male in town, and about me being "wild." They say more things about me than ten girls could live up to!

On September 27, 1931—to quell the rumors, perhaps—Rita La Roy married her agent, Ben Hershfeld. The marriage, alas, proved short-lived, lasting only until October of 1935. "It's Rita's idea that she wants her freedom and I am game to try it this way," Hershfeld explained to the press. His ex-wife concurred. "Our married life has been happy," she told the *Record*. "We haven't had a quarrel in our lives. We haven't talked divorce because there has been no reason for such talk. Anyway, I'm the worst person in the world to live with."*

In early 1932, Rita La Roy took over from an ailing Minna Gombell as David Landaus's seductive wife in *Amateur Daddy* (Fox, 1932), a rural melodrama starring Warner Baxter and Marian Nixon. When handsome construction worker Baxter spurns La Roy's amorous advances, she gets back at him in court by testifying that it was *she* who had been the victim of sexual harassment. "The generous fund of old-fashioned hokum in this feature appeared to find favor with the audience," a bemused Mordaunt Hall of the *New York Times* reported. The critic, however, found La Roy's small-town *femme fatale* to be somewhat of a "strange creature."

For Paramount, La Roy was Carole Lombard's golddigging friend who commits suicide when spurned by a playboy, in *Sinners in the Sun* (1932). She returned to Poverty Row right after that, however, to star opposite Edward J. Nugent in something called *Honor the Press* (Mayfair, 1932). According to *Film Daily*, she played a hat-check girl who helps a cub reporter to get the big scoop. Next came Taxi Belle Hooper, Marlene Dietrich, Josef von Sternberg, and *Blonde Venus*.

Conceived as Dietrich and Josef von Sternberg's first true "American film,"

---

*In the late 1930s, the world suddenly learned of a previous marriage. "I married early, for about an hour," the actress explained. "Or it may have lasted only fifteen minutes. My suitor threatened suicide if I didn't marry him!"

Rita La Roy in 1931 (photograph courtesy of the Danish Film Museum).

Blonde Venus (Paramount, 1932) told the lurid story of a German-born cabaret singer who, through a series of misunderstandings, is forced into prostitution and loses her young son as a consequence. Before she completely hits the skids, however, Dietrich's Helen Faraday languorously sings "Hot Voodoo" while wearing a gorilla suit topped by a blonde Harpo Marx wig. Her nightclub act is admired by a shady politician (a very young Cary Grant), but not by jealous rival performer "Taxi Belle" Hooper, with whom she shares a dressing-room and (in the original script) a great deal of spicy repartee. Most of that, alas, had been exorcised in the final shooting script. The Hays Office did, however, leave in a chance for Dietrich to inquire whether the trashy Taxi Belle "charged for the first mile."

As noted above, the role of "Taxi Belle" had been written for an earlier von Sternberg favorite, Evelyn Brent, but Paramount executive B. P. Schulberg, his gaze firmly on the Production Code, demanded a rewrite of the censurable script. Von Sternberg was forced to cut the role to the bare minimum (and, even more fatal to the end result, add a ludicrous happy ending!), with the result that Evelyn Brent, too big a star to waste in a bit role, was out. Inheriting what was left of the part, Rita La Roy does her best with her very few remaining scenes and manages to add some down-to-earth all–American nastiness to the otherwise oh so European flavor of the piece.

Rita La Roy suffered a career setback in September of 1932, when she suddenly walked off the Clara Bow vehicle, *Call Her Savage* (Fox, 1932), an all–*femme fatale* melodrama about a halfbreed who tries to become a debutante. According to the *Los Angeles Examiner*, the actress had left the company "because a director [John Francis Dillon] wanted her to wear scanty attire."

> She further emphasized her refusal to play the part in real life that she plays on the screen by slapping the heavy [Fred Kohler] in her picture, who tried to make love to her when the camera wasn't grinding.

La Roy was quickly replaced with Margaret Livingston, but a supporting actress walking off an important picture was unheard of in Hollywood and her career immediately hit a slump. Rita had appeared in ten films in 1932; the following year her output was two—and in one of them, *Song of Songs* (Paramount, 1933), her part was cut to a mere walk-on.

However, her fate in *Song of Songs* (Paramount, 1933) might not have had anything to do with La Roy's behavior on *Call Me Savage*. If she indeed had been Marlene Dietrich's lover during the making of *Blonde Venus*, as was rumored, she saw herself replaced during the filming of this, the first Hollywood film Dietrich made without von Sternberg, by writer Mercedes de Acosta. Marlene's attention span when it came to her *amours* was famously low. She certainly did not offer any help to La Roy, whose only other film role of the year was a bit part in *From Hell to Heaven* (Paramount, 1933), a horse-racing drama with Carole Lombard.

In late 1933, however, Ben Hershfeld, La Roy's agent and soon to be ex-husband, managed to secure her a contract with Columbia, a small studio still considered a struggling Poverty Row company and specializing in cheap crime dramas and Westerns. In *One Is Guilty* (Columbia, 1934), an *Inspector Trent* series entry starring Ralph Bellamy as the indefatigable sleuth, she played Willard Robertson's adulterous wife and is suspected throughout most of the film of murdering her lover, a prizefighter. (In the end, she proved to be a red herring.) In *Name the Woman* (Columbia, 1934), she was again a haughty socialite—this time involved in the murder of a district attorney. *Whirlpool* (Columbia, 1934), saw her as a nightclub singer, jealous of Jack Holt's preoccupation with Jean Arthur.

Following her stint at Columbia, La Roy was at liberty throughout 1935, giving her plenty of time to divorce her husband. She returned to the screen the following year, only to disappear in the crowd of former silent screen stars (Esther Ralston, Mae Marsh, Charles Ray, Maurice Costello, et al.) in Robert Florey's slow-moving paean to the American film industry, *Hollywood Boulevard*.

She was a bit more visible playing a gun moll in *Lady from Nowhere* (Columbia, 1936), a crime drama starring Mary Astor, and was quite good as one of the suspects in *The Mandarin Mystery* (Republic, 1936), a well-made version of the Ellery Queen whodunit starring a slightly miscast but still entertaining Eddie Quillan. "Rita La Roy is vivid as the questionable daughter of the stamp collector," *Varity*'s "Wear" commented.

She was "vivid" again as Rita Calmette, a temperamental opera diva who ends up a murder victim in *Find the Witness* (Columbia, 1937), a low-budget crime drama starring Columbia "B" movie stalwart Charles Quigley. While she went on to appear in nine films during the following three years, *Find the Witness* offered La Roy her last good role.

For the remainder of her screen career, Rita La Roy saw her fortunes dwindle from that of a supporting actress to an unbilled bit player. She appeared as a convict in *The Hit Parade* (Republic, 1937), a low-budget musical featuring talents ranging from Frances Langford to the Tic Toc Girls; and, along with fellow vamps Evelyn Brent and Natalie Moorhead, she was buried deep in the cast of *King of Gamblers* (Paramount, 1937), a minor crime drama which unsuccessfully attempted to make character actor Akim Tamiroff into another Edward G. Robinson.

Rosalind Keith and Rita La Roy in *Find the Witness* (Columbia, 1937) (photograph courtesy of the Danish Film Museum).

Rita was briefly restored to featured billing as a two-bit vixen out West in *Border G-Man* (RKO, 1938), a George O'Brien program Western so bad it premiered far away from those pesky reviewers—in Lincoln, Nebraska! *Fixer Dugan*, also from RKO, was her sole credit for 1939; she played a circus high-wire artist who plunges to her death, leaving her child (Virginia Weidler) to be raised by the fast-talking Lee Tracy.

Rita La Roy ended her screen career on Poverty Row, supporting the husband-and-wife team of James Dunn and Frances Gifford in *Hold That Woman* (1940), a low-budget (very low-budget!) drama about repo men. *Hold That Woman* was produced by a new studio, Producers Releasing Company, a penny-pinching entity lovingly known around Hollywood as "Prick Productions." La Roy played Lulu Driscoll, a jewel thief.

Retired from show business, Rita La Roy eloped to Yuma, Arizona, on May 14, 1943, with A. G. "Hank" Foley, "a well-known horse breeder." She came out of retirement in 1949, appropriately enough to play a fashion editor in *You're My Everything*, a minor backstage musical from Fox. Since then, she has completely disappeared from the public eye.

RITA LA ROY FILMOGRAPHY

- **1929:** *The Delightful Rogue; The Love Trap; Dynamite.*
- **1930:** *Lovin' the Ladies; Midnight Mystery; Check and Double Check (Amos 'n' Andy); Conspiracy; Sin Takes a Holiday; Lilies of the Field; Playthings of Hollywood.*
- **1931:** *A Holy Terror; Traveling Husbands; The Gay Diplomat; Leftover Ladies; The Yellow Ticket; Terror by Night; The Secret Witness.*
- **1932:** *While Paris Sleeps; Amateur Daddy; So Big; Sinners in the Sun; Honor of the Press; Bachelor's Affairs; Hollywood Speaks; Blonde Venus; Hot Saturday.*
- **1933:** *From Hell to Heaven; Song of Songs.*
- **1934:** *I've Got Your Number; Whirlpool; One Is Guilty; Name the Woman; Fugitive Lady.*
- **1936:** *Hollywood Boulevard; Lady from Nowhere; The Mandarin Mystery.*
- **1937:** *Find the Witness; Mountain Music; The Hit Parade; King of Gamblers; Flight from Glory.*
- **1938:** *Dangerous to Know; Condemned Women; Border G-Man.*
- **1939:** *Fixer Dugan.*
- **1940:** *Hold That Woman.*
- **1941:** *Sergeant York.*
- **1949:** *You're My Everything.*

16—Nina Mae McKinney

"Nina Mae McKinney wasn't mentally ready for the fame and fortune that enveloped her," a condescending Don de Leighbur of the Los Angeles *Sentinel* wrote in 1944. In actuality, it was Hollywood and the American film industry that were not mentally ready for the beautiful Nina Mae McKinney! Her startling debut as the cabaret dancer in King Vidor's all-black *Hallelujah* (M-G-M, 1929) resulted in the tag "the screen's first black love goddess" and Irving Thalberg, Metro's chief of production, euphorically called her "one of the greatest discoveries of the age." Needless to say, M-G-M did not know what to do with their "discovery of the age." There was little call for black *femmes fatales* and she wasn't exactly the mammy type or the typically subservient maid. Consequently, there wouldn't be another worthwhile role for Nina Mae McKinney until 1935 when she appeared opposite the even more neglected Paul Robeson in the British *Sanders of the River*. McKinney, who in Europe would be known as "the black Garbo," was an international star of stage and night clubs, but her sexuality frightened the ethnocentric Hollywood.

Nina Mae McKinney was born June 12, 1913, in Lancaster, South Carolina, and not in Harlem, as most contemporary biographies stated. She did make her professional debut there, however, and in 1928 appeared as one of Lew Leslie's *Blackbirds*.

McKinney's early years in show business remain obscure. It seems that she went from the backwoods of Harlem to becoming the black sex symbol of the 1920s as Chick, the *femme fatale* of *Hallelujah* (1929). Then again, the mainstream entertainment press rarely concerned themselves with what happened in "Darktown."

Today considered one of the finest films produced in the years of the "talkie revolution," *Hallelujah* was conceived by director King Vidor almost as an antidote to the musical travesty *Hearts in Dixie* (Fox, 1929), a silly "feel-good-among-them-colored-folks" extravaganza, which utilized every stereotype ever invented about happy cotton pickin' "darkies" (complete with Stepin Fetchit at his "lazy" worst). Vidor, to his eternal credit, went for "realism," depicting life among the black underclass of his beloved

South (Vidor was from Texas). With Irving Thalberg's help he managed to persuade the M-G-M brass not only to make the film in the first place (which was a considerable coup in itself, since it had very little chance of popular appeal in the same racist South that it depicted), but also to film it entirely on location in Memphis, Tennessee.

The story of *Hallelujah* is simple: The son of a sharecropper goes to the Big City, meets a fallen woman (McKinney), yields to temptation, squanders his family's hard earned money, and accidentally kills his own brother in a barroom brawl. He then proceeds to "get religion" and tries to inspire the *femme fatale* to change her life. She, of course, is too mired in her own selfishness to repent and instead betrays him. In a fit of jealousy, he kills her (and her lover), an act which convinces him to turn again to preaching the gospel. Repentant, he returns to the bosom of his family and the nice girl he had left behind.

In retrospect, *Hallelujah* is, as historian Alexander Walker points out, "better in intention than achievement." To play it safe, the film had an all black cast and consequently didn't really affect a white audience, who thus could study the mores of others in the comfort of their own segregated theaters. Mordaunt Hall of the *New York Times*, for example, is typical of the racism, conscious or unconscious, of white America:

> The humor that issues from *Hallelujah* is natural unto the Negro, whether it deals with hankering after salvation, the dread of water in baptism, the lure of the "come seven, come 'leven" or the belated marital ceremonies....

In casting his film, Vidor turned to the Harlem nightclub spots where he found William Fountaine, who plays McKinney's no-good lover; Victoria Spivey, the film's down-home girl, Missy Rose; and McKinney herself. The latter proved to be *Hallelujah*'s revelation, shimmying to Irving Berlin's "Swanee Shuffle," and vamping hero Daniel Haynes with the best of them. Mordaunt Hall noted her "chocolate color," which he preferred, it seems, over the pigmentation of Spivey, referred to as "black as coal."

Richard Watts, Jr., of the liberal *New York Post* appeared less bigoted in his assessment of McKinney, whom he deemed to be "assuredly one of the most beautiful women of our time." A more contemporary critic actually gave McKinney's acting some thought. "Her performance endures beyond any of the actors in the film," wrote Nancy Dowd:

> Miss McKinney's great beauty, her arrogance, her ambiguity, and her determination to get some pleasure out of life, no matter who tried to stop her, make her seem more modern and interesting than her chic Flapper counterparts.

The reaction to McKinney from white audiences, then and now, seems to be exactly what Vidor counted on when he cast her. Why else did he choose a girl who looked all but Caucasian for his sex symbol? Spivey, on the other hand, with her typically Negroid features, was considered homely if not actually ugly—acceptable for playing the nice, "safe" marrying kind. As with her successors (Lena Horne, Dorothy Dandridge et al.), McKinney was judged purely from a "white" criterion of beauty. (Her contemporary Josephine Baker, conversely, was considered a "savage" and had little chance for success in white America.)

16—NINA MAE McKINNEY   [133]

Daniel L. Haynes, Nina Mae McKinney and director King Vidor. Composite photograph from *Hallelujah* (M-G-M, 1929).

In the end, *Hallelujah* scored with "liberal-minded" white Northerners, who liked it better than their black counterparts. *Variety*, in its quaint prejudicial way, found from "sizing up the all-colored reception of the film from start to finish" at the Harlem Lafayette theater premiere, that "Negroes just won't take their big dramatic stuff seriously."

Maybe contemporary African Americans simply did not buy Vidor's version of "colored life." As the noted actor Clarence Muse said in the late 1930s,

> What we need are more Negro authors and screenwriters.... The Negro has lived in a world of conflict and struggle for generations and of such influences are sublime works created.

Needless to say, the future, bringing us Alex Haley, Alice Walker, Maya Angelou and scores of others, has proven him correct.

M-G-M was delighted with Nina Mae McKinney's near "crossover" appeal, and Irving Thalberg made a big deal of signing her to a long-term contract. That was an empty gesture, however, since M-G-M was not in the business of producing films for black audiences. The only place for black entertainers in mainstream fare was that of comic sidekick (painfully exhibited by the popularity of Stepin Fetchit and, later, Mantan Moreland), maids and "Mammys" (Hattie McDaniel and Louise Beavers come to mind), and various porters, elevator operators and shoeshine boys. Black *femmes fatales* were not even in the vocabulary. (Nor were, for that matter, "ordinary" working people; one rarely spots an African American extra in Hollywood films of the so-called "golden years.")

Since M-G-M didn't know what to do with her, McKinney was borrowed by First National, who cast her and Clarence Muse in a melodrama set in the Caribbean, *Safe in Hell* (1931). As a long delayed follow-up to *Hallelujah*, the film was, to put it mildly, anticlimactic; but McKinney did get to warble "When It's Sleepy Time Down South" (written by Muse) and, according to contemporary sources, was allowed to drop the script's stereotypical dialogue. "Nina Mae McKinney, the too seldom seen temptress of *Hallelujah!*, as a dark-skinned barmaid, is about the most entertaining item in the film," Andre Sennwald of the *New York Times* observed. Unfortunately, McKinney returned to M-G-M to find that the studio had dropped her option, the goodwill generated by her signing apparently having long since evaporated.

Ironically, it was M-G-M who brought her back to Hollywood after an interim during which she toured with a nightclub act. She appeared briefly as herself in Jean Harlow's *Reckless* (1935), but it was mainly the McKinney voice that the studio now desired. She dubbed Harlow's vocal numbers, but when the film was released they had been heavily cut for time. As a consequence, McKinney's main contribution to *Reckless* ended up mostly on the cutting room floor.

With the disappointment of *Reckless* behind her, Nina Mae McKinney followed the trail of black entertainers to Europe and toured there with great success, despite an ever threatening political situation. While in England, she signed to appear opposite the preeminent black American actor (and social activist) Paul Robeson, as his love interest in *Sanders of the River* (London Film, 1935).

Filmed on location in Nigeria, *Sanders of the River* is British imperialist filmmaking at its best (or worst, depending on the point of view), with Robeson as a peace-loving native helping District Commissioner Sanders (Leslie Banks) maintain tranquility between warring tribes. Happily, McKinney pops up and gets herself into trouble whenever the narrative bogs down to preachy, high-falutin' speeches. At one point, when kidnapped by a rebellious tribe, she is a typical damsel in distress whose

Opposite: **Paul Robeson and Nina Mae McKinney in** *Sanders of the River* **(London Films, 1935) (photograph courtesy of the Danish Film Museum).**

predicament seems straight out of a Universal cliffhanger. Robeson first attempts to rescue her, but ends up a hostage himself and it is up to the stalwart (and white) Leslie Banks to save the day for England. Andre Sennwald of the *New York Times* (who had taken over from the old-fashioned Mordaunt Hall) saw the imperialistic melodrama for what it was. Wrote Sennwald:

> The photoplay has cast a pall of sentiment over [the real life Sanders] and created a romantic portrait of the benevolent white father who guides the destinies of his black children for the greater glory of the empire on which the sun never sets.

Of the performances, Sennwald opined:

> Paul Robeson sings several English arrangements of native war songs, which are stimulating to hear, but a decided hindrance to his portrayal of the savage Bosambo. Similarly, the talented Nina Mae McKinney is likely to impress you more as a Harlem nightclub entertainer than a savage jungle beauty.

McKinney was offscreen again until 1938, when she did a specialty number in a cheap British musical comedy, *On Velvet*. She returned to the United States to play the female lead in the all black musical, *The Duke Is Tops* (Million Dollar Pictures,* 1938), but then had to withdraw because of illness. (Appropriately enough, she was replaced by Lena Horne.)

Recovered, she starred as a nurse turned torch singer in the *Gang Smashers* (Million Dollar Pictures, 1939), and then went to Kingston, Jamaica, for *Pocomania* (Domino, 1939), a melodrama with not a little similarity to *Hallelujah*. Again, she is a vamp, this time trying to scare away a rival sibling (Ida James) with phony voodoo rituals. As opposed to *Hallelujah*, however, *Pocomania* played exclusively black theaters. In something called *Straight to Heaven* (Million Dollar Pictures, 1939), she and detective James Baskett go after the mob who has framed her innocent husband (Lionel Monogas). Like *Pocomania*, *Straight to Heaven* was directed for black audiences only by Arthur Leonard.

It took McKinney a good four years to return to mainstream filmmaking. Upon her resurrection (for the melodrama *Dark Waters*, United Artists, 1944), de Leighbur of the *Los Angeles Sentinel* made an attempt to explain the absence:

> Young, perhaps a bit giddy she [had] succumbed to the adulation of the mob, developed an "attitude," and then started sliding down the well-greased runways that are all around for people on top to slip back upon if their feet are not firmly on the ground.

With writing like this reflecting mainstream thinking, it was no wonder that Hollywood had not changed for the better during her ten year absence. (Note how de Leighbur terms McKinney's admirers a "mob"!)

Dark Waters was, as Bosley Crowther of the *New York Times* reported, "a killer-diller

---

*A prolific producer of all-black screen entertainment, Million Dollar was headed by Harry M. Popkin and released on the states rights market.

of a thriller" set in a Louisiana bayou. The commonplace scenario (innocent girl arrives at strange old mansion) was made mildly interesting by the deft touches of its director, Andre de Toth, but McKinney added little more than "local color" to the proceedings. *Together Again* (Columbia, 1944), an Irene Dunne comedy, didn't help matters: Now truly "Mammy-fied," she appeared as Dunne's maid.

Twenty years after Irving Thalberg had named her "one of the greatest discoveries of the age," Nina Mae McKinney was finally given another notable screen role, that of Jeanne Crain's rival in *Pinky* (20th Century–Fox, 1949). Fox's publicity machine unabashedly hailed her return to the screen:

> Back in Hollywood again after three years of singing in New York nightclubs, Nina Mae McKinney still has all the exoticism of those past years. She plays another one of her come-hither roles in Darryl F. Zanuck's production of *Pinky*, the story which is based on Cid Ricketts Sumner's novel *Quality*. The script says that "her hips sway lazily and alluringly ... there's a savage exultation to her body." "In other words, it's my kind of a part," said Nina Mae who has brightened up many a movie. "I'm a man hunter and when I get one, I hold on to him."

Ostensibly the story of a black girl passing for white, *Pinky*, was less than honest in casting peaches-and-cream Jeanne Crain as its much maligned and discriminated against protagonist. Still, the drama, directed by Broadway's Elia Kazan, was considered a pioneer work on racial equality when it premiered and was probably the best anyone could expect from a Hollywood in the throes of the notorious HUAC hearings. (Kazan, to his friends' consternation, later testified as a "friendly" witness.)

Along with the similarly structured *Lost Boundaries* (Film Classics, 1949), *Pinky* was in reality a throwback to *Imitation of Life* (Universal, 1935), the soap opera in which McKinney's contemporary Fredi Washington had played a light-skinned black girl passing for white with tragic consequences, and its impact, as Gary Null points out in *Black Hollywood*, "was felt most profoundly by blacks who had no interest in passing for white."

> The implication in *Pinky* and *Lost Boundaries* [Null continues] was that all Negroes, certainly professional ones, wanted to be white, although the films tried to make the point that Pinky and [*Lost Boundaries*'] physician were forced to "pass" for purely professional reasons.

McKinney herself put a bit of distance between African American reality and Hollywood's pat version of it. "It's an exciting story" she said, "done with a lot of suspense. But it's about what happens to one girl. It doesn't take up any so-called problem as a whole and it doesn't say what the answer is for the kind of situations that girls like Pinky run into."

During the filming of *Pinky*, McKinney divorced her husband of many years, ship's steward Melvin Wolfolk, and eight days later, on April 8, 1949, married civil engineer Frank Mickey. The marriage, it appears, brought an end to her professional career. She died in New York City on May 3, 1967.

NINA MAE McKINNEY FILMOGRAPHY

1929: *Hallelujah.*
1931: *Safe in Hell.*
1935: *Reckless; Sanders of the River* (GB*).
1938: *On Velvet* (GB).
1939: *Gang Smashers; Pocomania* (Jamaica); *Straight to Heaven; Swanee Showboat.*
1944: *Together Again; Night Train to Memphis; Dark Waters.*
1947: *Danger Street.*
1949: *Pinky.*
1950: *Copper Canyon.*

*GB=Great Britain.

17—Sari Maritza

The beautiful, exotic Sari Maritza first came to the attention of Hollywood when she danced the tango with Charlie Chaplin following the November 1931 London premiere of *City Lights* (United Artists, 1931). It was widely assumed that she was to become the comedian's newest leading lady (on screen and off), but nothing materialized. The association with Chaplin, however, paid off in valuable publicity and in January of 1932 she swept into Hollywood on a wave of press releases and clutching a lucrative Paramount contract. The studio's interest in her was not a fluke: she was almost a double for Marlene Dietrich, Paramount's less than obedient top foreign star. Maritza, quaint accent, plucked eyebrows and all, was rushed into a strange concoction entitled *Forgotten Commandments* (Paramount, 1932), a morality tale "Glorified," as the advertisement promised, "by Spectacular Episodes from Cecil B. DeMille's *The Ten Commandments*" (Paramount, 1923). Maritza was the other woman trying to break up serious medical students Gene Raymond and Marguerite Churchill (and ultimately paying for that little indiscretion with her life). Heavily promoted, Maritza was top-billed and given the full star treatment by the studio, which apparently actually thought that she could become the next Continental superstar. Unfortunately, *Forgotten Commandments* was a mess and a box office disaster, and Mordaunt Hall of the *New York Times*, who offered a splendid review of DeMille's 20 minutes of padding, dismissed it as "not especially well written." Of the debuting Maritza, the critic was at least somewhat polite:

> Miss Maritza reminds one of Greta Nissen,* but her carefully plucked eyebrows and her make-up are not in her favor. She speaks English well and gives a competent performance of a Russian girl.

Sari Maritza did indeed speak English well—and why not? Contrary to her publicity, she wasn't "Continental" at all, but a nice English girl named Patricia Nathan.

*An earlier Paramount vamp whose career had been damaged by the coming of sound.

Sari Maritza in London, 1931.

When that was established, her Hollywood career went absolutely nowhere. She was never given a chance. Paramount played up the "mystery woman" bit with a massive publicity blitz, but her roles, apart from *Forgotten Commandments*, were standard ingenue types. It soon became obvious that her presence on the lot was solely to function as a threat to Marlene Dietrich, who had director approval and, for awhile, declined to work with anybody but her mentor Josef von Sternberg. However, when Dietrich was suspended for refusing to do *Blonde Venus* (1932) without von Sternberg, the studio called in Tallulah Bankhead, a clear indication that Sari Maritza had already outlived her usefulness.

The "mysterious" Sari Maritza was born Dora Patricia Detering-Nathan on March 17, 1910, in Tientsin, China, the daughter of Major Walter Nathan, a British industrialist, and his Viennese-born wife. At the age of 12 Patricia Nathan, as she was then known, traveled to Europe to get "a proper education." En route she stopped over briefly in Hollywood where she witnessed Douglas Fairbanks filming a scene from *Robin Hood* (United Artists, 1922). Then and there, she later said, the young girl decided to become a screen actress.

"I almost became an ice skater," she told John Scott of the *Los Angeles Times* in 1932. "I won several medals as a young girl and my mother wanted me to take up the sport in earnest. But it was such drudgery and all the time I was hoping to become an actress."

Patricia Nathan's aspirations were fulfilled via a chance meeting in Berlin, Germany, with Vivian Gaye, a former stage actress and now a talent agent. In the eyes of the industrious Miss Gaye, Patricia was prime for the big buildup and the pair traveled to Budapest, Hungary, where the teenager signed a contract with the Sascha Company.

Following a few of what she would later term "inconsequential roles," Patricia Nathan suddenly decided to change her name to the much more alluring Sari Maritza. "We selected it because we wanted a typical Viennese name that would not always be mispronounced by English people," she later explained. "Maritza," of course, was taken from the operetta *The Countess Maritza*.

Vivian Gaye next steered her charge toward London and the West End. It proved a very clever move, indeed. To complete her disguise as an intriguing foreigner, Maritza adopted a suitably guttural accent and was immediately inundated with theatrical offers. "I was told to lose the accent," she later admitted to Elizabeth Goldbeck of *Motion Picture*, "so in a week I learned to speak perfect English and was considered a very clever girl."

Signing with the Gaumont Company, Sari Maritza made her English language debut as a nightclub singer in the musical *Greek Street* (1930). She then shared *Bed and Breakfast* (1930) with Barry Lupino, and was *No Lady* (1931) trying to seduce comedian Lupino Lane while spying for some Ruritanian country. Next came her association with the visiting Chaplin and for the next several years she would vehemently deny having been intimate with the comedian. "I was appearing in films in London," she explained to Janet Burden of *Movie Classic* in 1932.

> His film, *City Lights*, was about to open there, and he arranged a large party for the theater and dancing afterwards. He was kind enough to invite me—and later on, at the cafe, we danced together.

But while Chaplin encouraged the young actress to go to Hollywood, "he never mentioned a contract or the possibility of my appearing in films with him," she would declare.

Her public statements to the contrary, the couple did indeed seem awfully "chummy," and no one bought the ruse that she was actually the girlfriend of Chaplin's press agent Carlyle Robinson.

The affair (if that was indeed what it was) lasted until Chaplin left for Berlin where he was warmly received by Marlene Dietrich. Ironically, Maritza also visited Berlin that year.

In the wake of her newfound notoriety, the "Austrian" actress accepted an offer to star in a lavish UFA production to be filmed in both an English and a German version. *Monte Carlo Madness* (or *Bomben auf Monte Carlo*) was a wild comedy based on the exploits of a certain Mr. Jaggers, the gentleman whose story inspired the hit song "He's the Man Who Broke the Bank at Monte Carlo." With the popular Hans Albers in the male lead, the end result proved rather pleasing. Mordaunt Hall of the *New*

York Times, always an admirer of Teutonic escapism, found the piece "an enjoyable diversion," and marveled at Maritza's "fluent English." The actress herself, however, later dismissed the comedy as "very, very bad."

Returning to England, Maritza was cast by producer Basil Dean as the female lead in a "much discussed" melodrama of gypsy life in London, *Water Gipsies* (British National, 1932). According to later reports, Dean "had scoured Europe for a girl with the face of an elf, and the sophistication of a siren." Maritza seemed to fill the bill, and when a reviewer remarked that she looked like "a pocket edition of Marlene Dietrich," Dietrich's home studio, Paramount, was quick to snap up the potential competitor.

In January of 1932, accompanied as always by the ubiquitous Vivian Gaye, Sari Maritza went Hollywood. Once in sunny California, she played the part of the Continental star to the hilt. Interviewed in the Hollywood apartment she shared with Gaye, the newcomer readily answered all questions, albeit, as one writer observed, "in an inexplicably disinterested and sullen way." She strongly denied having been Marlene Dietrich's understudy, as was widely rumored, pointing out that she "had been a star long before Miss Dietrich." She was not, she argued, in Hollywood to rival anybody, but was there "just to make money." And no, she didn't entertain the idea of becoming a platinum blonde like, say, Jean Harlow. "To me," she said, "platinum blond hair is almost vulgar."

Despite her resolutions, it was a decidedly blond Maritza who made her American screen debut as Irving Pichel's mistress in *Forgotten Commandments* (Paramount, 1932)—and her coloring certainly made an attractive corpse when Pichel shoots her after he discovers her affair with the handsome Gene Raymond. *Variety*, suffering under the delusion that she was from Germany, found Maritza to be "Vampish in an adolescent way. She speaks English very well, [but has] too much make-up around the eyes, a Continental habit."

If Paramount had thought that Maritza was going to be easier to deal with than the demanding *Fraulein* Dietrich, they were in for a rude awakening. In an interview with Faith Service of *Motion Picture*, the actress complained of being typecast as foreign sirens and hoped to eventually be cast in "the kind of roles offered to Norma Shearer." Maritza, according to Service, made clear that she did "not particularly admire the schools of Garbo and Dietrich." At the same time, however, the fan magazine writer painted a far from flattering portrait of the newcomer:

> She knows that she has lost her youth. She knows that she has crowded more time into her twenty-two years than is easily digestible. She looks older than she ought to feel.

Maritza actually achieved a "Norma Shearer role" in her second Hollywood film, *Evenings for Sale* (Paramount, 1932). A supposedly sophisticated comedy set in old Vienna, the romance centers on an impoverished count (Herbert Marshall) and the rich girl who considers him nothing but a gigolo. It could have been bright, breezy and flippant had it been directed by, say, an Ernst Lubitsch; in the heavy hands of the pedestrian Stuart Walker, however, *Evenings for Sale* was a rather leaden presentation, brightened only slightly by the presence of such veteran funsters as Mary Boland and Charles Ruggles.

17—Sari Maritza

In February of 1933, Sari Maritza was cast opposite Carole Lombard and Cary Grant in *Dead Reckoning*, a sort of *Grand Hotel* of the high seas. For some reason the film was suddenly recast (with lesser names Neil Hamilton and Shirley Grey) and ignominiously released by the studio's "B" movie department as *Terror Aboard* (Paramount, 1933).*

Maritza experienced some unwanted publicity in April of 1933, when she and her roommate Vivian Gaye were ordered to pay $732 in damages for trashing their apartment. Mrs. Helen Lee Barrie, the owner of their North Harper apartment complex, claimed that "burns, breakage, spots, torn upholstering, etc." eliminated "any suggestion of ordinary care." This otherwise minor court case received hefty coverage by the Hollywood press.

Maritza's life onscreen was not much easier: She was left at the altar by Stuart Erwin (who then went in mad pursuit of Peggy Hopkins Joyce) in *International House* (Paramount, 1933), a completely insane farce starring W. C. Fields and Burns and Allen. With such scene stealers front and center, it was all that Maritza could do just to hang on for the ride. "Measured in laughs," Andre Sennwald of the *New York Times* wrote, "this potpourri of unrelated talents is surprisingly good." It still is surprisingly good (and very, very funny), viewed six and a half decades later, and is the only Sari Maritza film to be regularly shown today.

By mid 1933 it was obvious that Sari Maritza had failed to become a threat to Marlene Dietrich—let alone Greta Garbo—and after having played a conventional ingenue in *A Lady's Profession* (Paramount, 1933), a tepid comedy about bootleggers starring the buxom Alison Skipworth, the studio let her go.

Freelancing, she was the ingenue again opposite Ann Harding in *The Right to Romance* (RKO, 1933) and, according to Mordaunt Hall of the *New York Times*, "appeared to advantage." Hall would not have been quite so kind had he bothered to review Maritza's next film, a little item entitled *Her Secret* (1933).

Produced by the inappropriately named Ideal Pictures Corp., *Her Secret* had Maritza appearing as a naive Georgia girl named, of all things, Waffles. In one scene, Waffles, to earn a few measly dollars to buy her dear old mother a bottle of perfume, does a quaint Southern dance in front of a group of rowdy fraternity brothers. That was about all there was to this cheaply made programmer which, for some reasons (inadequacy?) didn't earn a nationwide release until 1936. Maritza was top-billed along with former silent screen matinee idol Buster Collier and supported by Alan Mowbray and a group of amateur actors from the University of Arizona.

While *Her Secret* remained in limbo, Maritza was again in the headlines, when on May 24, 1934, she was found guilty of negligence in an automobile accident and ordered to pay a Mrs. C. W. Coberly of Wawona, California, $7500 in damages. This was the second time the English actress had been involved in a traffic mishap: In July of 1932 she had been slightly injured when her roadster hit another car in the Hollywood intersection of Gower and Fountain avenues.

October of 1934 brought happier news. On the 18th of that month the *Los Angeles Times* announced the Phoenix, Arizona, wedding of "the glamorous Sari Maritza

---

*Verree Teasdale (see below) inherited Maritza's role as the femme fatale.

Peggy Hopkins Joyce, W. C. Fields, Sari Maritza and Stuart Erwin in *International House* (Paramount, 1933).

and Sam Katz, Metro-Goldwyn-Mayer executive." The romance, it appeared, had been of some three years' duration and had resulted in an "elopement." Among the attendants were Vivian Gaye, Maritza's manager, and Randolph Scott, described as a "Western star and Miss Gaye's boyfriend.* The 42 year old groom was "the Russian-born son of an immigrant barber who had risen from Chicago's ghetto to the front ranks of the nation's showmen." Katz was indeed a top-ranked M-G-M executive and would go on to "supervise" such important films as *Captains Courageous* (1937). Following the nuptials, the couple took the opportunity to announce the bride's retirement from screen acting.

Sari Maritza did indeed retire, but not before having appeared as a Red Cross nurse battling through a low-budget version of World War I in *Crimson Romance* (Mascot, 1934), a melodrama co-starring her with, of all people, Erich von Stroheim. Stroheim's fall from grace since the early 1920s was now complete. "For the first time in my long career," the director of *Greed* and *The Merry Widow* later confessed, "I just acted like an automaton in order to bring home the shekels—and there were very few at that." For Maritza, who presumably appeared in this film for the same reasons, *Crimson Romance* proved an inglorious end to a once promising Hollywood career.

Sari Maritza divorced Sam Katz in May of 1938, claiming that her husband "declined to accompany her on social engagements and informed her that he no longer loved her." She seems to have completely retired from performing. "I don't care for the stage," she had once explained. "I should imagine it would grow terribly tiresome doing the same thing day after day." Instead, she returned to Europe and settled in her mother's native country of Austria. She died in the U.S. Virgin Islands in July of 1987.

Sari Maritza once candidly told a reporter that she couldn't act. Her few films do not belie that statement, but offscreen she seems to have been a colorful personality, typical of the "Continental" vamps imported from Europe to compete with Garbo and Dietrich. But she always fought the label of "mystery woman." "There is no use trying to be something you aren't," she explained. Maybe she should have stayed Patricia Nathan.

SARI MARITZA FILMOGRAPHY

1930: *Bed and Breakfast* (GB†); *Latin Love* (GB).
1931: *No Lady* (GB).
1932: *Water Gipsies [Water Gypsies]* (GB); *Monte Carlo Madness [Bomben auf Monte Carlo]* (Germany); *Forgotten Commandments; Evenings for Sale.*
1933: *A Lady's Profession. International House; Her Secret.*
1934: *Crimson Romance.*

---

*Vivian Gaye would later marry Ernst Lubitsch.

†GB=Great Britain.

18—Natalie Moorhead

"Her appearance is rather diamond-like," *Silver Screen*'s Wick Evans wrote of Natalie Moorhead in 1931, explaining that the *femme fatale*'s blonde beauty gave out "the impression of coldness." Typecast from the word go, Moorhead "slinked" her way through quite a few productions in the early 1930s, usually dressed to the teeth and dropping the odd acid remark here and there. Panther-like, Natalie played socialites and gang molls with the same devastating sense of *haute couture* and could always be counted on to lead a besotted man astray. While reaching a career apex as the conniving mistress who knew too much in *The Thin Man* (M-G-M, 1934), the offscreen Moorhead was once described as possessing "a very warm personality." Luckily, she kept that a secret from her audience and the typical frosty Moorhead performance could usually be counted as the highlight of the otherwise mediocre potboilers, with which she was saddled.

The future screen *femme fatale* was born Nathalia Messner on July 27, 1905, in Pittsburgh, Pennsylvania, and was educated at the Peabody High School there. According to later publicity, she was discovered on a shopping-spree in New York City in the mid–1920s.

"While trying out hats one afternoon her striking beauty attracted the attention of the [shop] owner who gave her an introduction to a friend who was a producer," Wick Evans told the readers of *Silver Screen* in 1931. The introduction led to a small role as a bridesmaid in the long-running hit *Abie's Irish Rose*.

"It wasn't pleasant living on $25 [a week] after I had been used to having everything I wanted," Moorhead would later say of her professional debut, "but I had a lot of pride and I guess I wouldn't trade that experience for anything now."

Moorhead had her first exposure as a trendsetter in George M. Cohan's *The Baby Cyclone*. During the run of the play her marcelled "Baby Cyclone bob" became all the rage and her trademark languid gait, complete with a sexy slouch, was much imitated. Hollywood duly took notice and snapped her up the following year while she was appearing with the Henry Duffy company in a Los Angeles production of *The Best People*.

During her 11 years in Hollywood, Natalie Moorhead never signed a studio contract, opting instead to freelance. As a result, she was rarely out of work but, on the flip side, also never benefited from the careful buildup that only a studio contract could provide. From her first film, *Thru Different Eyes* (Fox, 1929), a courtroom drama starring transition vamp Mary Duncan, Moorhead was pegged as a well-dressed siren. She successfully transferred her trademarks—the slouchy walk and severely marcelled hairdo—to a new, more visual medium. "She wears her hair back because she likes it that way, and because she realizes that it shows off her profile to advantage," Wick Evans explained.

Moorhead was busy in 1930, appearing in 10 films altogether, mostly as the second *femme* lead. Among them was an early run-in with William Powell, *The Benson Murder Case* (Paramount, 1930), a Philo Vance mystery. Draped in furs and dripping with diamonds, Natalie was the obvious suspect in the murder of a millionaire. (But was she indeed the culprit? As in most of her films, Natalie made a very convincing red herring.)

Next, both she and Powell turned up on the wrong side of the law in *Shadows of the Law* (Paramount, 1930), a fast-paced thriller in which she portrayed a blackmailer known as "The Black Widow."

Up until now it had all been very sobering stuff, but Moorhead could also play comedy and proved it with *Hook, Line and Sinker* (RKO, 1930), a typically madcap Wheeler and Woolsey comedy set in a hotel. As a farcical gun moll named Bessie Venessie, she managed to keep up with the low-brow comic team every step of the way.

The year 1931 brought mostly marital dramas with Moorhead playing a slinky home-wrecker or a frigid wife whose husband is "forced" to seek solace elsewhere. In Warners' *Illicit*, for example, Dick (James Rennie) and Anne (Barbara Stanwyck) suddenly find that their marriage has grown stale, whereupon good old Dick promptly starts dallying with Natalie—a sure sign of trouble ahead. In the end, of course, Anne makes Dick see the error of his ways and he cancels a planned trip to Europe with his trampish *inamorata*. As drama *Illicit* wasn't much, but the top-notch cast somehow made the trite situations work.

Moorhead was one of the *Women Men Marry* (1931) but inevitably get rid of, in a low-budget indie production that gave her second billing to Sally Blane. As Dolly Moulton, she played a married schemer who leads a naive newlywed (Blane) astray by introducing her to wealthy men. By the end of the film, Dolly's husband (Kenneth Harlan) is so fed up with her behavior that he takes a shot at her; luckily for Natalie, he proves as miserable a marksman as he is a husband. As this brief synopsis suggests, *Women Men Marry* was not exactly erudite or sophisticated filmmaking; the programmer, in fact, boasted a scenario that *Variety* termed "incredibly stupid."

Despite being firmly established as a villainess, Moorhead accepted her place in the Hollywood firmament with grace. "She doesn't care particularly for the screen roles she usually plays," Wick Evans of *Silver Screen* explained, "but prefers a 'heavy' part to more sympathetic ones that do not give her the chance to express herself."

More often than not, unfortunately, those kind of roles were in the supporting category and Moorhead usually had to rely on very few scenes in which to express herself.

The Menace (Columbia, 1932), a whodunit in which she played a wicked stepmother, is a good example. As Caroline Quayle she murders her elderly husband for his fortune and manages to frame her young stepson (Walter Byron) in the bargain. In due course, the clearly innocent youngster escapes from prison, alters his appearance by means of plastic surgery, and heroically returns to unmask the real killer and her conniving brother (William Davidson). Although fourth-billed, Moorhead still had enough good scenes in this programmer to upstage the ingenue, a very young Bette Davis!

Natalie Moorhead was given star billing for the first time in yet another Poverty Row mystery, *Discarded Lovers* (Tower Productions, 1932). As famous screen star Irma Gladden, she is observed having affairs with two men more or less at the same time, is harassed by several estranged husbands, receives threatening letters from her director's jealous wife, and has recently had to fire her chauffeur for theft. Needless to say, when the lady is found murdered in her automobile, suspects abound. The culprit, as it turns out, is a spurned screenwriter (Jason Robards). It was all very low rent, but at least Moorhead photographed well: "Miss Moorhead, who got the right side of the cameraman in this picture, looks well and does the almost inevitable strip for the customers," *Variety* observed.

Natalie, alas, did not always get on the right side of the cameraman. Although her striking appearance usually worked to her advantage, once in a while, when not lit properly, she would photograph ghostly. "Miss Moorhead uses too light a make-up, and in most scenes suggests she has been put in through double exposure," *Variety*'s anonymous reviewer, surveying *Love Bound* (Peerless, 1932), complained.

Moorhead was top-billed again in *Love Bound* and was once more cast as a malicious actress, this time blackmailing her married sugar daddy (Montagu Love) by threatening to tell his wife (silent screen star Clara Kimball Young) of their affair. In the middle of all this there is a former lover who wants in on the blackmail scheme, whereupon Natalie exercises extremely bad judgment by falling in love with her victim's handsome son (Jack Mulhall). Distributed on a states rights basis, *Love Bound* found very few takers.

In surveying these low-budget programmers, many critics found Moorhead to be the only tolerable ingredient. Of *The Fighting Gentleman* (Monarch, 1932), a poor drama about a mechanic with dreams of becoming a boxing champ, *Variety* discovered very little to admire—except Natalie's gusto: the "yarn is slow in starting with nothing happening until Miss Moorhead starts vamping [William] Collier, Jr. with the technique of Theda Bara," the reviewer observed.

Then 1933 brought more of the same: supporting roles (usually selfish wives) in "A" productions (or the lesser variety colloquially known as "nervous A's"), and leads in independently produced programmers. She was the victim of a charlatan (Warren William) in *The Mind Reader* (First National, 1933); Tully Marshall's easily corrupted daughter in *Corruption* (Imperial, 1933); Mathew Betz's sinister mistress in *The Big Chance* (Eagle Pictures, 1933), yet another boxing melodrama; one of the suspects in *Curtain at Eight* (Majestic, 1933), a backstage whodunit; and a "B" girl in *Only Yesterday* (Universal, 1933), the tearjerker that introduced Margaret Sullavan to the screen.

Theodore von Eltz and Natalie Moorhead in *Gigolettes of Paris* **(Equitable, 1933) (photograph courtesy of the Danish Film Museum).**

    Despite her busy schedule, Moorhead's career was already thought to be in decline when she was cast as the secretary Julia Wolf in M-G-M's splendid version of Dashiell Hammett's popular mystery *The Thin Man* (1934). As usual, she made everything she could of her few scenes. Not that anyone could miss her presence: Julia Wolf is the catalyst for the action—her murder is the whodunit's first puzzle. That she is more to her boss, the inventor Clyde Wynant (Edward Ellis), than a mere secretary is cleverly disclosed in the rapid-fire dialog. When the inventor (nicknamed "The Thin Man") interrupts her having a *tête-à-tête* with another man, Julia has a ready answer: "He isn't anybody," she purrs reassuringly, "just a fellow I used to know." "I thought you had given up that sort of 'friend,'" Wynant replies with disdain.

    The Thin Man, of course, was the detective comedy that made marriage look like fun—especially if it was pleasantly soaked in martinis. The teaming of William Powell and Myrna Loy as detectives Nick and Nora Charles was inspirational and the team was greatly helped by W. S. "Woody" Van Dyke's economical direction and a well-chosen supporting cast. But what made this quickly made programmer* so

---

*It was produced in little over two weeks—somewhat of a record for posh M-G-M.

Natalie Moorhead, Dorothy Short and Russell Hayden in *Heart of Arizona* (Paramount, 1938) (photograph courtesy of Janus Barfoed).

engaging, even when viewed with today's "political correctness," is the witty dialog provided by the husband and wife team of Albert Hackett and Frances Goodrich. ("What's that man doing in my drawers?" Loy inquires of a startled Powell at one point, when their domestic bliss is rudely interrupted by a police search.)

Despite its hurried production schedule, *The Thin Man* went on to earn four Academy Award nominations and was one of the 10 top-grossing successes of 1934. One of the few Moorhead films still to be shown regularly, its enduring popularity has made her a minor cult figure.

Moorhead appeared in several other whodunits in 1934—but in much less exalted company. She had an unusually sympathetic role in *Fifteen Wives* (Invincible, 1934), a thriller about the murder of a bigamist. As had become the rule regarding these pedestrian potboilers, Natalie was the only participant to receive any kind of praise. "Only three of the women are shown," *Variety*'s "Shan" wrote of *Fifteen Wives*, "and of the trio only Natalie Moorhead plays convincingly."

Natalie Moorhead was widowed in 1936 when her husband of six years, veteran director Alan Crosland, was killed in an automobile accident.* Her career had come to

---

Crosland, a major silent screen director, had put the struggling Warner Bros. on the map with the groundbreaking The Jazz Singer *(1927).*

a complete standstill, and in 1937 she filed a voluntary petition for bankruptcy. Forced to earn a living she returned to the screen in *King of Gamblers* (Paramount, 1937), but it was a mere walk-on. More followed, mostly at M-G-M, a studio known for hiring former "names" and offering them bit parts. She also appeared as, of all things, a demure Belle Starr in a Hopalong Cassidy program Western, *Heart of Arizona* (Paramount, 1938).

There were a couple of important pictures in 1939-1940, Moorhead's last year on screen, but one has to avoid blinking in order not to miss her. In the all-star *The Women* (M-G-M, 1939), she can be glimpsed as a customer in a fashion salon; and in *All This and Heaven Too* (Warner Bros., 1940), a Bette Davis romance, she and character actresses Mary Forbes and Georgia Caine were simply listed in the huge cast as "ladies." Her final screen appearance was a walk-on in *Margie* (Universal, 1940).

In 1942, Moorhead married former Chicago parks commissioner Robert J. Dunham, but was widowed for a second time in 1949. In the early 1950s she was reintroduced to Juan de Garchi Torena, a South American diplomat who, as Juan Torena, had enjoyed an erratic Hollywood acting career stretching from *The Gay Caballero* in 1932 to *Jeopardy* in 1953. The couple had first met 20 years earlier when working for the same studio. On July 27, 1957, Natalie Moorhead became Mrs. de Garchi Torena.

The de Garchi Torenas eventually settled away from Hollywood, in Montecito, California, an upscale suburb of Santa Barbara. Interviewed in her home in the early 1980s by author James Watters, Natalie Moorhead acknowledged that she had retired "with only few regrets." "Our life has been so rich in so many ways that the acting was only part of our happiness," the former screen *femme fatale* explained. The de Garchi Torenas were still living in Montecito when Natalie Moorhead died on October 13, 1992.

NATALIE MOORHEAD FILMOGRAPHY

1929: *Thru Different Eyes; The Girl from Havana; The Unholy Night.*
1930: *The Benson Murder Case; The Furies; Runaway Bride; Shadow of the Law; Manslaughter; The Office Wife; Hot Curves; Ladies Must Play; Spring Is Here; Hook, Line and Sinker.*
1931: *Illicit; Parlor, Bedroom and Bath; My Past; Dance, Fools, Dance; The Phantom of Paris; Women Men Marry; Morals for Women; The Deceiver; Maker of Men; Strictly Dishonorable.*
1932: *Three Wise Girls; Discarded Lovers; The Menace; Cross Examination; Love Bound; The Stoker; The King Murder; Pack Up Your Troubles; The Fighting Gentleman.*
1933: *Forgotten; The Mind Reader; Corruption; Private Detective 62; Dance Hall Hostess; The Big Chance; Curtain at Eight; Gigolettes of Paris; Secret Sinners; Only Yesterday.*
1934: *Long Lost Father; Dancing Man; The Thin Man; Fifteen Wives; The Curtain Falls.*
1936: *What Becomes of the Children? Two in a Crowd; 15 Maiden Lane.*

1937: *King of Gamblers; Torchy Blane, the Adventurous Blonde.*
1938: *The Beloved Brat; Heart of Arizona; Letter of Introduction.*
1939: *When Tomorrow Comes; Lady of the Tropics; The Women.*
1940: *Flight Angels; I Take This Woman; I Want a Divorce; Margie.*

19 — Esther Muir

"Closer, hold me closer," the Amazonian Esther Muir whispers seductively. "If I hold you any closer, I'll be in back of you," quips the eminent Dr. Hackenbush (Groucho Marx).

This amusing repartee comes from M-G-M's *A Day at the Races* (1937), the film for which Muir will always be remembered. Esther was the typical statuesque 1930s vamp, but with one difference: a keen sense of humor. And that sense came in handy—having to fend off the amorous advances of all three Marx Brothers, and, before them, Wheeler and Woolsey. Despite her success as the aggressive Flo, Hollywood rarely appreciated Muir for the expert comedienne she obviously was. All too often she was cast as your garden variety bitch—with nary a smile in sight. Sadly, *A Day at the Races*, while it has kept her name alive, did little for her career at the time. By the end of the decade she was down to bits and walk-ons and retired from the screen all too early in 1942. Still, Esther Muir remains one of our favorite *femmes fatales*.

She was born on March 1, 1907,* in Andes, New York. Following high school she was all set to attend Vassar on a scholarship but had to forgo the chance when her father suddenly died. Instead, she shocked everybody by leaving for New York City with hopes of a theatrical career. She proved all the naysayers wrong when she made her debut in the chorus of the *Greenwich Village Follies*. Muir quickly discovered her gift for comedy and went on to appear as a foil for Charlie Ruggles in two hit shows: *Mr. Battling Butler* (1923) and *Queen High* (1926). A starring role in the farce *His Girl Friday* (1929) eventually brought her to the attention of Hollywood.

For Muir, 1931 was a rather momentous year. She made her screen debut and married dance director Busby Berkeley. The union, it seems, was doomed from the start and lasted less than a year. Berkeley, Muir later explained, was "a lovely person but a real mama's boy." Most of the time she was "more his keeper than his wife."

On screen Muir played a jewel thief and a murderess in *A Dangerous Affair*

*The date does not quite make a "scholarship to Vassar" by the early 1920s seem likely.

(Columbia, 1931), a comedy mystery starring Jack Holt and Sally Blane. As Peggy Randolph, a kind of low-rent Mae West, she is not above using men (her husband and a crooked lawyer among them) to get what she wants, and the role, albeit small, would forever typecast her as a wisecracking vixen.

With marriage and divorce taking up most of her time, Muir did not return to the screen until 1933. She came back with a vengeance, however, appearing in 11 films for 10 different companies in 1933 alone. *So This Is Africa* (Columbia, 1933) introduced her to outright farce (*A Dangerous Affair* had, at best, been a black comedy). As Mrs. Johnson-Martini she was the rather unlikely director of a film expedition into darkest Africa. Once there, the company, which included the zany Bert Wheeler and Robert Woolsey, encounters a group of warring Amazon women lead by the fetching Raquel Torres. It was of course, all quite insane and flirted precariously with satire. Muir's role, it was whispered, was a take-off of real life explorer and filmmaker Osa Johnson, and Mordaunt Hall of the *New York Times* found her looking "quite attractive in her hunting costume."

Insanity also reigned over *Sailor's Luck* (Fox, 1933) an ethnic farce in which she had the opportunity to break a number of chairs over the heads of comedians Sammy Cohen and Frank Moran. A host of colorful bit parts followed as Muir turned up as a gun moll in a minor crime drama, *The Woman Who Dared* (William Berke, 1933); as Lilyan Tashman's wisecracking friend in *Wine, Women and Song* (Chadwick, 1933); and as a salesgirl in a drama about the building of a department store empire, *Sweepings* (RKO, 1933). She played tarts in *I Love That Man* (Paramount, 1933) and *The Bowery* (Fox, 1933); was a jailbird mother who returns to claim her "adopted" son in *Hell and High Water* (Paramount, 1933); and appeared as one of the "mail-order" brides (named, of course, Flo) in the cheap *Picture Brides* (Allied, 1933).

Muir achieved third-billing after Lola Lane and William Collier, Jr., in *Public Stenographer* (Screencraft, 1933), appearing as a typical 1930s dame—"fast-talking and quick to crack wise"—and was, according to *Variety*, "good for a couple of laughs from her blunt dialog."

Except for bit parts in *The Party's Over* (Columbia, 1934) and *Unknown Blonde* (Majestic, 1934), Muir was off the screen for most of 1934, having suffered a fall from a horse. The accident had happened on the set of a Kay Francis picture, *Dr. Monica* and was severe enough for Warner Bros. to replace her with George Raft's girlfriend Virginia Pine. During her convalescence Muir married lyricist Sam Coslow ("Cocktails for Two").

Muir returned to the screen in late 1934 and continued to do colorful walk-ons throughout 1935 and 1936. She turned up, for example, as Akim Tamiroff's tough looking wife in *The Gay Deception* (Fox, 1935); was Leon Errol's daffy girlfriend in *Coronado* (Fox, 1935); and did her gun moll routine in *The First Baby* (20th Century-Fox, 1936). After that, she briefly vamped Spencer Tracy in a night club scene in *Fury* (1936), the first of many films she did under a stock contract with M-G-M. She was briefly seen as a temperamental actress in the gigantic *The Great Ziegfeld* (M-G-M, 1936).

In mid-1936, M-G-M cast Esther Muir as Flo Marlowe, the scheming blonde in *A Day at the Races* (1937). Fully realizing that the Marx Brothers comedy was honed

19—Esther Muir

Groucho Marx and Esther Muir in *A Day at the Races* (M-G-M, 1937).

by trial and error, M-G-M chief of production Irving Thalberg set a precedent by sending the entire cast on a nationwide vaudeville tour. It was a fortunate move, for by the time filming began, Esther felt completely comfortable with the zany brothers' special brand of fast-paced, physical comedy.

A Day at the Races is a slapdash farce about a sanitarium, the crooks who aim to take it over, and a racehorse. It is all quite absurd, of course, and only meant as a framework for the Marxes' furious antics. When the eminent horse doctor Hugo Z. Hackenbush (Groucho), first spots the flirtatious Flo (Muir), he and wealthy Mrs. Upjohn (Margaret Dumont, naturally) are enjoying a spectacular Busby Berkeley–like production number (featuring specialty dancer Vivian Fay). "Isn't it beautiful!" Mrs. Upjohn exclaims. "The prettiest number I've ever seen," Groucho answers, leering at Flo.

Flo, as it turns out, is in cahoots with the crooked Whitmore (Leonard Ceeley) who wants her to frame the pesky Hackenbush. The plan is for her to get him in a compromising position in front of his benefactor, the lovesick Mrs. Upjohn. "When you knock on the door," Flo promises the worried Whitmore, "I'll have that moth-eaten Romeo playing the balcony scene!"

Needless to say, the seduction of Dr. Hackenbush does not go quite as planned. Chico and Harpo, wise to the situation, keep interrupting the *tête-à-tête* wearing a multitude of disguises and excuses and at times Flo (or is it Muir herself?) must fight not to lose it completely; it is one of the brothers' funniest bits and concludes with the sidekicks, now pretending to be house painters, wallpapering both Hackenbush and Flo, thus hiding them from the fast approaching Mrs. Upjohn.

Esther Muir worked so well with the Marx Brothers that it seems a pity they were never teamed again. In private life, however, she enjoyed a lasting friendship with the comedians.

Following her success in *A Day at the Races*, Muir returned to small roles in mostly indifferent productions. She was reunited with Wheeler and Woolsey (who certainly were no Marx Brothers) in *On Again—Off Again* (RKO, 1937); briefly appeared as a temperamental prima donna in a melodious but dull operetta starring Gladys Swarthout, *Romance in the Dark* (Paramount, 1938); and portrayed a character bearing the delightful name of Opal Updyke in *Battle of Broadway* (Fox, 1938), a backstage comedy with Victor McLaglen and Louise Hovick (Gypsy Rose Lee). Cast against type for a change, she showed versatility by playing a drab German *Hausfrau* in *Three Comrades* (M-G-M, 1938), a poignant tale of German youth during the early years of Nazism.

By the late 1920s, Muir would increasingly be found on Poverty Row playing lusty vamps in program Westerns such as *The Law West of Tombstone* (RKO, 1938) with Harry Carey, and *Western Jamboree* (Republic, 1938) with Gene Autry. There were several ultra low-budget indies and by the time of *Misbehaving Husbands* (PRC, 1941), she seemed to be sleepwalking through her assignments. In *Misbehaving Husbands* she actually had the female lead (opposite Ralph "Dick Tracy" Byrd), but the potboiler was geared to promote the comebacks of two former silent screen stars, Harry Langdon and Betty Blythe.

Esther Muir retired from the screen following a small supporting role in the crime drama *X Marks the Spot* (Republic, 1942). Instead, she concentrated on family life, with an occasional detour to the stage thrown in just to stay in shape. Divorcing Sam Coslow in 1947, Muir ventured into real estate. She retired a wealthy woman, owning homes in Green Valley, Arizona, San Dimas, California, and a summer residence in Kyparissi, Greece. Her daughter Jacqueline is married to television actor Ted Sorel and made Esther a grandmother twice. Esther Muir died in Mount Kisco, New York, August 1, 1995.

Esther Muir Filmography

1931: *A Dangerous Affair.*
1933: *So This Is Africa; Sailor's Luck; Wine, Women and Song; Sweepings; I Love That Man; The Bowery; Hell and High Water; Picture Brides; Public Stenographer; The Woman Who Dared.*
1934: *Unknown Blonde; The Party's Over; Caravan.*
1935: *The Gilded Lily; The Gay Deception; Here's to Romance; Racing Luck; Coronado.*

1936: *The First Baby; Fury; The Great Ziegfeld.*
1937: *High Hat; A Day at the Races; On Again—Off Again; I'll Take Romance; Love on Toast; Under Suspicion.*
1938: *City Girl; Romance in the Dark; Battle of Broadway; Three Comrades; The Toy Wife; The Law West of Tombstone; Western Jamboree; The Sunset Strip Case.*
1939: *The Girl and the Gambler; The Story of Vernon and Irene Castle.*
1940: *Misbehaving Husbands.*
1941: *Honky Tonk; Stolen Paradise.*
1942: *The Mayor of 44th Street; X Marks the Spot.*

20 — Ona Munson

The 1930s, the decade that earlier had ushered in Joan Crawford as Sadie Thompson in *Rain* (United Artists, 1932), ended with Ona Munson playing the most famous prostitute of them all: Belle Watling in *Gone with the Wind* (M-G-M, 1939). Belle, of course, as opposed to Sadie, was a whore with a heart of gold; in fact, she was *the* whore with a heart of gold. Yet, she was a loose woman and with the strict moral codes governing genteel society—in post–Civil War Atlanta as well as pre–World War II Hollywood—she found herself ostracized. Even in real life, as it turned out. Ona Munson remembered a reception given by the Atlanta Junior League in honor of the film's world premiere in that city. "The girls were very cordial to Miss [Vivien] Leigh, Mr. [Clark] Gable and Miss [Olivia] De Havilland but I found myself ignored for some reason," she wrote.

> After a while I discovered that they actually associated me with the character (which had been a real live one in Atlanta) and they were very hesitant about being photographed with me or seen talking to me. We finally got the little matter straightened out and the President of the Junior League wrote me a note of apology.

To many, Munson *was* Belle Watling—a testament to her fine performance—and the role pigeon-holed the actress who had come to films from musical comedy. "When the picture was released," she would later write, "I received a great deal of praise for my work, but it also proved to be somewhat of a boomerang." Her post–*GWTW* career proved fraught with whores of all sorts, culminating in the absurd Mother Gin Sling (Hollywood's more dignified version of Broadway's famous whore monger Mother Goddam), the blackmailing casino proprietress of *The Shanghai Gesture* (United Artists, 1941).

She was born Ona Wolcott on June 16, 1908, in Portland, Oregon, and was, she later wrote, destined to become a performer: "I was born to dance, and jiggled to music before I could even walk." That, despite the fact that the Wolcott family had no show business background (her father was a real estate agent). Mrs. Wolcott, however, was the typical stage mother and little Ona took dancing lessons from the age of four. "I went to a private school and my after hours were consumed with lessons. A private tutor for French, piano lessons, horseback, swimming, etc.," Munson remembered.

To assure success, Mrs. Wolcott brought Ona to New York City in 1920, hoping to launch her talented daughter on a stage career. Mother and daughter took up residence in a hotel on 103rd Street and Ona began "serious ballet training under a Russian ballet master and studied solidly for a year." The tutoring was interrupted, however, by Gus Edwards, who wanted her for one of his kiddie shows. Mrs. Wolcott dropped her lofty pretensions and Ona made her professional debut in *The Song Revue* (1922). The show was later revamped and played for 52 weeks on the Orpheum circuit. At the finish of the tour, mother and daughter went off to Europe, where Ona continued her schooling.

Returning to New York in 1926, Ona Munson's professional career took a dramatic turn in the right direction when she replaced Louise Groody in the title role of the musical comedy hit *No, No, Nanette*—"delighting," she later said, "numerous audiences and myself doing 'Tea for Two' and 'I Want to Be Happy' over and over again." In July of 1926, the busy actress took time out to marry Edward H. Buzzell, a former actor turned film director.*

From *No, No, Nanette*, the new Mrs. Buzzell went directly into *Twinkle, Twinkle* with Joe E. Brown, followed by George White's *Manhattan Lady* with Ed Wynn and *Hold Everything* with Bert Lahr and Victor Moore. The latter show, in which she sang "You're the Cream in My Coffee" and of which she later claimed to have owned 25 percent, was another smash hit and ran for a year and a half.

With sound now firmly established in Hollywood, Munson was quick to sign a contract with Warner Bros., making her screen debut opposite Joe E. Brown in *Going Wild* (1930), a pedestrian farce about a newspaperman mistaken for a famous aviator. Unfortunately, all she was asked to do in this and her following two assignments, *The Hot Heiress* and *Broadminded* (both First National, 1931), was decorate the background while the studio's second-tier comedians, Brown, Ben Lyon et al., took center stage.

Discouraged, she demanded dramatic roles, and lo and behold, the studio answered by casting her as a callous reporter in *Five Star Final* (First National, 1931), a hard-hitting newspaper yarn starring Edward G. Robinson. The role had some good lines ("I rode uptown in a taxi with him," she says, referring to a pervert played by a pre–*Frankenstein* Boris Karloff, "and I haven't any skin left on my knees"), and she received favorable reviews.

Alas, it was too little, too late; Munson, who had commenced studying with the veteran Laura Hope Crews, found Hollywood a decided comedown after Broadway, and with a newfound taste for high drama she returned to the stage. She appeared in

---

Born in 1897, Eddie Buzzell had abandoned acting in 1930 to become a director of lightweight screen fare, e.g. Hollywood Speaks *(1932),* The Girl Friend *(1935),* At the Circus *(1939), and* Best Foot Forward *(1943). He and Miss Munson divorced in January of 1931.*

Opposite: **Ona Munson, date unknown.**

two West Coast productions opposite Crews, *As Husbands Go* and *The Silver Cord*. Next, she did a season with the National Theater in Washington, D.C., toured with the William Brady Stock Company, and returned to Broadway opposite Dennis King in *Petticoat Fever* (1933).

In between her scores of stage engagements, Munson began a long career in radio. "As usual, along with everything else, I started this the hard way," she later wrote. "I liked the medium very much and realized its possibilities so I began to add other programs in which I could play characters." At the height of her radio activity, Munson was doing an average of 12 programs a week, including *Rich Man's Darling, David Harum, Cavalcade of America, March of Time,* and *Manhattan Merry-Go-Round.*

By 1935, Ona Munson had returned to Broadway and her first love, musical comedy. She starred opposite Joe Cook in *Hold Your Horses* at the Winter Garden, and supported British song-and-dance man Jack Buchanan in George Gershwin's *Pardon My English*.

Drama, however, was still first on her mind and in 1936 she appeared as Regina opposite Nazimova in a highly successful revival of Henrik Ibsen's *Ghost* staged at Broadway's Empire Theater. It was, in a way, a rebirth in serious drama for the actress and Hollywood paid attention. How much, was demonstrated when a talent scout from M-G-M convinced her to abandon a proposed stint in summer stock in order to give the screen another try.

As Munson tells it, her return to Hollywood was a complete waste. "I was placed under a six months' contract, made numerous tests and *sat*, along with Hedy Lamarr, Greer Garson, Ilona Massey and Ruth Hussey waiting for someone to give us something to do," she wrote in 1942. In actuality, M-G-M *did* put her to work, but considering the quality of the material, it is no wonder she chose forgetfulness: On loan-out to Universal, she played second fiddle to buxom Marion Martin in *His Exciting Night* (1938), which was not at all exciting; and her home studio completely wasted her as one of the students in *Dramatic School* (1938), a dreary melodrama that Luise Rainer certainly couldn't save.

That M-G-M squandered a veteran trouper like Ona Munson on such drivel was, however, par for the course. Realizing that her future still lay on Broadway, the actress asked for a release from her contract and returned to New York.

Although Munson had given up on Hollywood, Hollywood refused to let go of her. Soon after her return to New York, her agent called attention to the frantic search for an actress to play the prostitute Belle Watling in the screen version of Margaret Mitchell's enormously popular Civil War epic *Gone with the Wind*.

David O. Selznick's tumultuous search for the perfect Scarlett O'Hara has, of course, become Hollywood lore. Less remembered today is the likewise highly publicized casting of the supporting players, first among them Belle Watling, the careworn proprietress of Atlanta's house of ill repute whose kindness towards Vivien Leigh's Scarlett O'Hara is mightily rebuffed. Such disparate Hollywood vamps as Evelyn Brent, Estelle Taylor, Joyce Compton and Eve Arden vied for the role, but there was no clear favorite. As it turned out, Ona Munson ended the search, although that was not at all a certainty when she, "with great reluctance and complete dubiousness," returned to Hollywood.

Ona Munson in *Gone with the Wind* (M-G-M, 1939).

I felt certain the search would end with a big name [she later wrote]. Of course, had I read the book at this time I would have flown back and *fought* for the opportunity of portraying this character, but having been completely bored with the attendant publicity I merely decided to wait and see the picture.

Her agent, who would not take no for an answer, arranged a meeting with the film's producer, the illustrious, but overworked David O. Selznick. Preparing for the important meeting, Munson tried to dress like the character, even to the point of wearing platform shoes since the character was described as being tall. The metamorphosis, however, proved to be the bright red wig that all the Watling aspirants were given to wear. Wrote Munson in 1942,

> I really give that wig full credit for my doing Belle Watling—it completely changed the contours of my face, making it much broader and giving the robust quality the character needed. A steady stream of girls had had that same wig on and yet it did different things to all of them. It made some of them look like duchesses, others too tough, some too severe, etc. I walked into Mr. Selznick's office thus arrayed and he didn't even recognize me the change had been so complete. At this time they had already been shooting for quite a few weeks and without even a test I went to work the next day.

The rest, as they say, is history. Despite the huge cast vying for attention, Munson's performance stands out for the grace and warmth she gave an otherwise stereotypical character. With director Victor Fleming's attention occupied by the insecure Vivien Leigh and the sheer scope of his undertaking, Munson was pretty much left alone and her command is manifest in every scene. To Munson alone belongs the credit for making Belle Watling memorable.

Concurrent with her sporadic work on the endless *Gone with the Wind*, the busy actress starred opposite Edward G. Robinson on radio's *Big Town*. In the end, it was her success in this and other radio series that rescued her surprisingly anemic career. Playing Belle Watling had not suddenly elevated her to stardom and she languished in such potboilers as *Legion of Lost Flyers* (Universal, 1939), *Scandal Sheet* (Columbia, 1939), and *Big Guy* (Universal, 1939).

None of these mostly male-oriented action melodramas was worth her while, and Munson actually debated whether to return East, when a chance meeting with Herbert I. Yates of Republic Pictures suddenly changed her mind and the direction of her career.

Republic Pictures, a small San Fernando Valley company known mainly for their Westerns and serials, engaged Munson to pinch-hit for an ailing Claire Trevor at the Lawrence, Kansas, premiere of the Western *Dark Command* (Republic, 1940). Also attending was Republic's president, Herbert Yates. Remembered Munson two years later,

> On seeing me for the first time he [Yates] was so bowled over by the fact that my off-screen appearance was the antithesis to the illusion I created as Belle Watling, that he decided I could do anything and put me under contract then and there for three pictures a year.

Munson's first assignment for Republic, attempting to lure Chester Morris away from Anita Louise in *Wagons Westward* (1940), was negligible at best (although it did feature veteran Western star Buck Jones as the *villain!*), but in *Lady from Louisiana* (Republic, 1941) she starred opposite John Wayne as a conniving Southern girl with ideas of her own, not unlike Scarlett O'Hara.

Breaking with long observed tradition, Republic had spared no expense filming *Lady from Louisiana*, and the result was a sprawling tale of sin and redemption in the Deep South, complete with impressive special effects. For her own part, Munson felt that "the picture gave me an opportunity of being seen on the screen in my own true size."

Then 20th Century–Fox took notice and cast Munson as yet another hooker with a heart of gold, this time working the Alaskan lumber camps, in *Wild Geese Calling* (1941). While filming the robust melodrama, she was cast by veteran director Josef von Sternberg as Mother Goddam in the screen version of *The Shanghai Gesture*.

"When he first called my agent with that purpose in mind, I took the whole thing as a huge joke, never believing for one moment that he was serious," the actress later remembered.

> In fact, I thought he was having a little fun at Belle Watling's expense. It so happened that I was in the midst of another picture at the time, playing another "Belle" up in Alaska, when suddenly the calls (from Mr. von S.) began coming in with alarming frequency.

Munson managed to get time off to meet with von Sternberg and, as she had done earlier for David Selznick, endeavored to arrive in character—this time completing the tacky ensemble with a blond wig. Certain that the director had mistaken her for someone else, Munson had little faith in the meeting and was ill prepared for von Sternberg's enthusiasm.

> With utter disregard of my appearance his first words were, "You have simply *got* to do this part for me or I can't do the picture!" I dared not laugh now as I realized the deadly seriousness of the man. An incredulous "why?" was all I could muster forth in an answer, which was followed by an equally incredulous series of statements by Mr. von S., such as "This character is a cold and cynical woman which is why I want the softness and warmth of your personality. She is black haired with mobility of face, but I must have your blonde quality under a black wig and that immobile face which is so distinctly yours."

Based on a racy 1925 play by John Colton, *The Shanghai Gesture* is the melodramatic story of a white girl who is raised in a Chinese brothel by a madam. Of course, with typical melodramatic flair, the whore turns out to be the girl's long-lost mother.

The material was prime von Sternberg and could have made a classic erotic vehicle for Marlene Dietrich, had it not been too risqué even for the team that brought to the screen the somewhat similar *Shanghai Express* (Paramount, 1932). Censorship was, if anything, more stringent in 1941 than ever before and, in order to even contemplate a film version, von Sternberg had to change the locale from a brothel to a gambling casino and the lead character from Madam Goddam to the less profane Mother Gin Sling.

With those adjustments, unfortunately, the story lost most of its potency and *The Shanghai Gesture* (United Artists, 1941), despite von Sternberg's visual brilliance, proved a failure. ("The most gosh-awful piece of boredom that has come out of Hollywood in 20 years!" the *New York Daily News* remarked.) For Munson, new to von Sternberg's Svengali-like approach to filmmaking, the experience was the most exciting of her career. "I hardly knew whether I was having a fantastic dream or a horrible nightmare," she would later say. According to reviews, however, her efforts were somewhat in vain. "Ona Munson," wrote Bosley Crowther of the *New York Times*, "looks like an alabaster statue and acts like a gunman's moll."

The failure of *The Shanghai Gesture* seems to have disillusioned the actress, who returned to the screen only infrequently thereafter, busying herself instead with radio work. She starred in a silly jungle adventure, *Drums of the Congo* (Universal, 1942), which was so bad it kept her away from Hollywood for three years.

Ever on the lookout for somebody they could get on cheap, Republic lured Munson back to Hollywood in 1945, but all the studio could offer were supporting roles in *Cheaters*, a vapid comedy with Billie Burke, and *Dakota*, a mild Western starring John Wayne and Herbert Yates' newest "find" (and later wife), figure skater Vera Hruba Ralston. Two years elapsed before *The Red House* (United Artists, 1947), an atmospheric thriller starring her old friend Edward G. Robinson. Munson's role, however, was minuscule, and the film proved to be her last.

In 1949, semi-retired and living in Beverly Hills, Ona Munson took her third husband,* artist and designer Eugene Berman. She returned to the stage for the final time in 1951, supporting Helen Gahagan in a revival of *Kind Lady*. After that, she retired permanently.

There was no happy end for this, the most misused of Hollywood vamps: For years suffering from a mental disorder, Ona Munson committed suicide by overdosing on sleeping pills in her New York City apartment on February 11, 1955. She was found by her husband and left a note, "This is the only way I know to be free again.... Please don't follow me."

In an article for *Silver Screen* in 1941, Ona Munson had counted the 10 worst enemies of any actress. "Off hand," she had said, "I'd name Poor Pictures, Bad Publicity and Scandal,† Conceited Temperament, Losing Sense of Humor, Carousing, Putting on Front, Fair-Weather Friends, Obesity, and Middle Age." The greatest of these, she added, "seems to be Poor Pictures." With the notable exception of *Gone with the Wind*, it certainly was in Ona Munson's case.

ONA MUNSON FILMOGRAPHY

1930: *Going Wild*.
1931: *The Hot Heiress; Broadminded; Five Star Final*.
1938: *Dramatic School; His Exciting Night*.
1939: *Scandal Sheet; The Legion of Lost Flyers; The Big Guy; Gone with the Wind*.
1940: *Wagons Westward*.
1941: *Lady from Louisiana; Wild Geese Calling; The Shanghai Gesture*.
1942: *Drums of the Congo*.
1943: *Idaho*.
1945: *The Cheaters; Dakota*.
1947: *The Red House*.

---

*A second marriage to Stewart McDonald had proved short-lived.

†Munson dodged rumors of lesbianism her entire career. According to a new biography on Nazimova, the rumors were apparently based on some fact.

21—Vivienne Osborne

"Vivienne Osborne is a chameleon," her publicity read, "only far more vivid—physically and temperamentally—that's why she plays good-bad girls with such realism—and why she can separate the two and be sweetly romantic, or powerfully romantic, or just bad all over."

Truth be told, Vivienne Osborne was never very romantic. Dark-eyed and seething with passion, she played an aging French vamp trying to seduce the quietly befuddled Charlie Ruggles in *Wives Never Know* (Paramount, 1936). Of course, that was a comedy and her broad interpretation of a seductive *femme fatale* was at least good for a chuckle or two. It was an entirely different matter when she played it straight—such as in *Supernatural* (Paramount, 1933), where she is an executed murderess whose spirit takes over the body of Carole Lombard. The laughs here are unintentional and the film an embarrassment to Lombard, who had begged the studio to forget the whole thing. Carole, of course, went on to better things, but Osborne remained stuck in potboilers, trapped, one might say, like her anguished spirit in *Supernatural*.

Vivienne Osborne was born on December 10, 1896, in Des Moines, Iowa, the daughter of a wealthy rancher. A child prodigy of sorts, she went on stage at the age of five and as a teenager appeared for five years with a stock company in Spokane, Washington. In 1917 she toured extensively with a production of the old barnstormer *East Lynne* and starred the following year in *Dollars and Sense* at the Belasco Theater in Seattle, Washington. She made her New York bow in December of 1919, appearing in *The Whirlwind* at the Standard Theater.

Osborne was lured into making her screen debut opposite Joseph Marquis in *The Gray Brother* (MacManus Films, 1919), a message picture calling for more humane treatment of prisoners. Marquis played a good and decent boy innocently found guilty of some crime or another and sent to jail and Vivienne was his devoted sweetheart, patiently awaiting his release. A low-budget independent item, *The Gray Brother* never found a distributor and was withdrawn. (It was later released, in a truncated form, as *The Right Way*.)

While featured on Broadway in the comedy *The Bone Head* (1920), Osborne found time to appear in four films, only two of which had any merit: *The Restless Sex*, a Marion Davies comedy from Cosmopolitan, and *Over the Hill to the Poorhouse* from Fox. The latter, of course, was the quintessential mother-love melodrama and was "dedicated to mothers the world over." A third film, *Love's Flame*, in which Osborne played a French noblewoman saving an American flyer in World War I, was widely considered the year's worst! Not that it mattered much: The actress was by then regarded as a safe bet for Broadway stardom and would star in hit plays such as *The Silver Fox* (1921) and *The Love Child* (1922).

She reached her Broadway pinnacle two seasons later as Climene opposite Sidney Blackmer's *Scaramouche*, after which she played the title role in both the New York and London productions of *Aloma of the South Seas* (1926-1927).

In 1928 Florenz Ziegfeld chose her to play Milady de Winter to Dennis King's D'Artagnan in a lavish musical version of *The Three Musketeers*. That was a major triumph and Douglas Fairbanks wanted her for his up-coming sequel to his *The Three Musketeers* (1921), *The Iron Mask*. Osborne, who was all set to star on Broadway in *Weekend* (1929), declined Fairbanks' offer and the role eventually went to Dorothy Revier.

Despite her previous lack of success in films, Osborne was lured back in front of the cameras by the promise of sound. She appeared in several Vitaphone shorts filmed in New York and, after an absence of seven years, returned to features in something called *Morgan's Marauders* (Distinctive, 1929), a spoof of pirate films with an almost exclusively female cast.

Produced independently at Paramount's Astoria facilities, the comedy was a major embarrassment—the sound recording was crude and the sets laughable—so she cut her losses yet again and hurried back to the stage. In the end, however, the persistent offers from Hollywood were too good to pass up, and in 1931 she signed a contract with Paramount.

By now, of course, Osborne was no longer in the bloom of youth and Paramount's Ruth Chatterton seemed to have cornered the market for mature leading ladies. Instead, the studio launched her in character roles, albeit glamorous ones. Dark and elegant, she seemed perfect for the kind of overstuffed melodramas so much in vogue in the early days of sound. Being a rather commanding personality, she almost always lost her man or was cast as the interloper.

In her Hollywood debut, *The Beloved Bachelor* (Paramount, 1931), Osborne marries the wrong man and surrenders her lover (Paul Lukas) into the arms of his adopted ward (Dorothy Jordan). As preposterous as this sounds, the film proved popular at the box office, undoubtedly because of Lukas's popularity and Osborne's air of *hauteur*. (Jordan, the heroine, was rather vapid and soon enough left acting to marry producer Merian C. Cooper.)

Paramount actually did attempt to make Osborne into another Ruth Chatterton. In what looked suspiciously like a Chatterton reject, *Husband's Holiday* (Paramount, 1931), Vivienne, Clive Brook and Juliette Compton portrayed the usual triangle angst

James P. Laffey, Vivienne Osborne, Marcelle Carroll and Thomas Carrigan in *Love's Flame* (Fidelity, 1920).

of early "talkies." Unhappily, the film was all rather slow and dull. Explained *Variety*'s "Rush":

> Probably the quiet acting methods of Brook have something to do with the pale results, and Miss Osborne, who could play a spirited role with rich results, has been handled to keep in accord with her leading man. Anyhow, the outcome is not successful.

Despite the less than stellar reviews, *Husband's Holiday* was a money maker and Ruth Chatterton grew worried. To placate their reigning tragedienne, Paramount then cowardly demoted Osborne to eighth-billing as an aging gold digger in a Miriam Hopkins vehicle, *Two Kinds of Women* (1932).

With shabby treatment like that, it was no wonder that Osborne joined colleagues Kay Francis and William Powell (and, ironically, Ruth Chatterton who was already waning) in an exodus to Warner Bros. Not that the move improved her lot right away: the fast-paced Warner studio was geared more for the likes of Joan Blondell or Loretta Young than the aristocratic-looking Osborne. Relegated to supporting roles yet again, she was a murder suspect in *The Famous Ferguson Case*; briefly came between Loretta Young and Norman Foster in *Week-End Marriage*; and was one of the expecting mothers in *Life Begins* (all 1932).

Thankfully things improved considerably with *Two Seconds* (1932), the study of a condemned man whose life is seen via flashbacks, seconds before he is to die in the electric chair. The taut drama starred Edward G. Robinson as a construction worker who falls for the wrong woman and ends up a convicted murderer. Osborne, in what may be her finest performance, portrays the mercenary "taxi-dancer" who lures the inebriated Robinson into a loveless marriage. Not satisfied with one man, she takes up with the sleazy J. Carrol Naish while continuing to taunt and ridicule her increasingly despondent husband. It all ends in murder, of course, with Osborne and her paramour getting their just deserts.

Played with the accustomed grit by the Warner stock company, *Two Seconds* wasted no time on comedy relief but went straight for the gusto. Mordaunt Hall of the *New York Times*, for one, appreciated that, terming Robinson's performance "unusually impressive" and Osborne's "very real."

She was, again according to Mordaunt Hall, "sufficiently flint-hearted" as Maybelle, the former wife of a slick political campaign manager (Warren William) in the comedy *The Dark Horse* (Warner Bros., 1932). As a spoof of political intrigue, the farce was not exactly subtle, but it did offer Osborne a rare chance for parody amidst all the heavy breathing of her usual fare. A commendable professional, she came through with flying colors.

Despite her recent career upswing (or maybe because of it), Osborne left Warners in late 1932 and signed a three-picture deal with a new independent company, Jefferson Pictures Corp. It sounded good on paper, but Jefferson (releasing through RKO) did not have the cash flow to follow through with its rather lofty policies. In the end, none of Osborne's films for Jefferson were in the same league with what Warners had offered.

Men Are Such Fools (Jefferson, 1932) was claptrap about a war veteran (Leo Carillo) who marries a German Fraulein (Osborne). Unfortunately, the bride is not the faithful type (hardly any of the women Osborne was given to play were), and her latest affair results in a brawl that sends the luckless husband straight to the penitentiary. *Sailor Be Good!* (Jefferson, 1933), was cheerier: a comedy about a pugilist (Jack Oakie) who goes for the Navy boxing championship. This time, however, Osborne was cast against type as the lowly girl whom Oakie deserts for the flashier Gertrude Michael.

While no major shakes, *Sailor Be Good!* proved to be, in the words of Mordaunt Hall of the *New York Times*, "quite a lively hour and a quarter." Osborne's final film for Jefferson, *Tomorrow at Seven* (1933), offered her as the daughter of an intended murder victim and the romantic interest of Chester Morris, the chap who eventually solves the mystery. It was, to be generous, a standard programmer.*

In between these independent potboilers, Osborne freelanced as George Brent's unfaithful wife in *Luxury Liner* (Paramount, 1933), a not very good *Grand Hotel* imitation; inhabited the body of Carole Lombard in the aforementioned *Supernatural* (Paramount, 1933); and was a dance-hall hostess in *The Devil's in Love* (Fox, 1933).

Then there was a little item from Monogram entitled *The Phantom Broadcast* (1933), a rather unusual crime drama dealing with radio shows, gun molls, and gangsters.

In their book, Forgotten Horrors, George E. Turner and Michael H. Price overly praise both the film and Osborne, whom they (correctly in other instances but not in this) consider "unjustly forgotten."

Opposite: Vivienne Osborne in *Men Are Such Fools* (RKO, 1932).

Ralph Forbes starred as a hunchbacked "ghost voice," a sort of radio version of Cyrano de Bergerac, with Osborne as a siren whose allure is so strong that men would kill for her love. It was all rather bizarre and, as *Liberty Magazine* pointed out, "a swell story idea gummed up by a tiresome gangster plot."

By the end of 1933 movie offers were becoming scarce for an actress rapidly approaching middle age. Instead, she made a welcome stage comeback in the Los Angeles production of *Order, Please!* That took care of most of 1934, and when she returned to films, it was as a character woman. She was a haughty Lady Moulton to Joan Crawford's naive debutante in *No More Ladies* (M-G-M, 1935); and then supported a trio of tiresome singers: Bobby Breen in *Let's Sing Again* (Principal/Sol Lesser, 1936); Marion Talley (as Talley's untrustworthy sister) in *Follow Your Heart* (Republic, 1936); and Gladys Swarthout in *Champagne Waltz* (Paramount, 1937). In between, she took over from an ailing Verree Teasdale as the glamorous French actress Renee La Tour, briefly luring Charlie Ruggles away from Mary Boland in *Wives Never Know* (Paramount, 1936).

Osborne then had a strange part as a woman masquerading as her husband (and getting killed in the bargain) in *The Crime Nobody Saw* (Paramount, 1937), a whodunit based on a play by Ellery Queen and Lowell Brentano (a play which, the *New York Times* assured its readers, "hardly anybody saw"). Not much better was *She Asked for It* (Paramount, 1937), a pale *Thin Man* rip-off starring William Gargan as a mystery writer turned detective and Orien Heyward (Orien Heyward?) as his sidekick wife. Osborne was among the suspects in the hit-and-run killing of a millionaire.

Feeling rather dejected, Osborne left the screen again in late 1937, concentrating instead on summer stock, an area in which her name still carried some clout. She returned briefly to Hollywood in 1940, only to be wasted as a gun moll foil to Joe E. Brown in Columbia's *So You Won't Talk*.

Yet another dry spell followed, but she was back as Robert Lowery's mother in *I Accuse My Parents* (PRC, 1945), a low-budget exploitation drama about juvenile delinquents. Osborne's final screen appearance was as Vincent Price's first wife in the Gothic family drama *Dragonwyck* (20th Century–Fox, 1946). Her screen time in this semiclassic was brief.

Vivienne Osborne had always kept her offscreen life private (in the 1930s she had married and divorced millionaire Francis Worthington Hine), and in retirement she virtually disappeared. At one point, it seems, she worked as a sales clerk in a Los Angeles department store, but which one or when is unknown. She died at the age of 61 on June 10, 1961.

For a few moments in the early 1930s, Vivienne Osborne was a serious contender to become the screen's next great dramatic star. However, first at Paramount and then at Warners she ran into formidable competition from both Ruth Chatterton and Kay Francis. In retrospect, all three ladies, adept at the kind of moribund society melodrama so abundant in the early days of sound, were already anachronisms by 1932. It was the era of conversion to sound and "talkies" usually meant just that—a sea of dialogue. Once the studios had mastered the new technique, however, Hollywood returned to what it did best—painting exciting canvasses instead of still lifes. And theatrical ladies such as Osborne gave way to more exciting, more contemporary stars.

VIVIENNE OSBORNE FILMOGRAPHY

1919: *The Gray Brother.*
1920: *In Walked Mary; The Restless Sex; Love's Flame; Over the Hill to the Poorhouse.*
1921: *The Right Way.*
1922: *The Good Provider.*
1929: *Morgan's Marauders.*
1931: *The Beloved Bachelor; Husband's Holiday.*
1932: *Two Kinds of Women; The Famous Ferguson Case; Two Seconds; The Dark Horse; Week-End Marriage; Life Begins; Men Are Such Fools.*
1933: *Luxury Liner; Sailor Be Good! The Phantom Broadcast; Supernatural; Tomorrow at Seven; The Devil's in Love.*
1935: *No More Ladies.*
1936: *Follow Your Heart; Let's Sing Again; Sinner Take All.*
1937: *Champagne Waltz; The Crime Nobody Saw; She Asked for It.*
1938: *Wives Never Know.*
1940: *Primrose Path; Captain Caution; So You Won't Talk.*
1945: *I Accuse My Parents.*
1946: *Dragonwyck..*

22 — Gail Patrick

"She just went in and did her work," a good friend of Gail Patrick once said. "She knew she had a commodity, but she wasn't euphoric about acting."

Not being "euphoric" about her chosen craft proved in a strange way beneficial for the dark-haired actress, whose screen persona as a result was relaxed and subtle, if often dripping with irony. Patrick was never your average shrinking violet—for that she was much too intelligent. Usually, she was a member of society, but one who instinctively knew her exaltation in life might be borrowed and who was willing to fight to maintain her position. She certainly didn't share her daffy sister Carole Lombard's flighty sympathy for the downtrodden in *My Man Godfrey* (Universal, 1936), the screwball comedy where the glacial Patrick persona reached its zenith. And she was the least sentimental of the struggling actresses in *Stage Door* (RKO, 1937), never taken in by Katharine Hepburn's self-absorbed debutante or Ginger Rogers' streetwise, but ultimately naive and oh, so proper hoofer. Gail's controlled Linda Shaw knew she was a schemer with negligible talents, and she utterly rejected the self-righteous devotion to the theater exemplified by that pitiful old trouper Constance Collier. To Patrick's gold digger, Art would always come a distant third to diamonds and pearls.

Gail Patrick seems to have enjoyed her years in front of the camera, but she ultimately gave up her career in favor of the business side of Hollywood. A marriage to a former ad executive opened new doors for her creativity, and it was as the producer of the *Perry Mason* television series that she truly came into her own. As one of only a handful of women executives, Patrick seemed to live one of her old movie plots: succeeding in a male-dominated, cutthroat environment not suitable for "shrinking violets." Gail, off course, did it *her* way, with style and steely intelligence. Said Raymond Burr in March of 1961 of his boss:

> Gail is the most organized, the most fantastic woman I know. If she weren't married, I'd propose to her.

Like her screen characters, Patrick herself was never in doubt as to her priorities. "I don't have the soul of an actress," she admitted to Larry Walters of the *Chicago Tribune* in June of 1962. "I have a dollar sign as a soul."

She was born Margaret LaVelle Fitzpatrick on June 20, 1911, in Birmingham, Alabama, the daughter of a wealthy Irishman. Her mother, Paramount publicity would later insist, "descended from a long line of Southern forebears." The stated goal of the young Margaret was to become a lawyer and, eventually, the first woman governor of Alabama. In 1936, Gail Patrick, now a Hollywood starlet, still maintained that goal, advising her agent that she would be a candidate for the executive seat at Montgomery—in 1952.

While attending the prestigious Howard College, Patrick honed her leadership skills as captain of the girls' varsity basketball team and was active in college theatricals. In 1931, she was elected to College Humor's "Hall of Fame."

Earning a B.A. in 1932, she matriculated in law at the University of Alabama, but her studies were suddenly interrupted when, on a lark, she entered Paramount's nationwide "Panther Woman" contest, the prize of which was the female lead opposite Charles Laughton in the studio's upcoming *Island of Lost Souls* (1933). According to Paramount publicity, 60,000 young women entered the contest, which was ultimately won by the forgettable Kathleen Burke. Patrick later dismissed the experience, explaining that "it wasn't that I was so anxious [for the role], but the job paid $75 a week."

While Burke (a former dental assistant with no obvious acting talents) landed the coveted part, Patrick and Lona Andre, the runners-up as it were, were awarded Paramount contracts. Patrick, however, still not quite taking her stroke of luck seriously, greeted Hollywood on her own terms. "I came in borrowed clothes," she later told Hedda Hopper, "[and] refused to make cheesecake pictures, so everyone thought I was crazy. They offered me $50 a week, [but] I got them up to $75."

Despite failing to become the "Panther Woman," Patrick did make her screen debut opposite Charles Laughton: She had a bit part as a secretary confronted by the newly empowered Laughton in the multiplotted *If I Had a Million* (Paramount, 1932). Following that, she was somewhat more visible fighting alongside fellow contest loser Lona Andre in *The Mysterious Rider* (Paramount, 1933), a Zane Grey Western; and she played the ingenue in the grizzly *Murders in the Zoo* (Paramount, 1933). (Kathleen Burke, billed below her, turned up as the film's villainess.) Next, Patrick appeared as a novice in *The Cradle Song* (Paramount, 1933), and on loan to Monogram (her billing read "Courtesy of Paramount Pictures") was the ingenue in something called *The Phantom Broadcast* (1933).

With such a hectic schedule during her first full year in films, Patrick nevertheless found time for rather strenuous extracurricular activities. With Paramount publicity cameras happily cranking away she earned her pilot's license and visited the construction of the Boulder Dam, thus becoming "the first woman ever allowed to go down into the cavernous tunnels of the dam, where the presence of a member of the fair sex is regarded as bad luck by the workers." Later, as a successful television producer, the former actress could laugh at such an obvious publicity stunt. "When I was flying you'd think I was carrying the mail," she told Hedda Hopper in 1960. "And when they were told I'd studied law, you'd think I was a judge on the bench."

Prompted by moviegoers' interest in their brainy new starlet, Paramount quickly realized that they were harboring a *femme fatale* in sheep's clothing. Consequently, 1934 saw the actress in increasingly willful roles. She was, for example, the man-hungry Rhoda Fenton to Evelyn Venable's doe-eyed Grazia in Paramount's tasteful version of Alberto Casella's parable of love and immortality, *Death Takes a Holiday*. Mordaunt Hall of the *New York Times* found her to be "handsome and capable," and she certainly was both. But more importantly, she showed for the first time the "true" Gail Patrick, the no-nonsense, straight-in-your-face desire that would ultimately separate her from the pack.

Not quite as significant, but nevertheless worthy of contemplation, was *The Crime of Helen Stanley* (Columbia, 1934), a whodunit set on a Hollywood sound stage. Patrick played a haughty movie actress whose disagreeable personality soon marked her for murder. The murder itself was the old standby of someone switching a prop gun with the real thing, but that was of less importance than Patrick's cunning portrayal of a "typical" movie siren. The actress gave it her all, to the point where, according to a press release, she was injured during the filming of her death scene.

There were no mishaps on the set of *Murder at the Vanities* (Paramount, 1934), another show business whodunit. Again, Patrick played the victim, but this time she met her demise in the very first scene and had to play a corpse for nine consecutive days. "I fooled them on that one," she was later fond of saying. "I just stretched out comfortably, played corpse with one eye and kept the other open. I learned more than in all my other pictures put together."

Patrick was a bit more conventional as Randolph Scott's love interest in yet another Zane Grey adaptation, *Wagon Wheels* (Paramount, 1934). And yet, even in standard role in a routine program Western she was different. Here, she played a widow who kidnaps her own child from some hateful in-laws and treks west in order to start a new life as a frontierswoman. While not exactly a full-fledged modern feminist, Patrick's heroine was no blushing ingenue.

Next, she proved herself adept at comedy as a willful Southern belle who loses her man (Bing Crosby) to her less obstinate kid sister (Joan Bennett) in *Mississippi* (Paramount, 1935), a tuneful version of Booth Tarkington's *Magnolia*. It was the first of many roles in which a younger, more democratic sister runs off with Patrick's fiancé. In Walter Wanger's *Smart Girl* (1935), for example, the fiancé (whom she actually marries before bedding his enemy) is Kent Taylor and the kid sister is this time played by Ida Lupino (who herself would graduate to *femme fatale* roles in the 1940s).

Patrick returned to familiar settings in *The Preview Murder Mystery* (Paramount, 1936). Again she was an annoying screen star done in with a prop gun loaded with real bullets instead of blanks. The actress always looked back with amusement upon the fact that she so often played a murder victim. The reason, she claimed, was that she proved such an effective screamer.

There was no call for screaming while on loan to Universal for *My Man Godfrey* (1936). Nevertheless, Patrick was in her element as the shrewd Cornelia Bullock, a socialite who is not fooled by kid sister Irene's (Carole Lombard) scavenger hunt prize, the polished, too-good-to-be-true butler Godfrey (William Powell). To get rid of the irritating factotum (who was never fooled by her superior attitude), Cornelia sets him up by planting her valuable pearls under his bed and calling the police. Godfrey, of course, turns out to be a society scion fallen on hard times and only impersonating a derelict, so Cornelia's little trick misfires.

My Man Godfrey remains one of the era's most delightful comedies and is a deserved classic. Contemporary reviews were for the most part complimentary, with Frank S. Nugent of the *New York Times* pronouncing it "the daffiest comedy of the year." As the snobbish Cornelia Bullock (of the Park Avenue Bullocks), Patrick was the only sane member of her family and basically served as straight woman to her dizzy relatives (including her giddy mother, played by Alice Brady, who earned an Academy Award nomination for her scatterbrained performance). Being sane in a screwball comedy, however, meant being the villain, and Cornelia Bullock was no exception. It was Gail Patrick's most polished performance, and the role for which she will be remembered.

On December 17, 1936, in Tijuana, Mexico, Gail Patrick wed Hollywood restaurateur Robert Cobb, the owner of the Brown Derby and "inventor" of the famous Cobb salad.

Concentrating on her private life, Patrick bowed out of *Clarence* (Paramount, 1937), a minor comedy with Roscoe Ates, but she was back in full force, top-billed as the torch-singing wife of a notorious gangster (Ricardo Cortez) in *Her Husband Lies* (Paramount, 1937). Ostensibly depicting the life and crimes of real-life gangster Arnold Rothstein (but rather resembling a modern-day *Robin Hood* in its whitewashing of the notorious thug), *Her Husband Lies* was a remake of *Street of Chance* (Paramount, 1930). Patrick thus took over the role of the suffering wife from Kay Francis, an actress whom she physically somewhat resembled. But while Francis was believable as a dupe, Gail was too intelligent to portray a poor, neglected wife and in the end seemed rather miscast.

She was far from miscast as the calculating would-be actress Linda Shaw in RKO's much praised screen version of Edna Ferber and George S. Kaufman's comedy-drama about struggling thespians in New York, *Stage Door* (1937). Gregory La Cava (who had previously guided Patrick through *My Man Godfrey*) assembled a top-notch cast to portray the denizens of a theatrical boarding house. Katharine Hepburn (who had just been voted "box office poison" by exhibitors) shared top billing with Ginger Rogers, and both stars offered keen portrayals. The film, however, was all but stolen by a splendid supporting cast that included Constance Collier as a melodramatic has-been turned acting coach; Andrea Leeds, as an eternally promising newcomer who chooses suicide over career death; Eve Arden, as a wisecracking cynic (complete with a live cat draped around her shoulders); and Patrick, as the glamour girl whose solution to unemployment is to sleep with the producer. Patrick's Linda Shaw, however, is too shrewd for libertine Adolphe Menjou, who throws her over, first for the naive Rogers, then for the self-possessed (but equally naive) Hepburn. When Menjou inevitably shows his real face, the two girls discover that they need each other to survive. Patrick, whose illusions have long been broken, needs nobody and naturally proves much more capable of weathering the ups and downs of show business than her gullible fellow boarders. *She* is the ultimate survivor, and one is never in doubt of her

Opposite: Gail Patrick, date unknown.

bright, comfortable (and unapologetic) future—if not as a star, then as the wife (or mistress) of a rich "stage Johnny."

Patrick's Linda was almost a repeat of her Cornelia Bullock. Again she was the most level-headed (with the possible exception of the sarcastic Arden) in a group of naifs—and again the screen-writers tried to punish her for her uncompromising honesty. Contemporary reviews dismissed her in favor of Andrea Leeds, whose tortured actress was much admired. Today, Leeds comes across as somewhat banal, while Patrick's performance seems shaded and multifaceted.

Following a couple of low-budget crime dramas, Patrick was again borrowed by Universal, this time to play Deanna Durbin's mother in *Mad About Music* (1938). As a widowed actress who is duped by an over-zealous press agent to hide away her teenaged daughter in a Swiss boarding school, the actress finally played a thoroughly sympathetic character—and played her well. Patrick often complained of type-casting and professed a desire to play decent women, providing, she said, that

> the character has strength, stamina and sound dramatic situations to confront and conquer. Bad-girl roles are flashier, of course, but there's not the satisfaction in them that I get from the homespun type ... and by this type of role I don't mean a sweety-sweet character. I can't stand this sort of person. I mean a woman of sound character who thinks and fights her way through obstacles until she wins out in the end.

In *Mad About Music* Patrick is no "sweety-sweet" and her Gwen Taylor does show strength of character. Still, in accordance with convention, she naturally cannot quite make it alone, but has to rely on a nice marriageable composer (Herbert Marshall) to provide Durban with what the youngster mostly desires: a "normal" family life. Apart from these modern reservations, *Mad About Music* is, as Frank S. Nugent of the *New York Times* pointed out, "a friendly and wholesome show." It was also one of the year's biggest box office hits.

Patrick's career then took a seemingly unexpected nosedive. She later admitted to have lost interest in her screen career around this time and thus did little to fight uninspiring parts in such potboilers as *Disbarred* and *Grand Jury Secrets* (both Paramount, 1939). She had good billing but very few scenes as a woman who briefly dallies with Sam Houston on his way to the Alamo in Republic's *Man of Conquest* (1939), but a proposed turn as the other woman in 20th Century–Fox's *20,000 Men a Year* (1939), never materialized.* Instead, she publicly battled her husband Robert Cobb and was squired around town by comedian Freeman Gosden (of *Amos 'n' Andy* fame). The Cobbs finally divorced on October 29, 1940, with Gail Patrick charging "mental anguish."

Leaving Paramount after seven years, Patrick freelanced but found little to inspire her in such potboilers as *The Doctor Takes a Wife* (Columbia, 1940), in which she was Ray Milland's snobbish fiancée, or *Gallant Sons* (M-G-M, 1940), a juvenile delinquent melodrama which had her as Bonita Granville's mother (shades of *Mad About Music*, but only shades).

Happily, in *My Favorite Wife* (RKO, 1940), Patrick finally returned to playing the

---

*The role was eventually played by Patrick's counterpart at Fox, Margaret Lindsay.

Gail Patrick and Paramount still photographer William Walling (extreme right) during a "Miss 1939" promotion.

quintessential other woman, this time cashing in on Irene Dunne's "death" to nab Cary Grant. When Dunne returns very much alive, the scene is set for one of the last of the great screwball comedies. Bosley Crowther of the *New York Times* found the concoction "a rondo of refined ribaldries and an altogether delightful picture," and commended Patrick on her excellent performance, especially, he noted, since she had to spend "most of her time in negligee."

There was little to cheer about in the dreary *Kathleen* (M-G-M, 1941), in which she was Laraine Day's rival for the affections of Herbert Marshall (and, in effect, for those of Marshall's screen daughter, Shirley Temple). She did a low-budget whodunit with George Sanders, *Quiet Please, Murder* (20th Century–Fox, 1942); and then went the propaganda route as a disillusioned Nazi in *Women in Bondage* (1943), a minor effort from minor studio Monogram. Next, she was trapped in a couple of antique bedroom farces from independent producer Edward Small: *Up in Mabel's Room* (United Artists, 1944), and *Brewster's Millions* (United Artists, 1945). Although popular, neither was anything to write home about.

Patrick's private life, it seems, was more dramatic than her screen roles. She had met Arnold Dean White, a former Navy man, at the fabled Hollywood Canteen, and on July 11, 1944, in Jacksonville, Florida, she became Mrs. White. Returning from their honeymoon, the Whites embarked on a business venture, a toy store which proved quite successful.

The marriage, unfortunately, did not: The couple separated in 1945 following the stillbirth of their twin daughters. The tragedy was amplified by White's inability to obtain outside work, and in the divorce agreement he was listed as an unemployed toy manufacturer.

Gail Patrick forged ahead, alone again, running her store and obtaining sporadic screen work. For Republic, she starred in such potboilers as *The Madonna's Secret* (1946) with Francis Lederer, and *The Plainsman and the Lady* (1946) with William "Wild Bill" Elliott and the dreadful Vera (Hruba) Ralston. Her final screen appearance came in *The Inside Story* (Republic, 1948), a "comedy" with William Lundigan. These run of the mill efforts certainly did nothing to belie her later statement that "it's debatable if I ever was an actress." With a new husband, ad executive Cornwall Jackson, whom she had wed on July, 25, 1947, she happily left her acting career behind.

Gail Patrick was, of course, far from finished with show business. On Saturday, September 21, 1957, at 7:30 PM the CBS television network premiered its newest courtroom drama, *Perry Mason*. The series was based on the popular whodunits by Erle Stanley Gardner and featured Raymond Burr, a hulking supporting actor, as the eminent defense attorney who never lost a case; Barbara Hale, a former screen starlet, as Mason's faithful secretary Della Street; William Hopper (the son of columnist Hedda Hopper) as private detective Paul Drake; William Talman as the luckless district attorney Hamilton Burger; and Ray Collins as the no-nonsense police lieutenant Tragg. It was an unbeatable combination and the series, which lasted until September of 1966, became television's most successful and longest running courtroom show. The producer behind the success was Gail Patrick Jackson.

"My husband and [Gardner] were partners in several properties," Mrs. Cornwall Jackson explained her surprising change of venue to Hedda Hopper in June of 1960.

> They had a show on radio and a couple of other things they owned jointly. When I came into Corney's life I became a partner too. *Life in Your Hands* was one. We still own it. One third belongs to Jack Simpson, one third to Corney and a third to Erle. We'd turned down several offers for Erle's stories to be televised because we had to be certain they'd be handled with care. Then after a vacation in Honolulu we were open to offers.

Both Gardner and Jackson thought Gail would be the perfect person to produce the series, and, along with former child star Bonita Granville (the producer of the *Lassie* series) and director Ida Lupino, she became one of the few women to hold power in Hollywood. Being a woman in a man's world did not pose any problems, she informed an inquiring Louella Parsons in 1960.

> I've never felt self-conscious as a woman dealing with men. I think it's because the men are concerned, as I am, only with the business at hand. I guess you'd say we meet on a mental level.

The hard work, however, in addition to raising two adopted children and the death of Erle Stanley Gardner, took its toll on the Jackson marriage, which ended in divorce in April of 1969. "It was an interesting situation, since we are still partners together in Erle's Paisano Productions," Cornwall Jackson said of the divorce. "The estrangement between Gail and me led to some real battles in Paisano, but the conflict got *Perry Mason* moving again."

It did indeed, and in September of 1973, seven years after the original had left the air, CBS inaugurated a new series starring Monte Markham and Sharon Acker as Perry and Della. This time Cornwall Jackson was the executive producer while Gail Patrick held the title of "executive consultant." The new cast (which included Albert Stratton as Drake, Harry Guardino as Burger, and Dane Clark as Tragg) failed to catch on, however, and the show was canceled in January of 1974.*

With the demise of the second series, Gail Patrick retired to concentrate on her many charitable duties. In 1970, for example, she was the national honorary chairman of the Easter Seals campaign and, a life-long diabetic, became chairman of the American Diabetes Association in 1973. On September 28, 1974, in Neully, France, she married her fourth husband, Illinois businessman John Velde, Jr., a marriage that lasted until her death from leukemia in 1987.

In her heyday Gail Patrick came across as Hollywood's most intelligent other woman. She was rarely as nasty as Claire Dodd nor quite as vindictive as Helen Vinson, and it was often difficult to root against her as the studio obviously meant us to. Patrick was so sane, so composed—an island of lucidity in a sea of daffiness. And although the screenwriters asked us to sympathize with Andrea Leeds (which we dutifully did), we rather suspected that Gail was the better actress. She certainly was more fun.

GAIL PATRICK FILMOGRAPHY

1932: *If I Had a Million.*
1933: *The Mysterious Rider; The Phantom Broadcast; Pick-Up; Murders in the Zoo; To the Last Man; Cradle Song.*
1934: *Death Takes a Holiday; The Crime of Helen Stanley; Murder at the Vanities; Take the Stand; Wagon Wheels; One Hour Late.*
1935: *Rhumba; Mississippi; Doubting Thomas; No More Ladies; Smart Girl; The Wanderer of the Wasteland; The Big Broadcast of 1936; Two Fisted; The Lone Wolf Returns.*
1936: *Two in the Dark; The Preview Murder Mystery; Early to Bed; My Man Godfrey; Murder with Pictures; White Hunter.*
1937: *John Meade's Woman; Her Husband Lies; Artists and Models; Stage Door.*
1938: *Mad About Music; Dangerous to Know; Wives Under Suspicion; King of Alcatraz.*
1939: *Man of Conquest; Disbarred; Grand Jury Secrets; Reno; The Hunchback of Notre Dame; The Doctor Takes a Wife; My Favorite Wife; Gallant Sons.*

---

*The Perry Mason *series was given new life in the 1980s via a string of made-for-television movies, again featuring Burr and Hale. In all likelihood, not even the 1993 death of Raymond Burr will put an end to the amazing career of Hollywood's favorite defense lawyer.*

1941: *Love Crazy; Kathleen.*
1942: *We Were Dancing; Tales of Manhattan; Quiet Please, Murder.*
1943: *Hit Parade of 1943; Women in Bondage.*
1944: *Up in Mabel's Room.*
1945: *Brewster's Millions; Twice Blessed.*
1946: *Claudia and David; Rendezvous with Annie; The Madonna's Secret; The Plainsman and the Lady.*
1947: *Calendar Girl; King of the Wild Horses.*
1948: *The Inside Story.*

23 — Dorothy Revier

"The Caviar of Poverty Row," they called patrician-looking Dorothy Revier. For most of her career, Revier was under contract to Columbia Pictures, at the time a marginal proposition at best. Dorothy always saw herself as a dancer and when sound came around felt positioned to compete with the musical comedy stars imported from the East by Warner Bros. and M-G-M. Harry Cohn, the cigar-chomping czar of Columbia, saw things differently.

"Harry told me to 'forget it'," Revier later recalled. "He wanted me to be a great dramatic actress—a Bette Davis. I thought, 'Bette Davis is the greatest actress in America! He has to be kidding!'"

Unfortunately, Cohn was dead serious. Later in the decade he came to his senses and established his latest acquisition, Rita Hayworth, via a series of lavish (for Columbia, at least) musical comedies, in which Hayworth's not inconsiderable terpsichorean talents were fully spotlighted. He even brought in Fred Astaire as her partner in a few notable occasions. Dorothy Revier was never given such consideration. On the contrary, she was doomed to appear in a deluge of utterly implausible melodramas, in which she more often than not was asked to seduce the immobile Jack Holt—an actor completely inadequate in romantic clinches.

The exotic looking Revier had been typed as a vixen from the very beginning of her career, but the turning point had come in 1929 when Douglas Fairbanks borrowed her from Cohn to play Milady de Winter in United Artists' *The Iron Mask*. The film, and her performance in it, was quite a triumph, but Cohn failed to act; or rather, his struggling company was ill equipped to respond. So Dorothy Revier continued her modest reign as Columbia's resident vamp until 1931, when she finally left the studio to freelance.

Unhappily, her career quickly went from Cohn to worse. Instead of Columbia's modest but still adequate budgets, she now had to contend with hardly any budgets at all from fly-by-night organizations such as Action Pictures, Maxim, Mayfair, Peerless (which should have been named Cheerless), and Ajax. "Caviar of Poverty Row," indeed! She finally called it quits after having played a schoolmarm in *The Cowboy and the Kid* (Universal, 1936), a Buck Jones program Western in which the best scenes went to the Kid (Billy Burrud).

"I really think my family background is more interesting than my career!" Dorothy Revier wrote in 1983. She was born Dorothea (Doris) Valegra on April 18, 1904, in San Francisco, the daughter of "the first chair, solo cornetist of the San Francisco Symphony." Her aunt, Ida Valegra, was a noted opera singer, and Dorothea herself was all but "born in a trunk." "I studied ballet mostly as a child," she recently told writer Michael Ankerich. "I would get up early every morning and study about four hours before going to school." The hard work paid off and by 1922 she was dancing professionally at Tait's Cafe in San Francisco. Her specialty, she recalls, was "Italian and Russian ballet, ballroom and eccentric dancing." She claims to have danced in prologues and in vaudeville, but it was at Tait's that she met screen director Harry Revier,* who was to become her first husband. Revier, it seems, was her ticket to Hollywood and stardom.

The newly renamed Dorothy Revier made her screen debut in *Life's Greatest Question* (Quality Films, 1921), a Western starring an also-ran cowboy named Roy Stewart; and *The Broadway Madonna* (Quality Film, 1922), a society melodrama. Both were directed by her husband and produced by two aggressive newcomers in Hollywood, the brothers Sam and Harry Cohn. Needless to say, she was the star, and while the films weren't much, their modest success earned her a featured role in Universal's *The Wild Party* (1923), a newspaper farce starring Gladys Walton. *The Supreme Test* (Cosmosart, 1923), a gangster melodrama with Johnny Harron, followed, after which she signed with indie company Goldstone for a series of low-budget action adventures.

Directed by outdoor specialists like Alvin Neitz and Duke Worne, the Goldstone series teamed her mostly with William Fairbanks, a stuntman turned action star and no relation to Doug (a fact that he hoped audiences would overlook). Most of these quickly made five- or six-reelers were Westerns, but a few had other locales.

The Virgin (Goldstone, 1924), a religious melodrama set in Spain, in which Fairbanks for some reason was replaced with the more "domesticated" Kenneth Harlan, had pretensions, but the bulk of the films bore titles like *Border Women*, *The Cowboy and the Flapper*, and *That Wild West* (all 1924) — simple potboilers geared toward the juvenile trade. For the most part, the series was ignored by critics, but a few of the entries attracted notice in the trade papers. A *Variety* review of *Down By the Rio Grande* (Goldstone, 1924), for example, gives a good idea of the kind of fare found in the small neighborhood theaters frequented mainly by the small fry:

> Just one of those things, and full to the brim with maudlin subtitles, of which the first is the tip off to the merits of the picture, with the following footage living up to the expectations invoked by the initial wording. The story is negligible, neither Fairbanks or Miss Revier mean anything, and the interest aroused took form in a general restlessness throughout the audience, which only relaxed when the finish had been reached.

---

*Harry Revier came to films in the mid-teens and went on to direct Evelyn Brent in The Weakness of Strength *(1916) heavyweight boxing champion Jess Willard in* The Challenge of Chance *(1919) and Western star Roy Stewart in* Heart of the North *(1921), in addition to the films featuring his wife. Revier, who later established his own production company, retired following* The Lash of the Penitentes *in 1937.*

Needless to say, it was quite a step up from Goldstone when Revier returned to Universal for a supporting role opposite Mary Philbin in *Rose of Paris* (1924), a "Roaring Twenties" melodrama set in a Paris nightclub. From that, she went to First National (supporting Claire Windsor in *Just a Woman*, 1925), before landing at the newly-formed Columbia where old friend Harry Cohn offered her a long-term contract.

According to Revier, it was her agent who promoted the idea of signing with Cohn. "He told me that within a few years Columbia would be one of the biggest studios in Hollywood," she would later recall. The agent was about ten years off the mark, and by the time the little studio was finally solvent, Revier had long since departed.

Dorothy once acknowledged that she had an affair with the irascible and often foul-mouthed Harry Cohn. More often, however, she would insist that their relationship was on a purely professional level. "Harry was a very kind man," she explained in 1983, "but volatile and quick tempered. He was also a very handsome man. His [first] wife, Rose, was very kind and helpful to me. She was extremely intelligent. A Christian Scientist." At least the two women thus had more in common than just Harry: Revier was herself a lifelong follower of Christian Science.

The immediate reason for Harry Cohn's interest in Dorothy Revier is not difficult to understand: She was quite simply an actress on her way up. Prior to signing with Columbia she had been awarded the female lead opposite Rudolph Valentino in *The Hooded Falcon*, a spectacular costume drama written by his (domineering) wife, Natacha Rambova. Unfortunately, Mrs. Valentino, who also was to design the production, became overly ambitious and the project ultimately was abandoned for lack of funds. Nonetheless, being considered by the Valentinos added extra prestige to a newcomer with no major films to her credit and Harry Cohn was quick to sign her up. The publicity, he realized, was already paid for by somebody else.

Revier's budding career got yet another boost when the members of the Western Association of Motion Picture Advertisers (WAMPAS) elected her a 1925 Baby Star. The select group of 13 young starlets were intensively publicized and were feted at a well-attended ball. None of them, however, with the possible exception of Revier herself, made it to stardom.*

In her first film for Columbia, *The Danger Signal* (1925), Revier merely supported the veteran Jane Novak, but she received co-star billing opposite Cullen Landis in her next, *An Enemy of Men* (1925), an exploitation melodrama set in a nightclub. Nightclubs and the dimpled Landis were also the major ingredients in *Sealed Lips* (1925), and she was awarded star billing for the first time as a secretary who poses as her boss' wife in *Steppin' Out* (1925), with Ford Sterling. Next, First National borrowed her for *The Far Cry*, a Blanche Sweet vehicle, and she actually managed to upstage the star in her few scenes as a French vamp.

Meanwhile, back at Columbia, Harry Cohn had discovered Revier's flair for comedy. She was still playing vamps, but now she often portrayed them as more funny

---

Among the year's other "Babies" were Olive Borden, a "flapper" who ended her life on Los Angeles' Skid Row; Madeline Hurlock, a Mack Sennett comedienne with a penchant for marrying literary giants (first Marc Connolly, then Robert E. Sherwood); and Borden's cousin Natalie Joyce.

than lethal, romping through such farces as *When Husbands Flirt* (1925), with Forrest Stanley, and *When the Wife's Away* (1926), with droll little George K. Arthur. Universal paid attention and borrowed her for *Poker Faces* (1926), a pleasant bedroom farce with Laura La Plante and Edward Everett Horton.

Nevertheless, melodrama and action-oriented fare continued to be Columbia and Revier's "bread and butter": she and Helene Chadwick fought over Gayne Whitman in *Stolen Pleasures* (1927), and she played a runaway flapper who gets involved with a burglary ring in *Wandering Girls* (1927). In *Poor Girls* (1927), she was a naive young woman who learns that her mother (Ruth Stonehouse) is a notorious nightclub owner.

The Tigress (1927), a melodrama set in Old Spain, was a milestone of sorts: it was the first of seven films, in which she appeared opposite action hero Jack Holt. According to Revier herself, the two got along "very well," but the association must have been somewhat strenuous. The Holt pictures were square-jawed juvenile fare with very little time out for characterization let alone romance; consequently, they offered very little time for the leading lady.

In retrospect, the Holt films were actually quite entertaining if unsophisticated programmers. The most popular entry proved to be *Submarine* (1928), a better than average underwater thriller directed by newcomer Frank Capra. For some reason, Holt decided on the spot to give a little more of himself than usual. In one scene, the usually unemotional actor felt that his character required to be filmed with teary eyes. "Frank Capra kept arguing with Jack, telling him all the reasons he felt that wasn't necessary," Revier remembered 60 years later. "Finally Frank just threw up his hands and said, 'For God's sake let him cry!' Then we all sat around for hours waiting." Ultimately, Capra made the actor do two "takes," one with tears and one without. The dry one made it into the film.

In between the Holt pictures, Revier returned to less hectic fare where she could lounge about being the *femme fatale*. One of her better efforts was an old-fashioned society melodrama with Tom Moore, entitled, appropriately enough, *The Siren* (1927). Directed by Byron Haskin, it was, according to *Film Daily*, "strong, dramatic stuff," and *Variety*'s "Mori" found it "an interesting [melodrama] for the Honky Tonk," adding that "Harry Cohn may be given the entire credit for turning out a production of this quality against [Columbia's] cost limitations."

Hollywood actresses were clamoring for the chance to play the nefarious Milady de Winter opposite Douglas Fairbanks' D'Artagnan in *The Iron Mask* (United Artists, 1929), the long awaited sequel to the phenomenally popular *The Three Musketeers* (United Artists, 1921). Barbara La Marr had skyrocketed to stardom as the original Milady, but the beautiful and troubled star had died in 1925 at the age of 28. When Fairbanks came knocking on Hary Cohn's door in search of a replacement (his original choice, Vivienne Osborne, had turned him down flat), the sly tycoon quickly offered him Dorothy Revier. It was a situation almost too good to be true. While United Artists was spending a fortune publicizing the newest Fairbanks blockbuster, promoting Revier in the bargain, Harry, who owned her contract, would collect a hefty loan-out fee while paying his star her usual (low) weekly salary.

The Iron Mask, as it turned out, became the silent era's last great swashbuckler. The dawn of sound had arrived and movie spectaculars would, for a while at least, be replaced by moribund society dramas saturated with an overabundance of talk. The enjoyable and relaxed circumstances under which *The Iron Mask* was created were no longer possible.

Dorothy Revier vividly remembers the day when the Duke of Kent paid the company a visit. "At the end of the set was a replica of a cathedral window," she told writer Michael Ankerich.

> It was a huge arch which appeared to be gorgeous stained glass pane. It was actually papier mâché. Fairbanks left the set, only to return in a spectacular way. Suddenly the "cathedral windows" shattered and [he] came leaping through astride his horse. Everyone—the cast, the audience (he always had an audience) and the Duke—applauded. Fairbanks loved to do stunts, and he did all his own. He was a wonderful athlete.

Such derring-do, onscreen or off, would not be manageable on a soundstage, which would often truly resemble a cathedral—quiet and reverent, built to worship a new "god," the sound engineer.

On February 12, 1929, Revier, a divorcee of two years, married Charles Schoen Johnson, "a Philadelphia socialite" with a knack for marrying glamorous actresses (his first wife was the exquisite silent star Katherine MacDonald). Cohn was far from pleased: "When Harry found out about Charles, he came to me and told me he cared for me and asked me to wait before getting married," she later recalled. "I finally realized that Harry really did love me."

Trying to recover from a broken heart, Harry Cohn busied himself with converting his facilities to accommodate sound, thus enabling Revier to make her "talkie" debut in a comedy-mystery, *The Donovan Affair* (1929). Jack Holt, who starred as a bumbling detective, had by this point in his career given up pretending to be a romantic leading man so Revier instead had to vamp the second male lead, William Collier, Jr. In their next outing together, *Father and Son* (1929), she was a man-hungry Countess and Holt a widower with a young son. It still was not so much romantic as sappy.

Possibly because he felt rejected, Cohn increasingly lent Revier to other studios—a situation, of course, that also made him a fair amount of money. First National borrowed her to play the other woman opposite Nancy Carroll and Hal Skelly in *The Dance of Life* (1929), and she was a gun moll in a Paramount crime drama with George Bancroft and Esther Ralston, *The Mighty* (1929). The following year, she played a nasty socialite vamping Joe E. Brown in the boxing farce *Hold Everything* (Warner Bros., 1930), and she starred opposite Douglas Fairbanks, Jr., in *The Way of All Men* (First National, 1930), a strange drama about an underground speakeasy threatened by rising floodwaters!

If nothing else, Revier's loan-outs were better than what Harry Cohn had to offer. At Columbia, she continued to support Jack Holt in potboilers such as the trite *The Squealer* (1930), in which she played his unfaithful wife and an unfit mother (to Davy Lee of "Sonny Boy" fame). *Vengeance* (1930), was even worse: A lurid triangle drama set in Africa, it won no awards.

According to Revier herself, Cohn suddenly fired her without warning. She went straight over to Fox to discuss a contract. "I returned to Columbia to get my personal belongings, and told Harry I was going to Fox," she recalled in 1983.

> He was furious! He didn't think I had the nerve to leave. The entire incident turned into a real scene. I was young and unsophisticated or I would have had an attorney represent me. But I stayed on.

Not long after, Revier did indeed leave Columbia, but apparently under less passionate circumstances, and she would return to the studio on several occasions in the future. Her final film under the old contract proved to be *The Avenger* (1931), a Buck Jones "B" Western in which the stalwart Buck, not too convincingly, was Joaquín Murieta to Revier's South-of-the-Border señorita. She and the pleasant Jones became fast friends, a fact that would help her in a less rosy future.

Following her departure from Columbia, Revier did make a stopover at Fox, but as a freelance player. She appeared as Shelah Fane, a temperamental movie star whose murder is solved by the eminent Chinese detective Charlie Chan (Warner Oland) in *The Black Camel* (Fox, 1931). This was only the second entry in the long-running series and was still considered a prestige project (complete with location filming in Hawaii) and not the throwaway budget filler that later editions became. *The Black Camel* was also one of Revier's last films of any importance, a turn of events, it is safe to say, that she had not bargained for when leaving Columbia.

From Fox, Revier went to Universal where she was demoted to third billing (after Regis Toomey and Sue Carol) in *Graft* (1931), a newspaper drama. *Leftover Ladies* (Tiffany-Stahl, 1931), a marital drama with Claudia Dell and Arthur Byron followed, after which she starred as a columnist who goes on the trail of her brother's killer in *Anybody's Blonde*.

Produced seemingly without any budget by an outfit calling itself Action Pictures (a definite misnomer), *Anybody's Blonde* boasted of a cast of former silent stars,* but it made Columbia's output look like superior filmmaking in comparison. Dismissing the film as junk, *Variety*'s "Mark" nevertheless found that Revier "looked okay and not stagey in her big scenes."

As miserable as *Anybody's Blonde* was, it was better than *Sally of the Subway* (1932), also from Action Pictures. The far-fetched plot had no Sallys and no subways, but it did have a naive Grand Duke Ludwig of Saxe-Thalberg (Jack Mulhall) stranded in New York who gets involved with a jewel thief (Huntley Gordon) and his moll (Revier). The film was so bad that a co-star, Blanche Mehaffey, later vigorously tried to keep it off television via a "defamation of character" suit. Unfortunately, she lost.

Revier had a potential change of pace playing a female *Raffles* in *The Widow in Scarlet* (1932), but the film, produced by Mayfair (which was actually Action Pictures in a disguise that fooled no one) received very few bookings. She was much better served by *Night World* (Universal, 1932), a nifty little thriller set in a nightclub, which Andre Sennwald of the *New York Times* termed a "symphonic arrangement of songs and snatches of human experience." While not quite as well received, *The Secrets of Wu Sin* (Invincible, 1932), was a not-too-bad yellow-peril melodrama in which she was mean to the so very decent Lois Wilson.

Dorothy Revier returned ignominiously to Columbia in January of 1933 for *The Thrill Hunter*, a comedy with her friend Buck Jones, who, since it wasn't a Western,

---

*Including the former "Arrow Collar Man" Reed Howes and "flapper" Edna Murphy.

Bela Lugosi, Dorothy Revier and Warner Oland in *The Black Camel* (Fox, 1931).

billed himself as Charles Jones for the occasion. That film was so bad the studio kept it on the shelf for seven months before finally releasing it on a double bill.

Dorothy Revier's final film of any importance was Universal's *By Candlelight* (1933), James Whale's romantic comedy of errors about commoners masquerading as nobility and vice versa. It was fluff, but expensive fluff, and had a strong cast that included Elissa Landi, Paul Lukas, and Esther Ralston. Dorothy's role, however, was merely background decoration.

From the elegance of *By Candlelight*, it was back to Columbia, Buck Jones, and the realm of "B" Westerns: In *The Fighting Ranger* (1934) she was Tonita, a fiery below-the-border belle (Jones apparently enjoyed masquerading as a *bandito* complete with a sombrero and a rather uneasy accent); alas, she had little to do beyond looking sultry.

She played an unfaithful wife yet again in *Unknown Blonde* (1934), from Majestic ("A sorry illustration of puppet-dangling," Mordaunt Hall of the *New York Times* complained); supported Henrietta Crossman (an especially tiresome theater veteran) in *The Curtain Falls* (Chesterfield, 1935), a sentimental tale of a homeless actress who impersonates a wealthy colleague; and was an aerialist (and heroine Dorothy Wilson's *mother*, an rather ominous turn of events) in *Circus Shadows* (Peerless, 1934). After

Buck Jones, Frank Rice and Dorothy Revier in *The Fighting Ranger* (Columbia, 1934). (Photograph courtesy of Janus Barfoed.)

that, she was reunited with Buck Jones (who had quit Columbia for Universal) in *When a Man Sees Red* (1934). For old times' sake, she was given star billing, but the picture was not very good.

There was little improvement in 1935: She was a spoiled socialite in *$20 a Week* from something called Ajax Pictures; played the unfaithful wife of a publisher (Claude King) in Chesterfield's *Circumstantial Evidence*; was a dance-hall girl in a Hopalong Cassidy Western from Paramount, *The Eagle's Brood*; and played a former actress suspected of murdering her husband in *The Lady in Scarlet*, also from Chesterfield.

Dorothy Revier came to the end of the road cinematically with *The Cowboy and the Kid* (Universal, 1936), which, appropriately enough, was yet another Buck Jones Western. This time, however, she was cast against type as a demure schoolmarm. As we have seen, portraying kind and understanding women was not her strength and *Variety*'s "Wear" found her "slightly too dramatic for the role."

After more than 80 films in 14 years, Dorothy Revier disappeared almost completely from the limelight. She rarely granted interviews and when she did, proved suitably modest about her accomplishments. Remarked one columnist:

Most of the people who have achieved great prominence on the screen have more showmanship in their manner—but if you meet Dorothy Revier in person you would love her for the lack of it.

She divorced her second husband, Charles Johnson, sometime in the 1940s and in the following decade wed commercial artist William Pelayo. That marriage failed in 1964 and she remarried Johnson. It was, she later said, a very happy relationship. Johnson left her a widow in 1976 and she moved from their house in Beverly Hills to an apartment in West Hollywood. In her later years she was rather more outgoing and willingly shared her memories with the many young film buffs who seem to descend like vultures on elderly movie stars. Her only regret, she said, is that she had turned down an opportunity to play Belle Watling in *Gone with the Wind*. "Little did I know it was to be *the* picture of the century," she explained.

In preparation for their book on former screen luminaries, *Return Engagement*, James Watters and the photographer Horst visited the actress in her home in the early 1980s. Watters found her to be not unlike the ghost of Ophelia "with a distant, haunted yet aristocratic aura." At that late stage in her life, the actress, according to Watters, had only one remaining wish. "I'd just like to see my star put in the sidewalk on Hollywood Boulevard," she said. Sadly (as of December of 1998) that has yet to happen. Dorothy Revier died at the age of 89 on November 19, 1993.

DOROTHY REVIER FILMOGRAPHY

- **1922:** *The Broadway Madonna.*
- **1923:** *The Wild Party; The Supreme Test.*
- **1924:** *Marry in Haste; Do It Now; The Martyr Sex; Down By the Rio Grande; The Other Kind of Love; Call of the Mate; The Sword of Valor; Border Women; The Virgin; The Cowboy and the Flapper; Man from God's Country; The Wild West; Rose of Paris.*
- **1925:** *Dangerous Pleasure; Just a Woman; The Danger Signal; An Enemy of Men; Sealed Lips; Steppin' Out; When Husbands Flirt; The Fate of Flirt.*
- **1926:** *The Far Cry; Poker Faces; The False Alarm; When the Wife's Away; The Better Way.*
- **1927:** *Stolen Pleasures; Wandering Girls; The Price of Honor; Poor Girls; The Clown; The Drop Kick; The Tigress; The Warning; The Siren.*
- **1928:** *The Red Dance; Beware of Blondes; Sinners Parade; Submarine.*
- **1929:** *The Iron Mask; The Quitter; The Donovan Affair; Father and Son; The Dance of Life; Light Fingers; Tanned Legs; The Mighty.*
- **1930:** *Murder on the Roof; Hold Everything; The Squealer; Vengeance; The Way of All Men; The Bad Man.*
- **1931:** *The Blonde Camel; The Avenger; Graft; Leftover Ladies; Anybody's Blonde; The Last Ride.*
- **1932:** *Sally of the Subway; Sin's Pay Day; Night World; Arm of the Law; Beauty Parlor; The Widow in Scarlet; The King Murder; No Living Witness; A Scarlet Week-End; The Secret of Wu Sin.*
- **1933:** *Love Is Like That; Thrill Hunter; Above the Clouds; By Candlelight.*

1934: *The Fighting Ranger; Unknown Blonde; Green Eyes; The Curtain Falls; When a Man Sees Red.*
1935: *Circus Shadows; $20 a Week; Circumstantial Evidence; The Lady in Scarlet; The Eagle's Brood; Frisco Waterfront.*
1936: *The Cowboy and the Kid.*

24 — Gale Sondergaard

Dark and sinister-looking, Gale Sondergaard entered the record books by winning the first ever Best Supporting Actress Academy Award. She won for playing the reptilian Faith Paleologus, Edmund Gwenn's scheming housekeeper in the sprawling *Anthony Adverse* (Warner Bros., 1936). It was a remarkable feat, made no less so by the fact that *Anthony Adverse* marked her screen debut. A three year veteran of the Theater Guild, Sondergaard had come to Hollywood with her writer husband Herbert Biberman. Recognizing that Hollywood in reality was obsessed with the mundane, the striking-looking actress had never truly believed in a screen career—until, that is, Mervyn LeRoy tested her for *Anthony Adverse*. Winning the role (over, among others, Bette Davis), Sondergaard embarked on one of Hollywood's more interesting, if artistically unfulfilled, careers. She is known today primarily as *The Spider Woman* of 1940s cult films; it is often forgotten that Sondergaard gave a carefully shaded portrayal as the brave wife of Alfred Dreyfuss in *The Life of Emile Zola* (Warner Bros., 1937) and was highly touted for her role as Bette Davis' Eurasian adversary in *The Letter* (Warner Bros., 1940).

In the mid–1940s, fighting to overcome stereotyping, Sondergaard offered yet another vivid performance in a role that could easily have been a liability in the hands of a lesser actress, that of Lady Thiang, the King's patient and loving first wife in *Anna and the King of Siam* (20th Century–Fox, 1946). It was, alas, to become her last role of any importance; along with her husband, one of the original "Hollywood Ten," Sondergaard, a lifelong liberal who had served her country well in the 1930s fighting against the rising tide of fascism, was to endure a decade of blacklisting. Surviving this, the most shameful chapter in Hollywood history, she remained a dignified presence in American culture until her death in 1985.

Amazingly, the actress who would come to be known for portraying exotic villainesses was born Edith Holm Sondergaard on February 15, 1899, in Lichtfield, Minnesota, the daughter of Danish immigrant parents. Her father was a professor at the University of Minnesota and the Sondergaards were extremely politically aware. "I was raised by progressive parents," she told the *Village Voice* in the mid 1970s. "Now you'll understand why I have a historical point of view about what goes on—politically, and in every way."

Not surprisingly, Sondergaard was educated at the University of Minnesota, where she obtained a B.A. in English. She was, however, stagestruck from an early age, already in grade school reading passages from *Ivanhoe*. A high school drama teacher remarked that her personality would probably be too exotic for anything other than the stage. "You'll never be an average girl at a tea party," he advised her—and then promptly cast her as a domestic in a school play.

Realizing that the high school teacher probably had been correct, Sondergaard one day simply quit a career in academia for a stint with the Minneapolis School of Dramatic Arts. It proved to be a courageous and ultimately perceptive move: Leaving the Academy, she was immediately engaged by the John Kellard Shakespeare Company of Milwaukee and made her professional debut as Jessica in *The Merchant of Venice*. She was then engaged by the renowned Jessie Bonstelle Stock Company of Detroit and was Gertrude to Melvyn Douglas' *Hamlet*. Despite her tender age she excelled in character parts, tackling any role offered her, "hags and ingenues, mothers and daughters, wantons and nuns." In 1922 she took time out to marry a Neill O'Malley but otherwise kept her focus firmly on the stage. Thus, with her new husband in tow, she relocated to New York City.

Sondergaard made her Broadway debut in *What's Your Wife Doing?* in 1923, but success only came her way in 1928, when the Theater Guild engaged her to understudy Judith Anderson as Nina in Eugene O'Neill's *Strange Interlude*. Complying with convention for the only time in her long career, Sondergaard, not unlike a Ruby Keeler, stepped in when Anderson suddenly had to withdraw. "I did it on two hours' notice and without ever having met the cast," she later said. "But Nina was my role and I knew I couldn't fail." She didn't, and as a reward earned a three year contract with the prestigious company.

Nursed by the Theater Guild she stretched her talents further with major roles in *Major Barbara*, *The American Dream*, *Alice's House*, *Dr. Monica*, *Invitation to a Murder*, *Karl and Anna*, and *Red Dust*. In the latter two she was directed by Herbert Biberman, a well-known progressive writer and director. In 1930 she divorced O'Malley and married the much more compatible Biberman.

Having established himself as a comer, Biberman signed a contract with Columbia in 1934 and the couple relocated to the West Coast.* Sondergaard, unselfishly sacrificing her own career, left the Theater Guild to be with her husband. "I'm not going to stay behind. I'll give up my career, but I'm going with you," she told him.

Once in Hollywood, Sondergaard spent her time as Biberman's script editor and general "sounding board," never seriously considering a career as a screen actress. Incredibly, Gale Sondergaard, one of the most striking women in Hollywood, did not think herself beautiful enough for movies.

In Hollywood, Biberman was to work on projects such as Eight Bells *(1935),* Meet Nero Wolfe *(1938) and* King of Chinatown *(1939).*

24—GALE SONDERGAARD

In late 1935, however, a friend convinced her to meet with director Mervyn LeRoy, who was searching for the right actress to play the evil Faith Paleologus in his upcoming version of Hervey Allen's historical bestseller *Anthony Adverse*. LeRoy had tested Warners' top female star, Bette Davis, but the part was deemed too small and the director was determined to find a "new face." He found it the minute he laid eyes on the exotic-looking Gale Sondergaard. "Mervyn LeRoy told me afterwards that as soon as I walked in the door—I had some silver earrings on—he wanted me," the actress explained to Leonard Maltin 36 years later.

Filming the mammoth 1,200 page novel about an orphan who grows up to become a wealthy merchant (and, for a while, slave trader), but gives it all up for the love of Napoleon's mistress, would become a giant undertaking costing Warner Bros. an unprecedented $1,050,500. Contemporary opinion found the money well spent (modern critics are more dubious as to its merits, most finding it tediously overlong), and *Anthony Adverse* was named one of the National Board of Review's top ten pictures of 1936. Fredric March starred as the idealistic Anthony, with Olivia de Havilland as his romantic interest; Claude Rains as his evil stepfather; Edmund Gwenn as the kind-hearted father-in-law; and Sondergaard as Gwenn's conniving housekeeper, who conspires with the corrupt Rains in getting rid of the pesky Adverse. Sondergaard had only a few scenes in the long narrative, but she made every minute count and turned Faith Paleologus into one of the decade's most malicious females. Tricking a defenseless old man into willing her his fortune, she proceeds to conspire with a depraved nobleman to rid the world of the one man that stands in their way of total dominance. Today the performance seems almost a cliché, but Sondergaard's Faith came four years in advance of that standard-bearer of Machiavellian housekeepers, Judith Anderson's Mrs. Danvers of *Rebecca* (1940).

Sondergaard's reaction to seeing her own snarling and not a little reptilian performance for the first time was pure shock. "I remember going to the rushes with Mervyn LeRoy and wanting to crawl under my seat when I saw myself," she later said.

> After it was over [LeRoy] said, "Well what do you think of yourself as a motion picture actress?" And I said, "I think I look so self-conscious." He said, "If that's what you think, just go on being self conscious."

Sondergaard's reviews were overwhelmingly favorable, although Frank S. Nugent of the *New York Times* complained that her interpretation of the role was "a complete departure from the character in the novel." The members of the Academy of Motion Picture Arts and Sciences, voting for supporting players for the first time, thought the performance one of the year's finest and nominated her for Best Supporting Actress along with Beulah Bondi of M-G-M's *The Gorgeous Hussy*; Alice Brady, who had been daffy in Universal's *My Man Godfrey*; Bonita Granville, the tiny terror of Goldwyn's *These Three*; and Maria Ouspenskaya's aristocrat in Goldwyn's *Dodsworth*. Handicapping the competition, the industry papers considered Ouspenskaya and Sondergaard the front-runners, odds about even.

The winner, of course, was Sondergaard who, despite Awards presenter George

Jessel's nice speech on the importance of supporting players, only received a plaque, not the coveted statuette.*

Winning the very first Best Supporting Actress Award hardly made Gale Sondergaard a star. "I think if the award ever did anyone any good, it wasn't me. Because a supporting award in no way enhances a career or salary in the way that Best Actress does," she told Boze Hadleigh of *Scarlet Street* in 1984.

Instead of graduating to leads, Sondergaard could do nothing but stand by and watch while Paramount eliminated most of her part in the witch-hunt melodrama *Maid of Salem* (1937). "That's the one time I was left on the cutting-room floor," she told Leonard Maltin of *Film Fan Monthly* in 1971. "What you saw in that was not representative of what I did in it." What she did do was make sure that innocent Claudette Colbert would be hanged for murder.

In retrospect, Sondergaard's participation in *Maid of Salem*, a powerful (if somewhat romanticized) indictment of intolerance, was ironic, to say the least. In July of 1936, the Bibermans, along with such theater luminaries as Eddie Cantor, Oscar Hammerstein and Dorothy Parker, and political bigwigs J. W. Buzzell (AFL) and John Lechner (American Legion), joined in the formation of the Hollywood Anti-Nazi League, a group of concerned Americans, mostly liberals (and some Communists), but also comprised of several conservatives. The League took out full-page ads in the Hollywood trade papers denouncing "The Menace of Hitlerism in America," and published the newsletter *Hollywood Now*.

Their participation in this and other antifascist causes would come back to haunt the Bibermans. "I wouldn't know about the communists," Sondergaard said 40 years later to writer Victoria Hodgetts of the *Village Voice*. "We were antifascists. We were anti–Nazis."

When writers Dorothy Parker and Lillian Hellman visited Spain in the throes of civil war in 1937, they returned to Hollywood brimming with horrifying stories of atrocities. To combat what they correctly perceived as a dangerous turn of events in Europe, they gathered together other like-minded film industry notables† and founded the Motion Picture Artists Committee to aid Republican Spain. This commendable group, of which Gale Sondergaard and her husband were among the founders, was to prove yet another nail in their coffins.

Onscreen, Sondergaard was less civic minded. She was very evil indeed as Simone Simon's brutal sister, a seedy cafe owner (read: bordello madam) in 20th Century–Fox's remake of *Seventh Heaven* (1937). When the naive Simon refuses to "entertain" a wealthy customer, Sondergaard beats her to a pulp and throws her out into the mean streets of Paris to fend for herself.

Janet Gaynor had won an Academy Award for portraying the little French waif in the original 1927 version, but the melodrama of lost souls trying to survive in the slums of Paris had been better suited to the silent era. The French Simone Simon was not up to the challenge of making the heroine believable to a modern audience, but

---

*The Academy did not give out "Oscars" in the supporting categories until 1943. The governing body did not remedy that appalling situation until Charlton Heston (of all people!) awarded Sondergaard the statuette 33 years later.

†Including writers Dashiell Hammett, Donald Ogden Stewart and the Epstein Brothers, and actors Melvyn Douglas, Luise Rainer, Paul Muni and John Garfield.

Sondergaard was at her menacing best as the brutish sister and Frank S. Nugent of the *New York Times* thought she gave "by far the outstanding performance in the picture."

After playing a compassionless tormentor of street urchins, Sondergaard showed a remarkable acting range by immediately shifting gears to portray the noble wife of the much maligned Alfred Dreyfuss (Joseph Schildkraut) in *The Life of Emile Zola* (Warner Bros., 1937), a lavish bio-pic starring, as the credits declared, *Mr.* Paul Muni. Again, however, her part was brief ("built up from nothing," wrote Nugent), yet Sondergaard once more managed to create a full-fledged character with little help from the screenwriters.

She had scarcely more to do as Doris Clandon, a malicious thief who leads young boys into a life of crime in *Lord Jeff* (M-G-M, 1938), a sentimental adventure tailored to the much overrated talents of Freddie Bartholomew and Mickey Rooney; but she was very good indeed as Madame Charlot, the aging proprietress of a *Dramatic School* (M-G-M, 1938). Jealous of her promising, young students, the onetime stage star simmers with envy and resentment and is, in other words, the antithesis of the spirited old trouper played by Constance Collier in the similar *Stage Door* (RKO, 1937). "It is an interesting role, played with understanding and assurance," wrote the *New York Times'* Nugent, who felt that Sondergaard stole the film from its lead, the fey Luise Rainer.

Had Mervyn LeRoy not been persuaded otherwise, Sondergaard would have made a very glamorous Wicked Witch of the West in M-G-M's amazingly durable *The Wizard of Oz* (1939). It was the studio brass, however, who decided to conform with children's perceptions of a wicked witch rather than their parents'. Sondergaard refused to go along; "I *won't* be an ugly witch," she told producer Arthur Freed, who replaced her with the hatchet-faced Margaret Hamilton, a former kindergarten teacher with no such compunction. Fanny Brice had been tapped to play Glinda, the Good Witch, but M-G-M felt that a little glamour was needed after all, and she in turn was replaced with former Ziegfeld Girl (and Florenz Ziegfeld's widow) Billie Burke. In retrospect it was the correct call, but it would still have been entertaining to have watched Brice and Sondergaard going at each other.

Instead of terrorizing Judy Garland, Sondergaard menaced Martha Raye and Bob Hope in a silly comedy, *Never Say Die* (Paramount, 1939). She was an impressive but immobile Empress Eugenie in Warners' gigantic production of Franz Werfel's *Juarez* (1939), after which she returned to scare Bob Hope witless in *The Cat and the Canary* (Paramount, 1939). In the latter, she is Miss Lu, a clairvoyant housekeeper who, it turns out, is merely a "red herring"—clever casting on the part of producer Arthur Hornblow, Jr., who made sure that Sondergaard, very Mrs. Danvers–like, would appear the prime suspect in a series of gruesome murders spooking the proverbial haunted mansion.

As a consolation prize, perhaps, for losing out on *The Wizard of Oz*, 20th Century–Fox cast Sondergaard as the treacherous but very glamorous house cat Tylette in the second screen version of *The Blue Bird* (1940). Shirley Temple (who had once been considered for the part of Dorothy Gale) starred as Mytyl, the little girl who, with her brother Tyltyl (Johnny Russell), goes off to search for the blue bird of happiness. It is Tylette, who, in an attempt to thwart the children's quest, admonishes the trees of the forest to frighten them into returning home.

Gale Sondergaard, Bob Hope and Paulette Goddard in *The Cat and The Canary* (Paramount, 1939). (Photograph courtesy of the Danish Film Museum.)

Fox, going for laughs instead of drama, had first cast pratfall comedienne Joan Davis as Tylette, but then thought better of it and offered the part to Sondergaard, who played it for all it was worth. It was all for naught, however; *The Blue Bird* was a bit too ethereal to appeal to children, and many reviewers found the adult cast members somewhat over the top. "If children are to represent the children," Frank S. Nugent of the *New York Times* complained, "then it seems incongruous to turn the dog and the cat into grown-up [Eddie] Collins and sheath-gowned Gale Sondergaard, who are a bit too large to be playing games." As an attempt to duplicate the charm and freshness of *The Wizard of Oz*, *The Blue Bird* was a costly failure.

Sondergaard's most important role of the year came at Warner Bros., who cast her as the widow of Bette Davis' victim in *The Letter*. Based on a W. Somerset Maugham play, *The Letter* details a triangle drama set among planters in the Malaysian jungle. Davis starred as the bored wife of a rubber planter (Herbert Marshall), who shoots her lover in what she claims is self defense. While Davis, who ultimately confesses her guilt, is redeemed by the love of her husband, Sondergaard, as the victim's

Eurasian wife, is not so forgiving. In an act of revenge, she brutally stabs her erstwhile rival to death. "I did my best to look evil, to think evil, and hoped it wouldn't seem foolish," she told Leonard Maltin many years later.

Unfortunately for the outcome, *The Letter* had undergone some critical changes before reaching the screen. In Maugham's original play, for example, the Davis character is never punished (except for the fact that she must continue her boring, empty life in a country she doesn't understand), and Sondergaard's "Mrs. Hammond" is actually the lover's Chinese mistress, not his wife. To mollify the Hays Office, Warners felt obligated to punish Davis for her evil deed and, to avoid charges of miscegenation, changed Sondergaard's character into a Eurasian woman. According to Sondergaard, however, the studio didn't change her enough. "I went to wardrobe to be fitted before we were to begin, and they brought out all these cheap, horrible things of a second-class whore." The actress felt sure that the character was to be vilified only because she was part Chinese, and together with director William Dieterle she proceeded to restore her by making her more glamorous and dignified. "I must say that in all the wicked women I've had to play in my life, and I've done a number, I refused them being made ugly," Sondergaard later said.

While Bosley Crowther of the *New York Times* felt that Sondergaard "cryptically conveys through appearance and attitudes only the enigmatic menace of the native woman," most thought her portrayal intriguing, W. Somerset Maugham himself among them. Maugham, in fact, had been delighted with her casting. "I remember meeting Mr. Maugham before the picture was even made," Sondergaard later told Boze Hadleigh. "He took to me right away, and I to him."

Offscreen, Sondergaard and her husband Herbert Biberman were in trouble with the so-called Dies Committee, the first of many congressional "inquiries" into leftwing "infiltration" of Hollywood. Congressman Martin Dies, a rabid rightwing Democrat from Texas, had earlier labeled the Anti-Nazi League a "Communist front organization," and now he turned his paranoid gaze toward a Hollywood establishment that he considered a "hotbed of Communism." Having managed to "turn" several former members of the Communist Party, Dies compiled a list of 42 motion picture personalities suspected of being Communists. Among the "suspects" were, along with the Bibermans, Humphrey Bogart, Fredric March, James Cagney, Franchot Tone and Lionel Stander. Both Sondergaard and Biberman were subpoenaed by a Los Angeles grand jury to answer questions "concerning operations of Communists in the film colony." Dies, alone in so-called executive session (at his mansion in Beaumont, Texas), promised clearance to all those who would "cooperate." By August of 1941 all but Stander (who was fired by Republic Pictures as a consequence) had been "cleared," but the Dies lists would resurface ten years later with terrible consequences.

To get away from it all, Sondergaard returned to the Broadway stage in *Cue for Passion* (1941). The play ran a successful three months, but when it was over, the actress felt more than ready to return to Hollywood. "It was an interesting role, and it was fun to get back to the theater, [but] when it was over I was so frustrated because I couldn't see it on the screen," she later told Leonard Maltin.

Although Gale Sondergaard had emerged as one of Hollywood's most interesting character actresses of the late 1930s, the new decade would prove rather anticlimactic.

Through such programmers as *The Black Cat* (Universal, 1941), *Enemy Agents Meet Ellery Queen* (Columbia, 1942), *Isle of Forgotten Sins* (PRC, 1943), and *The Strange Death of Adolf Hitler* (Universal, 1943), Sondergaard was fast becoming a cliché of her old screen persona. She might have resurrected her career playing the resentful Mrs. Danvers in *Rebecca* (Selznick, 1940), but the plum role went to her old "nemesis" Judith Anderson. Instead, she played foils for Bob Hope in *My Favorite Blonde* (Paramount, 1942) and Ralph Bellamy in *Enemy Agents Meet Ellery Queen* (RKO, 1942).

Signing with "B" movie factory Universal, Sondergaard was announced to star opposite Lon Chaney, Jr., in a series loosely based on pulp fiction and radio's *Inner Sanctum* mysteries. In the end, only the mediocre Chaney was made to suffer through these hapless little chillers ground out by Universal as so much sausage.*

Universal basically wasted Sondergaard's talents—with one notable exception. She was absolutely wonderful playing cat-and-mouse with Basil Rathbone and Nigel Bruce in *Sherlock Holmes and the Spider Woman* (1944), one of the better entries in the seemingly endless (and highly anachronistic) series. This time Holmes and Watson delve into a series of "suicides"—actually murders of wealthy, heavily insured men. The murder weapon is a poisonous spider carried around by an African pygmy (Angelo Rositto) and the brain behind the attacks is the fiendish "Spider Woman," played with malignant glee by Sondergaard in what would become her pivotal 1940s role.

Although realizing the limitations of the genre, Sondergaard still found it "fun playing with Basil and Nigel Bruce." And although critics were generally harsh (Bosley Crowther, for instance, turned highbrow and declared her "sinister in a soporific way"), audiences made the cheaply produced programmer a "sleeper" hit. Viewed today, the film manages to walk a thin line between outright campiness and true suspense.

Two years later, *Sherlock Holmes and the Spider Woman* spawned *The Spider Woman Strikes Back* (1946), a potboiler with few qualities other than the fact that Gale Sondergaard appeared in it. "They thought they would do a series starring me as the Spider Woman and it had nothing to do with [Sherlock Holmes], she later complained. "Well, I almost had hysterics at one time out of hating it so." It pained her, she told Philip Scheuer of the Los Angeles *Times*, "to be considered catty—let alone predatory—the kind that pounces on her prey." It also disconcerted her to be always cast as a Eurasian.

In between *Spider Woman* assignments, Sondergaard was wasted in typical 1940s Universal dreck, always giving a commendable performance but usually merely thrown into the stew as a red herring. She was, for example, completely innocent of any wrongdoing in *The Invisible Man's Revenge* (1944), but, read by Sondergaard, lines such as "Don't worry, you'll get all that's coming to you" took on a decidedly sinister bent. In *The Climax* (1944), a virtual remake of the previous year's *Phantom of the*

---

*A Sondergaard-like role of a murderous nurse was eventually played by lookalike Patricia Morison in the first of the series, Calling Dr. Death *(1943). In the second installment,* Weird Woman, *the role of a vengeful widow, a classic Sondergaard part, was played by RKO's Houri of Horrors (as the* Hollywood Reporter *named her) Elizabeth Russell. And in* Dead Man's Eyes *(1944), the pedestrian Acquanetta sports a coiffure highly reminiscent of Gale's. In all cases, the parts were probably deemed too secondary for an actress of Sondergaard's stature.*

Opera, she was again on the side of the angels, this time as Boris Karloff's housekeeper, skulking around to prove her boss guilty of murder.

Fortunately, Sondergaard was rescued from the horrors of Universal (if not typecasting) when 20th Century–Fox cast her as Lady Thiang, the King's number one wife in the screen version of Margaret Landon's popular biography *Anna and the King of Siam* (1946). Like she had in *The Letter*, however, the actress fought front office dictums tooth and nail to give the character the refinement and elegance she felt it deserved. "I really pleaded for the dignity of these women," she later said.

The story of an English teacher who travels to Thailand in the 1860s to tutor the harem and 67 children of a "savage" potentate, *Anna and the*

Gale Sondergaard in 1943.

King of Siam today seems more engaging and less sentimental than its later musical reincarnation *The King and I* (20th Century–Fox, 1956). Not the least of the reasons are the enjoyable performances by Irene Dunne and Rex Harrison in the title roles, Lee J. Cobb as the king's chief minister, and Sondergaard. Lady Thiang was one of the actress' own favorite characterizations. "I got deep, deep pleasure out of [it]," she later said. "I just loved this woman—such a noble, wise, farseeing woman, who accepted her fate." For her performance, Sondergaard earned her second Academy Award nomination, but lost to Anne Baxter of Fox's *The Razor's Edge*.

No one expected it at the time, but *Anna and the King of Siam* proved to be Sondergaard's last film of any merit for more than a decade. She appeared opposite Bob Hope for the fourth (and final) time in *Road to Rio* (Paramount, 1947), and lent her services to a weak Maria Montez costume "epic," *Pirates of Monterey* (Universal, 1947). After that, she suddenly found herself all but unemployable.

In October of 1947, Sondergaard's husband, Herbert Biberman, became a member of the sacrificial "Hollywood Ten," a group of screen artists who, instead of collaborating with the House Un-American Activities Committee (HUAC), invoked the Fifth Amendment's provision against self-incrimination when asked the infamous question, "Are you now or have you ever been a member of the Communist Party?" Biberman, along with Dalton Trumbo, Edward Dmytryk,* Ring Lardner, Jr., and others, was cited for contempt of Congress and sentenced to one year in prison. Sondergaard, at this point only a victim of guilt by association, found herself placed on a so-called "gray-list," unable to secure work in a film industry nervous about the outcome of the hearings in Washington.

She did return briefly to the screen in 1949, when old friend Mervyn LeRoy hired her for a supporting role in a glossy M-G-M soap opera starring Barbara Stanwyck, *East Side, West Side*. But after that, no other offers came her way and she instead devoted her time to work on behalf of the "Ten," narrating a documentary about their case.

The Hollywood Ten (1950) was, according to writers Larry Ceplair and Steven Englund, "noteworthy for its utter lack of self-pity." The film was, of course, like its protagonists, blacklisted, although a group of "Ten" wives, including Sondergaard, dutifully "carted [it] from meeting hall to auditorium to living room."

In March of 1951, during a new round of hearings into film industry subversion, Sondergaard was "named" by "friendly" witness and Columbia star Larry Parks as a member of the Communist Party USA.† For Sondergaard, who was subpoenaed to testify before the committee, this turn of events did not come as a surprise. On March 13, 1951, she had written to the board of Screen Actors Guild that "I would be naive if I didn't recognize that there is a danger that I may have arrived at the end of my career as a motion picture actress." She continued,

> Today I read that this particular Inquisition is not directed against the industry but is directed at individuals. This would seem to imply that any number of individual actors could be destroyed without further injuring the industry—and that the employer, having been guaranteed that they would not be personally involved, have given the committee carte blanche to attack individuals to their own purpose.

Sondergaard went on to state that she believed in the freedom of speech, religion and association described in the First Amendment, but realized that the sitting Supreme Court would not come to her aid. She therefore saw no other option than to invoke her Fifth Amendment right to silence and the right not to incriminate herself. The Guild, in a carefully worded letter, basically washed their collective hands of the entire affair.

It was, in retrospect, an unfortunate choice to invoke the Fifth: Since the Communist Party had never been illegal, Sondergaard had broken no laws. The Fifth Amendment, however, guaranteed that she could not be asked to "name names," the most infamous practice of the Inquisition in Hollywood, but several "unfriendly" witnesses achieved the same goal by invoking the First Amendment, the right to freedom of speech.

---

*Dmytryk later distanced himself from the other "Ten" and turned informer.

†Parks also "named" 1930s actresses Karen Morley, Dorothy Tree and Anne Revere, all of whom were blacklisted.

Unfortunately, not all Hollywood radicals were as steadfast in their beliefs, but instead, like Larry Parks, turned informers when their livelihood was suddenly threatened. Consequently, Sondergaard would be informed on by several former colleagues, among them the screenwriter Martin Berkeley* and the actor Lee J. Cobb (Sondergaard's co-star in *Anna and the King of Siam*).

Appearing before the Un-American Activities Committee in late March 1951, Sondergaard, as pledged, invoked the Fifth Amendment when asked about her affiliation with the Communist Party. "May I say everybody is branding every progressive organization which has done good work as subversive. This I find very sad and very shocking," she expressed to Committee counsel Frank Tavenner. Returning from Washington she told the press that she "felt sorry about Larry Parks being an informer. I'm sorry he didn't stick by his guns."

Unlike the "Hollywood Ten," Sondergaard was not carted away to prison, but she did face total blacklisting from the motion picture industry. She resurfaced briefly in 1954, when she turned down an offer to play a leading role in Herbert Biberman's docu-drama about striking mine workers in New Mexico, *Salt of the Earth*, explaining that her presence would detract from the film's important message. "The role was written for me, but only a Mexican could have played it," she later said.† When reactionaries in and out of Hollywood made distribution of the film all but impossible, Biberman sued the motion picture industry for conspiracy, but ultimately lost the case.

Now a Hollywood outcast, Sondergaard spent several years raising her adopted children, Joan and Daniel Biberman, did some summer stock (the stage was not nearly as affected by the blacklist as were motion pictures), and from 1956 to 1958 toured in a one-woman show bearing the unwieldy (but tenacious) title of *Woman, Her Emergence into Fuller Status as a Human Being in Relation to Her Mate*. A modern feminist, Sondergaard was again well ahead of her time.

By the late 1960s, the stigma of the Hollywood blacklists had all but disappeared; in fact, having been on a list was now thought of almost as an act of heroism—which, for many, it certainly had been.

Sondergaard found a measure of resurrection when she returned to her native Minneapolis in 1967 to appear in repertory at the Tyrone Guthrie Theater. The following year the University of Minnesota (her alma mater) gave her the "outstanding achievement award."

She returned to the screen after 20 years playing a small supporting role in a sincere, if somewhat naive, pre–Civil War melodrama, *Slaves* (1969), which was produced in part by survivors of the Theater Guild (including founding father Philip Langner) and directed by Herbert Biberman. Compared to the modern civil rights movement, the pioneering radicals proved somewhat out of touch and the film, dealing with miscegenation and starring Stephen Boyd and Dionne Warwick, was easily dismissed by critics as just so much hokum.

More important in the scheme of things was Sondergaard's much belated television

---

Berkeley led the name-calling before HUAC, informing on 162 persons.

Rosaura Revueltas replaced her.

debut in a segment of *It Takes a Thief* (1969). Television became a whole new career for the veteran actress, who went on to appear on such shows as *Get Smart*, *The Bold Ones*, *Night Gallery*, and *Medical Center*. In between television shows, she returned to the stage in productions of *The Crucible*, *John Gabriel Borkman*, *Uncle Vanya*, and *Goodbye Fidel*.

Sondergaard slowed down her career considerably after Herbert Biberman's death in 1971. In 1973, Curtis Harrington directed her in a telefilm scripted by Robert Bloch, *The Cat Creature*, in which she was her old villainous self while terrorizing a new generation of actors. She returned to the screen three years later, appearing in *Pleasantville* (KCET, 1976), a minor drama detailing the relationship between a 12-year-old girl and her grandmother, and *Return of a Man Called Horse* (United Artists, 1976).

In the latter, her role was highly reminiscent of the one played by Dame Judith Anderson in *A Man Called Horse* (1970). In this rather nonessential sequel, Richard Harris again plays the aristocratic Englishman Out West, this time returning to save the Indian tribe that had adopted him in the original film. Visiting the set of *Return*, writer Victoria Hodgetts was struck by a small figure in heavy brown skins and pigtails.

> Immobile in the blistering sun [Hodgetts wrote in the *Village Voice*], then—"CUT"—she breaks. Rises. I had thought from behind that it was a young girl: now I notice that the braids are grey—this is an older woman—the shaman, the witch doctor, the one who instigates the Sun Wow Ritual to try to save the tribe. This is Gale Sondergaard. She comes toward us, suede boots neatly skirting red and black volcanic boulders and directors' chairs, something tiny in her hand. She's been squatting in the sun for hours; only able to do so because of the discipline of yoga 90 minutes every day and the stamina of a life of yogurt, wheat germ bran, and healthy living.

Interviewed on the set of her first worthwhile movie in 20 years, Sondergaard did not find it ironic that the former Hollywood "outcasts" had become revered members of their profession. "No, it's not ironic," she explained. "I have no ironies or bitterness. I *understand*. I'm very objective—I see it all as the March of History. The progressives are *always* being pushed down by the establishment. And the establishment *has* to do it, too. To preserve themselves! It is not *nice*—but that's the way it is."

A few weeks later, she reiterated her position to the Los Angeles *Times*:

> I feel no bitterness. If you allow yourself to grow bitter, you only hurt yourself. I'm very proud of having been a part of that period. I am proud to have taken a stand. I don't want to go on living in that period, but I realize that if I can understand it, then I must help other people understand it.

Gale Sondergaard returned to the screen for the final time in *Echoes* (Continental, 1983), a strange, dreamlike allegory of an art student's descent into madness. By this late date she looked, as the writer James Watters noted, frail and parched and not unlike the late Danish writer Isak Dinesen (Karen Blixen). Offscreen, she would admit to a sense of loss, the loss of work that might have been.

True to her beliefs, the actress spent her final years living in a small frame house in the unfashionable Hispanic Los Angeles neighborhood of Echo Park. In early 1985, however, she moved to the Motion Picture Country Home and Hospital, which is where she died on August 14, 1985. She was survived by her son Daniel Biberman, two grandchildren and her sister, Hester De Lacey Sondergaard.*

GALE SONDERGAARD FILMOGRAPHY

1936: *Anthony Adverse.*
1937: *Maid of Salem; Seventh Heaven; The Life of Emile Zola.*
1938: *Lord Jeff; Dramatic School.*
1939: *Never Say Die; Juarez; The Cat and the Canary; The Llano Kid.*
1940: *The Blue Bird; The Mark of Zorro; The Letter.*
1941: *The Black Cat; Paris Calling.*
1942: *My Favorite Blonde; Enemy Agents Meet Ellery Queen; A Night to Remember.*
1943: *Appointment in Berlin; The Strange Death of Adolf Hitler; Isle of Forgotten Sins.*
1944: *Sherlock Holmes and the Spider Woman; Follow the Boys; The Invisible Man's Revenge; The Climax; Christmas Holiday; Gypsy Wildcat; Enter Arsene Lupin.*
1946: *The Spider Woman Strikes Back; A Night in Paradise; Anna and the King of Siam; The Time of Their Lives.*
1947: *Pirates of Monterey; Road to Rio.*
1948: *East Side, West Side.*
1969: *Slaves.*
1976: *Return of a Man Called Horse; Pleasantville.*
1983: *Echoes.*

---

*Hester Sondergaard appeared in the American version of a Soviet film, Seeds of Freedom *(1943), and two Hollywood productions,* The Naked City *(1948) and* Jigsaw *(1949).*

25 — Lilyan Tashman

The newspaper headlines were cold and impersonal that Thursday in March of 1934. What else could they have been? Mere words seemed inadequate to describe the grief and sorrow felt collectively from New York to Hollywood, from London to Paris. Lilyan Tashman had died. "Gay, happy, brilliant Lilyan Tashman is gone," wailed columnist Louella Parsons.

> Hollywood found it difficult yesterday to grasp the sad import of the news that "Lil," as her friends called her, had passed away, following an emergency operation in New York.

A few days later the streets around the Universal Funeral Chapel on Lexington Avenue were blocked off to accommodate the 3,000 mourners who showed up to bid Lilyan Tashman farewell. Not since Rudolf Valentino's death eight years earlier had New York City experienced such an outpouring of grief for a screen star.

Lilyan Tashman has become, Jack Hamilton wrote in 1974, "a dim, legendary figure in movie history, a tough worldly actress who died young." Even in the nostalgic 1990s has she been virtually forgotten. Yet, Tashman held an enormous influence over women in the late 1920s and early 1930s. Not as an actress, although she enjoyed a long screen career, but because of her keen use of fashion. She was what they used to call a "clotheshorse"—*The* clotheshorse! Women the world over imitated her. "She was daring in her style," Louella Parsons explained.

> She could wear a hat at an angle that would make any other woman look ridiculous. Her costumes were chic, and she adored appearing in something individual that would make other women turn and look at her.

Tashman was just as "daring" in her personal life. A lesbian, she married Edmund Lowe, one of Hollywood's more overt homosexuals, and they became each other's "beard," so to speak. American morality was appeased and Hollywood insiders could enjoy the "if they only knew" aspect of the union.

With the advent of "talkies," moviegoers the world over discovered what those same Hollywood insiders had known all along: Tashman was not only elegant, she was also one of the wittiest women around. Offscreen, sometimes even cruelly so. (She once warned Norma Shearer away from dating Jack Pickford by referring to him as "Mr. Syphilis"!) Party givers always considered her high on their "A" lists, and now producers would make sure that the public could enjoy her caustic remarks as well (or at least as many of them as the Hays Office would allow).

The vehicle or size of role never really mattered; her *modus operandi* was almost invariably the same. Usually she would enter in some extraordinary outfit, say something sparkling or scathing, then quickly exit. Often you wouldn't remember the film itself—only her. And what she had worn. When she died at only 34, sob-sisters everywhere speculated that she had been on the verge of breaking through as a leading lady. Probably not. Girls like Lilyan were too bright, too independent, and too worldly to have bothered placating the Hollywood elite.

She was born as plain Lillian Tashman on October 23, 1899, in Brooklyn, the daughter of Maurice Tashman, a children's clothing manufacturer. As a teenager she nurtured dreams of becoming a schoolteacher when, as they say, fate intervened: Florenz Ziegfeld spotted her having tea at the Cafe de Paris. According to later reports, an underling came up to her table with the message that Ziegfeld would like to meet her. "I thought it was sort of a gag," she later admitted. "So I said, 'If Mr. Ziegfeld wants to see me, tell him to come over to my table'." As legend has it, the great impresario did just that and Tashman became one of his "Glorified Girls" in the 1916 edition of the *Ziegfeld Follies*.

It is a congenial story with one major flaw: It didn't happen that way. In reality, Tashman had already gained quite a reputation as a fashion model and made her Broadway debut in the chorus of *The Lilac Domino*. That show opened to good reviews in October of 1914—two years *before* she entered the *Follies*. She then appeared with Gus Edwards, singing "You Gotta Stop Pickin' on My Little Pickaninny" in his *Song Revue of 1914*.

Nevertheless, a *Follies* girl she did become (in June of 1916), and Ziegfeld was so impressed with her potential that he later ushered her into his other 1916 hit, *The Century Girl*. She was just as busy the following year, appearing in both the *Follies* and *Miss 1917*. If ever there was a born "Glorified Girl" it was Lilyan Tashman, who could descend a staircase wearing a mammoth headdress like no one else.

Tashman's fellow performers knew early on that she possessed an almost deadly wit, but Ziegfeld himself was primarily interested in her striking looks. By 1919, however, she had discovered farce and left the *Follies* to make a sensational legit debut as Pansy in *Come On Charley*. She also married for the first time that year—Al Lee, a vaudevillian whom she had met through Eddie Cantor.* The marriage, unfortunately, proved short-lived, lasting less than a year.

Tashman's breakthrough performance came in 1921, when she gave Ina Claire a run for her money as the man-hungry Trixie in *The Gold Diggers*. The comedy about three Broadway hopefuls on the make was very popular and enjoyed a healthy run. It

---

Lee enjoyed a minor screen career which included Marriages Are Made *(1918).*

also made Tashman a household name: Soon theatergoers asked shopkeepers for "Lilyan Tashman gowns" and begged hairdressers to create a "Lilyan Tashman coiffure"—even if that meant a blonde dye job.

Needless to say, Tashman's newfound popularity proved a lightning rod to film companies searching for new and exciting faces, and she was soon inundated with offers. In the end, Paramount won out and she made her screen debut supporting Richard Dix in *Experience* (1921).

Experience was the old story of the country bumpkin who goes to the Big City and is exploited by an assortment of unsavory city slickers. Midway through the film Tashman saunters in (playing a temptress known as "Pleasure"), does her vamp routine and exits. She did not think much of the experience, merely collected her (not insubstantial) salary and promptly forgot about the whole thing.

There was another stage success the following year, *A Bachelor's Night*, and again she played a character named Trixie (she was that kind of girl in those years). Sam Goldwyn followed Paramount's lead and hired her for a day or two at an impressive salary to support Mabel Normand in *Head Over Heels* (1922). That experience also did not make her forget Broadway, nor did a third film, again for Goldwyn, a little parody of *Sturm und Drang* melodrama entitled *Nellie, the Beautiful Cloak Model* (1924). In between these potboilers she starred on stage in *Lady Bug* (1923) and toured extensively.

Tashman returned to Broadway as Hazel, "a de luxe pirate on the highway to Eros," in *The Garden of Weeds*. The screen rights to the play was sold to Famous Players–Lasky, a division of Paramount who wanted her to repeat the performance before the cameras in Hollywood. This time she was ready: Not only did she have a new man in her life, but that man was an actor based in Hollywood.

Tashman had met Edmund Lowe back in 1919 when he was appearing on Broadway opposite Lenore Ulric in *The Son-Daughter* and she was busy with *Come On Charley*. It was love at first sight, she later admitted, but he was married. Soon, she was too and they lost contact. They met again in 1924 and got engaged, both having divorced their respective spouses. But Lowe had a contract waiting for him in Hollywood, and she was now the "toast" of Broadway.

The offer from Famous Players changed all that. "She knew she wasn't saccharinely beautiful as film beauty is gauged," Dorothy Spenseley of *Photoplay* later wrote.

> But she well knew she had something that every pretty cinema aspirant has not got. She had an urban air of *distingué*—a positive assurance—a radiating self-confidence. And then, too, there was Lilyan's figure—of which she did not boast, but which has been before observed. It is her dryad-like form—and the caressing way her frocks embrace her—that convinces you she is a lineal descendant of sinuous Salome.

Despite her "positive assurance" and the encouraging presence of Edmund Lowe, Tashman kept her options open: "I came to Hollywood with the idea that I would give myself three months in which to make good in pictures," she later recalled. "If I was not well on my way to success within that time, I would return to Broadway."

The Garden of Weeds (Famous Players–Lasky, 1924) did nothing to change her mind: while she had been one of the principals in the stage version of the play, her role was drastically cut in the screen version—possibly on orders from the star, Betty Compson. But before the film was released, *Manhandled* (Famous Players–Lasky, 1924), filmed in New York prior to Tashman's leaving for the Coast, had already premiered. And here she sparred (on screen) with the studio's top box office attraction, Gloria Swanson.

A typical Swanson vehicle, *Manhandled* centered on a little shop girl (Swanson) who leaves her boyfriend for a fling in society. Once there, of course, she runs afoul of the likes of Tashman (whose wardrobe at any time matched Swanson's own), and quickly decides that happiness, after all, is to be found behind the counter at Gimbel's. It was the kind of theme that had made Swanson a star and the film was a big success. It also made Tashman a viable screen commodity.

She quickly settled into her new surroundings. Perhaps Southern California was not as cerebral as New York City, but in Hollywood there were just as many parties and, as Dorothy Spenseley would write, "Lilyan was Lilyan—clever, entertaining, witty—a brilliant addition to any social affair, be it tea or a dinner party."

It was fortunate that she had such a stimulating social life. Her films were rarely as interesting: She supported Alma Rubens in a dreary society melodrama, *Is Love Everything?* (Associated Exhibitors, 1924), and upstaged Marie Prevost in *The Dark Swan* (Warner Bros., 1924), a family drama. Then came *Ports of Call* (Fox, 1924), and in that she at least played opposite her fiancé, Edmund Lowe. Working side by side must have proved blissful: On September 1, 1925, they were finally married.

Despite the fact that Lowe was well-known to Hollywood insiders as a homosexual (or maybe because of it), the marriage was, from all accounts, a happy one. After Tashman's sudden death, the columnists not only mourned her, but also the tragic end to one of Hollywood's most serene alliances. "Edmund Lowe and Lilyan Tashman," wrote *Photoplay*'s Margaret Sangster,

> had nine years of happiness. Complete, thrilling happiness. That's a long-time marriage for Hollywood—and it's more joy than mere mortals are privileged to crowd into an entire lifetime.

The couple's Beverly Hills home soon reflected the new Mrs. Lowe's personal taste. Again according to Sangster, it was Lilyan who started the vogue for white—draperies, upholsteries, carpets—everything in bright white. "One would imagine that a home with a plethora of white upholstery might be a hard place in which to live—but it was not so with the Tashman-Lowe domicile," Sangster wrote shortly after the actress' death.

> Lilyan never told Eddie, I'll warrant, to be careful of ashes and beware of muddy feet. And her guests didn't feel, ever, that they were posed against the background of a modern museum. Despite the elegance of fabric, and the delicacy of design, and utter good taste, they felt at home.

At the studio (whichever studio the freelancing Tashman was working for at the time) the buzzword was also "elegance." But elegant ladies in the latter part of the Roaring Twenties were more often than not vamps. And Tashman could vamp with the best of them. "Very few women of the screen are as cleverly naughty as Lilyan," Dorothy Spenseley of *Photoplay* opined. "Or should it be naughtily clever? And there are so many charming heroines!"

The question on Spenseley's mind was whether the now married Tashman should graduate to less seductive roles. The answer, the fan magazine writer suggested, was a definite no! Unless, she added, Tashman would

> inject into her good interpretations a bit of the tang that made her wicked women so absolutely fascinating. I should not be surprised if she did, for Lilyan has the inbred knack of seasoning the most insipid roles with a goodly share of personality.

If producers were trying to soften the image of the new Mrs. Edmund Lowe, the result was not readily detectable. She was her naughty and glamorous self opposite Corinne Griffith in a society melodrama entitled *Declassee* (First National, 1925), and then played more or less herself in *Pretty Ladies* (Metro-Goldwyn, 1925), a dramatized look behind the scenes of the *Follies*. She and Andre de Beranger portrayed a bored (but elegant) dance team who decided to dally with other people in *So This Is Paris* (Warner Bros., 1926), not exactly a Pollyanna story either.

In late 1925, Tashman signed for two films with a newly organized company, Metropolitan Pictures Corporation. The company (which was supported by Cecil B. DeMille) offered the public the usual promise: From now on Miss Tashman would appear in "nice roles."

The producers made good on their pledge in her first film, *Rocking Moon* (1926), a trivial action drama filmed on location in Alaska, but her sugary heroine was not memorable. In *Whispering Smith* (1926), a railroad story with H.B. Warner, she was back to form playing an outlaw's untrustworthy wife.

Tashman was more fashionable than ever as the Duchess of Lincolnwood, giving Pauline Starke a bad time in *Love's Blindness* (M-G-M, 1926), a slick Elinor Glyn romance; British nobility had never experienced anything like her. Neither, for that matter, had Paris, and in the Norma Talmadge version of *Camille* (1927), Tashman's first film under a new contract to First National, she appeared as the outrageously haughty Olympe and in the process managed to upstage the star.

She continued to upstage First National stars throughout 1927, making life difficult—at least for a moment or two—for Priscilla Bonner in *The Prince of Headwaiters*; Billie Dove in *The Stolen Bride*; Will Rogers in *A Texas Steer*; and Clive Brook in *French Dressing*. The following year she added the studio's most popular commodity, Colleen Moore, to her list of victims (in *Happiness Ahead*).

Although usually cast in supporting roles, once in a while Tashman nabbed a starring part—but always on Poverty Row. In *The Woman Who Did Not Care* (Gotham, 1927), for example, she was star billed as a poor lass who resolves to become a "party girl" in order to further her lot in life. It was essentially the same role she always played, but here she was the whole show, and despite the miserable production values, she did rather well. *Variety*'s "Abel" found that the piece "more than hit the mark," and that Tashman "carried her assignment in a difficult, unsympathetic part."

However, few people actually saw this low-budget independent release and the film did little to bolster her career as a star. Consequently, she remained stuck in secondary roles, some of them better than others.

Frequently, she was a designing chorus girl (*Phyllis of the Follies* [Universal, 1928] and *Take Me Home* [Paramount, 1928]), but once in a while her part had a bit more substance. She was, for example, a clever Mrs. Passmore to Irene Rich's Helen Craig in the first screen version of George Kelly's play *Craig's Wife* (Pathé, 1928). And she was well cast as Paul Lukas' unsympathetic wife in *Manhattan Cocktail* (Paramount, 1928), a Nancy Carroll vehicle that featured musical interludes, but was essentially a silent.

Already a stage star, Tashman made an auspicious talkie debut (featuring a splendid courtroom scene—the ideal situation for any actress at the dawn of sound) in *The Trial of Mary Dugan* (M-G-M, 1929). If nothing else, the film proved that Tashman was not to be one of the legion of silent screen stars left behind by the advent of sound.

Although her professional career seemed to have taken an upswing, it was the private Lilyan Tashman—her style and devastating wit—that as always commanded center stage. In early 1929 she accompanied Greta Garbo to New York where the Swedish actress was to embark on her first trip home since becoming an American icon. The Edmund Lowes were good friends of John Gilbert, Garbo's sometime paramour, and Tashman had hosted the couple on several occasions. She was also, it was rumored, Garbo's latest in a long line of female lovers.

Now, she was to help select a suitable wardrobe for what was to be Garbo's triumphant return to Stockholm. "She has bought some really divine things," Lilyan reported to a friend.

> Several smart tweed traveling suits, two lovely velvet dresses, a gorgeous gray fur coat, heavenly evening gowns in which [she] will look—well, as only Garbo can look. She has also bought some beautiful things with lace on them. I was surprised—she can't tell real lace from machine-made. She would always turn to me and ask, "But Tashman, how do you *know* it is handmade?"

While Tashman remembered in detail every item of Garbo's shopping list, she remained mum on more personal events. She had to, if she valued the Swedish star's friendship—a friendship that, from all accounts, lasted until Tashman's untimely death. Certainly it lasted longer than their romance, which allegedly ended when Garbo met the equally flamboyant writer Mercedes De Acosta.

Sound definitely brought new life to Tashman's career. Not only could audiences salivate over her amazing wardrobe, now they were also able to enjoy her caustic remarks. As a result, casting directors scrambled to come up with roles that would fit her unique delivery.

She was, for example, allowed to be witty as well as menacing as Emma Peterson, the villainous mastermind behind a fraudulent asylum scheme in *Bulldog Drummond* (Goldwyn, 1929), one of the most successful early sound films. And she was absolutely ready to play Mary Brian's selfish mother in Paramount's screen version of Edith Wharton's "The Children," a Cinderella story released (with a keen eye to the box office) as *The Marriage Playground* (1929).

Lilyan Tashman and Ronald Colman in *Bulldog Drummond* (United Artists, 1929).

Not that there were not a few naysayers who thought her line delivery left a bit to be desired; Mordaunt Hall of the *New York Times*, for example, considered her "sure enough of herself" but then added that "more often than not she makes the grievous error of reciting rather than talking."

Fortunately, by the time of *New York Nights* (United Artists, 1929), Tashman was an old pro in the talkie game—which is more than could be said for the gangster drama's heroine, Norma Talmadge, whose second to last film it was to be.

Like most of her peers, Tashman had to endure a steady succession of moribund screen operettas—many of them so awful that by the end of 1929, the word "musical" on a marquee would often spell box office disaster. Thankfully, since she did not have to carry the burden of top billing, she emerged virtually unscathed. The same could not be said for the nominal stars of these flops: Nancy Welford in *The Gold Diggers of Broadway* (Warner Bros., 1929), Bernice Claire in *No, No Nanette* (First National, 1930), or Harry Richman in *Puttin' on the Ritz* (United Artists, 1930). All top draws on Broadway, none of them would make it to screen stardom.

Increasingly Tashman's unique way with a quip would be used for comedy purposes. She was still a vamp, but now the result was laughter rather than bosom-heaving drama.

She was tantalizing as always as the gangster's moll in *On the Level* (Fox, 1930), a comedy about two Cajuns (Victor McLaglen and the delightful but underused Fifi D'Orsay), and had several funny moments as Frank Fay's errant wife in *The Matrimonial Bed* (First National, 1930). As a matter of fact, these early years of sound were to prove Tashman's most consistently gratifying period in Hollywood.

By 1931, however, trite material was taking its toll. There was nothing Tashman could do to save Samuel Goldwyn's *One Heavenly Night*, a hackneyed story in which a flower girl is persuaded to pose as a cabaret singer. Unwisely, Tashman, as the *real* cabaret star, was asked to take a back seat to Evelyn Laye, a British import who came highly recommended but proceeded to lay one of the biggest eggs of the decade. The entire affair, as a result, was a box office disaster.

There was a bit more spirit in *Finn and Hattie* (RKO, 1931), a comedy in which Tashman vamped Leon Errol; but *Millie* (RKO, 1931) was a rather distasteful melodrama about a mother (the humdrum Helen Twelvetrees) who kills the man who seduced her young daughter. Tashman played the heroine's gold digging friend, and she had similar roles later that year in a couple of Paramount potboilers: *Up Pops the Devil*, in which she replaced an ailing Wynne Gibson, and *Girls About Town*. In the latter she and Kay Francis portrayed call girls and, it must be said, she was a great deal more believable in her part than was the lisping, patrician Miss Francis.

As a reward for these monotonous assignments, Paramount gave her star billing in *The Road to Reno* (1931), a self-explanatory tale of a divorcee whose bad influence all but ruins the life of her young daughter (Peggy Shannon). Unfortunately, Peggy Shannon, whom the studio thought would become a new Clara Bow, did not and the drama only proved that Tashman should not have been asked to carry a film all by herself.

Murder by the Clock (Paramount, 1931), however, has emerged as a minor classic of the horror-comedy genre. Tashman appears as Laura Endicott, a shady lady who is thought to be behind a series of murders taking place in the proverbial old mansion. Lilyan, as it turns out, is merely a red herring and is soon marked for death herself. To her rescue comes police officer William Boyd, whom she proceeds to vamp mercilessly in an outrageous parody of her own persona.

In between the (intentional) bouts of high camp, *Murder by the Clock* has enough eerie ghosts, clutching hands, sliding panels, and damp mausoleums to satisfy even the most devoted fan of the genre. Paramount was not exactly known for their *Grand Guignol* melodramas, but here the studio matches Universal's best offerings almost shudder for shudder, and in addition, the film contains one of Tashman's most ingratiating performances.

She was equally good as a schemer who lures unsuspecting men into her boyfriend's gambling den in *The Wiser Sex* (Paramount, 1932), but the drama, starring Claudette Colbert, was a dud. So was *Scarlet Dawn* (Warner Bros., 1932), a lavish but empty costume drama set during the Bolshevik Revolution. Tashman looked the part, but had little to do as a Russian temptress who sets her sights on dashing Douglas Fairbanks, Jr. As Mordaunt Hall of the *New York Times* indicated in his review, she did little more than a bit of "purring and flirting," and the film was consequently much the weaker.

Opposite: **Lilyan Tashman in 1931.**

25—LILYAN TASHMAN

In October of 1932, Lilyan Tashman was suddenly hospitalized with acute appendicitis, a situation gravely complicated, it was suggested, by too much work. Recovering from the ordeal she told a friend, Princess Alexandra Kropotkin, that she didn't deserve any sympathy. "I am sure I gave myself appendicitis just by thinking about it," she explained to the Princess. "The idea of getting it always terrified me. So, of course, I got it."

Tashman returned to the screen for a bit part in *Gold Diggers of 1933* (Warner Bros., 1933), and she played her usual vamp routine opposite Charlie Ruggles and Mary Boland in the comedy *Mama Loves Papa* (Paramount, 1933).

It was obvious, however, that all was not well. In early September of 1933 she took over the role of a gangster's moll in *Broadway Thru a Keyhole* (20th Century, 1933), replacing Peggy Hopkins Joyce who had suffered a nervous breakdown. Two days into filming, alas, Tashman had to withdraw because of adhesions resulting from the appendectomy and was herself replaced with Blossom Seeley. As it turned out, she was never to fully recover. (The film, incidentally, contains the final appearance of Broadway's Texas Guinan, who died four days after its release.)

Despite illness and the necessary career slowdown, Tashman was still very much in the news. A public "feud" with actress-columnist Hedda Hopper had readers everywhere taking sides. John L. Haddon, writing in *Motion Picture*, offered a blow by blow account of the skirmish:

> War has been declared in Hollywood—a strictly feminine war, polite but deadly. The battle-cry was sounded when Hedda Hopper not only intended but boldly asserted that Lilyan Tashman, far from deserving her repute as Hollywood's best dressed woman, "wears the Theater on her back." To which Miss Tashman replied, just as boldly, "At least, I am not actually *dowdy*." The barbs went back and forth—and not always tongue-in-cheek. "Understand," Hedda said, "any remarks that I make about Lilyan's clothes are not a reflection on her personality. I like her. Adore her. And I think her clothes are lovely. They ought to be—*she spends enough on them, heaven knows*" [italics added by Haddon].

As Haddon so subtly hinted, the "feud" might have started as a publicity gag, but soon the gloves seem to have been removed. Every time Hopper's snide remarks appeared in print, Tashman would respond, never allowing the condescending columnist the last word. "I really do not care to discuss Miss Hopper," Lilyan was quoted as having said.

> I consider that I have been very kind and given her all the *publicity* that even *she* could want. Knowing how badly she needs publicity, I have been very tolerant, but of course, there is a limit. If she were an authority on clothes, I would pay some attention to her. But—of course it is really too absurd. One is either smart—or one simply isn't. One is chic—or one is not chic. Unfortunately, Miss Hopper is *not noted* for her chic.

This very public exchange can easily be seen as trivial. But Hedda Hopper, whose career as a character actress had never overcome a certain archness and was about to come to an end, was determined to become a rival and eventually surpass the

Opposite: **Irving Pichel and Lilyan Tashman in** *Murder by the Clock* **(Paramount, 1931).**

increasingly powerful Hearst columnist Louella Parsons. And Louella, of course, was one of Tashman's dearest friends.

With her much heralded fashion know-how being publicly vilified while she was still trying to recover from a serious illness, it is no wonder that Tashman had little time, or inclination, to vigorously pursue her acting career. There was something called *Too Much Harmony* (Paramount, 1933), in which she vamped an incessantly crooning Bing Crosby, and she had a small supporting role as Norma Shearer's sister in the melodrama, *Riptide* (M-G-M, 1934), but fans had the right to feel cheated.

In early February of 1934, Tashman arrived at the old Biograph studios in the Bronx, New York, to appear as a greedy saloon singer in *Frankie and Johnnie*, a screen version of the old ballad about cardsharps and riverboat belles during Reconstruction. Before she departed for New York, she called her old friend Louella Parsons: "I'm happy," she told the columnist. "It's going to be my kind of role and Ed [Lowe] is going with me."

By the time she reached New York, she was exhausted. The long train journey had taken its toll and her health was visibly deteriorating. Yet, "the show must go on," and she had contracted to do *Frankie and Johnnie*. The filming proved a nightmare. Details would only emerge after her death, but they were grim.

"She was gravely ill during the entire time [*Frankie and Johnnie*] was being made," the *Los Angeles Times* reported in March.

> On her last day on the [Biograph] lot, she remained on the set from seven a.m. until midnight in order that she might finish the production. She urged the director [Chester Erskine] to hurry, telling him she feared her strength would not last.

It barely did, and her scenes finally "in the can," she and Lowe rushed to Connecticut to recuperate. Fan magazine writer Margaret Sangster later hailed the actress' great courage:

> Lilyan Tashman wasn't the sort to let down in the privacy of her own boudoir, for the simple reason that she didn't approve of, or enjoy, letting down. If she had been careless about clothes, I have no doubt that she might have been careless in other matters—but carelessness was a word that had been let out of Lilyan Tashman's vocabulary. If she had let down in the matter of grooming she might even have murmured at the end, "I'm tired. I can't work any longer. Give me rest." *But she didn't*. She practically died on the set, finishing her last picture. The physician who operated on her said, "It was her indomitable will—and her courage—that kept her going."

On March 21, 1934, Lilyan Tashman suddenly underwent emergency surgery to remove a cancerous tumor. It was all too late and she died on the operating table.

Despite a year of increasing ill health, Tashman's death at only 34 came as a shock to the motion picture industry and, needless to say, to her grieving husband.

"When the reporters besieged [Edmund] Lowe, the day of his wife's death, he hadn't much to say," Margaret Sangster later commented. "We like him because he hadn't. He faltered, 'I can't believe it—' Which is, in a way, the perfect tribute."

Ironically, *Wine, Women and Song* (Chadwick, 1933), a programmer in which Tashman was top billed, opened in New York the day before her death. "She had been featured in films for nine years [sic]," the *Los Angeles Times* noted, "but this production brought her initial role as a leading lady. In the movie, as in life, she died young."

As we have seen, *Wine, Women and Song* did not bring Tashman her "initial role as leading lady," poignant as that might have been. Rather, she had occasionally been top billed as far back as 1925 (Metropolitan's *Rocking Moon*). Always, however, the vehicles had been low-budget indie productions, and *Wine, Women and Song* proved no exception (some contemporary news stories to the contrary).

An ordinary backstage melodrama, the film stars Tashman as a chorus girl pushed over the edge by a slick, unscrupulous entrepreneur (Lew Cody).* Mordaunt Hall of the *New York Times*, obviously unaware of Tashman's tragic death, was rarely as disparaging as he was this time:

> After witnessing *Wine, Women and Song*, one is apt to conclude that the director [the veteran Herbert Brenon] and the players have treated this story with the disdain that it deserves. Lilyan Tashman not only gives an inefficient portrayal, but she is also poorly made up.

Wrong, Mr. Hall—she was dying!

Unaware of its tragic production, the eminent critic concluded his review by terming the film "tawdry, amateurish and frequently offensive."

Republic finally released Tashman's last film *Frankie and Johnnie* in May of 1936. Although she was obviously the film's second female lead,† Lilyan appeared unbilled. Presumably, Republic was loath to remind the public of the fact that the film was two years old. Not that it mattered much—*Frankie and Johnnie* was largely ignored and quickly disappeared from view.

So did, it seems, the memory of Lilyan Tashman herself. It was, as we have seen, the actress' offscreen *joie de vivre* that had made her famous and not her film roles. In that respect, her fame is comparable to today's Madonna—the difference being, of course, that Tashman also possessed elegance, wit, and talent.

Margaret Sangster, who seems to have been more of a friend and confidante than a casual fan magazine interviewer, accorded Tashman her most appropriate eulogy:

> A block or two, in New York, often measures more than a quarter of a mile. It is sometimes the distance between happiness and heartbreak, between sunshine and sorrow, between life and death. And so it is strange that, while Lilyan Tashman lay quietly at rest in a white chapel on an upper East Side street, the lights of Broadway were making magic with her name. I fancy she would have wished it so. To know that, even as her friends knelt at her bier and sobbed their last farewell—even as curious crowds stormed the very doors of the funeral church—she was still moving and laughing and talking on the street she had loved. For Lilyan Tashman did not typify quiet and repose—she was quicksilver and the flash of sequins and the perfume of gardenias and the gaiety of dance music. Her life was very sky-rocket; she rose suddenly in brilliance, shone against the clouds—and disappeared when the brilliance was at its height.

A strange postscript to Tashman's death occurred in July of 1936: Kathryn Lambert, a chorus girl turned writer for the *Sunday Mirror*, related in an article titled "Six

---

Cody, a veteran silent screen star, also died in early 1934—from acute alcoholism.

†*The heroine was the equally tragic Helen Morgan who would succumb to alcoholism in 1941.*

Girls" how she and five other *Ziegfeld Follies* chorines in 1916 had made a pact to meet again in 20 years. The "convention," as it were, never took place. Of the six, Miss Lambert was the only survivor: Olive Thomas, the beauty of the group and later Mrs. Jack Pickford, had perished under mysterious circumstances in Paris in 1920; Martha Mansfield, a promising starlet, burned to death on the set of *The Warrens of Virginia* (Paramount, 1924); Bessie Poole had died after "an incident in a Manhattan Night Club"; Effie Alsop, who had once married and divorced a millionaire, was found dead in a rooming house for destitute women; and Lilyan Tashman, "the gayest of them all," was now also gone.

Miss Lambert, as a matter of fact, sued the producers of *Walking Down Broadway*, a minor programmer from 20th Century–Fox, for plagiarism, alleging that the drama was based on her *Sunday Mirror* article. (Tashman, it seems, was in the film portrayed by Fox's "Queen of the B's," Lynn Bari.) No information as to the outcome of the suit has been found.

LILYAN TASHMAN FILMOGRAPHY

1921: *Experience.*
1922: *Head Over Heels.*
1924: *Nellie, the Beautiful Cloak Model; Winner Take All; Manhandled; The Garden of Weeds; Is Love Everything?; The Dark Swan; Ports of Call.*
1925: *A Broadway Butterfly; The Parasite; Declassee; I'll Show You the Town; Pretty Ladies; Seven Days; The Girl Who Wouldn't Work; Bright Lights.*
1926: *Rocking Moon; The Skyrocket; Siberia; Whispering Smith; So This Is Paris?; For Alimony Only; Love's Blindness.*
1927: *Don't Tell the Wife; Camille; The Woman Who Did Not Care; The Prince of Headwaiters; The Stolen Bride; A Texas Steer; French Dressing.*
1928: *Lady Raffles; Happiness Ahead; Phyllis of the Follies; Craig's Wife; Take Me Home; Manhattan Cocktail.*
1929: *The Lone Wolf's Daughter; Hard-boiled; The Trial of Mary Dugan; Bulldog Drummond; The Gold Diggers of Broadway; The Marriage Playground; New York Nights.*
1930: *No, No Nanette; Puttin' on the Ritz; On the Level; The Matrimonial Bed; Leathernecking; The Cat Creeps.*
1931: *The House That Shadows Built* (documentary); *Millie; Finn and Hattie; Up Pops the Devil; One Heavenly Night; Murder by the Clock; The Mad Parade; The Road to Reno; Girls About Town.*
1932: *The Wiser Sex; Those We Love; Scarlet Dawn.*
1933: *Wine, Women and Song; Mama Loves Papa; Too Much Harmony.*
1934: *Riptide.*
1936: *Frankie and Johnnie.*

26—Verree Teasdale

The term usually employed to describe Verree Teasdale was "chic." With marcelled blonde hair, an inborn sense of *haute couture*, and a penchant for dropping icy remarks without ever, as publicist John Springer once put it, "cracking that surface polish," she was the perfect counterpart to her real-life husband, the suave and devilishly debonair Adolphe Menjou.

Teasdale could be malicious with the best of them, but she added a certain poise to her nastiness—a quality often lacking in contemporaries such as Lilyan Tashman or Natalie Moorhead. Verree was not a gun moll or floozy; in fact, she made an extremely regal Hippolyta in Reinhardt's lavish version of *A Midsummer Night's Dream* (Warner Bros., 1935).

As the social climbing Irene Hibbard in *First Lady* (Warner Bros., 1937), arguably the quintessential Teasdale role, she gave it her all to become the "hostess with the mostest" of Washingtonian cafe society. That she was eventually defeated in her endeavor by the higher-billed Kay Francis made no difference to Frank S. Nugent of the *New York Times*, who proclaimed her "First Lady of the Strand Theater" on the occasion of the film's December 23, 1937, New York premiere.

Verree Teasdale was born on March 5, 1906, in Spokane, Washington, the daughter of Clement and Mattie Wharton Teasdale; two of her cousins, her later publicity would state, were the poet Sara Teasdale and the novelist Edith Wharton.

A child of affluence, Verree grew up on Manhattan's Park Avenue, attending Mrs. Perkins' School for Girls and later Brooklyn's Erasmus Hall. Stagestruck since childhood, she studied at the New York School of Expression and the American Academy of Dramatic Art, making her professional debut in 1924 in *Cheaper to Marry*. Recognition, however, came later that year, when she appeared opposite Henry Hull in Philip Barry's *The Youngest*.

In 1927 Teasdale married musical comedy star William J. O'Neal, but the union proved unsuccessful and she divorced him in 1933.

The highlight of Teasdale's near decade-long stage career came with a two year run opposite Ethel Barrymore in *The Constant Wife*. She went on several tours with the play, returning to Broadway in 1931 as the predatory Jean in *The Greeks Had a Word for It* by Zoe Akins.

In the early days of sound films most major Hollywood studios had production arms located in or near New York City in order to enlist fresh talent with badly needed stage experience. Teasdale was one of the many Broadway luminaries attracted to the kind of salary that only movies could offer, and she made her screen debut in 1929 opposite Barbara Bennett and Bobby Watson in RKO's first musical, *Syncopation*.*

The film, a tepid backstage yarn about a struggling vaudeville team shot on what amounted to a shoestring in the old Pathé studios in Harlem, completely wasted Teasdale in a small supporting role, but she presumably gained some needed camera experience. She made another try the following year, playing a con artist in Paramount's *The Sap from Syracuse* (Ginger Rogers starred), but that experience likewise failed to ignite much interest.

In early 1932, following a starring role on Broadway in *Experience Unnecessary*, Teasdale finally succumbed to the insistent calls from Hollywood and signed a contract with M-G-M. She made her West Coast debut (and gave a "highly commendable" performance, according to Mordaunt Hall of the *New York Times*) as Warren Williams' elegant mistress in *Skyscraper Souls* (M-G-M, 1932), a sort of poor man's *Grand Hotel* about lives in a Manhattan high-rise. She then had to bow out of playing Conrad Nagel's long-suffering wife in *Divorce in the Family* (M-G-M, 1932) due to a severe case of tonsillitis (veteran actress Lois Wilson replaced her), but was back in form as Charles Laughton's fashionable French mistress in *Payment Deferred* (M-G-M, 1932), a rather theatrical melodrama about a milquetoast who is suspected of murder. It was a minor part but rather showy, and Mordaunt Hall found her performance "satisfactory."

While M-G-M had dished Teasdale up as a run-of-the-mill *femme fatale*, other studios recognized her as the ideal foil for comedians. Universal, for example, borrowed her for two comedies starring the bucolic team of Slim Summerville and ZaSu Pitts: *They All Had to Get Married* and *Love, Honor and Oh, Baby!* (both 1933); and she played a merry hide-and-seek with the unflappable Charlie Ruggles (the couple pretending to be more exotic than they really were) in *Goodbye Love* (Jefferson/RKO, 1933), a gentle farce about a millionaire with alimony troubles.

Next, she did two shipboard dramas for Paramount, *Luxury Liner* (1933), yet another ersatz *Grand Hotel*, as an opera singer romancing Frank Morgan, and the bizarre *Terror Aboard* (1933). The latter was a salty whodunit in which her character was suffocated in a ship's deep freezer! Wrapping up the year on a high note she portrayed the evil Empress Agrippa in Sam Goldwyn's million dollar musical comedy *Roman Scandals* (United Artists, 1933).

In the time-honored fashion of Mark Twain's *A Connecticut Yankee in King Arthur's*

Prominent in the supporting cast was tenor Morton Downey who had recently married Miss Bennett. That short-lived union produced the infamously abrasive television talk show host.

Court, *Roman Scandals* had Eddie Cantor falling asleep on a statue of Agrippa in the "Museum of Roman Art" in West Rome, New York, only to wake up at the court of Emperor Valerius (Edward Arnold). Hilarity and much singing and dancing (by, among others, Ruth Etting and the famed Goldwyn Girls) ensue. Andre Sennwald of the *New York Times* found both the statue and the actress herself "unusually good-looking."

After leaving M-G-M for Warner Bros., 1934 proved a banner year for the actress. She was uncharacteristically but very becomingly subdued as Kay Francis' levelheaded confidante in *Dr. Monica*, a good role that did much to humanize her. Then, conversely, she was elegant and high-handed as a Hoboken girl impersonating a Russian duchess (and being blackmailed for her efforts) in *Fashions of 1934*, and arrogant and forbidding as Duchess de Grammont opposite Dolores Del Rio in *Madame Du Barry*.

On August 24, 1934, Teasdale became the third wife of veteran actor Adolphe Menjou,* and never did two individuals complement each other more. The couple was among Hollywood's most elegant and their combined *joie de vivre* became legendary.†

Verree Teasdale's finest performance was arguably that of Helen Walbridge, a celebrated actress whose image is shattered when a grown daughter (Jean Muir) suddenly shows up on her doorstep, in *Desirable* (Warner Bros., 1934). Behaving alternately pathetic and duplicitous she tries to shield the naive girl from life's more unsavory aspects. Her schemes misfire, however, when the girl inevitably meet and falls for her mother's rakish lover (George Brent). Fortunately, Teasdale's anguish is buffered somewhat by 17 lavish wardrobe changes, courtesy of Orry-Kelly, Warner's preeminent costume designer.

Needless to say, *Desirable* was pure soap opera, but well made and acted with typical assuredness by the superb Warner stock company. "Miss Teasdale, in particular, is impressive in a role which demands the expression of her personal hatred for her daughter's presence without at the same time losing her charm and urbanity," observed Andre Sennwald of the *New York Times*.

Teasdale maintained her "charm and urbanity" (in addition to receiving top billing) in *The Firebird* (Warner Bros., 1934), in which she was the prime suspect in the murder of a narcissistic actor (Ricardo Cortez). Sennwald this time thought that she played her part with "appropriate finesse," but, alas, the whodunit was a rather static reproduction of a minor Lajos Zilahy play and won no prizes.

A chauvinist on and off the screen, Adolphe Menjou discouraged his newest wife from accepting too many screen offers, and Teasdale's only 1935 release was Warner's pretentious screen version of *A Midsummer Night's Dream*.

In films from the mid-teens, Adolphe Menjou reached a pinnacle of urbanity early on as the wealthy rake in Chaplin's A Woman of Paris *(1923). His second wife had been silent screen vamp Kathryn Carver, whom he divorced when he didn't feel that marriage conformed with his image as a roué.*

†*Despite his earlier views on the subject of marriage, the union with Teasdale lasted until the actor's death in 1963. In 1937 the Menjous adopted a son, Peter Adolphe Menjou. Their legacy has, however, been tainted by Adolphe's rabid rightwing politics. In 1947 he proved a very friendly witness during the House Un-American Activities hearings into subversiveness in Hollywood.*

Max Reinhardt had produced Shakespeare's immortal fantasy at the Hollywood Bowl, and the studio hired him to restage it for the cameras.* Visually beautiful, *A Midsummer Night's Dream* suffers from the egregious miscasting of certain key roles, especially among the juveniles (Dick Powell, for example, is an atrocious Lysander) and the comics—with the possible exception of James Cagney who makes a capital, if very un–Shakespearean, Bottom. Yet, Teasdale had, in the words of Andre Sennwald, "a queenly bearing" as Hippolyta, and Ian Hunter nicely complemented her by performing an aristocratic Theseus, Duke of Athens.

A Midsummer Night's Dream, although somewhat of a failure at the box office, was a prestige project and earned an Academy Award nomination for Best Picture (it lost to M-G-M's gigantic *Mutiny on the Bounty*), winning the award for Hal Mohr's breathtaking photography.

Verree Teasdale in *A Midsummer Night's Dream* (Warner Bros., 1935).

Virtually retired to accommodate the wishes of her husband, Teasdale nevertheless returned to the screen in 1936 (replacing an ailing Gail Patrick, who in turn had replaced Gertrude Michael) as a fight manager's classy girlfriend in *The Milky Way* (Paramount, 1936), a Harold Lloyd vehicle about a milquetoast milkman who inadvertently becomes a prizefighter. Menjou could hardly protest her participation: The film was directed by his friend Leo McCarey, and he himself co-starred as the fight promoter. In any case, it was a propitious return: Verree Teasdale teaching Harold Lloyd to box in waltz-time is one of the comedy's highlights.

With the success of *The Milky Way*, Paramount convinced Teasdale to forget about retirement and play the *femme fatale* (again opposite Menjou) in the bedroom farce *Wives Never Know* (1936). The actress agreed but then had to withdraw from the project because of illness (to be replaced by Juliette Compton).

*Unfortunately, following a breach of contract suit by a French company, Reinhardt was barred from directing the film himself and William Dieterle was subsequently given full control over the production.

Opposite: **Verree Teasdale and Adolphe Menjou (1931). (Newspaper clipping.)**

The following year, however, she was ready to accept the role of the very social Irene Hibbard in *First Lady* (Warner Bros., 1937), and Menjou approved even though he wasn't in it. As the wife of a bumbling Supreme Court Justice (the droll Walter Connolly), Teasdale is completely in her element battling the refined Kay Francis over who is the best hostess in Washington. The ladies are aided immeasurably by the sharp dialogue of George S. Kaufman and Dorothy Dayton, and although Francis as the ambitious wife of the Secretary of State emerges the winner, most critics felt that the honors should have gone to her opponent. Especially, the *New York Times*' Frank S. Nugent suggested, since "Miss Teasdale is the perfect mouthpiece for the Kaufman-Dayton insolences, while Miss Francis—even discounting her difficulty with the letter 'r'—has been trained in a far gentler school of drama."

> There is an art of insult and Miss Francis has not mastered it [Nugent continued]. She delivers her lines with the self-conscious unction of an actress who has just discovered how good they were when reading the script that morning. Miss Teasdale, on the other hand, lets them rip out and curl about her opponent's ears, and rarely bothers to wait for the welts to rise.

Samuel Goldwyn wanted Teasdale for the role of the evil Nazama, the wife of the Mongol leader (Alan Hale) in his gigantic production of *The Adventures of Marco Polo* (United Artists, 1938), but again illness was blamed for preventing her participation (or did the dictatorial Menjou nix the idea?), and the role was given to Binnie Barnes.

She had recovered sufficiently by August of 1938 to accept a good supporting role as Billie Burke's troublemaking friend Mrs. Parkhurst in *Topper Takes a Trip* (Hal Roach/United Artists, 1938), the second in the series of unearthly comedies based on Thorne Smith's popular "Topper" stories; and nothing could have prevented her from reteaming with Walter Connolly in Gregory La Cava's screwball comedy, *Fifth Avenue Girl* (RKO, 1939). Teasdale plays Connolly's snobbish wife, whose discarded mink coat is the preamble to a mad satire involving a penniless girl (Ginger Rogers), who is suddenly mistaken by everyone for a millionaire's "kept woman."

Then considered "cheerful and cheerfully unimportant" (Nugent of the *New York Times*), the comedy is today seen as a rather mediocre example of the genre (Leonard Maltin goes so far as to call it "tiresome"), but Teasdale, as always, is right on the money as a vain and supercilious society matron.

She returned to M-G-M for *I Take This Woman* (1940), a monotonous melodrama starring Spencer Tracy and Hedy Lamarr about a doctor who sacrifices his social standing for an unworthy woman. It was a troubled production that underwent several script changes and was in turn abandoned by two directors before journeyman W. S. Van Dyke came to its rescue. When *I Take This Woman* was finally released more than a year after its October 1938 start date, Hollywood wags referred to it as "I Re-Take This Woman." Teasdale, although third billed as one of Tracy's society friends, had very little screen time in the final cut and probably regretted her involvement.

I Take This Woman, as a matter of fact, may have soured the actress on filmmaking

Opposite: Verree Teasdale in *Topper Takes a Trip* (Hal Roach, 1939).

completely: In any case her final three screen performances were merely routine: She and hubby Adolphe Menjou turned up briefly (although Menjou received top billing!) in Thorne Smith's cross-dressing farce *Turnabout* (Hal Roach/United Artists, 1940); she was Fred Allen's wife in a funny screen version of the Allen–Jack Benny radio "feud," *Love Thy Neighbor* (Paramount, 1940); and returned to M-G-M one final time as Ian Hunter's wife in a comedy starring James Stewart and Hedy Lamarr, *Come Live with Me* (1941). After that, apparently, she was content with being Mrs. Adolphe Menjou.

Now in its third decade, Menjou's screen career was still going strong. In between testifying against former co-workers in the notorious witch-hunt trials of the late 1940s, the dapper veteran found time to appear in such classics as *State of the Union* (M-G-M, 1948), in which he played an unscrupulous political boss (typecasting?) and fought on the set with co-star Katharine Hepburn, a confirmed liberal; *Man on a Tightrope* (20th Century–Fox), where he played, of all things, a Communist policeman; and, best of all, Stanley Kubrick's *Paths of Glory* (Bryna/United Artists, 1957), arguably the finest antiwar film ever made. As the imperious General Broulard who sends his men on a futile suicide mission, Menjou gave the performance of a lifetime. His participation in this important film almost makes up for his past "misdeeds." His final film role was as the strange hermit Mr. Prendergast to Hayley Mills' *Pollyanna* (Buena Vista, 1960).

Through it all, Mrs. Menjou stayed retired in the couple's Beverly Hills home, rarely, according to insiders, giving any thoughts to her own, mostly forgotten, career. After her husband's death on October 29, 1963, she was little heard from, although David Ragan, a tireless chronicler of forgotten movie stars, reported in 1976 that she was still keenly interested in fashion. One of Hollywood's most elegant citizens, Verree Teasdale died on February 17, 1987.

Verree Teasdale Filmography

- **1929:** *Syncopation.*
- **1930:** *The Sap from Syracuse.*
- **1932:** *Skyscraper Souls; Payment Deferred.*
- **1933:** *They Just Had to Get Married; Luxury Liner; Terror Aboard; Love, Honor, and Oh-Baby! Goodbye Love; Roman Scandals.*
- **1934:** *Fashions of 1934; A Modern Hero; Dr. Monica; Desirable; Madame Du Barry; The Firebird.*
- **1935:** *A Midsummer Night's Dream.*
- **1936:** *The Milky Way.*
- **1937:** *First Lady.*
- **1938:** *Topper Takes a Trip.*
- **1939:** *Fifth Avenue Girl.*
- **1940:** *I Take This Woman; Turnabout; Love Thy Neighbor.*
- **1941:** *Come Live with Me.*

27—Helen Vinson

Helen Vinson was not your typical doll-faced Hollywood starlet. Far from it! There was something disturbingly feline about her. Yet, we never doubted that she was a lady—usually not a very nice lady, but a lady nonetheless. In the 1930s nobody could hold a candle to her when it came to that prototype of female villainy, the other woman. In fact, she was the other woman even when legally married to the hero! In *The Life of Vergie Winters* (RKO, 1934), for example, her wealthy husband (John Boles) has a love child with the lowly Vergie (Ann Harding). But when Boles finally comes to his senses and begs to be released from a loveless marriage so he, at long last, can find some happiness, Vinson shoots him down in cold blood.

Vinson was a murderess again in *Private Worlds* (Walter Wanger, 1935), but that fact is cleverly kept hidden long enough for her to drive poor Joan Bennett, her lover's wife, utterly insane. Joan, who was not yet the *femme fatale* she would become in the 1940s, was so dim and ingenue-ish here, that she rather deserved her awful fate.

Helen Vinson was so adept at playing bad, that she often inadvertently won the audience over to her side—an unfortunate side effect that many a Hollywood leading lady, completely upstaged by the other woman, had to confront. As Andre Sennwald of the *New York Times* once remarked:

> Miss Vinson's cool and clear-eyed intelligence, even when it is enlisted on the side of the devil, has an unhappy way of winning our sympathy.

She was born Helen Rulfs on September 7, 1907, in Beaumont, Texas, the daughter of a Texas Oil Company executive. Like so many other young people, she became interested in the theater performing in college shows while attending the University of Texas. In May of 1925, however, she suddenly abandoned all ambitions to elope with Philadelphia carpet manufacturer Harry N. Vickerman, determined, she later told Ruth Biery of *Motion Picture*, "to become what most Southern girls are usually trained for: an entrancing wife and an adorable mother."

Vinson may have been an "entrancing wife," but she also returned to the theater—despite her new husband's wishes—making her professional debut in a Houston production of *The Charm School* in 1927. That same year she made her New York bow opposite Jack LaRue and Alison Skipworth in the short-lived play *Los Angeles*, embarking on a busy if unexceptional Broadway career. Among her more noteworthy efforts were *Death Takes a Holiday* (1929) as Rhoda (with Rose Hobart as Grazia); *Berlin* (1931) with Sydney Greenstreet; and *The Fatal Alibi* (1932) with Charles Laughton.

In between her Broadway stints, Vinson found time to make a ignoble screen debut in something called *It's a Deal* (Majestic, 1930), a "comedy" about poor white trash duped by a slick huckster into buying nonexistent real estate. Filmed on location in Florida, *It's a Deal* also featured Claire Dodd, who was later to become Vinson's chief rival for the title of "Queen of the Hollywood Other Women."

It's a Deal was not, of course, the vehicle to persuade Vinson to abandon Broadway, but in mid-1932 she accepted an offer from Warner Bros./First National and left for Hollywood. Once there, however, the picture business proved not quite as glamorous as she had expected. "The studio seemed like an absolute sea of short men to [Vinson]," explained Ruth Biery. "James Cagney, [Paul] Muni and [George] Raft had to stand on boxes when they acted in scenes with the five feet, seven and a half inch Helen." With that in mind, the tall newcomer quickly realized that she might not be ingenue material!

Not that Vinson was thought of as anything but a starlet in her first few films. She gained much needed camera experience but not much else playing bit parts such as Kay Francis' friend in a programmer, *Jewel Robbery* (1932); was Constance Bennett's confidante in *Two Against the World* (1932); and was dumped by David Manners for Loretta Young (her first other woman role) in *They Call It Sin* (1932).

She was notable, however, as the girl who falls for the prison escapee (Paul Muni) in Mervyn LeRoy's indictment of the penal system, *I Am a Fugitive from a Chain Gang* (1932). Seen today, the film's haunting finale is still quite effective: Having escaped death row with the law hot on his trail, Muni shows up at Helen's apartment to bid her a final good-bye. Fearful for his future, she probes, "How do you live?" "I steal," he answers laconically, before disappearing into the night.

"The producers do not mince matters in this melodrama," reported Mordaunt Hall of the *New York Times*, "and even at the close there is none of the usual bowing to popular appeal."

As a result of *Chain Gang*, Vinson was prominently featured in eight films released in 1933, one of them a true classic and considered one of the era's finest accomplishments: *The Power and the Glory* (Fox, 1933).

A rags-to-riches story of an unscrupulous industrialist, the drama, directed by William K. Howard (from an original screenplay by Preston Sturges), has often been favorably compared to the later *Citizen Kane* (RKO, 1941), and, on a less grandiose scale, Sturges' own *The Great McGinty* (Paramount, 1940). Starring Spencer Tracy (who gave what the *Nation* described as "one of the fullest characterizations ever achieved") and 1920s flapper Colleen Moore, the film offered Vinson fourth billing as the protagonist's second wife, whose affair with his young son (Clifford Jones) ultimately leads to his suicide.

Although Vinson's vitriolic Eve Borden in *The Power and the Glory* was by far her most effective characterization, the year brought several other notable performances: She was "attractive" (Hall in the *Times*) as a good girl involved with, and eventually dumped by, slum lawyer William Powell in *Lawyer Man*; came between Paul Lukas and (again!) Loretta Young in the gambling comedy *Grand Slam*; was the socialite who unsuccessfully tries to interest rough bootlegger Edward G. Robinson in the upper-class sport of polo in *Little Giant*; and replaced Claire Dodd as one of the suspects in the fifth whodunit based on S.S. Van Dine's popular detective Philo Vance, *The Kennel Murder Case*.

Next, Paramount borrowed her (and gave her co-star billing with Clive Brook and George Raft) for the crime drama *Midnight Club* (1933). Vinson was a jewel thief who reforms for the love of a man (Brook), and Andre Sennwald of the *New York Times* thought she displayed "a handsome and pleasing personality."

The busy schedule seems to have taken its toll on Vinson's private life and on November 25, 1933, she filed for divorce from Harry Vickerman. According to newspaper reports, one of the reasons for the break-up was that Vickerman "wouldn't permit 'people of the Theater' to enter their home." Ironically, Vinson's first release after the divorce was the romantic comedy *As Husbands Go* (Fox, 1933), in which she and hubby Warner Baxter, after much marital travail, end up living "happily ever after."

The year 1934 brought some on-screen happiness, but not a lot. Now freelancing, Vinson had signed a three picture deal with RKO. She only made two, however; for some reason she was replaced by Kay Johnson in *Their Big Moment*, a silly comedy-mystery starring ZaSu Pitts and Slim Summerville. But as we have seen, she did appear as Ann Harding's nemesis in *The Life of Vergie Winters*, and she was the other woman in *Let's Try Again*, a triangle drama that also included Diana Wynyard and Clive Brook.

In late June of 1934, Columbia signed her to replace an ailing Florence Rice in *The Captain Hates the Sea*, a Poverty Row version of *Grand Hotel* (M-G-M, 1932). Playing a jewel thief posing as a vacationing librarian, Vinson received above-the-title billing, *Grand Hotel* style, along with the likes of Victor McLaglen, Wynne Gibson and, in his final film, the former heartthrob John Gilbert. The film, unfortunately, was a misfire despite assertive direction from Lewis Milestone, who must have wondered what he was doing there.

At Universal, meanwhile, Vinson was second billed to Charles Bickford (who actually played the villain) in *A Notorious Gentleman* (1935), a crime drama in which she played an actress innocently accused of murdering her fiancé. She was rather sympathetic in her attempt to clear herself (with the help of District Attorney Onslow Stevens), and was even more emphatic in *The Wedding Night* (United Artists, 1935), although losing her husband (Gary Cooper) to Polish immigrant Anna Sten (Sam Goldwyn's highly publicized but ultimately unsuccessful Russian import).

Cooper plays an author studying the manners and customs of a Polish settlement in Connecticut for an upcoming novel. Using the lovely Manya (Sten) as the model for his heroine, the novelist, unintentionally of course, falls for her piquant charms. As the wronged wife, Vinson is remarkably collected: When Manya is mortally wounded by her enraged fiancé (Ralph Bellamy), she, in fact, quietly leaves her husband to his grief—disappearing from his life, it is implied, without any rancor.

Clive Brook, Helen Vinson and George Raft in *Midnight Club* **(Paramount, 1933). (Photograph courtesy of the Danish Film Museum.)**

It is a remarkably restrained performance, and Andre Sennwald of the *New York Times* thought that she was "excellently right, playing the part with such intelligence and sympathy that she definitely [contributed] to the power of the climax."

Despite her recent success playing sympathetic women, Vinson was reinstated as one of Hollywood's best villainesses in *Private Worlds* (Walter Wanger/United Artists, 1935), the medical drama in which she drove poor Joan Bennett insane. And she was bad to the bone again in *Age of Indiscretion* (M-G-M, 1935), a Lenore Coffee concoction about a publisher (Paul Lukas) whose extravagant wife (Vinson) leaves him when he gets into debt. Not only does she go to Reno for a divorce (and immediately takes a new lover), she also abandons her small child (David Holt), an unpardonable sin in 1930s melodramas. Fortunately, the publisher's adoring secretary (Madge Evans) has been standing in the wings all along, ready to nurse father and son back to happiness.

Having again misbehaved, this time toward a child at that, Vinson was all set up to be hissed off the screen when *Age of Indiscretion* premiered. That didn't quite happen, according to at least one reviewer. "It is unfortunate that the part of the evil wife is performed by the most charming player in the film, Helen Vinson," Andre Sennwald of the *New York Times* complained.

> You may recall that Miss Vinson played hob with that excellent photoplay *The Wedding Night* by interpreting the brazen wife with such sympathetic understanding that many of us resented her husband's bad taste in falling out of love with her. This sort of thing has been happening in Miss Vinson's pictures for several years, the audience admiring and feeling sorry for her instead of reacting according to the script.

Offscreen, Vinson had a new man in her life, and on September 12, 1935, in Harrison, New York, she married British tennis star Fred Perry. "Our marriage will be successful," she told the press,

> because I'm a thorough-going American woman and I exercise my prerogative of being independent. It's all right with my husband. He agreed to it before we were married.

After that statement, the couple must have been in agreement to jeopardize Vinton's burgeoning Hollywood career by settling in England. Fan magazine writer Ruth Biery echoed many in Hollywood when she wrote:

> "Why should she go?" Her Hollywood friends had demanded when the offer to go had first arrived. Well, why should she go? She had big pictures to her credit. Six in a single year; a real record for a freelance player [sic]. Why should an actress with such success leave Hollywood? And she'd had offers for as many more.

"Perhaps it was the adventure," the actress herself later explained. "Or perhaps it was just meant to be."
Or was it simply love? Perry was England's premier tennis player and an icon in his homeland; it was unlikely that he would even be "allowed" to live that far away from Wimbledon.
It could also be, of course, that the actress was tired. It had been suggested that she was "getting too many pictures. That too many was as bad as not enough." In any case, she didn't *have* to act to be happy, she told Ruth Biery.

> I like acting but it isn't all of life. It takes a lot out of you. It can give you grey hair before your time. I could stop being an actress without dying *from* it. I can go on being an actress without dying *for* it, I hope. I think it's so foolish to say we *can't* do this; we *can't* do that.

Once in England, of course, Vinson did not give up acting. Her continued demand was helped in no small way by the so-called "quota quickies," American-financed films made in Britain in order for Hollywood companies to be allowed distribution rights of their regular product. *Transatlantic Tunnel* (Gaumont-British, 1935), for example, was a silly science fiction tale about the building of a tunnel between England and the United States (!).
Infused with Hollywood talent such as Richard Dix and Madge Evans, in addition to Vinson, *Transatlantic Tunnel* was quite successful, even in the United States,

despite the typically meager budget. Andre Sennwald called it "an imaginative drama in the best Jules Verne tradition," but found that although Vinson played with "her customary skill," she was "wasted in the role of the siren."

Transatlantic Tunnel was followed by another "quota quickie," *King of the Damned* (British Gaumont, 1936), a prison melodrama in which Vinson, as the commandant's daughter, manages to curb an uprising among the inmates; and the topical *Love in Exile* (Capital Films, 1936), a romantic drama about a king (Clive Brook) who relinquishes the throne for the love of a foreign woman. Within weeks of the film's release, Edward VIII abdicated to marry Wallis Simpson. A coincidence? We think not!

Despite her mild success in British-made films and her former statements to the contrary, Vinson returned to Hollywood in mid–1936, along with her husband who apparently suddenly wanted to go Hollywood. The marriage, however, was showing signs of strain and Perry began seeing an awful lot of Marlene Dietrich.

Unfortunately, Hollywood was (and still is) notoriously capricious and there were few offers for the returning Vinson. She played an estranged wife reunited with her husband by the kindly Dr. Luke (Jean Hersholt) in *Reunion* (20th Century–Fox, 1936), the second film "starring" the famous Dionne Quintuplets (who received above-title billing, no less). That was merely routine, however, and so was *Vogues of 1938* (United Artists, 1937), a musical comedy *cum* fashion show in which she played Warner Baxter's faithful wife whom he discards in favor of Joan Bennett.

Next, Vinson was Rosalind Russell's snobbish friend in a minor comedy from M-G-M, *Live, Love and Learn* (1937); but she was off the screen for all of 1938, concentrating instead on her personal life. She finally divorced the philandering Perry in December of 1938, and soon thereafter wed New York socialite Donald Hardenbrook.

Returning to the screen in April of 1939, she found that her roles had become smaller or the productions cheaper. She was one of Kay Francis' society friends in *In Name Only* (RKO, 1939), a marital drama starring Carole Lombard (as the other woman) and Cary Grant; briefly tried to seduce the uninteresting Richard Carlson in *Beyond Tomorrow* (Academy Productions, 1940), a strange indie about three wealthy codgers spending Christmas with a group of downtrodden youngsters; dallied with married Alan Marshal in *Married and in Love* (RKO, 1940), a trite programmer with Barbara Read; and was a temperamental Broadway star in *Curtain Call* (RKO, 1940), a minor Anne Shirley vehicle.

There was a nice return to her alma mater, Warner Bros., as plantation owner Jerome Cowan's disagreeable wife in *Torrid Zone* (1940), a tropical melodrama set in Honduras and starring James Cagney and Ann Sheridan. This is the film where Vinson is admonished by "Oomph" girl Ann Sheridan for not carefully disposing of her cigarette. "After all," says Miss Sheridan, "that's how the Chicago fire started." "The Chicago fire was started by a cow," answers haughty Helen, allowing Sheridan to retort, "History repeats itself?"

But *Enemy Agent* (Universal, 1940), was bottom-of-the-barrel entertainment (she was a dime-store Mata Hari), and *Bowery Boy* (Republic, 1940), as a socialite trying to steer Dennis O'Keefe astray, did even less to restore her position in Hollywood. Following *Nothing but the Truth* (Paramount, 1941), where she briefly vamped Bob Hope, she semiretired.

Universal managed to lure Vinson back (how, we will never know) to play Ann Blyth's mother in *Chip Off the Old Block* (Universal, 1944), one of those annoying little "B" musicals featuring the precocious charms of Donald O'Connor and Peggy Ryan. She stayed around long enough to appear, briefly, in Republic's *The Lady and the Monster* (1944), a plodding horror melo with Erich Von Stroheim (at his most hammy) and Vera Hruba Ralston in the title roles; and she received top billing as Noel Neill's long-suffering mother in *Are These Our Parents?* (Monogram, 1944). Thomas M. Pryor of the *New York Times* pronounced the juvenile delinquency drama, "a mediocre screen entertainment at best."

Vinson was very mysterious as Helena Draque, one of the many suspects involved with murder and possibly espionage in *The Thin Man Goes Home* (M-G-M, 1945), the second to last in the long running saga of the crime-solving Charleses (William Powell and Myrna Loy). Despite being the weakest entry in the series, *The Thin Man Goes Home* was Vinson's best film in years. It proved, alas, to be her last.

Helen Vinson in 1940.

Helen Vinson gave up her screen career after the mediocre *The Thin Man Goes Home*. Instead of pursuing a career that was obviously going nowhere, the wife of socialite Donald Hardenbrook became one of the doyennes of New York society. Apparently, she gives little thought to her long ago show business career.

In the early to mid–1930s, Helen Vinson received consistently good reviews and was well on her way to stardom. It was obvious from the start that here was an actress out of the ordinary. Had she fought for better roles (like Bette Davis) and had a bad marriage not proved a costly detour, in all probability Vinson would have emerged as one of the decade's more luminous leading ladies. Instead, we can thank her for a series of keen portrayals of that oft-neglected Hollywood constant, the other woman.

HELEN VINSON FILMOGRAPHY

1930: *It's a Deal.*
1932: *Two Against the World; Jewel Robbery; The Crash; They Call It Sin; I Am a Fugitive from a Chain Gang.*
1933: *Lawyer Man; Second Hand Wife; Grand Slam; The Little Giant; Midnight Club; The Power and the Glory; The Kennel Murder Case; As Husbands Go.*
1934: *The Life of Vergie Winters; Let's Try Again; Gift of Gab; The Captain Hates the Sea; Broadway Bill.*
1935: *The Notorious Gentleman; The Wedding Night; Private Worlds; The Age of Indiscretion; Transatlantic Tunnel* (GB*); *King of the Damned* (GB*); *Reunion.*
1937: *[Walter Wanger's] Vogues of 1938; Live, Love and Learn.*
1939: *In Name Only.*
1940: *Married and in Love; Enemy Agent; Curtain Call; Beyond Tomorrow; Torrid Zone; Bowery Boy.*
1941: *Nothing but the Truth.*
1944: *Chip Off the Old Block; The Lady and the Monster; Are These Our Parents?*
1945: *The Thin Man Goes Home.*

*GB=Great Britain.

28 — Thelma White

Thelma White was a minor comedienne who spent most of her screen career in short-subject comedies opposite second rate comedians like Leon Errol and Billy Wayne. She would probably have been completely forgotten had it not been for *Reefer Madness* (1936).

Yes, White co-starred as Mae, the hard-boiled but unenthusiastic dope dealer who plied innocent young things with the "devil weed," thereby ruining their lives forever!

Originally entitled *Tell Your Children*, the cheap exploitation drama was produced by a well-meaning religious group and played for years in small town theaters under a variety of titles, including *Reefer Madness*, the name that eventually stuck and under which it was re-released to much laughter and derision in the drugged-out 1960s. White, who was under contract to RKO when she made the film, never wanted to play Mae, the dope peddler.

"I was a musical comedy actress, I didn't want to make a movie about drugs," she explained to the *Los Angeles Times* in 1987.

Nobody remembers Thelma White's other feature films (mostly low-budget musicals and comedies), but thanks to late night television and innumerable "Worst Movies" festivals, Mae is still with us, still plying her nefarious trade while corrupting naive young things like Dorothy Short and Lillian Miles.

Born Thelma Constance Wolpa on December 4, 1911 (this is the official date, but Thelma's true year of birth was probably closer to 1908), in Lincoln, Nebraska, White was the daughter of itinerant carnival performers. With her parents she moved from town to town in the Midwest, working carnivals and sideshows. (She herself made her professional debut at the age of two as a cooing Kewpie doll in a shooting gallery!)

Her father, she later said, sidestepped the so-called Gerry Society* "by using a bottle of whiskey and a sob story to obtain a back dated birth certificate from a courthouse

---

*A children's welfare organization who wanted her in a schoolroom instead of a shooting gallery.

clerk." Although she had a private tutor for three years, the education was cursory and she never finished elementary school.

Mr. Wolpa disappeared from Thelma's life when she was ten and she moved with her mother to Omaha, Nebraska, where she attended the Chambers Dancing School. While there, she won first prize in an amateur contest at Omaha's Empress Theater, energetically belting out "When I Knock the 'L' Out of Kelly." The win resulted in a three month vaudeville engagement with George Jessel on the Orpheum Circuit and a tour of Canada with the Winnipeg Kiddies.

Returning from the tour, White teamed up with 13-year-old Marjorie Guthrie, a child soprano with a remarkable likeness to Thelma herself. Together they became the White Sisters and toured the vaudeville circuits extensively for two years. The culmination of the tour was a stint at New York's famed Palace Theater: "Marjorie and I were booked into the Palace ten times one year. So far as I know, that's a record," White told writer Harry Preston in 1965.

The White sisters were managed by Thelma's very ambitious mother (shades of Mama Rose!), who apparently kept the team's earnings in her corset, unwilling to trust the banking system. "Sure, I was exploited, but I didn't know it at the time," White explains today.

In 1925, Marjorie Guthrie married and the team split up. As a solo act, Thelma was quickly booked to appear in the 1926 edition of *Earl Carroll's Vanities*. "I was only fourteen, but with some heavy padding and an adult hair style I looked old enough."

On January 1, 1927, Thelma married for the first time, sneaking off between shows to tie the knot with vaudevillian Claude Stroud. "The marriage went downhill from there," she later said. "I loved Claude, but we were just kids."

In 1930, divorced from Stroud, Thelma wed Max Hoffman, Jr., and made her screen debut. This second marriage, however, also proved short-lived, but her screen career was soon blossoming.

White had found her niche in two-reel comedies and signed a contract with Pathé, one of the busiest producers in the field, appearing in such series as *Pathé Melody Comedies* and *Pathé Folly Comedies*.* From Pathé she went to the competing Vitaphone (Warner Bros.), where she starred in *The Honeymooners* series with a knockabout comic named Billy Wayne. She now felt ready for Hollywood, signed a contract with RKO (the new owners of Pathé, incidentally), and arrived amidst some fanfare on the West Coast in early 1932.

The RKO studio spent quite a bit of money promoting Thelma White, hoping to launch a new star with a tailor-made vehicle entitled "Blonde Poison." For unknown reasons the project never got off the ground, nor did a starring role opposite Wheeler and Woolsey, RKO's top comedy team, in *Hips, Hips, Hooray!* (1934). At the last minute, RKO felt that the farce needed more box office appeal and replaced her with Thelma Todd. Dejected, but not defeated, she returned to New York and by August was back on Broadway opposite Milton Berle in *Salute*.

The indomitable White, still under contract to RKO, returned to Hollywood in

---

*One of the items, A Night in a Dormitory, also featured a very young Ginger Rogers, whose early career was comparable to Thelma White's.

Thelma White in *Tell Your Children* (1938).

September of 1935, but the studio still had nothing lined up for her, and all she did was a bit in *Two in the Dark* (released 1936). There was, however, a co-starring role opposite former stuntman Richard Talmadge in something called *Never Too Late* (Reliable, 1935), in which they were detectives trying to get the goods on some jewel thieves. Alas, few people saw the film, which was distributed on the states'-rights basis and quickly disappeared from sight.

One cannot say that Thelma White made much of a splash in films in this period (or any other for that matter). She was still under contract to RKO, but that studio lent her services to Paramount for what were insignificant bit parts in more or less insignificant potboilers. Then, of course, there was *Tell Your Children*, or *The Burning Question*.

This probably heartfelt plea to say no to smoking dope was produced (some sources say in 1936) by a company calling itself G and H Productions and released on a states'-rights basis in 1938. It was, as Bad Film fans everywhere know, a rather inept warning about the dangers of marijuana smoking. Based, as they say, "on an original story by Lawrence Meade," the drama opens with a stern written warning:

> The story you are about to witness may startle you. It would not have been possible, otherwise, to sufficiently emphasize the frightful toll of the new drug menace which is

destroying the youth of America in alarmingly increasing numbers. *Marihuana* is that drug—a violent narcotic—an unspeakable scourge—*The Real Public Enemy Number One!* Its first effect is sudden, violent, uncontrollable laughter, then come dangerous hallucinations—space expands—time slows down—almost stands still ... fixed ideas come next, conjuring up monstrous extravagance—followed by emotional disturbances, the total inability to direct thought—the loss of all power to resist physical conditions ... leading finally to acts of shocking violence ... ending often in incurable insanity. In picturing its soul destroying effects no attempt was made to equivocate. The scenes and incidents, while fictionalized for the purpose of this story, are based on actual research into Marihuana addiction. If this stark reality will make you *Think*, will make you aware that something *must be done* to wipe out this ghastly menace, then the picture will not have failed in its purpose.... Because the dread *Marihuana* may reach forth for your son or daughter ... *or yours* ... *or YOURS*" [italics are in the original].

After that introduction, audience members presumably weren't ready for the hilarity that ensued. Veteran director Louis Gasnier, a holdover from the early silent era who had recently found himself employable only on Poverty Row, painted his picture with an extremely thick brush.

The story he told was the otherwise cautionary tale of high school students lured into becoming maniacal marijuana addicts by an unscrupulous older couple, Jack (Carleton Young) and Mae (White). Actually, Mae is not quite as eager to lead the young innocents down the garden path as is her hubby, but once they are hooked on reefers, she delivers the "goodies" without much complaint. In between serving the kiddies hop, Thelma shows a generous amount of leg—a clear sign that the filmmakers, religious educators or not, knew their target audience well.

Tell Your Children was inept filmmaking on all levels—hilariously so. The acting is either completely over the top (as when a wild-eyed Dave O'Brien admonishes his girlfriend to play the piano "faster, faster!") or simply nonexistent. The "scourge" of marijuana is here treated as if it was the equivalent of today's "crack" cocaine, but the action is constantly interrupted by pompous speeches delivered by wooden actors impersonating authority figures (teachers, doctors, judges, and the like).

White, who never smoked or used alcohol in real life, she says, had a scene where she did both: "Boy did it make me sick," she later recalled. "The director wanted us to 'hoke' it up. He wanted us to show the madness." For her troubles, she said, she earned $2,500 a week (from RKO apparently; the studio might have backed the film: George A. Hirliman, its producer, was an associate producer there).

Forty years later White looked back with contempt at RKO, who forced her to do a film she disliked from the start. "I hide my head when I think about it. It was a dreadful film," she told the *Los Angeles Times*.

Tell Your Children went on to become one of the most successful exploitation films of all times and is still delighting audiences everywhere. In 1939 it was re-released as *The Burning Question* and in 1947 as *Reefer Madness*. New Line picked it up in 1973 and has given it a new life on videotape. "It's unintentionally funny," comments Howard Suber, a UCLA film historian and professor. "You laugh at people for being so uptight and emotional. Its popularity comes from feeling superior to these people who were ranting and raving."

With controversy still raging over *Tell Your Children* (it was, needless to say, banned in many places), White returned to the Broadway stage where she co-starred with Joe E. Lewis in *Right This Way* (1938), introducing the standard "I'll Be Seeing You." She did a gangster melodrama for Monogram, *Wanted by the Police* (1938), and toured Australia with *Folies d'Amour*.

When America finally entered the war, White became one of the busiest entertainers on the USO tours. Unfortunately, ill health put a momentary stop to her career; appearing with the USO in Alaska, she came down with pneumonia and later suffered a nervous breakdown. By the late 1940s, she says, a debilitating series of new malaises virtually crippled her and forced her to retire from performing.

Throughout the 1940s, despite her various bouts with illness, Thelma White continued to appear in comedy shorts with Leon Errol and, periodically, in feature films: *A Man's World* (Columbia, 1943); *Spy Train* (Monogram, 1943), as a passenger aboard a train carrying a bomb; *Bowery Champs* (Monogram, 1944), as a gangster's moll; and *Mary Lou* (Columbia, 1948), her final film, a musical at long last!

Thelma White returned to Hollywood in the late 1950s, but this time as an artists' manager. (Among her clients were Robert Blake and Ann Jillian.) More recently, she developed her own television production company for release of independent films.*

In 1957 she was the subject of television's *This Is Your Life* program. Ten years later she married for the third time, to actor and costume designer Tony Millard. The couple resides in Panorama City, where she reputedly has been busy writing her autobiography. In August of 1992 the veteran performer was hospitalized for a bleeding ulcer, but, happily, seems to have fully recovered.

THELMA WHITE FILMOGRAPHY

1935: *Never Too Late.*
1936: *Two in the Dark; The Moon's Our Home; Forgotten Faces.*
1938: *Tell Your Children* [*Reefer Madness*]; *Wanted by the Police.*
1942: *A Man's World.*
1943: *Spy Train.*
1944: *Bowery Champs.*
1948: *Mary Lou.*

---

*E.g., Tom Jones Rides Again *(date unknown)*.

29 — Anna May Wong

Today, the name Anna May Wong elicits either outright snickers or a vague recollection of "high camp." Some historians portray her as the only Chinese actress to become a major star. In reality, Wong was never a star in the true sense of the word; her ethnicity precluded such luxury. She was a considerable draw in Europe, but in Hollywood, Wong skulked about as the vengeful daughter of Fu Manchu, or was merely mysterious in that stereotypical screenwriter's idea of Oriental inscrutability.

To a certain extent, the mediocrity of her roles was of her own doing. Time and again she turned down potentially star-making roles, considering them—often quite rightly so—stereotypical and demeaning. She refused, for example, to play the spy Mah-Li in Frank Capra's *The Bitter Tea of General Yen* (1932), and turned down the role of the concubine in *The Good Earth* (1937). In either case, she felt it belittling that she, the only genuine Asian among the principal players, should be offered the role of the villain. Neither of the actresses who replaced her (Toshia Mori and Tilly Losch, respectively) became major stars, but Wong certainly had the capacity or notoriety to succeed where they failed.

Of course, in a better world Wong should have been offered the female lead in *The Good Earth*, a part she was obviously born to play. Not the company to rock the ethnocentric boat, however, M-G-M went with the Austrian Luise Rainer, who thus garnered her second Academy Award in a row.

Certainly Anna May Wong had some memorable parts along the way. She burst to prominence slinking across the screen as the Mongolian slave girl in Douglas Fairbanks' *The Thief of Baghdad* (1924), and if the role was stereotypical in the worst way, Wong gave it her own stamp of elegance and refinement. Eight years later, appearing seemingly dipped in ink, she played the mysterious cigarette-smoking traveler in Josef von Sternberg's *Shanghai Express* (1932). A "fallen woman," she selflessly offers her body to a brutal warlord in order to save a group of Westerners stranded in the middle of a Chinese revolution and, in the process, manages to upstage the film's female lead,

Marlene Dietrich. In fact, *Shanghai Express* is Wong's best remembered film and the only one in which she is treated by a director with the respect she deserved.

Born Wong Liu Tsong (Chinese, it was said, for "Frosted Yellow Willow") in Los Angeles on January 3, 1905, Anna May Wong was the daughter of the Chinese-born proprietor of a laundromat. According to the actress herself, her humble but hard working and proud background offered a stability much needed later in the whirlwind life of show business. "Some girls might get up-stage about the laundry," she explained in 1923.

> Not for Me. Pictures are fine, and I'm getting along all right, but it's not so bad to have the laundry back of you, so you can wait and take good parts and be independent when you're climbing. Not to have to worry about where your next meal is coming from.

Later, Mary Winslip of *Photoplay* rather patronizingly described a happy childhood:

> She has never been to China; Los Angeles' Chinatown is her home. The public schools gave her an education and her association with American youth filled her with vitality and joyousness and freedom that is as quaint in her as a cluster of red balloons tied to a cherry tree.

Behind the "vitality and joyousness and freedom," however, was a deep desire to become somebody. And somebody in Los Angeles inevitably meant a screen actress. Emma Gee, in her biography of Wong in *Notable American Women*, wrote,

> As a youngster she often played truant and frequented the local nickelodeon. This precocious interest brought her into conflict with her father, who considered the world of film disreputable [and] unfit for a proper Chinese-American daughter. Strong-willed and fiercely independent, she decided upon an acting career in her early teens....

Despite her father's misgiving, Wong (who invented her stage name at the age of 11) made her screen debut as an extra in *The Red Lantern* (Metro, 1919), a melodrama starring Alla Nazimova. She had been working at Hollywood's Ville de Paris department store when she heard that Metro was seeking 300 girls as extras.

According to some sources, Wong was not a complete novice when she made her screen debut, having done some dancing and amateur stage work before setting out to conquer Hollywood. Not that it mattered much. She still had to accept extra work and bit parts for two years before being "discovered."

The official discovery of Anna May Wong came about in 1922. The previous year she had achieved some recognition as Lon Chaney's abused wife in a three-part miscegenation drama from First National, *Bits of Life*, and as a half-caste in Fox's *Shame*. She was therefore the obvious choice to play Frances Marion's version of *Madame Butterfly* opposite Kenneth Harlan's Pinkerton in *The Toll of the Sea* (Metro, 1922), an early technicolor experiment.

Despite misgivings about the film itself, reviewers praised Wong as the Chinese girl who loves a Britisher only to commit suicide when he is forced to marry a white woman. The *New York Times* commented,

> Miss Wong stirs in the spectator all the sympathy her part calls for, and she never repels one by an excess of theatrical "feeling." She has a difficult role, a role that is botched nine times out of ten, but hers is the tenth performance.... She should be seen again and often on the screen.

With reviews like that, Anna May Wong was heralded as a new star. Not that it mattered much; Hollywood moguls did not exactly go out of their way to create vehicles for an Oriental leading lady. And that despite the fact that there existed a precedent: in the mid-teens, Paramount had tailored a series of intelligent, well received melodramas around Japan's Sessue Hayakawa, who became the first (and, arguably, only) Asian, able to cross the racial barricade.

Anna May Wong's ethnicity also affected her private life. She had fallen in love with her director in *Bits of Life*, the roguishly charming Marshall (Mickey) Neilan. According to some sources, the two wanted to marry (and almost eloped to Mexico), but were halted by the stringent miscegenation laws, which were to stay on the books until 1945.

In later interviews, the actress sugarcoated her rise to prominence, rarely discussing anything so myth shattering as racism. "I feel I am a very fortunate person," she told *Motion Picture* in 1931.

> All people have their dreams, and it's wonderful just to have them. But when they actually come true you are happy and lucky beyond what you have any right to expect. And it's very wonderful. I think it was my fatalism that made me able to start working out my seemingly impossible ambition. That, and the fact that I am very imaginative—it was possible for *anything* to happen, it seemed to me. I was so young when I began that I knew I still had youth if I failed, so I determined to give myself ten years to succeed as an actress. Ten years is not a long time in the Chinese mind.

It was lucky indeed, that Wong permitted herself ten years to succeed in her chosen profession. For every step forward, it must have seemed, she took two backwards.

Following the success of *Toll of the Sea*, all she could get were bits as honky-tonk girls or somebody's concubine in films such as Tod Browning's *Drifting* (Universal, 1923), a cheap melodrama about opium smuggling. The next step forward had to wait until 1924, when Douglas Fairbanks picked her to play the Mongolian slave girl in his colorful production of *The Thief of Baghdad*.

With Fairbanks at his precipitous best flying through the air on a magic carpet to locate a treasure, United Artists' *The Thief of Baghdad* is, still today, a wondrous, imaginative fairy-tale produced in the very best Hollywood tradition.

Not that the production did not have its problems, large and small. To the latter category belonged Anna May Wong's skimpy slave girl attire, which, according to Fairbanks, the actress needed her father's permission to wear.

Permission gracefully granted, Wong's treacherous Mongol was an exciting sight to behold—and the realization of many a young boy's fantasies. Observed *Photoplay*,

> From crown to sole, Anna May Wong is Chinese. Her black hair is of the texture that adorns the heads of maidens, who live beside the Yang-tse-Kiang. Her deep, brown eyes, while the slant is not pronounced, are typically Oriental. These come from her Mongol

father. But her Manchu mother has given her height and a poise that Chinese maids seldom have.

Such condescending drivel was the prose used to describe one of Hollywood's most beautiful and extraordinary women, whose talent and appeal could easily have made her one of the world's leading screen actresses. Her appearance in *The Thief of Baghdad* should have catapulted her forwards, but instead she only received more of the same.

She had little to do as Tiger Lily in *Peter Pan* (Famous Players, 1924), and her roles in potboilers such as the Pathé serial *The 40th Floor* (1924) and the espionage drama *Forty Winks* (Famous Players, 1925) only gave impetus to her nickname as the movies' Oriental Siren.

In the spring of 1925, dejected by her shabby treatment in Hollywood, Wong briefly tried the stage but met with negligible success. Along with a group of fellow silent screen actors that included once popular serial stars Ruth Stonehouse and Helen Holmes, she embarked on a disastrous tour of the vaudeville circuits. In his *Encyclopedia of Vaudeville*, historian Anthony Slide describes the group's arrival at the Kansas City Convention Hall:

> Seats were $2 each, and the audience was promised the opportunity to dance with the stars after the show. On opening night, the company drove to the hall, accompanied by a police escort and marching band, only to be confronted with eighteen thousand empty seats. There was an immediate display of temperament until the stars realized that reporters were present, at which point they decided to present their show anyway. Their misfortunes had only just begun, for before they could leave town for their next booking in Atchison, Kansas, the local agent for the show filed an attachment on the admittedly very small box-office receipts. After that was straightened out, the troupe left for Atchison and Omaha, where the final blow was struck. The orchestra conductor's paycheck bounced, and he attached the receipts. Discouraged, the stars returned to the safety of Hollywood, where such dramas were played out only on the screen.

Anna May Wong returned to Hollywood for still more abuse. She was Oneta, a "fiery Indian maiden" in *The Desert Trail* (M-G-M, 1926), a low-budget mining drama, and was forced to take seventh billing in *Fifth Avenue* (PDC, 1926), an old-fashioned tearjerker.

She was back to seething jealously in an opium den in *Old San Francisco* (Warner Bros., 1927), an unabashedly old-fashioned melodrama; and was then Renee Adoree's rival in *Mr. Wu* (M-G-M, 1927).

Adoree, who received second billing (to Lon Chaney), and was heavily promoted by M-G-M, also played a Chinese girl, and therein lay the trouble. Wong (tenth billed in *Mr. Wu*), constantly had to compete for roles with non–Asians such as Adoree and newcomer Myrna Loy. In *The Crimson City* (Warner Bros., 1928), for example, Loy starred as a girl sold into slavery by a cruel Mandarin (Japanese actor Sojin), whereas Wong had to make good with a minor supporting role.

In late 1928, tired of typecasting and the constant struggle for good parts, she left Hollywood behind to enjoy the less stringent atmosphere of Europe. Like it had so many other racially oppressed entertainers before her, Berlin welcomed the émigrée

Anna May Wong in *The Thief of Baghdad* (United Artists, 1924).

with open arms, and she starred in the German film *Song* (1928).* She was warmly received in London in 1929, where producer Basil Dean bought the play *A Circle of Chalk* especially for her and the young Laurence Oliver. The composer Constant Lambert saw her in that and, completely enamored, dedicated his *Eight Poems of Li Po* to her.

And while appearing on stage at night, she filmed *Piccadilly* (British, International, 1929), a backstage melodrama, during the day. Wong played a poor dishwasher who becomes a dancer and, eventually, a murderess.

Directed by the German E. A. Dupont, *Piccadilly*, despite its technical crudeness (it was a silent with a few dialog scenes added), was a great deal better than what Hollywood had offered. Later in her life, however, Wong refused to attend revivals of the film, claiming she had been in too great an emotional state when it was made.

The talk of the town, Wong and Sessue Hayakawa (who was also seeking greener pastures overseas) were received as "Goodwill Ambassadors" by the British Royal family—not on behalf of the United States, incidentally, but China and Japan, respectively. With this kind of acceptance, the two stars had conquered race and prejudice—as *Motion Picture* so quaintly put it.

A proven success, Wong toured Europe, appearing before audiences in France, Austria and Germany and proving a hit everywhere she went. While in France, she filmed *L'amour maitre des choses* (1931), the French version of a British film she had made, *The Flame of Love*, and in Germany, she surprised everyone by speaking fluent German on stage in *Tschain Tschi*. Also in Germany she was befriended by actress (later director) Leni Riefenstahl, from whom she for a while seemed inseparable.

She met little, if any, prejudice. "That's one reason why I was so happy there," she later told Betty Willis of *Motion Picture*. "Of course," she clarified, "it depends a lot where you are. People who might ordinarily have racial feelings would make an exception in the case of a celebrity. But there, everyone was lovely to me."

Realizing, however, that on the whole, her European films were as bad as (if not worse than) what Hollywood had offered, Wong decided to return. On her way back, however, she made a successful Broadway debut in *On the Spot* (1931). The play enjoyed a healthy 30-week run and the American film industry again showed interest.

"When I left Hollywood I vowed that I would never act for films again," she told writer Doris Mackie upon her return to Los Angeles.

> I was so tired of the parts I had to play. Why is it that the screen Chinese is always the villain? And so crude a villain—murderous, treacherous, a snake in the grass! We are not like that. How could we be, with a civilization that is so many times older than the West?

In spite of Wong's not inappropriate rhetorical questions, her Hollywood comeback showcased her as the murderous and treacherous Ling Moy, vengeful daughter of that perennial snake in the grass, Dr. Fu Manchu (Warner Oland). The film was *Daughter of the Dragon* (Paramount, 1931), and it was the third installment in the

---

Released in Great Britain as Show Life *and in the United States as* Wasted Love. *"Anna May Wong is a competent little actress, but it would take far more than good acting to make this production half-way diverting," Mordaunt Hall of the* New York Times *complained in December of 1929.*

series depicting Sax Rohmer's pulp fiction menace, an estimable but quite homicidal Chinese doctor. It was all rather lurid and not a little demeaning (despite the presence in the cast of Wong's fellow "Ambassador," Sessue Hayakawa), but Paramount had held a carrot in front of the actress. In her next film, she would be directed by Josef von Sternberg.

The story of a group of travelers stranded in the midst of a Chinese revolution, *Shanghai Express* (Paramount, 1932) began filming in late 1931 with a cast that included Marlene Dietrich as a whore known as the Shanghai Lil; Clive Brook as a stiff upper lip Britisher, who was once her paramour; Warner Oland (taking a break from his duties as Charlie Chan and Fu Manchu) as an impervious rebel leader; and Anna May Wong as Hui Fei, a delicate but ultimately strong courtesan.

Despite von Sternberg's notoriously imperious ways, filming went smoothly for Wong, who struck up a lasting friendship with Dietrich.* In between takes, the two actresses would relax together in Marlene's luxurious dressing room, listening to the German star's extensive collection of Richard Tauber records. Filming an uprising in China more or less to the strains of Tauber must indeed have been an unforgettable experience.

Happily, von Sternberg lavished as much care in lighting and photographing Wong as he did Dietrich (which was considerable), and the result is striking. Beautiful and seemingly detached from the horrors happening around her, Wong managed to convey the mental anguish, aversion and despair the character experiences without resorting to obvious melodramatics, even when raped by the cold-blooded rebel leader. It is a finely shaded performance, just as calculated maybe, but not nearly as mannered as Dietrich's stunning but ultimately vacuous Shanghai Lil. Naturally, Wong's performance was more or less overlooked by contemporary critics, so completely caught up were they by the Dietrich mystique and von Sternberg's virtuosity. But it is a performance that has withstood the test of time—despite the film's embryonic racism.

If Anna May Wong had counted on her European celebrity and the popularity of *Shanghai Express* to earn her some respect in Hollywood, she was sadly mistaken. Rumored to be the front runner for the starring role as Lien Wa, a beautiful Chinese-American caught up in San Francisco's Tong wars in *The Son-Daughter* (M-G-M, 1932), she ultimately lost the part to an embarrassingly miscast Helen Hayes. It would have been unseemly, Hollywood reckoned, had Wong been allowed to make passionate love with her leading man, the Mexican-born Ramon Novarro. The Hays Office had stringent rules about miscegenation and was not about to "lower" their standards; that the male lead could have been played by, say, Korean-born Philip Ahn, Wong's off-screen fiancé, apparently occurred to no one.

Dejected after losing *The Son-Daughter*, and having turned down the stereotypical role of the malicious spy in Frank Capra's *The Bitter Tea of General Yen* (Columbia, 1933), Wong played Mrs. Pyke in a whodunit loosely (very loosely) based on Sir Arthur Conan Doyle's *A Study in Scarlet* (K. B. S., 1933). In fact, the drama had only the title and the character of Sherlock Holmes (played by Reginald Owen) in common with Conan Doyle's original and was written (by director Robert Florey and

---

Her friendship with women like Riefenstahl and Marlene Dietrich greatly helped persistent rumors of lesbianism.

Owen) especially for her. Moreover, despite receiving second billing, Wong was indeed again the villain of the piece. Filmed on the cheap by a Poverty Row company, *A Study in Scarlet* was nevertheless better than expected and Wong was praised for her performance.

She returned to Paramount for *Limehouse Blues* (1934), but was yet again cast as a jealous Chinese girl who loses her man (an incongruously made-up George Raft) to the lily-white Jean Parker. *Limehouse Blues* bore more than a passing resemblance to D.W. Griffith's classic melodrama *Broken Blossoms* (1919), but was vastly inferior and reminded reviewers more of the "Yellow Peril" melodramas of the early teens. Wong, again fed up with Hollywood's treatment of her, returned to England. (On a stopover in New York, she delivered dialogue retakes on a transcontinental link to Hollywood.)

Although Wong found less racism in her daily life overseas, her British films were as tasteless as the worst from Hollywood. She was yet again a vengeful slave girl in the anachronistic musical *Chu Chin Chow* (Gainsborough, 1934); and in *Java Head* (Basil Dean, 1935), she once more commits suicide when her white lover (John Loder) leaves her for a woman "of his own kind." Based on a Joseph Hergesheimer novel, *Java Head* was, in the words of Andre Sennwald of the *New York Times*, "windy and poorly accented."

Anna May Wong had for years expressed interest in playing O-Lan, the meek farmer's wife in a screen version of Pearl S. Buck's 1931 bestseller *The Good Earth*. Plans to film the sprawling saga of Chinese peasants battling the elements had been dropped in 1933 (because of difficulties both in casting and in assembling a workable script), but in 1935 Irving Thalberg of M-G-M resurrected the project. Sweden's Nils Asther (who had played *General Yen* in 1932) and Charles Boyer from France were at one point or another announced to play Miss Buck's stoic hero, the farmer Wang Lung. In the end, however, the studio borrowed Jewish actor Paul Muni from Warners.

For O-Lan, Wang's first wife, M-G-M considered Broadway's Katherine Cornell and Brooklyn's Barbara Stanwyck. Luise Rainer, the studio's prized Viennese import, finally won the part that would earn her the second Academy Award in a row.*

As it turned out, Anna May Wong was never even in the running! She was, however, mentioned as a strong possibility for Lotus, Wang's selfish second wife. But again, M-G-M demurred. As Lotus, Wong would have love scenes with Muni, and that would be in conflict with the production code.

According to the actress herself, alas, it was she who turned down the role, in part due to M-G-M's demand that she screen-test, and in part because she didn't like the role. "I'll be glad to take the test but I won't play Lotus," she is quoted as having told Thalberg.

> If you let me play O-Lan, I'll be very glad. But you're asking me—with my Chinese blood—to do the only unsympathetic role in the picture, featuring an all–American cast [sic] portraying Chinese characters.†

The previous year she had won for playing Florenz Ziegfeld's wife, Anna Held, in The Great Ziegfeld. *The experience proved somewhat of a jinx for Rainer, who never again appeared in a worthwhile film.*

†*M-G-M instead cast Wong's friend, the Austrian dancer Tilly Losch, as Lotus.*

Anna May Wong, circa 1935.

Instead of portraying the sympathetic, hard working and somewhat realistic O-Lan, Anna May Wong traveled to China for the first time. "I took what money I had and said I would stay as long as it lasted," she later told the *Hollywood-Citizen News*.

[Swedish-born] Warner came over and was well received. He was frequently called Charlie Chan. Because I had been the villainess so often in pictures, it was thought I had not been true to my people. It took four hours one afternoon to convince the government this was not so.

Like countless black American entertainers, then and now, Wong was given the impossible responsibility of being a role model instead of what she really was: a hard working actress trying to earn a living without completely compromising her ideals.

Returning once again to Hollywood, Wong found herself the victim of a lunatic who sent her letters with threats of disfigurement; fortunately, the man was quickly apprehended. On a somewhat calmer note, she repudiated the rumor that she was about to wed Philip Ahn, commenting that "it would be like marrying my brother."

Professionally, things were pretty much as before the trip to China. Wong was again denied the Asian role of the year, this time Princess Kukachin in Samuel Goldwyn's *The Adventures of Marco Polo* (United Artists, 1938). Goldwyn's choice of the pedestrian Sigrid Gurie must have seemed like a slap in the face to Wong, who could only stand by while Gary Cooper and the infamous "Siren of the Fjords" made considerable fools of themselves.

The films Wong *did* do were programmers: She was the daughter of a murder victim who helps the police solve the case in *Daughter of Shanghai* (Paramount, 1938), which, despite its lurid title, was a straightforward whodunit. Philip Ahn played the cop and the statuesque Cecil Cunningham was the villainess, the brains of a smuggling ring. Wong and Cunningham became fast friends, a friendship that lasted until Anna May's death.

Daughter of Shanghai was followed by yet another crime drama from the Paramount "B" unit, *Dangerous to Know* (1938). A reworking of her 1931 Broadway play *On the Loose*, the potboiler had Wong, although star billed, playing second fiddle to Akim Tamiroff's mobster who wants to marry a socialite (Gail Patrick). Bosley Crowther of the *New York Times* found it "second-rate melodrama hardly worthy of the talents of its generally capable cast."

Equally unworthy, at least of Anna May Wong, was Warner's *When Were You Born* (1938), a silly whodunit which employed the gimmick of listing the astrological signs of its cast members in the credits.

While Wong turned down Grand National's *Panama Patrol* (1939), a minor espionage thriller (Adrienne Ames was substituted), she accepted whatever Paramount handed her, including *King of Chinatown* (1939), in which she again played opposite Tamiroff, whom the studio for some reason was promoting in leading roles. Offscreen, she was Dorothy Lamour's coach on *Disputed Passage* (Paramount, 1939) and she became the studio's all purpose consultant on things Chinese.

She returned to screen acting in 1941, but was now mired in Poverty Row productions. Having more or less been reduced to a parody of herself, she starred as a schoolteacher turned intelligence agent in *Bombs Over Burma* (PRC, 1942), and was the leader of the Chinese resistance in *Lady from Chunking* (PRC, 1943). With no other offers materializing, she announced her retirement from the screen and instead worked for China relief through the USO.

"I first walked through the gates of the Moongate Apartments at 326 San

Vicente Boulevard in Santa Monica in 1948," Conrad Doerr, a distant relative of Cecil Cunningham, wrote in *Films in Review* in December of 1968.

> The Chinese red moongates were the only thing Chinese about that L-shaped Spanish house, which had been converted into apartments. I was somewhat nervous as I rang the bell and my landlady-to-be for the next eight years opened the door. She was Anna May Wong, in black sweater and slacks, and the perennial bangs.

Doerr got to know the former actress well and has given a good account of her later years. She was, for example, terrified of returning to acting, although she often received offers. Not long after Doerr had rented the room, his landlady signed to do a television series.

Anna May Wong, circa 1940.

"The night before she was to leave for the East," Doerr wrote, "she had a few people over for dinner, and, early in the evening, she began to come apart—terrified not only over returning to work but doing so in a new medium."

The program was to be done live and the stint would last for 13 weeks. Wong managed to collect herself (she was, if nothing else, a professional of the old school), went to New York "and came back stimulated and anxious to work. Alas, the teleseries was never made."

Wong *did* return to performing, but not on television. In 1949 her good friend Arthur Lubin directed her in the crime drama *Impact* (United Artists), a *film noir* about a man who comes "back from the dead." Contemporary reviewers did not like the film ("a dull thud," wrote Bosley Crowther of the *New York Times*), but it has later gained a reputation as a "sleeper."

Wong finally did appear on television when, in 1951, she starred in *The Gallery of Madame Liu Tsong* on the Dumont network.

Subsequently, she did a few guest spots, but her main source of income remained the apartment building on San Vicente and she became a well known figure around her Santa Monica neighborhood.

"It was difficult not to notice that whenever Anna May appeared in public she created a stir," Conrad Doerr later remarked. "She was tall for a Chinese woman, had remained striking-looking, and her public wardrobe had an Oriental flavor." In 1956, however, the actress sold the apartment building and moved in with her brother Richard at his home on 21st Place in Santa Monica.

Producer Ross Hunter, always willing to engage Hollywood veterans, brought Wong back to the screen as Lana Turner's maid in the melodrama *Portrait in Black* (Universal, 1960). She probably should not have bothered ("Miss Wong is merely inscrutable as the suspicious housekeeper," wrote the *New York Times'* A. H. Weiler), but she had accepted in order to work with Anthony Quinn, the film's male lead.

Quinn and his then wife, Katherine DeMille, had for a long time been among her best friends, and the actor subsequently convinced her to do *The Savage Innocents* (Paramount, 1960). She went on location to Alaska for this pseudodocumentary about an Eskimo (Quinn) battling the influence of "civilization." Wong played Quinn's mother-in-law, but when the film was released, her voice had been dubbed.

She had been seriously ill during the arduous location filming of *The Savage Innocents*, but had recovered enough for Ross Hunter to cast her as Madame Liang in his upcoming version of *Flower Drum Song* (Universal, 1961). She never got to play the role: on February 3, 1961, she died of a heart attack in her sleep and was replaced with Juanita Hall.

Anna May Wong always felt out of place in the ethnocentric Hollywood. In fact, she thrived in Continental Europe, and had it not been for the threatening political situation of the late 1930s, she probably would have relocated there permanently.

The leftwing writer Cedric Belfrage thought that she belonged in Europe. "Some are born European; some achieve Europe; some have Europe thrust upon them," Belfrage wrote in *Motion Picture* (1930), describing a group of expatriate Hollywood actresses that included Wong, Betty Blythe and Louise Brooks.

> In Hollywood they were, in a way, square pegs in round holes. They were well on the upward path to the starry heights; some [Blythe, presumably] had actually achieved stardom. There was nothing to stop them except their temperaments.
>
> They had restless souls, like Chekhov's heroines who sit on the wide-open steppes and moan all day long: "God! I'm stifling here! I can't breathe! When, oh when, do we go to Moscow? ... So, in the end, they packed their grips and lit out for their spiritual home. Hollywood saw them no more—for a time, at least.

ANNA MAY WONG FILMOGRAPHY

1919: *The Red Lantern.*
1920: *Dinty.*
1921: *Bits of Life; Shame.*
1922: *Toll of the Sea.*
1923: *Drifting; Thundering Dawn.*

1924: *The Thief of Baghdad; The Alaskan; Peter Pan; The 40th Door.*
1925: *Forty Winks.*
1926: *The Desert's Toll; Fifth Avenue; A Trip to Chinatown; Silk Bouquet.*
1927: *Old San Francisco; Mr. Wu; Driven from Home; Streets of Shanghai; The Devil Dancer; The Dove.*
1928: *The Chinese Parrot; Across to Singapore; Chinatown Charlie; Song* (German); *The Crimson City.*
1929: *Piccadilly* (GB*); *Wasted Love* (GB*).
1930: *The Flame of Love* (GB*).
1931: *L'amour maitre des choses* (France); *The House That Shadows Built* (documentary); *Daughter of the Dragon.*
1932: *Shanghai Express.*
1933: *A Study in Scarlet.*
1934: *Limehouse Blues; Chu Chin Chow* (GB*).
1935: *Java Head* (GB*).
1938: *Daughter of Shanghai; Dangerous to Know; When Were You Born.*
1939: *Island of Lost Men; King of Chinatown.*
1941: *Ellery Queen's Penthouse Mystery.*
1942: *Bombs Over Burma.*
1943: *Lady from Chungking.*
1949: *Impact.*
1953: *Ali Baba Nights.*
1960: *Just Joe* (GB*); *Portrait in Black; The Savage Innocents* (GB*).

*GB=Great Britain.

Bibliography

Baskette, Kirtley. "Binnie with a Grin." *Photoplay*, Oct, 1934, pp. 67, 101 and 102.
Biery, Ruth. "Looking at Life with Helen Vinson." *Motion Picture*, January, 1936, pp. 29 and 62.
_____. "Suicide Never Pays." *Photoplay*, May 1928, pp. 33 and 120.
"Binnie Making a Comeback." *Los Angeles Times*, December 1, 1972, part IV, pp. 1, 10 and 11.
Bodeen, DeWitt. "Evelyn Brent." *Films in Review*, June 1976, pp. 339–360.
Brownlow, Kevin. *The Parade's Gone By*. New York: Alfred A. Knopf, 1968.
Ceplair, Larry, and Steven Englund. *The Inquisition in Hollywood*. New York: Anchor Press, 1980.
Crivillo, Kirk. *Fallen Angels*. Secaucus, N.J.: Citadel Press 1988.
Dawson, Esther. "Baclanova." *Photoplay*, August 1928, pp. 66 and 129.
de Leighbur, Don. "Dark Waters." *Los Angeles Sentinel*, June 15, 1944.
Gehman, Richard, and Michael McFadden. "The Golden Sex." *Los Angeles Herald Examiner*, May 14, 1963, pp. B1 and B8.
Goldbeck, Elisabeth. "How Sari Maritza Was Made a Star." *Motion Picture*, February 1933, p. 51.
Gray, Charleson. "Mary Mary *Not* Contrary." *Motion Picture*, April 1930, p. 42.
Haddon, John L. "What a 'Battle'." *Motion Picture*, July 1933, pp. 58 and 87.
Hadley, Boze. "Last Kiss of the Spider Woman." *Scarlet Street*, summer 1993, pp. 24–32.
Hall, Gladys. "Evelyn Brent: Confessions of the Stars." *Motion Picture Classic*, July 1929, pp. 28–29 and 66.
Hampton, Erle. "Saved from the Law." *Photoplay*, June 1928, pp. 63 and 96.
Hanson, Patricia King, executive ed., and Alan Gevinson, assoc. ed. *The American Film Institute Catalog, Feature Films, 1931–1940*. Berkeley: University of California Press, 1993.
Hoaglin, Jess. "Where Are They Today?" *Hollywood Reporter*, March 29, 1972.
_____. "Wherever Is...?" *Meredith Newspapers*, July 9, 1980.
Hobart, Rose. *A Steady Digression to a Fixed Point*. Metuchen, N.J.: Scarecrow Press, 1994.
Hodgetts, Victoria. "The Spider Woman Must Be Doing Something Right." *Village Voice*, February, 1976.
Howe, Herbert. "Hollywood's New Slayer." August 1929, p. 43.
Humphrey, Hal. "Evelyn Brent." *Los Angeles Mirror*, December 4, 1960, part 2, p. 4.
Kobal, John. "Evelyn Brent," in *People Will Talk*. New York: Alfred A. Knopf, 1985, pp. 99–117.
_____. "Louise Brooks," in *People Will Talk*. New York: Alfred A. Knopf, 1985, pp. 71–97.

_____. "Olga Baclanova," in *People Will Talk*. New York: Alfred A. Knopf, 1985, pp. 44–55.
Kyle, Richard Garland. "The Legend of Anna May Wong." *AsiAm*, August 1987, pp. 12–14.
Lewis, David, and James Curtis, eds. *The Creative Producer*. Metuchen, N.J.: Scarecrow Press, 1993.
"Madness: Actress Recalls Cult Movie." *Los Angeles Times*, February 15, 1987.
Maltin, Leonard. "Gale Sondergaard." *Film Fan Monthly*, April 1971, pp. 6–15.
Manners, Dorothy. "How It Feels to Play the Other Woman." *Motion Picture*, pp. 66 and 105.
_____. "Plenty Smart Girl." *Motion Picture Classic*, December 1930, pp. 65 and 102.
_____. "She Thought She Was Dunn." *Motion Picture*, p. 71.
Munden, Kenneth, ed. *The American Film Institute Catalog of Feature Films, 1921–1930*. New York: R.R. Bowker Co., 1971.
Navasky, Victor S. *Naming Names*. New York: Viking Press, 1980.
Null, Gary. *Black Hollywood*. Secaucus, N.J.: The Citadel Press, 1975.
Paris, Barry. *Louise Brooks*. New York: Doubleday, 1989.
Parsons, Louella. "Gail Patrick." *Los Angeles Herald Examiner*, April 17, 1960.
Peak, Mayme Ober. "Binnie Started Her Life in Slum." *Boston Globe*, May 19, 1939.
Preston, Harry. "Thelma White." *Films in Review*, November 1965, pp. 589–591.
Ragan, David. *Who's Who in Hollywood, 1900–1976*. New York: Arlington House, 1976.
Rainey, Buck. "Ruth Royce," in *Those Fabulous Serial Heroines*. Metuchen, N.J.: Scarecrow Press, 1990, pp. 400–404.
Revier, Dorothy. "Que Sera Sera." *International Collector*, August 1983.
Robinson, David. *Chaplin, His Life and Art*. New York: McGraw-Hill, 1985.
Rosen, Marjorie. *The Popcorn Venus*. New York: Coward, McCann & Geoghegan, 1973.
Sangster, Margaret. "Cinderella of Broadway." *Photoplay*, June 1934, pp. 43–44.
Service, Faith. "Maybe She's Another Dietrich." *Motion Picture*, May 1932, p. 51.
Shale, Richard, ed. *Academy Awards*. New York: Frederick Ungar, 1978.
Sheuer, Philip. "Gale Sondergaard." *Los Angeles Times*, July, 14, 1946.
Skolsky, Sidney. "Tintypes." *Hollywood Citizen News*, September 28, 1944.
Slide, Anthony. *The American Film Industry*. New York: Limelight Editions, 1990.
"Sondergaard's Upward Nobility." *Los Angeles Times*, January 18, 1976.
Spenseley. Dorothy. "3170 Miles from Broadway." *Photoplay*, March 1926, pp. 33 and 118.
Springer, John, and Jack Hamilton. *They Had Faces Then*. Secaucus, N.J.: Citadel Press, 1974.
Stenn, David. *Clara Bow: Runnin' Wild*. New York: Doubleday, 1988.
Thorp, Dunham. "White Shadows and Sable." *Motion Picture Classic*, January 1929, pp. 63 and 86.
Turner, George E., and Michael H. Price. *Forgotten Horrors*. New Brunswick, N.J., and New York: A.S. Barnes, 1979.
Uselton, Roi A. "The Wampas Baby Stars." *Films in Review*, February, 1970, pp. 73–97.
Vaughn, Robert. *Only Victims*. New York: Putnam, 1972.
Walker, Alexander. *The Shattered Silents*. New York: William Morrow, 1979.
Watters, James. "Dorothy Revier," in *Return Engagement*. New York: Clarkson N. Potter, 1983, p. 144.
_____. "Gale Sondergaard," in *Return Engagement*. New York: Clarkson N. Potter, 1983, p. 20.
_____. "Natalie Moorhead," in *Return Engagement*. New York: Clarkson N. Potter, 1983, p. 154.
Willes, Betty. "Famous Oriental Star Return to the Screen." *Motion Picture*, October 1931, p. 45.
Wilson, Elizabeth. "The Ten Worst Enemies of Any Actress." *Silver Screen*, June 1941, pp. 36 and 90.
Winslip, Mary. "The China Doll." *Photoplay*, June 1923, p. 35.

Index

Abie's Irish Rose (play) 147
Absolute Quiet (1936) 114
Academy Awards 7, 21, 39, 50, 197, 199–200, 205, 229, 247, 254
The Accusing Finger (1936) 114
Acker, Sharon 185
Adelatori, Yolanda 70
Admirals All (1935) 109
The Adorable Liar (play) 49
Adorée, Renée 250
The Adventures of Marco Polo (1938) 23, 230, 256
Adventures of Smiling Jack (1943) 122
Again, Pioneers (1950) 46
The Age for Love (1931) 85
Age of Indiscretion (1935) 236–237
Aggie Appleby, Maker of Men (1933) 108–109
Aguglia, Mimi 53
Ahn, Philip 253, 256
Air Police (1931) 92
Albers, Hans 141
Aldridge, Kay 122
Alfred, Julian 104
Alias the Doctor (1932) 74
All About Eve (1950) 81
All at Sea (1929) 91
All This and Heaven Too (1940) 152
Allen, Fred 25, 232
Allen, Gracie 143
Allwyn, Astrid 85
Aloma of the South Seas (play) 170
Aloma of the South Seas (1941) 70
Alper, Murray 117
Alsop, Effie 224

Amateur Daddy (1932) 125
Ameche, Don 24, 67, 68
Ames, Adrienne 256
Ames, Robert 97
"Amos 'n' Andy" 123, 124
Anderson, John Murray 58
Anderson, Dame Judith 198, 199, 208
Andre, Lona 178
Andre Charlot's Revue (play) 20
Angel, Heather 19, 20
Angelou, Maya 134
Ankrum, Morris *see* Stephen Morris
Ann Carver's Profession (1933) 75
Anna and the King of Siam (1946) 197, 205, 207
Anson, A.E. 14
Anthony Adverse (1936) 197, 199
Anybody's Blonde (1931) 192
Arbuckle, Roscoe 5n
Arden, Eve 164, 180, 182
Are These Your Parents? (1944) 239
Are You There? (1931) 14
Arlen, Richard 14, 89
Armstrong, Robert 17
Arnold, Edward 22, 227
Arthur, George K. 91, 190
Arthur, Jean 67, 91n, 127
As Husbands Go (play) 163
As Husbands Go (1933) 235
Askam, Percy 104
Astaire, Fred 76, 187
Asther, Nils 254
Astor, Mary 97, 109, 127
Ates, Roscoe 180
Attorney for the Defense (1932) 42
Atwill, Lionel 14, 114, 122

Auer, Mischa 22
Autry, Gene 158
The Avenger (1931) 192

Babbitt (1934) 76
Baby Cyclone (play) 147
Bachelor Apartment (1931) 97
A Bachelor's Night (1922) 213
Back Street (1932) 107
Baclanoff, Vladimir 9
Baclanova, Olga 9–17
Bainter, Fay 49, 57
Baker, Josephine 132
Ball, Lucille 25
Ball, Suzan 70
Bancroft, George 12, 13, 38, 39, 191
Banjo on My Knee (1936) 68
Bankhead, Tallulah 58, 60, 140
Banks, Leslie 134, 136
Banton, Travis 6, 38
Bara, Theda 5, 13, 149
Bari, Lynn 224
Barnes, Binnie 19–29, 230
Barratt, Robert 75
Barraud, George 58
Barrett, Edith 55
Barrie, Wendy 21
Barringer, Barry 92
Barrington, Phyllis 124
Barrymore, Ethel 226
Barrymore, John 43, 86
Barrymore, Lionel 33
Barthelmess, Richard 54
Bartholomew, Freddie 201
Bartram, James 61, 62
Baskett, James 136
Battle of Broadway (1938) 158
Baum, Vicki 109

[263]

INDEX

Baxter, Anne 205
Baxter, Warner 24, 50, 83, 125, 235, 238
Beau Geste (1926) 38
Beau Sabreur (1928) 38–39
Beaudine, William 46
Beaumont, Harry 105
Beavers, Louise 134
Bed and Breakfast (1930) 141
Beebe, Marjorie 97
Beery, Noah 51
Beery, Wallace 54, 66
Behold My Wife (1935) 60
Belfrage, Cedric 258
Bellamy, Madge 82
Bellamy, Ralph 127, 235
Belle of the Nineties (1934) 66
The Beloved Bachelor (19301) 170
Bennett, Barbara 226
Bennett, Constance 25, 234
Bennett, Joan 179, 233, 236, 238
Bennett, Richard 104
Benny, Jack 24, 232
Benson Murder Case (1930) 148
Berkeley, Busby 75, 155, 158
Berkeley, Martin 207
Berkeley Square (1933) 61
Berlin, Irving 132
Berman, Pandro S. 81
Between Fighting Men (1932) 92
Betz, Matthew 149
Beyond Tomorrow (1940) 238
Biberman, Herbert 197, 200, 203, 205–207, 208
Bickford, Charles 235
The Big Chance (1933) 149
Big Guy (1939) 166
Big Town (radio show) 166
The Billion Dollar Scandal (1932) 17
Birell, Tala 118
Birth of a Baby (1938) 93
The Bitter Tea of General Yen (1932) 247, 253, 254
Bits of Life (1922) 248, 249
The Black Camel (1931) 192, 193
The Black Cat (1941) 79, 204
Black Gold (1947) 70
Black Magic (1929) 91
Black Moon (1934) 54
The Black Widow (1947) 122
Blackbirds (stage presentation) 131
Blackmer, Sidney 170
Blane, Sally 91n, 148, 156
Blind Alleys (1927) 37
Blixen, Karen 208
Bloch, Robert 208
Blockade (1938) 69
Blonde Crazy (1931) 50, 97
The Blonde Venus (1932) 40–41, 123, 125–126, 140
Blondell, Joan 55, 75, 97, 98, 171
Blondie Johnson (1933) 75

Blood and Sand (1922) 6
Blood Money (1933) 100
Blue, Monte 51
The Blue Bird (1940) 201–202
Blystone, John G. 83
Blyth, Ann 239
Blythe, Betty 158, 258
Boardman, Eleanor 35, 58
Bodeen, Dewitt 31, 44, 46
Bogart, Humphrey 203
Boland, Mary 142, 174, 221
Boles, John 233
Bombs Over Burma (1942) 256
Bondi, Beulah
The Bonehead (play) 170
Bonner, Priscilla 215
Bonstelle, Jessie 198
Borden, Olive 189n
Border G-Man (1938) 128
Border Women (1924) 188
Borzage, Frank 82
The Boudoir Diplomat (1930) 85
Bow, Clara 6, 32, 58, 89, 106, 126, 218
The Bowery (1933) 156
Bowery Boy (1940) 238
Bowery Boys 46
Bowery Champs (1944) 46, 245
Boyd, William 103, 105, 116, 218
Boyer, Charles 62, 254
Brady, Alice 22, 180, 199
Breen, Bobby 174
Breen, Joseph I. 7, 66
Breese, Edmund 33
Brendel, El 96
Brenon, Herbert 223
Brent, Evelyn 6, 31–46, 92, 123, 125, 126, 127, 164, 188n
Brent, George 172, 227
Brewster's Millions (1945) 183
Brian, Mary 42n, 105, 216
Brice, Fanny 201
Broadminded (1931) 162
Broadway (1929) 32, 40
A Broadway Madonna (1922)
Broadway Melody of 1936 (1935) 114
Broadway Thru a Keyhole (1933) 221
The Broken Wing (1932) 74
Bronson, Betty 91
Brook, Clive 38, 46, 58, 170–171, 215, 235, 236, 238, 253
Brooks, Louise 31, 37, 42, 43, 47, 54, 89, 258
Brown, Joe E. 24, 54, 99, 162, 173, 191
Brown, Johnny Mack 46, 51, 97
Browne, Lucille 120–121
Browning, Tod 9, 15, 37
Bruce, Nigel 204
The Buccaneer (1938) 69
The Buccaneer (1958) 69, 70
Buchanan, Jack 164

Bulldog Drummond (1929) 216, 217
Bunco Squad (1950) 113, 118
Bureau of Missing Persons (1933) 99
Burgess, Dorothy 49–56, 100
Burgess, Grace 49
Burke, Billie 168, 201, 230
Burke, Kathleen 178
Burning Question see *Reefer Madness*
Burns, George 143
Burr, Raymond 177–178, 184–185
Burrud, Billy 188
Buzzell, Edward H. 162
By Candlelight (1933) 193
Bye Bye Bonnie (play) 49
Byrd, Ralph 158
Byron, Arthur 192
Byron, Walter 51, 149

Cagney, James 6, 50, 53, 75, 97, 114–115, 203, 229, 234, 238
Caine, Georgia 152
The Californian (1937) 68
Call Her Savage (1932) 126–127
Call of the Wild (1935) 66
Camille (1927) 215
Cantor, Eddie 74, 200, 212, 227
Capra, Frank 190, 253
Captain Hates the Sea (1934) 235
Captains Courageous (1937) 145
Carey, Harry 158
Carlisle, Mary 53
Carlson, Richard 238
Carol, Sue 124, 192
Carmen (play) 11
Carmenzita and the Soldier (play) 11
Carrigan, Thomas 171
Carrillo, Leo 75, 172
Carroll, Madeleine 171
Carroll, Nancy 191, 216
Carver, Kathryn 227n
The Case of the Curious Bride (1935) 76
The Case of the Howling Dog (1934) 76
Case of the Velvet Claws (1936) 76
Castles in the Air (play) 104
Cat and the canary (1939) 201, 202
The Cat Creature (1973) 208
Cavalcade (play) 20
Cavalcade (1933) 21
Cavanagh, Paul 60
Caught (1949) 118
Ceeley, Leonard 157
Celestin, Jack 14
The Century Girl (play) 212
Chadwick, Helene 190
Chained for Life (1950) 15
Champagne Waltz (1937) 174
Chaney, Lon, Jr. 204

Index

Chaney, Lon, Sr. 12, 248, 250
Change of Heart (1938) 69
Chaplin, Charles Spencer 35, 139, 141
Chaplin, Lita Grey 93
"Charlie Chan" 253
Charlie Chan at the Olympics (1936) 68
Charlie Chan in Honolulu (1939) 78
Chatterton, Ruth 7, 60, 62, 73, 75, 107, 170, 174
Cheaters (1945) 168
Check and Double Check (1930) 123, 124
Cheer Up and Smile (1930) 14
Chevalier, Maurice 41, 52, 92
Children of Pleasure (1930) 105
China Bound (1929) 91
Chip of the Old Block (1944) 239
Christian, Linda 28
Christine, Virginia 122
Christopher, Kay 118
Chu Chin Chow (1934) 254
Churchill, Marguerite 139
Cianelli, Eduardo 25
Circle of Chalk (play) 252
Circus Clown (1934) 54
Circus Jim (1921) 34
Circus Shadows (1934) 193
City Chap (play) 104
City Girl (1930) 84–85
City Lights (1931) 139
City Streets (1931) 103, 105–106
Claire, Bernice 217
Claire, Ina 212
The Clam Diggers (play) 104
Clare, Pauline 104
Clarence (1937) 180
Clark, Dane 185
Clarke, Mae 6, 41n, 115
Claudia (1943) 17
Cleopatra (1934) 65
The Climax (1944) 204
Cobb, Lee J. 116, 205, 207
Cobb, Robert 180, 182
Cochrane, C.B. 58
Cody, Lew 98, 223
Cohan, George M. 55, 147
Cohen, Sammy 156
Cohn, Harry 187, 188–192
Cohn, Rose 189
Colbert, Claudette 200, 218
Collier, Constance 177, 180, 201
Collier, William "Buster," Jr. 92, 143, 149, 156, 191
Collins, Eddie 202
Collins, Ray 184
Colman, Ronald 217
Colton, John 167
Columbia Pictures 127, 187, 188–192
Come On Charley (play) 212

Compson, Betty 12, 58, 85, 214
Compton, Joyce 164
Compton, Juliette 57–63, 106, 170, 229
Connolly, Walter 229
The Constant Wife (play) 226
Conway, Jack 54, 66
Coogan, Jackie 42
Cook, Joe 164
Cooper, Gary 23, 38–39, 66, 103, 106, 143, 235, 256
Cooper, George 97
Cooper, Merian C. 170
Cornell, Katherine 254
Coronado (1935) 156
Correll, Frank 124
Corruption (1933) 149
Cortez, Ricardo 68, 180, 227
Coslow, Sam 156, 158
Counsel's Opinion (1933) 23
Count of Monte Cristo (1934) 61
Countess Maritza (operetta) 141
Cowan, Jerome 238
Coward, Noël 20, 24
Cowboy and the Flapper (1924) 188
The Cowboy and the Kid (1936) 188, 194
Craig's Wife (1928) 216
Crain, Jeanne 137
Crabbe, Larry (Buster) 67, 121n
Cradle Sing (1933) 178
Crawford, Joan 6, 47, 161, 174
Crews, Laura Hope 162–163
Crime Doctor (1934) 109
Crime Nobody Saw (1937) 174
The Crime of Helen Stanley (1934) 179
The Crime of the Century (1933) 108
The Crimson City (1928) 250
Crimson Romance (1934) 145
Crooner (1932) 75
Crosby, Bing 78, 179, 222
Crosland, Alan 152
Crossman, Henrietta 193
Crouching Beast, The (1936) 109
The Crusader (1932) 42
The Crusades (1935) 66–67
Cue for Passion (play) 203
Cummings, Constance 108
Cunard, Grace 120
Cunningham, Cecil 156, 257
Curtain at Eight (1933) 149
Curtain Call (1940) 238
Curtain Falls (1935) 193

Dakota (1945) 168
Damita, Lily 74
Dance of Life (1929) 191
Dancing Mothers (play) 49
Dandridge, Dorothy 132
Dane, Karl 91
Danger Island (1931) 120–121
The Danger Signal (1925) 189

Dangerous Affair (1931) 155–156
The Dangerous Flirt (1924) 37
Dangerous to Know (1938) 256
A Dangerous Woman (1929) 9, 13
Dark Command (1940) 166
The Dark Horse (1932) 172
Dark Streets of Cairo (1941) 70
The Dark Swan (1924) 214
Dark Waters (1944) 136–137
Darkened Rooms (1929) 40
Darmour, Larry 69, 70
Darrow, John 109
Daughter of Shanghai (1938) 43, 256
Daughter of the Dragon (1931) 252–253
Daughter of the Tong (1939) 44
Davidson, William 149
Davies, Marion 60, 85, 170
Davis, Bette 7, 44n, 75, 76, 149, 152, 187, 197, 199, 202–203, 239
Davis, Joan 202
Davis, Owen, Jr. 85
Davis, Richard 17
Daw, Marjorie 58
Day, Laraine 183
A Day at the Races (1937) 155, 156–157
De Acosta, Mercedes 127, 216
"Dead Reckoning" (proposed film) 143
Dean, Basil 142, 252, 254
Dear Girl (play) 89
Death Takes a Holiday (play) 234
Death Takes a Holiday (1934) 179
De Beranger, Andre 215
Decameron Nights (1953) 26
Declasse (1925) 215
Dee, Frances 58
De Havilland, Olivia 161, 199
De Leon, Jack 14
The Delightful Rogue (1929) 124
Dell, Claudia 192
Del Rio, Dolores 76, 227
The Demi Tasse Revue (play) 89
DeMille, Cecil B. 65–67, 69, 105, 108, 139, 215
DeMille, Katherine 65–71, 258
Derr, E. B. 117
The Desert Trail (1926) 250
Desirable (1934) 227
De Toth, Andre 137
Devil and the Deep (1932) 60
The Devil Is Driving (1932) 108
DeVoe, Daisy 58, 106
Diamond Jim (1935) 22
Dick Tracy's Dilemma (1947) 113, 117–118
Dies, Martin 203
Dieterle, William 203, 229n
Dietrich, Marlene 12, 38, 40, 58, 123, 125–126, 127, 139, 140, 141, 142, 143, 167, 238, 248, 253

INDEX

Dietrichstein, Leo 82
Dillon, John Francis 126
Dinehart, Alan 108
Dione, Rose 15
Dionne Quintuplets 238
Disbarred (1939) 182
Discarded Lovers (1932) 149
Disputed Passage (1939)
Divorce in the Family (1932) 226
The Divorce of Lady X (1938) 23
Dix, Richard 89, 104, 213, 237
Dmytryk, Edward 206
Docks of New York (1928) 9, 12
"Dr. Fu Manchu" 252-253
Dr. Monica (1934) 156, 227
The Doctor Takes a Wife (1940) 182
Dodd, Claire 7, 73-80, 97, 103, 185, 234, 235
Dollars and Sense (play) 169
Donat, Robert 21
The Donovan Affair (1929) 191
Don't Bet on Blondes (1935) 76
Don't Gamble with Strangers (1946) 117
Dorr, Conrad 257-258
D'Orsay, Fifi 218
Double Cross (1941) 110
Douglas, Melvyn 24, 74, 198
Dove, Billie 85, 215
The Dove (1927) 12
Down by the Rio Grande (1924) 188
Downey, Morton 226n
Downey, Morton, Jr. 226n
Downstairs (1932) 17
Dracula (1931) 15
The Drag Net (1928) 6, 31, 39
Dragonwyck (1946) 174
Dramatic School (1938) 164, 201
Drew, Roland see Walter Goss
Drift Fence (1936) 67
Drifting (1923) 249
Drums of the Congo (1942) 168
Duffy, Henry 148
The Duke Is Tops (1938) 136
Dull, Orville O. 25
Du Maurier, Sir Gerald 58
Dumont, Margaret 157-158
Duncan, Mary 81-86, 148
Dunn, James 128
Dunn, Josephine 87-93
Dunne, Irene 7, 14, 76, 137, 183, 205
Dupont, E.A. 252
Durante, Jimmy 100
Durbin, Deanna 19, 23, 182
Duse, Eleanora 82
D'Use, Margo 121n
Dvorak, Ann 110

The Eagle's Brood (1935) 194
Earles, Harry 15-16
East Lynne (play) 169

East Side, West Side (1949) 206
Echoes (1983) 208
Eck, Johnny 15
Eddy, Nelson 92
Ederle, Gertrude 89
Edwards, Gus 162, 212
Edwards, Harry 40, 41, 43
Eilers, Sally 125
Ellery Queen and the Murder Ring (1941) 44
Ellery Queen, Master Detective (1940) 70
Elliott, William 184
Ellis, Edward 150
Ellison, James 67
Emergency Landing (1941) 44
Enemy Agent (1940) 238
Enemy Agents Meet Ellery Queen (1942) 204
Entwhistle, Peg 86n
Errol, Leon 156, 218, 241, 245
Erskine, Chester 222
Erwin, Stuart 143-144
Esper, Dwain 15n.
Evans, Madge 236, 237
Evenings for Sale (1932) 142
Excess Baggage (1928) 89-91
Experience (1921) 213

Fairbanks, Douglas, Jr. 75, 191, 218
Fairbanks, Douglas, Sr. 21, 35, 77, 140, 170, 187, 190-191, 247, 249
Fairbanks, William 188
The Falcon Strikes Back (1943) 110
The Fall Guy (1930) 105
The Famous Ferguson Case (1932)
Farmer, Frances 24
Farrell, Charles 82, 83, 84-85, 109
Farrell, Glenda 50-51, 98
Fascinating Youths (1926) 89
Fashions of 1934 (1934) 227
Fast Company (1929) 40
Fast Company (1938) 77
Father and Son (1929) 191
Fay, Frank 218
Fay, Vivian 157
Fenton, Leslie 14
Ferber, Edna 180
Ferguson, Al 121
Fetchit, Stepin 131, 134
Field, Lew 104
Field, Virginia 121
Fields, W.C. 89, 121n, 143-144
Fifteen Wives (1934) 100, 151
Fifth Avenue (1926) 250
Fifth Avenue Girl (1939) 230
The Fighting Gentleman (1932) 92, 149
The Fighting Ranger (1934) 193, 194

Fille de Madama Angot (opera) 11
Film-Booking-Office (FBO) 35
Fineman, B. P. 31, 35, 37, 38, 39
Find the Witness (1937) 127, 128
Finn and Hattie (1931) 218
Fire Over Africa (1954) 26
The Firebird (1934) 227
Fireman, Save My Child (1927) 89
The First Baby (1936) 156
First Lady (1937) 225, 230
Five and Ten (1931) 85
Five Star Final (1931) 162
Fixer Dugan (1939) 128
The Flame of Love (1929) 252
Flames (1932) 97-98
Fleming, Victor 166
Florey, Robert 32, 127, 254
Flower Drum Song (1961) 258
Flynn, Errol 77n
Folies Bergère de Paris (1935) 114
Follow Your Heart (1936) 173
A Fool There Was (1915) 5
Footlight Parade (1933) 75
Forbes, Mary 152
Forbes, Ralph 173
Forced Landing (1941) 44
Ford, Wallace 15, 75, 114
Forgotten Commandments (1932) 139-140, 142
Forgotten Girls (1940) 110
Forman, Carol 122
The 40th Floor (1924) 250
Forty Carats (1973) 28
Forty Winks (1925) 250
Foster, Norman 171
Foster, Stephen 117
Fountaine, William 132
Four Devils (1929) 81, 82
Fox, Harry 44
Fox, William 82
Fox Film Corp. 50, 56, 82, 191-192
Fox Movietone Follies (1930) 96
Framed (1930) 41
Francis, Kay 24, 60, 73, 75, 77, 156, 171, 174, 180, 218, 225, 227, 230, 234, 238
Francis, Noel 6, 50, 95-101
Frankenstein (1931) 15
Frankie and Johnny (1936) 222, 223
Franklin, Howard B. 55
Frankowitch, M.J. 24-26, 28
Frawley, William 49
Freaks (1932) 9, 14-17
Freed, Arthur 201
French Dressing (1927) 215
Freuler, John R. 92
Frisco Jenny (1932) 98
From Hell to Heaven (1933) 127
Frontier Marshall (1939) 24
The Fugitive Lady (1952) 25

Index

Furness, Betty 109
Fury (1936) 156

G-Men (1935) 115
Gable, Clark 66, 114, 161
Gahagan, Helen 168
Gallagher, Richard "Skeets" 100
Gallant Sons (1940) 182
Gambling (1934) 55
Gambling Lady (1934) 75
The Gang Buster (1931) 103, 105
Gangs of New York (1937) 109–110
Garbo, Greta 9, 12, 39, 57, 58, 142, 143, 216
Garden of Weeds (1924) 213
Gardner, Erle Stanley 76, 184
Gardner, Helen 82
Gargan, William 67, 174
Garland, Judy 201
Garson, Greer 164
Gasnier, Louis 107, 244
The Gay Brother (1919) 169–170
The Gay Caballero (1932) 152
The Gay Deception (1935) 156
The Gay Diplomat (1931) 125
Gaye, Vivian 140, 142, 143, 145
Gaynor, Janet 56, 78, 81, 82, 85, 200
The Gentleman from Mississippi (1914) 33
Gerber, Neva 119, 121
Gerry Society 241
Gershwin, George 164
Gest, Maurice 11
Get Your Man (1927) 89
Getting Gertie's Garter (1945) 25
Ghost (play) 164
Gibson, Wynne 6, 97, 103–111, 218, 235
Gifford, Frances 122, 128
Gigolettes of Paris (1933) 150
Gilbert, John 17, 35, 216, 235
The Gingham Girl (play) 104
Girl Loves Boy (1937) 116
Girls About Town (1931) 74, 218
Girls in Chains (1943) 55
The Glass Key (1935) 77
Gleckler, Robert 115
The Glorious Lady (1919) 33
Glyn, Elinor 215
Goddard, Paulette 70, 202
Going Wild (1930) 162
The Gold Diggers (play) 212
Gold Diggers of 1933 (1933) 221
The Golden Eye (1948) 46
Goldstone, Phil 188–189
Goldwyn, Samuel 213, 218, 226, 230, 235, 256
Gombell, Minna 125
Gone with the Wind (1939) 43, 161, 163–166, 195
Good Dame (1933) 100
The Good Earth (1937) 247, 254–255

Good Morning, Dearie (play) 87
Good Night Ladies (play) 110
Goodrich, Frances 151
The Goose and the Gander (1935) 77
Gordon, Huntley 192
Gosden, Freeman 124, 182
Goss, Walter 89
Grable, Betty 43
Graft (1931) 192
Grand Jury Secrets (1939) 182
Grand National Films, Inc. 114–116
Granville, Bonita 182, 184, 199
Grant, Cary 183, 238
Gray, Lawrence 105
Gray, Lorna 122
Great Guy (1937) 114–115
The Great Lover (play) 82
The Great Lover (1931) 14
Great Ziegfeld (1936) 156
Greek Street (1930) 141
Greeks Had a Word for It (play) 226
Green, Alfred E. 97
The Green Gang (play) 89
Greene, Graham 54
Greenwich Village Follies (play) 155
Grey, Nan 23
Grey, Shirley 143
Griffith, Corinne 109, 215
Griffith, David Wark 35
Groody, Louise 162
Guardino, Harry 185
Guilbert, Yvette 81
Guilty as Hell (1932) 98
Guinan, Texas 6
Gurie, Sigrid 256
Guthrie, Marjorie 242
Gwenn, Edmund 197, 199

Hackett, Albert 151
Haines, William 89, 91
Hale, Alan 51, 230
Hale, Barbara 76n, 184–185
Haley, Alex 134
Hall, Juanita 258
The Hall Johnson Choir 68
Hallelujah (1929) 131–133, 136
Halperin, Nan 104
Hamilton, Hale 100
Hamilton, Margaret 201
Hamilton, Neil 143
Hammett, Dashiell 58, 106
Hammerstein, Oscar 200
Hands Across the Table (1935) 67
Happiness Ahead (1928) 215
Hardenbrook, Donald 238, 239
Harding, Ann 143, 233, 235
Harker, Gordon 109
Harlan, Kenneth 92, 121, 148, 188, 248
Harlow, Jean 15, 95, 134, 142

Harolde, Ralf 124
Harrington, Curtis 208
Harris, Richard 208
Harrison, Rex 205
Harron, Johnny 188
Hart, Mary 68
Haskin, Byron 190
Hawks, Howard 54, 66
Hayakawa, Sessue 249, 252, 253
Hayden, Russell 116, 151
Hayes, Bernadene 113–118
Hayes, George "Gabby" 69, 116, 121n
Hayes, Helen 49, 107n, 253
Hayes, Lorraine *see* Lorraine Randall
Haynes, Daniel L. 132, 133
Hays, Will H. 6, 7
Hays Office 7, 53, 124, 126, 203, 212
Hayward, Louis 25
Hayworth, Rita 187
He Married His Wife (1940) 24
Head Over Heels (1922) 213
Heart of Arizona (1938) 151, 152
The Heart of a Painted Woman (1915) 33
Hearts in Dixie (1929) 131
Hecht, Ben 25, 38, 46
Held to Answer (1923) 35
Hell and High Water (1933) 156
Hellman, Lillian 200
Hendricks, Ben, Jr. 100
Henie, Sonja 23
Hepburn, Katharine 23, 81, 177, 180, 232
Her Bodyguard (1933) 108
Her Husband's Lies (1937) 180
Her Resale Value (1933) 99
Her Secret (1933) 143
Heroes of the Flames (1931) 120
Hershfeld, Ben 125, 127
Hersholt, Jean 108, 238
Heston, Charlton 200n
Heyward, Orien 174
Hilton, Daisy 15
Hilton, Violet 15
High Pressure (1932) 42
Hips, Hips, Hooray! (1934) 242
Hirliman, George A. 245
His Exciting Night (1938) 163
His Girl Friday (play) 155
His Tiger Lady (1928) 39–40
The Hit Parade (1937) 127
Hobart, Rose 122, 234
Hold Everything (play) 162
Hold Everything (1930) 191
Hold That Woman (1940 128
Hold Your Horses (play) 164
Holiday (1938) 23
"Hollywood Anti-Nazi League" 200, 203
Hollywood Boulevard (1936) 43, 127

INDEX

"Hollywood Ten" 197, 206
Holmes, Helen 250
Holmes, Phillips 107
Holt, David 236
Holt, Jack 44, 69, 127, 156, 190, 191
Holt of the Secret Service (1942) 44
A Holy Terror (1931) 125
Home on the Range (1934) 42
The Honeymooners, series (1930s) 242
Honor of the Press (1932) 125
Hook, Line and Sinker (1930) 148
Hopalong Cassidy Returns (1936) 43
"Hopalong Cassidy" (series) 43, 113, 116–117, 152
Hope, Bob 201, 202, 205, 238
Hopkins, Miriam 92, 107, 171
Hopper, Hedda 178, 184, 221–222
Hopper, William 184
Hornblow, Arthur 201
Horne, Lena 132
Horton, Edward Everett 190
The Hot Heiress (1931) 162
House Un-Activities Committee (HUAC) 206, 227n
Hovick, Louise *see* Gypsy Rose Lee
Howard, William K. 234
Hughes, Carol 44
Hughes, Howard 85, 118
Hull, Henry 225
Human Desires (1924) 58
The Human Side (1934) 114
Hunter, Ian 232
Hunter, Ross 258
Hurlock, Madeline 189n
Husband's Holiday (1931) 58, 170–171
Hussey, Ruth 164
Hutchinson, Josephine 77
Hutton, Beulah 119–122
Hyams, Leila 15

I Accuse My Parents (1945) 174
I Am a Fugitive from a Chain Gang (1932) 98–99, 108, 234
I Give My Love (1934) 103, 109
I Love That Man (1933) 156
I Sell Anyhting (1934) 76
I Take This Woman (1940) 230
I Want a Divorce (1940) 55
Idiot's Delight (1939) 117
If I Had a Million (1932) 103, 108, 178
If I Had My Way (1940) 79
Illicit (1931) 148
Imitation of Life (1934) 100, 137
Impact (1949) 257
The Important Witness (1933) 100
In Name Only (1939) 238
In Old Arizona (1929) 49, 50, 55, 83

In Old Caliente (1939) 69
In Old California (1942) 25
Ince, Ralph 51, 98
Inescort, Frieda 79
"Inner Sanctum" 204
The Inside Story (1948) 184
Interference (1928) 32, 40
International House (1933) 143–144
The Invisible Man's Revenge (1944) 204
The Iron Mask (1929) 170, 187, 190–191
Is Love Everything? (1924) 214
Island of Lost Souls (1933) 177
Isle of Destiny (1940) 70
It Couldn't Have Happened (But It Did) (1936) 43
It Takes a Thief (television series) 208
It's a Deal (1930) 74, 234
It's Great to Be Alive (1933) 52–53
It's the Old Army Game (1926) 89

Jackson, Cornwall 184–185
The Jade Cup (1926) 37
James, Ida 136
Jannings, Emil 12, 39
Jarnigan (play) 104
Java Head (1935) 254
The Jazz Singer (1927) 6, 87
Jeans, Ursula 21n
Jefferson Pictures Corp. 172
Jeopardy (1953) 152
Jessel, George 199–200
Jewel Robbery (1932) 234
Johnson, Charles Schoen 191
Johnson, Kay 235
Johnson, Osa 156
Jolson, Al 87, 91
Jones, Buck 35, 43, 166, 188
Jones, Clifford 234
Jordan, Dorothy 170
Jory, Victor 75
Joseph, Samuel 20, 22
Joslyn, Allyn 78
Journal of a Crime (1934) 75
Joyce, Natalie 189n
Joyce, Peggy Hopkins 143–144, 221
Juarez (1939) 44, 201
The Judge (1949) 70
Judgment Book (1935) 114
June Love (play) 104
June Moon (1931) 105
Jungle Girl (1941) 122
Jungle Jim (1937) 43
Jurado, Katy 70
Just a Woman (1925) 189

Kane, Helen 104
Katz, Sam 145
Karloff, Boris 162, 205
Kathleen (1941) 183

Kaufman, George S. 180
Kazan, Elia 137
Keeler, Ruby 49, 198
Keith, Rosalind 128
Kelly, Nancy 24
Kelly, Paul 114
The Kennel Murder Case (1933) 75, 235
Kent, Duke of 191
Kent, Sydney 20
Kent, Willis 124
Kibbee, Guy 76
Kick In (1931) 58, 106–107
Kid Boots (play) 89
Kilgallen, Dorothy 25
King, Dennis 164
The King and I (1956) 205
King of Chinatown (1939) 256
King of Gamblers (1937) 43, 127, 152
King of the Damned (1936) 238
Kirkwood, James 98
Kismet (play) 85
Kismet (1920) 85
Kismet (1930) 81, 84
The Kiss Burglar (play) 58
Knapp, Evalyn 97, 98
Kohler, Fred 126
Kolker, Henry 115
Komisarjevsky 11
Konrad, Dorothy 46
Koo Coo 15
Korda, Alexander 21, 23, 61
Kropotkin, Princess Alexandra 221

La Cava, Gregory 180, 230
Lackteen, Frank n121
Ladies Must Love (1933) 53–54
Ladies of the Big House (1931) 97, 107
The Lady and the Monster (1944) 239
Lady from Chunking (1943) 256
Lady from Louisiana (1941) 166–167
Lady from Nowhere (1936) 127
A Lady's Profession (1933) 143
Laemmle, Carl 22
Laffey, James P. 170
Lahr, Bert 162
Lake, Arthur 14
La Marr, Barbara 190
Lamarr, Hedy 164, 130, 232
Lambert, Jack 118
Lambert, Katherine 223–224
Lamour, Dorothy 24, 43, 256
Lanchester, Elsa 21
Landau, David 125
Landi, Elissa 125, 193
Landis, Cullen 189
Lane, Lola 156
Lane, Lupino 141
Langdon, Harry 158

Index

Langford, Frances 127
La Plante, Laura 35n, 190
Lardner, Ring, Jr. 206
La Rocque, Rod 124
La Roy, Rita n41, 123–129
LaRue, Jack 233
Lasky, Jesse L. 9, 41
Last Command (1928) 39
The Last of the Mohicans (1936) 19, 22
Last Train from Madrid (1937) 43
Laughter and Tears (1921) 34
Laughton, Charles 19, 20, 21, 25, 27, 178, 226
Law West of Tombstone (1938) 158
Lawyer Man (1933) 235
"Leave It to the Girls" (radio show) 25
Lederer, Francis 184
Lee, Al 212
Lee, David (Davy) 91, 191
Lee, Dixie 14
Lee, Gypsy Rose 28, 158
Lee, Lila 54
Lee, Rowland V. 13
Leeds, Andrea 180, 182, 185
Left-Handed Gun (1936) 100
Leftover Ladies (1931) 124, 192
Legion of Lost Flyers (1939) 166
Lehman, Lily 81
Leiber, Fritz 104
Leigh, Vivien 61, 161, 166
Leisen, Mitchell 67
Leni, Paul 12
Leonard, Arthur 136
Leonard, Barbara 98
Leonard, Eddie 91
LeRoy, Mervyn 197, 198, 201, 207, 234
Leslie, Lew 131
Lester, Cecile Culani 65
Lester, Captain Edward Gabriel 65
Let's Sing Again (1936) 174
Let's Try Again (1934) 235
The Letter (1939) 197, 202–203, 205
Lewis, David 9, 13
Lewis, Mitchell 12
Lewis, Sinclair 76
Lewton, Val 44
Life Begins (1932) 171
Life of Emile Zola (1937) 197, 201
Life of Vergie Winters (1934) 233, 235
Life's Greatest Question 188 (1921)
Lillie, Beatrice 14
Limehouse Blues (1934) 254
Linden, Eric 116
Lindsay, Margaret 182n
Little Giant (1933) 235
Little Jessie James (play) 104
Live, Love and Learn (1937) 238

Livingston, Margaret 97, 127
Lloyd, Harold 229
Lombard, Carole 7, 67, 125, 127, 143, 169, 172, 177, 179, 238
Lord Jeff (1938) 201
Losch, Tilly 247, 254n
Lost Boundaries (1949) 137
The Lost City (1935) 121n
Louise, Anita 166
Love, Montagu 51, 149
Love Bound (1932) 149
The Love Child (play) 170
Love 'Em and Leave 'Em (1927) 31, 37, 47
Love in Exile (1936) 238
Love Thy Neighbor (1940) 232
Love Under Fire (1937) 68
Love's Blindness (1926) 215
Love's Flame (1920) 170, 171
Love's Greatest Mistake (1927) 37
Lowe, Edmund 42, 50, 108, 211, 213–215, 216, 222
Lowery, Robert 174
Loy, Myrna 15, 54, 86, 117, 150–151, 239, 250
Lubin, Arthur 257
Lubitsch, Ernst 40, 92, 93, 142, 145n
Lucky Night (1939) 117
Lugosi, Bela 193
Lukas, Paul 103, 106, 109, 170, 193, 216, 235, 236
Lulu Belle (play) 55
Lund, Lucille 120, 121
Lundigan, William 113, 117, 184
Lupino, Barry 141
Lupino, Ida 179
Lupino, Stanley 20
Luxury Liner (1933) 172, 226
Lyon, Ben 162
Lysistrata (play) 11

MacArthur, Charles 25
McCarey, Leo 229
McCoy, Tim 120
McCrea, Joel 24, 68, 75–76
McDaniel, Hattie 134
MacDonald, Jeanette 14, 89, 92
MacDonald, Katherine 191
McGuire, Dorothy 17
McGuire, Tom 85
Mack, Helen 109
McKinney, Nina Mae 131–138
McLaglen, Victor 218, 235
McLeod, "Tex" 20
Mad About Music (1938) 182
The Mad Empress (1939) 43–44
The Mad Parade (1931) 41
The Mad Turtle (play) 85
Madame Du Barry (1934)
Madame Satan (1930) n65, 105
Madame X (play) 107
Madison, Mae 51, 97
Madonna 223

Madonna of the Streets (1930) 41, 92
The Madonna's Secret (1946) 184
Maid of Salem (1937) 200
Malay Nights (1933) 51
Maltin, Leonard 199, 200, 203
Mamoulian, Rouben 106
Man About Town (1939) 24
The Man Called Back (1932) 60
A Man Called Horse (1970) 208
Man from Del Rio (1956) 70
Man from Down Under (1943) 25, 27
The Man I Love (1929) 14
Man of Conquest (1939) 182
Man of the World (1931) 105
Man on a Tightrope (1953) 232
Man Wanted (1932) 75
The Man Who Laughs (1927) 12
The Man Who Reclaimed His Head (1934) 100
The Mandarin Mystery (1936) 127
Manhandled (1924) 214
Manhattan Cocktail (1928) 216
Manhattan Lady (play) 162
Mankiewicz, Herman J. 14
Manners, David 75, 234
Mannors, Sheila 124
A Man's Man (1929) 91
A Man's World (1942) 110, 245
Mansfield, Martha 33, 224
March, Fredric 60, 199, 203
Margie (1940) 152
Maris, Mona 54, 84
Maritza, Sari 139–145
The Mark of Zorro (1920) 35
Markham, Monte 185
Marquis, Joseph 169
The Marriage Playground (1929) 216
Married and in Love (1940) 238
Marsh, Mae 127
Marshal, Alan 238
Marshall, Herbert 142, 182, 183, 202
Marshall, Tully 149
Martin, Marion 164
Martin, Tony 68
Marx, Chico 158
Marx, Groucho 157–158
Marx, Harpo 158
Marx Brothers 155, 156–158
Mary Lou (1948) 245
Massey, Ilona 24, 25, 164
Mathis, June 33
The Mating Call (1928) 37
The Matrimonial Bed (1930) 218
Maude, Cyril 34
Maugham, W. Somerset 42, 202, 203
Maurice 34
Mayer, Louis B. 15
Maynard, Ken 92
Maynard, Kermit 43

INDEX

Mehaffey, Blanche 192
Meighan, Thomas 37, 89
Melody Lane (1929) 87, 91
Men Are Such Fools (1932) 172
Men Call It Love (1931) 85
The Menace (1932) 149
Mendes, Lothar 106
Menjou, Adolphe 14, 39, 75, 85, 89, 180, 225, 227–228, 229, 230, 232
Metro 33
Metro-Goldwyn-Mayer 131–134, 163
Metropolitan Pictures Corp. 215
Michael, Gertrude 172, 229
Michael O'Halloran (1937) 110
Michaels, Beverly 118
The Midnight Club (1933) 235, 236
Midsummer Night's Dream (1935) 225, 227–229
Midwest (play) 114
The Mighty (1929) 191
Miles, Lillian 241
Milestone, Lewis 235
Miljan, John 66
The Milky Way (1936) 229
Milland, Ray 182
Millar, Adelqui 34
Miller, Marilyn 74
Miller, Walter 120, 121
Millie (1931) 218
Million Dollar Pictures 136
The Millionaire's Double (1917) 33
The Mind Reader (1933) 149
Minnevitch, Borrah 68
The Miracle (play) 11
Misbehaving Husbands (1941) 158
Mississippi (1935) 179
Mr. Battling Butler (play) 155
Mr. Broadway (1933) 93
Mr. Wu (1927) 250
Mitchell, Margaret 164
Mix, Tom 98
A Modern Hero (1934) 54
Mohr, Hal 229
Molly Magdalene (play) 105
Monogas, Lionel 136
Monte Carlo Madness (1931) 141–142
Montez, Maria 205
Montgomery, Robert 78
Monti, Carlotta 121n
Moore, Colleen 6, 215, 234
Moore, Tom 190
Moore, Victor 162
Moorhead, Natalie 123, 127, 147–153, 225
Moran & Mack 40
Moran, Frank 156
Moreland, Mantan 134
Morgan, Claudia 117
Morgan, Helen 223n
Morgan, Frank 21, 226

Morgan's Marauders (1929) 170
Mori, Toshia 247
Morison, Patricia 204n
Morley, Karen 109, 206
Morning Glory (1933) 81, 86
Morocco (1930) 58
Morris, Chester 40, 166, 172
Morton, Charles 82
Mother Sings (play) 114
The Mouthpiece (1932) 98
Movietone (sound system) 50
Mowbray, Alan 143
Muir, Esther 155–159
Muir, Jean 227
Mulhall, Jack 92, 105, 149, 192
Muni, Paul 44n, 98, 201, 234, 254
Munson, Ona 43, 161–168
Murder at Dawn (1932) 92
Murder at the Vanities (1934) 179
Murder by an Aristocrat (1936) 77
Murder by the Clock (1931) 218, 220
Murders at the Zoo (1933) 178
Murnau, F.W. 12, 82
Murray, James 107
Muse, Clarence 133–134
Music Box Revue (play) 49
Mutiny Ahead (1935) 100
My Favorite Wife (1940) 182–183
My Man Godfrey (1936) 177, 179–180, 199
My Old Kentucky Home (1937) 117
My Pal the King (1932) 98
My Woman (1933) 75
Myers, Carmel 54
Mysterious Rider (1933) 178

Nagel, Conrad 226
Naish, J. Carrol 172
Naldi, Nita 6
Name the Woman (1934) 127
Navy Born 77
Nazimova, Alla 164, 168n, 148
Neagle, Anna 58, 61
Negri, Pola 9, 12, 13
Neilan, Marshall 249
Neill, Noel 239
Nell Gwynn (1926) 58, 61
Nellie, the Beautiful Cloak Model (1924) 213
Nemirovitch-Danchenko, Vladimir 11
Never Say Die (1939) 201
Never Too Late (1935) 243
New Wine (1942) 25
New York Nights (1929) 217
Night After Night (1932) 108
Night Club Scandal (1937) 43, 98
A Night in a Dormitory (1932) 242n
A Night in Montmartre (1931) 20
A Night of Mystery (1928) 39
Night World (1932) 192

Ninotschka (1939) 39
Nissen, Greta 14n, 37, 89, 139
The Nit Wits (1935) 43
Nixon, Marian 56, 85, 125
No Foolin' (play) 95
No Lady (1931) 141
No More Ladies (1935) 174
No No Nanette (play) 162
Normand, Mabel 213
North of the Rio Grande (1937) 116
North West Mounted Police (1940) 70
Nothing But the Truth (1929) 104
Nothing But the Truth (1941) 238
Notorious Gentleman, The (1935) 235
Novarro, Ramon 253
Novak, Jane 189
Nugent, Elliott J. 125
Null, Gary 137

Oakie, Jack 14, 40, 105, 172
Oberon, Merle 21, 23
O'Brien, Dave 244
O'Brien, George 96, 125, 128
O'Brien, Pat 96n, 107
O'Connor, Donald 239
O'Connor, Una 20
Officer 444 (1926) 119
Oh, Johnny (play) 104
O'Keefe, Dennis 238
Oland, Warner 192, 193, 252, 256
Old San Francisco (1927) 250
Olivier, Laurence 23, 61, 252
On Again—Off Again (1937) 158
On the Level (1930) 218
On Velvet (1938) 136
One Exciting Adventure (1934) 22
One Heavenly Night (1931) 218
One Hour with You (1932) 93
One Is Guilty (1934) 127
O'Neal, William J. 225
O'Neil, Sally 53
O'Neill, Barbara 70
Only Yesterday (1933) 100, 149
Oppenheimer, George 26
Order, Please! (play) 174
Orient Express 54
Orry-Kelly 227
Osborne, Vivienne 58, 169–175, 190
Our Blushing Brides (1930) 74
Ouspenskaya, Maria 199
Out of Singapore (1932) 51
Over the Hill to the Poorhouse (1920) 170
Owen, Reginald 243–254
Owsley, Monroe 61

Pabst, Georg Wilhelm 54
Page, Anita 91n
The Pagan Lady (1931) 41
The Painted Desert (1931) 50

Index

Panama Patrol (1939) 256
"Panther Woman" 178
Parachute Jumper (1933) 75
Paramount 37, 41, 43, 60, 89, 142, 170–171, 178
Paramount Junior Stars 89
Paramount on Parade (1930) 41
Pardon My English (play) 164
Parker, Cecilia 116
Parker, Dorothy 200
Parker, Jean 254
Parks, Larry 206, 207
Parsons, Louella 24, 211, 221
The Party's Over (1934) 156
Pascal, Ernest 85
Paterson, Pat 62
Pathé 50
Pathé Folly Comedies 242
Pathé Melody Comedies 242
Paths of Glory (1957) 232
Patrick, Gail 7, 177–186, 229, 256
Payment Deferred (1932) 226
The Payoff (1935) 73, 77
Peg o' My Heart (1933) 60–61
Perils of Nyoka (1942) 122
Perils of Pauline (1914) 119
Perry, Fred 237, 238
"Perry Mason" 76–77, 177, 184–185
Personality Kid (1934) 76
Peter Pan (1924) 250
Peters, House 35
Petrova, Olga 33
The Phantom Broadcast (1933) 172–173, 178
The Phantom of Crestwood (1932) 86
Philbin, Mary 189
"Philo Vance" 148, 235
Phyllis of the Follies (1928) 216
Piccadilly (1929) 252
Pichel, Irving 142, 220
Pickford, Jack 33n, 212, 224
Pickford, Mary 35
Picture Brides (1933) 156
Pine, Virginia 156
Pine-Thomas Productions 44
Pinky (1949) 137
Piper Paid (play) 55
Pirate Treasure (1934) 120, 121
The Pirates of Capri (1949) 25
Pirates of Monterey (1947) 205
The Pit (1914) 33
Pitts, ZaSu 114, 226, 235
The Plainsman (1937) 67, 69
The Plainsman and the Lady (1946) 184
Play Girl (1932) 51
Playing with Fire (1916) 33
Playthings of Desire (1934) 93
Playthings of Hollywood (1930) 124
Pleasantville (1976) 208

Pleasure Crazed (1929) 50
Pocomania (1939) 136
Poker Faces (1926) 190
Pollyanna (1960) 232
Pomeroy, Roy 40
Poole, Bessie 224
Poor Girls (1927) 190
Popkin, Harry M. 136n
Ports of Call (1924) 214
Portrait in Black (1960) 258
Post, Guy Bates 43
Powell, Dick 55, 229
Powell, William 22, 37, 39, 42, 82, 105, 148, 150–151, 171, 179, 235, 239
The Power and the Glory (1933) 234–235
The President's Mystery (1936) 43
Pretty Ladies (1925) 215
The Preview Murder Case (1936) 179
Prevost, Marie 97, 214
Price, Vincent 174
The Prince of Headwaiters (1927) 215
Prison Nurse (1938) 117
The Private Life of Don Juan 21
The Private Life of Henry VIII (1933) 19, 21
Private Worlds (1935) 233, 236
Producers Releasing Corp. 128
Production Code 7, 38, 49, 126
Public Stenographer (1933) 156

Quarantine (play) 49
Queen Christina (1933) 39
Queen High (play) 155
Quiet Please, Murder (1942) 183
Quigley, Charles 127
Quillan, Eddie 127
Quinn, Anthony 68–70, 258

Racketeers in Exile (1937) 109
Raft, George 98, 108, 156, 234, 235, 236, 254
Ragan, David 232
Raiders of the Ghost City (1944) 122
Rain (1932) 161
Rainer, Luise 7, 164, 247, 254
Rains, Claude 199
Ralston, Esther 127, 191, 193
Ralston, Jobyna 35n
Ralston, Vera Hruba 168, 184, 239
Rambeau, Marjorie 117
Rambova, Natacha 189
Ramona (1936) 67–68
Randall, Lorraine 113
Rappe, Virginia 5n
Raridon 15
Rathbone, Basil 204
Ray, Allene 119
Ray, Charles, 127

Ray, Terrance 58
Raymond, Gene 139, 142
Raymond, Ray 104
The Razor's Edge (1946) 205
Read, Barbara 23, 238
Rebecca (1940) 199
Recaptured Love (1930) 50
Reckless (1935) 134
The Red House (1947) 168
The Red Lantern (1919) 248
Reed, Philip 74
Reefer Madness (1936) 241, 243–245
Reform Girl (1933) 100
Regas, George 68
Reid Wallace 5
Reinhardt, Max 11, 229
Rendezvous (1935) 22
Rennie, James 148
Republic Pictures Corp. 166–167
The Restless Sex (1920) 170
Return of a Man Called Horse (1976) 208
Reunion (1936) 238
Revere, Anne 206
Revier, Dorothy 170, 187–196
Revier, Harry 188
Rice, Florence 77, 235
Rice Frank 194
Rich, Irene 216
Rich Man's Folly (1931) 58
Richards, Grant 117
Richardson, Ralph 23
Richman, Harry 217
Richmond, Kane 117
Ricketts, Tom 120
Riefenstahl, Leni 252
Riggs, Betty *see* Evelyn Brent
The Right to Romance (1933) 143
Rio Rita (play) 95
Riptide (1934) 222
Ritz Brothers 19, 24
The River (1928) 82
RKO Radio Pictures 41, 242
The Road to Reno (1931) 218
Road to Rio (1947) 205
Robards, Jason 149
Robbins, Tod 14
Roberta (1935) 76
Roberts, Beverly 110
Robertson, Willard 127
Robeson, Paul 134–136
Robin Hood (1922) 140
Robin Hood of Monterey (1947) 46
Robinson, Carlyle 141
Robinson, Edward G. 6, 95, 97, 127, 162, 166, 168, 172, 235
Robinson, Pete 15
Robson, Mark 44
Rocking Moon (1926) 215
Roderick, Olga 15
Rogers, Charles "Buddy" 89
Rogers, Ginger 76, 177, 180, 226, 230, 242n

Rogers, Roy 69
Rogers, Will 85, 215
Roland, Gilbert 46, 70
Roland, Ruth 119
Roman Scandals (1933) 226–227
Romance in the Dark (1938) 77, 158
Romance of the Rio Grande (1929) 83
Rooney, Mickey 98, 201
Roosevelt, Eleanor 93
Roosevelt, Franklin Delano 93
Rose of Paris (1924) 189
Rosen, Al 13
Roth, Lillian 105n
Roulien, Raoul 52
Royce, Ruth 119–120, 121, 122
Royer, Fanchon 99
Rubens, Alma 214
Ruggles, Charles 142, 155, 169, 174, 221, 226
The Ruined Lady (play) 34
Russell, Elizabeth 204n
Russell, Johnny 201
Russell, Rosalind 24, 28
Rustler's Valley (1937) 116
Ryan, Peggy 239
Ryan, Robert 118

Sabu 24
Safe in Hell (1931) 134
Sailor Be Good! (1933) 172
Sailor's Luck (1933) 156
Sally of the Subway (1932) 192
Salt of the Earth (1954) 207
Sanders, George 183
Sanders of the River (1935) 131, 134–136
Santa Fe Marshall (1940) 116–117
The Sap from Syracuse (1930) 226
The Savage Innocents (1960) 258
Sawyer, Joe 115
Scandal Sheet (1939) 166
Scaramouche (play) 170
Schildkraut, Joseph 201
Schlom, Herbert 117
Scott, Fred 50
Scott, Randolph 24, 42, 55, 76, 145, 179
Sealed Lips (1925) 189
The Secret Call (1931) 74)
The Secret of the Chateau (1934) 76
The Secrets of Wu Sin (1932) 192
Seegar, Miriam 51
Seeley, Blossom 221
Seitz, George B. 114
Selznick, David O. 66, 164–166, 167
Selznick, Lewis 33
Seventh Heaven (1937) 200–201
The Seventh Victim (1943) 31, 44
Shadows of the Law (1930) 148
Shame (1922) 248

Shanghai Express (1932) 167, 247–248, 253
The Shanghai Gesture (play) 82
Shanghai Gesture (1941) 161, 167–168
Shannon, Peggy 218
Shaw, Oscar 87
She Asked for It (1937) 174
She Gets Her Man (1935) 114
Shearer, Norma 117, 142, 212, 222
Sheridan, Ann 238
"Sherlock Holmes" 204, 253
Sherlock Holmes and the Spider Woman (1944) 204
Sherman, Harry 116
Sherman, Lowell 97
Sherwood, Robert E. 85
Shirley, Anne 238
Short, Dorothy 151, 241
Shuttle of Life (1920) 34
Sidney, Sylvia 61, 97, 106, 107
The Sign of the Cross (1932) 108
The Silent Witness (play) 14
The Silent Witness (1933) 14
Silk Stocking Sal (1924) 37
The Silver Cord (play) 163
The Silver Fox (play) 170
The Silver Horde (1930) 41
Silver Tassie (play) 20
Simon, Simone 200
Sin of Madelon Claudet (1931) 107
The Sin Sister (1929) 91
Sinatra, Frank 28
The Singing Fool (1928) 87, 91
Sinners in the Sun (1932) 125
The Siren (1927) 190
Skelly, Hal 40, 104, 191
Skinner, Otis 85
Skipworth, Alison 147, 234
The Sky Parade (1936)
Skyscraper Souls (1932) 226
Slaves (1969) 207
Slide, Anthony 46, 250
Small Town Girl (1936) 22
Smart Girl (1935) 179
Smart Money (1931) 95, 97
Smart Woman (1931) 97
Smile (play) 74
Smith, C. Aubrey 34
Smith, Kent 28
Snapshots of 1921 (play) 104
So Big (1932) 98
So This Is Africa (1933) 156
So This Is Paris (1926) 215
So You Won't Talk (1940) 173
The Son-Daughter (1932) 253
Son of a Sailor (1933) 99
Sondergaard, Gale 7, 44n, 197–209
Song (1928) 252
Song of Kentucky (1929) 50
Song of Songs (1932) 127
Song of the Trail (1936) 43
The Song Revue (play) 162

Sorel, Ted 158
The Soul Market (1916) 33
Soussanin, Nicholas 13, 14, 17
The Spanish Jade (1922) 34, 35
Speed Limits (1935) 43
The Spell of the Yukon (1916) 33
The Spider Woman Strikes Back (1946) 204
Spivy, Victoria 132
Springer, John 87
Spy Train (1943) 45, 46n, 245
The Squall (play) 49, 55
The Squealer (1930) 191
Stack, Robert 24
Stage Door (1937) 177, 180–182, 201
Stander, Lionel 203
Stanley, Forrest 190
Stanwyck, Barbara 47, 68, 148, 206
Starke, Pauline 215
State of the Union (1948) 232
State's Attorney (1932) 86
Sten, Anna 235
Steppin' Out (1925) 189
Stepping Stones (play) 87–89
Sterling, Ford 189
Stevens, Inger 70
Stevens, Onslow 235
Stewart, James 232
Stewart, Roy 188
Stiller, Mauritz 12
Stirling, Linda 122
The Stoker (1932) 51
The Stolen Bride (1927) 215
Stolen Pleasures (1927) 190
Stone, Milburn 70
Stone of Silver Creek (1935) 99, 100
Stonehouse, Ruth 190, 250
Sraight to Heaven (1939) 136
The Strange Case of Clara Deane (1932) 103, 107, 109
Strange Death of Adolf Hitler (1943) 204
Strange Interlude (play) 198
Strangers in Love (1932) 60
Stratton, Albert 185
Stratton-Porter, Gene 110
Street of Missing Women (1940) 110
Street of Sin (1928) 12
Strictly Dynamite (1934) 100
Stroud, Claude 242
Strozzi, Kay 14
Stuart, Gloria 69
Stuart, Sir James 123
A Study in Scarlet (1933) 253–254
Sturges, Preston 234
Submarine (1928) 190
Success at Any Price (1934) 109
Sudden Bill Dorn (1938) 43, 100–101
Sullavan, Margaret 100, 149

INDEX [273]

Sullivan, Ed 93
Summerville, Slim 226, 235
Sunrise (1927) 12, 82, 85
Superman (serials) 122
Supernatural (1933) 169, 172
Sutherland, A. Edward 105
Sutter's (1936) 22
Swanson, Gloria 25, 214
Swarthout, Gladys 77, 158, 174
Sweepings (1933) 156
Sweet, Blanche 32–33, 189
Sweethearts of the Navy (1937) 116
Swim, Girl, Swim (1927) 89
Swing High (1930) 50
Symphony of Living (1935) 43
Syncopation (1929) 226

Take Me Home (1928) 216
Talley, Marion 174
Talmadge, Norma 12, 215, 217
Talmadge, Richard 121
Talman, William 184
Tamiroff, Akim 127, 156, 256
Tangerine (play) 104
Tarzan the Fearless (1935) 121n
Tashman, Lilyan 156, 211–224, 225
Tavenner, Frank 207
Taxi! (1932) 51, 53
Taylor, Estelle 37, 164
Taylor, Kent 179
Taylor, Ray 120, 121
Taylor, Robert 22, 117
Taylor, William Desmond 5n
Tearle, Conway 114
Teasdale, Verree 143n, 174, 225–232
Tell Your Children see *Reefer Madness*
Temple, Shirley 23, 85, 183, 201
The Ten Commandments (1923) 139
Ten Nights in a Barroom (play) 113
Terror Aboard (1933) 143, 226
A Texas Steer (1927) 215
Thalberg, Irving 15, 131, 132, 134, 137, 157, 254
Thanks for Everything (1938) 23
That Hamilton Woman (1941)
That Wild West (1924) 188
That's My Story (1937) 113
Theater Guild 198
Their Big Moment (1934) 235
There's Always Tomorrow (1934) 21
They Call It Sin (1932) 234
The Thief of Bagdad (1924) 247, 249–250, 251
The Thin Man (1934) 147, 150–151
Thin Man Goes Home (1945) 239
Think Fast, Mr. Moto (1937) 121
Thirteen Women (1932) 86

This Is the Night (1932) 74–75
This Thing Called Love (1941) 24
Thomas, Jameson 116
Thomas, Olive 5, 33, 224
Thomson, Kenneth 75
Thompson, Carlos 28
Thorpe, Richard 92
Three Blind Mice (1938) 23
Three Comrades (1938) 158
Three Loves Has Nancy (1938) 78–79
The Three Musketeers (play) 170
The Three Musketeers (1921) 190
The Three Musketeers (1939) 19, 24
Three Sinners 12
Three Smart Girls (1936) 19, 22–23
Three Wise Crooks (1925) 37
The Thrill Hunter (1933) 192
Thru Different Eyes (1929) 82–83, 148
Thunderstorm (1955) 28
Tic Toc Girls 127
Tiger Woman (1944) 122
Tigress, The (1927) 190
'Til We Meet Again (1940) 24
Tip-Off Girls (1938) 43
Tobin, Genevieve 76n, 92, 125
Todd, Thelma 89, 242
Together Again (1944) 137
The Toll of the Sea (1922) 248–249
Tomorrow at Seven (1933) 172
Tone, Franchot 203
Tonight at 8:30 (play) 24
Too Much Harmony (1933) 222
Toomey, Regis 106, 192
Topaz (play) 67
Topper Takes a Trip (1938) 230, 231
Torena, Juan de Garchi 152
Torrence, David 85
Torres, Miguel C. 43
Torres, Racquel 156
Torrid Zone (1940) 238
Tourneur, Maurice 33
Tracy, Lee 128
Tracy, Spencer 96, 156, 130
Transatlantic Tunnel (1935) 237–238
Trapped by G-Men (1937) 109
Trapped in the Sky (1939) 69
Traveling Husbands (1931) 41, 125
Travis, June 76n
Tree, Dorothy 206
Trenholme, Helen 76
Trevor, Claire 24, 121, 166
The Trial of Mary Dugan (1929) 216
The Trouble with Angels (1966) 28
Trumbo, Dalton 206
Tryon, Glenn 40
Tucker, Forrest 44

Tucker, Richard 97
Turnabout (1940) 232
Turner, Lana 28, 258
Tuska, Jon 119
Twelvetrees, Helen 7, 50, 75, 91n, 218
Twentieth Century (play) 25
20,000 Men a Year (1939) 182
Twinkle Twinkle (play) 162
Two Against the World (1932) 234
Two in the Dark (1936) 242
Two Kinds of Women (1931) 74, 92, 107–108, 171
Two Seconds (1932) 171–172

Ullman, Liv 28
Ulric, Lenore 42
El último varón sobre la tiara (1933) 53
Unconquered (1947) 69, 70
Under Cover Man (1932) 98
Under 18 (1932) 74
Underworld (1927) 6, 31, 37–38, 46, 47
Unfaithful (1931) 60
Union Pacific (1939) 69
United Artists 35
Universal 22, 23
Unknown Blonde (1934) 156
Up in Mabel's Room (1944) 25, 183
Up Pops the Devil (1931) 218
Up the River (1930) 96

Valegra, Ida 188
Valentino, Rudolph 6, 189, 211
Van Dine, S.S. 235
Van Dyke, W.S. 150–151, 230
Veidt, Conrad 12
Velez, Lupe 39, 93
Venable, Evelyn 117, 179
Vengeance (1930) 191
Vernon, Billie 104
Victor, Henry 15
Vidor, King 131–133
Village Tale (1935) 55
Vinson, Helen 7, 74, 75, 98, 103, 108, 233–240
The Virgin (1924) 188
Viva Villa (1934) 54, 66
Viva Zapata! (1952) 70
Vogues of 1938 (1937) 238
Von Eltz, Theodore 150
Von Sternberg, Josef 6, 9, 12, 31, 37–39, 47, 58, 125–126, 127, 140, 167–168, 247–248,, 253
Von Stroheim, Erich 145, 239

Wagon Train (TV series) 46
Wagon Wheels (1934) 179
Wagons Westward (1940) 166
Walcamp, Marie 119
Walker, Alexander 132
Walker, Alice 134

Walker, Johnnie 93
Walker, Nella 23
Walker, Stuart 142
Wallace, Richard 106
Walsh, George 52
Walton, Gladys 188
WAMPAS Baby Stars 35, 87, 91, 189
Wandering Girls (1927) 190
Wanger, Walter 69, 179
Wanted by the Police (1938) 245
Warner, H.B. 215
Warner Bros. 50, 96–97
Washington, Fredi 137
Water Gipsies (1932) 142
Watters, James 152
The Way All Men (1930) 191
Wayne, Billy 241, 242
Wayne, John 166
Weaver, Marjorie 68
The Wedding Night (1935) 235
Week-End Marriage (1932) 171
Weidler, Virginia 128
Welford, Nancy 217
Wellman, William 14, 40
West, Mae 14, 66, 108, 156
Western Association of Motion Picture Advertisers 189
Western Jamboree (1938) 158
Whale, James 193
What's My Story (1937) 117
What's Your Racket (1933) 100
What's Your Wife Doing? (play) 198
Wheeler, Bert 43, 156
Wheeler & Woolsey 95, 148, 155, 156, 158, 242
What Price Decency (1933) 51–52
When a Man Sees Red (1934) 194
When Husbands Flirt (1925) 190
When the Wife's Away (1926) 190

When Were You Born (1938) 256
When You Smile (play) 104
Where Angels Go—Trouble Follows (1968) 28
Whirlpool (1934) 127
Whirlwind (play) 169
Whispering Smith (1926) 215
White, Arnold Dean 183–184
White, George 162
White, Pearl 119, 121
White, Thelma 46, 241–245
White Cockatoo (1935) 100
The White Parade (1934) 100
Whitman, Gayne 190
Whitney, Renée 50, 97
Whoopee (1930) 74
Why Bring That Up? (1929) 40
Wicked Woman (1953) 118
Wickes, Mary 28
Wide Open Town (1941) 44
The Widow in Scarlet (1932) 192
Wife, Husband and Friend (1939) 24
Wilcox, Herbert 58, 61
Wilcoxon, Henry 66, 79
Wild Geese Calling (1941) 167
Wild Gold (1935) 121
The Wild Party (1923) 188
Wilder, Billy 22
Willard, Jess 188n
William, Warren 76–77, 149, 172, 226
Wilson, Lois 22, 192, 226
Windsor, Claire 189
Wine, Women and Song (1933) 156, 222–223
Wise, Thomas 33
The Wiser Sex (1932) 218
Without Children (1935) 43
Wives Never Know (1936) 169, 173, 229

The Wizard of Oz (1939) 201, 202
The Wolf of Wall Street 13
Woman to Woman (1928)
Woman Trap (1929) 40
Woman Who Dared (1933) 156
The Woman Who Did Not Care (1927) 215
The Women (1939) 152
Women in Bondage (1943) 182
Women in the Night (1948)
Women Love Once (1931) 58
Women Men Marry (1937) 77, 148
Wong, Anna May 43, 247–259
Wood, Ernest 105
Woolsey, Robert 43, 156
Working Girls (1931) 74
The World Gone Mad (1933) 42
Wray, Fay 12, 54, 75
Wrecking Crew (1942) 44
Wynn, Ed 162
Wynyard, Diana 21, 235

X Marks the Spot (1942) 158

Yates, Herbert 166, 168
The Yellow Ticket (1931) 125
Young, Carleton 244
Young, Clara Kimball 149
Young, Loretta 7, 23, 53, 67, 68, 85, 91n, 171, 234, 235
You're My Everything (1949) 128–129

Zanuck, Darryl F. 66, 137
Ziegfeld, Florenz 74, 82, 95, 170, 201, 212
Ziegfeld Follies 58, 89, 95, 212, 224
Zoppi, Vladimir 11
Zucco, George 77